THE GENUS
GALANTHUS

A BOTANICAL MAGAZINE MONOGRAPH

The Genus
GALANTHUS

Aaron P. Davis

Illustrations by Christabel King

Series Editor—Brian Mathew

Published in association with
The Royal Botanic Gardens, Kew

Timber Press
Portland, Oregon

Published in 1999 by
Timber Press, Inc.
133 S.W. Second Avenue, Suite 450
Portland, Oregon 97204

Reprinted 2000

Printed in Hong Kong

Library of Congress Cataloging-in-Publication Data

Davis, Aaron P.
      The genus Galanthus / Aaron P. Davis ; illustrations by
   Christabel King.
            p.   cm.
      "Published in association with The Royal Botanic Gardens, Kew."
      "A Botanical magazine monograph."
      Includes bibliographical references and index.
      ISBN 0-88192-431-8
      1. Snowdrops. 2. Snowdrops—Classification. I. Royal Botanic
   Gardens, Kew. II. Title.
   QK495.A484D28   1999
   584'.34—dc21   96-56148
                                                                       CIP

For my mother and father

CONTENTS

Colour plates 1–19 follow page 81.
Colour plates 20–35 follow page 112.
Colour plates 36–56 follow page 192.

LIST OF
COLOUR PLATES

PAINTINGS

PHOTOGRAPHS

11

ACKNOWLEDGEMENTS

In common with other taxonomic studies, this monograph would not have been possible without the help and co-operation of a great number of people. I would like to offer my sincere gratitude to the following persons and organizations. I make no excuses for the length of these acknowledgements and apologize to those whom I may have forgotten to mention.

I would like to start by thanking the Botany Department at Reading University and at the Royal Horticultural Society (RHS), where the research for this monograph was undertaken (as a PhD thesis). This project was supported by a grant from the Science Engineering Research Council (SERC), and the Royal Horticultural Society, as a SERC-CASE award. I would like to thank my supervisors at Reading University, Professor Jeffrey Harborne and Dr. Stephen L. Jury, and the staff at the Botany Department for their technical assistance, logistic support, and for the use of their facilities. I am grateful to the staff of the Reading University Plant Sciences gardens and experimental glasshouses for their assistance in growing and maintaining the collection of *Galanthus* that was used in this study. I would also like to thank Ronnie Rutherford for his innumerable talents, and Roger Hyam, with whom I spent cold winter mornings photographing snowdrops. At the RHS, I would like to thank my PhD supervisor Christopher D. Brickell for his advice, support, and encouragement, and the staff at Wisley for making the *Galanthus* collection available for study.

Throughout my studies on the genus *Galanthus*, and afterwards to the present day, I have received every assistance from the staff at the Royal Botanic Gardens, Kew. I would particularly like to thank Dr Sasha Barrow, Dr R.K. Brummitt, Paul Bygrave, Jill Cowley, Justin Fletcher Moat, Tony Hall, Dr Petra Hoffmann, Brian Mathew, and Richard Wilford.

I am grateful to the directors of the herbaria at ATH, AUBSN, BM, C, E, ISTE, JE, K, FI, G, HUB, L, LE, LD, P, PR, PRC, RNG, SAAR, TBI, TGM, UPA, and MHA (abbreviations after Holmgren, Holmgren, and Barnett, 1990) for providing facilities and/or making herbarium specimens available for study. I would particularly like to acknowledge the staff at AUBSN (Nalchik), LE (St. Petersburg), and TBI (Tbilisi) for their assistance, expertise, and hospitality during extended study visits. During my studies I spent a number of months in Russia and Georgia, and I had the great pleasure of working with the following people: Dr Helen Mordak and Dr Yuri Roskov from LE, and Sasha Lebedeva and Dr Boris Turniev from the Caucasian Biosphere Reserve in Sochi. I would also like to thank Professor Georgia Kamari (UPA), Professor Neriman Özhatay (ISTE), Dr Johan van Scheepen (KAVB, Hillegom, The Netherlands) and Dr Arnis Seisums (Academy of Sciences, Latvia).

Many individuals have greatly contributed to this work through their knowledge and enthusiasm for *Galanthus*, including Ruby Baker, Matt Bishop, Dr Gwen Black, Dr John Grimshaw, Harry Hay, Manfred Koenen, Dr John Marr, Dr Ronald Mackenzie, Colin Mason, Richard Nutt, Dr Martin Rix, Nigel Rowland, the late Ole Sønderhousen, Audrey Vockins, and the late Primrose Warburg. And to those enthusiasts, in addition to those persons just mentioned, who kindly donated plant material: Erna and Ronald Frank, Will McLewin, and Roger Poulett. During the latter part of my studies I made a visit to northeastern Turkey, and I would like to thank John Drake, Mehmet Karahan, and Liz Thompson for making it a worthwhile and enjoyable trip.

I am especially grateful to the late Ole Sønderhousen, who went to great lengths to place at my disposal his invaluable knowledge of *Galanthus* in Turkey; and to Richard Nutt and the late Primrose Warburg who offered a great deal of information, advice, and encouragement at the very beginning and throughout this project.

I also wish to mention those who have had little interest in snowdrops, but who have offered sound and erudite advice concerning the many systematic and taxonomic difficulties of this work, particularly Dr Estrela Figueirdo, Dr David Gower, Dr Terry Hedderson, and Dr Paul Wilkin.

The distribution maps were created by Justin Moat, and the artwork for this monograph has been undertaken by Christabel King. I am extremely grateful to her for bringing this volume to life with her descriptive and beautiful paintings.

INTRODUCTION

Galanthus L. is a genus of bulbous, petaloid monocotyledons, consisting of 18 species. It belongs to the family Amaryllidaceae J. St.-Hil. The genus is confined to Europe, Asia Minor, and the Near East. It is found from the Pyrenees in the west to the Caucasus and Iran in the east, extending as far south as Sicily, the Peloponnese, and Lebanon. The northern limit of distribution is difficult, if not impossible, to ascertain, due to introduction and cultivation by humans. The majority of the species occur in woodlands, at the edge of woodlands in grass areas, or by streams, usually in mountainous regions (800–1500m). One or two species, however, occupy quite different habitats. *Galanthus platyphyllus* is found at altitudes up to 2600 m in the high Caucasus, growing in wet snow-melt alpine grasslands. At the other extreme is the newly described *G. peshmenii* from the East Aegean, which can be found growing a mere 10 m from the sea.

The genus *Galanthus* was established by Linnaeus in *Systema Naturae* (1753), the name being derived from the Greek words *gala*, meaning milk, and *anthos*, flower. Commonly known as SNOW-DROPS, the genus is a well-known and much-loved group of plants, cherished as harbingers of spring. According to Church (1908), the origin of the common vernacular name snowdrops can be traced back to the German *Schneetropfen*, which refers to the tear-shaped earrings or pendants worn by ladies of the sixteenth and seventeenth centuries. According to *The Oxford English Dictionary* (edn. 2, 1989), the first published use of the name snowdrops is in the book *Colours*, written by Boyle in 1664: 'These purely white flowers that appear about the end of winter, and are commonly called snowdrops'. In the same year, Evelyn (1664) wrote in *Kalendar Hortens:* 'December. Flowers in prime. Snow flowers or drops, yucca, &c'. English vernacular names, which pre-date the use of snowdrops, are FAIR MAIDS OF FEBRUARY, CANDLEMAS BELLS, and WHITE LADIES. These names are all associated with the Church festival of Candlemas Day which takes place each year on 2 February, and which refers to a procession of white-robed maidens during the Feast of Purification. In other countries similar names have been used in connection with this religious festival: in France, the name VIOLETTE DE LA CHANDALEUR was used; and in Italy, PURIFICATION FLOWER. These names are very appropriate for a flower with such a quality of pureness; moreover, Candlemas Day coincides perfectly with the peak of the flowering season. The common modern German vernacular for *Galanthus* is the wonderfully euphonious SCHNEEGLOCKCHEN, meaning little snowbell.

In the British Isles, the genus *Galanthus* is one of the best known and most frequently cultivated of all bulbous plants. A number of reasons account for its popularity, but foremost must be the simple beauty of this little plant and the timeliness of its flowering season. The hardiness of the snowdrop in addition to its longevity and disease resistance make it a very amenable subject for cultivation. The pure-white perianth segments, pristine on even the dullest winter day, have an almost indescribable beauty. Like many other members of the Amaryllidaceae the snowdrop has segments that are thick and robust, and are not spoilt by harsh weather. The value of the snowdrop is increased because it flowers when little else is in the garden or countryside. In the British Isles, the peak of the flowering season is late January to mid-February, a time of year when most plants are still in the hold of winter's rest. Indeed, the snowdrop can withstand even the harshest of winter weather, surviving many degrees below freezing, even for prolonged spells. When other hardy plants, such as *Helleborus* spp. and *Arum* spp., have become flaccid because of low temperatures (c. $-10°C$), many species of *Galanthus* appear almost untouched. Even when the plant collapses after a particularly hard night's frost (below c. $-15°C$), it will rise again and open its flower as soon as it is touched by the warmth of the new day.

The genus *Galanthus* has also become popular, especially during the twentieth century, because of the large number of species, cultivars, and clones that are available for cultivation. Hundreds of garden cultivars have been listed or described, and many have received certificates and awards for their horticultural worthiness. Even today, despite the reluctance of some firms to stock large numbers of cultivars, many different cultivars are available in commerce. Indeed, beginning in the 1980s the popularity of growing snowdrops has seen a renewal reminiscent of the passion for these plants that flourished during late nineteenth and early twentieth centuries.

The genus *Galanthus* is closely allied with the genus *Leucojum* L. According to Müller-Doblies and Müller-Doblies (1978) these genera should be placed in their own subtribe, the *Galanthinae* Pax (Pax, 1887); they are closely relatd to *Narcissus* and *Sternbergia*, which are placed together within the tribe *Narcissinae* Endl. (after Endlicher, 1836). Although the morphology of *Leucojum* is far more divergent than *Galanthus*, the many morphological similarities that unite these two genera are easy to identify. The most conspicuous similarity between *Galanthus* and *Leucojum* is their small white pendent flowers, each composed of six free perianth segments (arranged in two series, inner and outer). Other characteristics uniting these two genera are the arrangement and structure of the anthers, morphology of the bulb, small size of the pollen grains, a number of anatomical features, and habit. Despite the similarities between the two genera they are easily set apart by a few salient characters. The simplest way to tell them apart is by the difference in size between the outer and inner whorl of segments: in *Galanthus* the inner segments are smaller than the outer ones (about half the size), whereas in *Leucojum* both whorls of segments are always equal. The genus *Galanthus* always possesses a green mark or marks on each of the inner perianth segments, whereas in all species of *Leucojum*, except *L. aestivum* and *L. vernum*, the segments are always plain white. Further useful distinguishing characteristics are that *Galanthus* has one flower per scape (rarely two), and two leaves per bulb (rarely three or more) whereas *Leucojum* usually has two to several flowers per scape and several leaves. These genera have other differences between them, particularly in floral morphology, but these are less obvious on casual examination.

INTRODUCTION TO THE
TAXONOMY OF *GALANTHUS*

Galanthus has been the subject of a number of taxonomic revisions (Beck, 1894; Gottlieb-Tannenhain, 1904; Kemularia-Nathadze, 1947b; Traub and Moldenke, 1948; Stern, 1956; Artjushenko, 1965, 1966, 1970), but each one disagrees with all the others in the enumeration of the species and the division of the genus. At the present time, despite such an investment in research, the taxonomy of *Galanthus* is in disorder: species limits and affinities are obscure and the taxa difficult to identify with any certainty. Many possible factors contribute to the taxonomic confusion that prevails. Previous workers have commented on the paucity of material available

17

for study (Stern, 1956), poor preservation of vital characters when plants are prepared as herbarium specimens (Artjushenko, 1965), and inadequate field observations (Brickell, 1984; Kamari, 1982). Regarding herbarium material, three major characters—leaf vernation, the amount of wax on the leaf, and the number of marks on the inner perianth segment—are frequently lost upon pressing and drying. The last two of these characters are sometimes preserved if the material is dried quickly, but leaf vernation is often still difficult to ascertain, unless it is of the most extreme type. Taxonomic investigation of *Galanthus* therefore necessitates the study of living specimens, preferably at their place of origin.

A further problem, and one common in taxonomic research, is that most studies have been limited to areas defined by geo-political boundaries and not natural distributions. In the case of *Galanthus*, the division has been obvious between studies undertaken in the former USSR and those done outside that area. Soviet scientists worked in partial isolation on taxa occurring in the Soviet states, without having easy access to material in Europe and Asia Minor. Likewise, taxonomic studies elsewhere were biased towards taxa occurring outside the Soviet areas. This situation is epitomized by the studies of Stern (1956), who did not have access to material from the Caucasus, and Artjushenko (1965, 1966, 1970, 1974) who was not able to review much material for the species occurring outside the USSR.

Added to the above difficulties with taxonomy, and typical of horticulturally desirable plant groups, has been the over-zealous naming of taxa, particularly of species and varieties. This has created a plethora of superfluous names, making the nomenclature large and chaotic.

From 1991 to 1994 I had the opportunity to undertake a systematic investigation of the genus *Galanthus* as a doctoral thesis project at the University of Reading. During this study I had at my disposal many resources, materials, and modern methods for conducting a sophisticated, systematic enquiry. Those facilities enabled me to make progress into the understanding of the taxonomic relationships of this challenging genus. The main product of this research was the construction of an updated classification of the genus, which is published here as a new monograph of *Galanthus*.

18

TAXONOMIC HISTORY OF THE GENUS

Chapter One of *Snowdrops and Snowflakes* by Stern (1956) provides a useful overview of the early literature and pre-Linnaean classifications of *Galanthus*. According to Stern, the genus *Galanthus* was listed as early as the fourth century BCE by Theophrastus (370–285 BCE), the Greek philosopher and naturalist. Theophrastus used the name Leucoion to denote at least two different plants, one was the gilliflower (*Matthiola incana*) and another was *Galanthus*, or what is assumed to be this genus, as the description refers to a bulbous plant with white flowers. The Greek name Leucoion, literally translated, means 'white violet', a name which was not used exclusively for *Galanthus*, or indeed even for bulbous plants.

In the herbals of the sixteenth and seventeenth centuries, prior to Linnaean classification, the genus *Galanthus* was most often called Leucoium (or Leucoion), but the names Narcissus (and Narcisee), Leuconarcissolirion, Narcisolyrion, and Narcisso-Leucojum were used also. The first of the sixteenth-century herbals to include *Galanthus* was Mattioli's *Commentarii in sex libros Pedacii Dioscoridis* (1544), in which it was called 'Narcissus'. The 1554 edition of Mattioli's *Commentarii* includes what could be the earliest printed illustrations of *Galanthus*. These early plates do not always, however, provide a very faithful description of the plant we know today. In the case of Mattioli's work, for example, *Galanthus* is depicted as a plant with six leaves (instead of two).

As the early literature of *Galanthus* has been covered in some detail by Stern (1956), I do not want to go into any further detail on the subject here. For those readers who do want more information Appendix 4 provides a guide to the pre-Linnaean literature.

In *Systema Naturae* Linnaeus (1735) used the genus name *Galanthus*, to accommodate those entities which he considered separate from *Leucojum*. In *Species Plantarum* Linnaeus (1753) described the first species of *Galanthus*: *G. nivalis*, the familiar and widespread species of central Europe.

Figure 1. Narcissus—*Galanthus.* Mattioli, *Commentarii, in sex libros Pedacii Dioscoridis*, 1554.

20

LEVCO-
NARCIS-
SOLIRION
minimum.

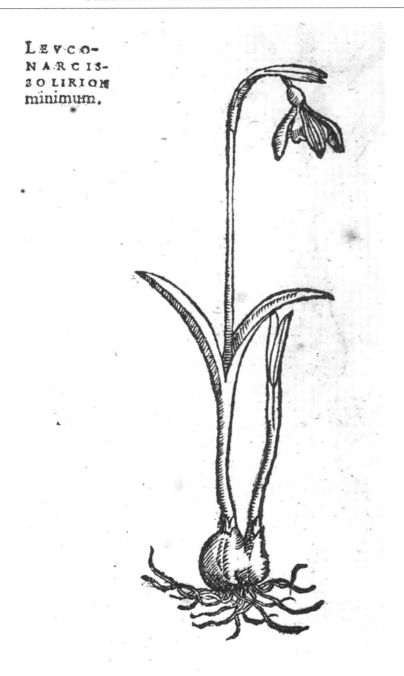

Figure 2. Leuconarcissolirion minimum—*Galanthus nivalis*. Lobel, *Plantarum seu stirpium historia*, 1576.

21

1 *Leucòium Bulbosum præcox.*
Timely flowring Bulbus violet.

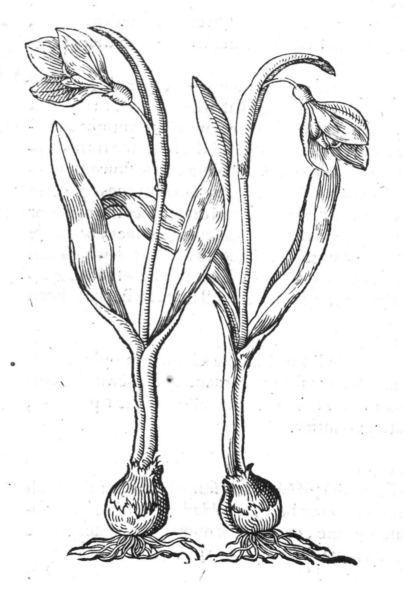

Figure 3. Leucoium bulbosum preacox. Timely flowring Bulbus violet—*Galanthus nivalis.*
Gerard, *Herball,* 1597.

22

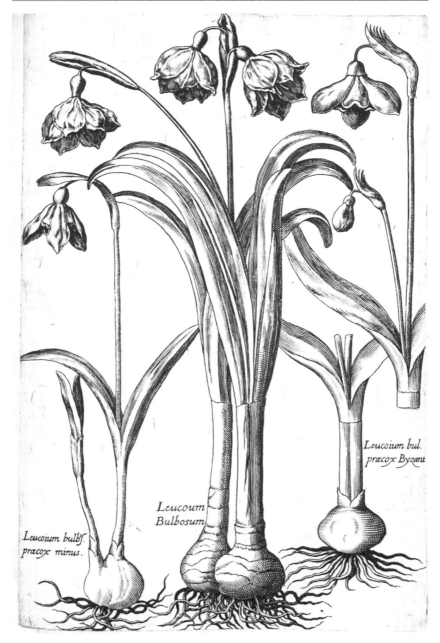

Leucoium bulbꝭ.
præcox minus.

Leucoum
Bulbosum

Leucoium bul.
præcox Byzant

Figure 4. Leucoium bulbosum praecox minus—*Galanthus nivalis*—and **Leucoium bulbosum praecox Byzantinus**—*Galanthus plicatus.* De Bry, *Florilegium novum,* 1611.

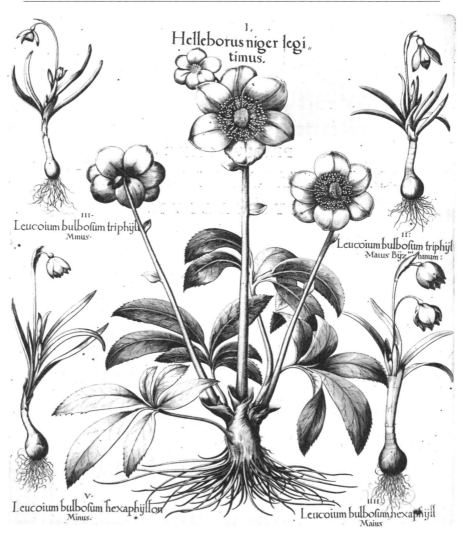

Figure 5. Leucoium bulbosum triphyll. Maius Byzantinum—*Galanthus* sp.—and **Leucoium bulbosum triphyll. Minus**—*Galanthus nivalis.* Besler, *Hortus eystettensis,* vol. 2, 1613.

24

When Boissier (1882) presented the first classification of the genus in *Flora Orientalis*, six species of *Galanthus* had been described. Boissier's enumeration included *G. nivalis* L., three species from Greece (*G. graecus* [Boissier, 1882], *G. reginae-olgae* [Orphanides, 1876], and *G. elwesii* [Hooker, 1875]), one species from the Crimea (*G. plicatus* [Marschall von Bieberstein, 1819]), and one from the Caucasus (*G. latifolius* [Ruprecht, 1868]). Boissier divided the genus into three groups on the basis of flowering time and the shape of the apex of the anther: *G. latifolius* was separated from the rest on account of having anthers with blunt apices; *G. reginae-olgae* was separated from the others because of its autumn-flowering habit.

The account of *Galanthus* by Baker (1888) in *Handbook of the Amaryllideae*, was similar to Boissier's, except that Baker recognized two subspecies for *G. nivalis*: subsp. *imperati* Bertol. and subsp. *caucasicus* Baker. Baker, probably following Boissier, also used flowering time to separate *G. reginae-olgae* from the other species, and added one further character—'edges of leaf reduplicate'—to identify *G. plicatus*. In less than a decade after the publication of *Handbook of the Amaryllideae*, Baker described seven new species of *Galanthus*: *G. fosteri* (1889), *G. allenii* (1891), *G. ikariae* (1893a), *G. perryi* (1893b), *G. maximus* (1893c) [later renamed *G. grandiflorus* (Baker 1893e)], *G. byzantinus* (1893d), and *G. cilicicus* (1897). Each of these species was sent to him at the Royal Botanic Gardens, Kew, either directly from the increasingly explored Balkans and Asia Minor, or indirectly via the gardens of horticulturists who were beginning to become interested in the genus at that time.

Owing to an increasing horticultural interest in *Galanthus* during the end of the nineteenth century, a plethora of horticulturally derived names appeared in the literature of the day. *The Garden (London)*, *Gardeners Chronicle*, and the *Journal of the Royal Horticultural Society* were the most frequent media for the publication and use of these new species, varieties, forms, and cultivars. Much of this information is brought together in two important references, both published in the *Journal of the Royal Horticultural Society*. The first is a collection of papers by Allen, Melville, and Burbidge, all written after a conference on snowdrops and published in 1891. The second is a single well-illustrated and very informative paper on snowdrops written by Bowles (1918).

In an attempt to put some taxonomic order to the increasing number of names, Beck (1894) enumerated all the taxa that he

25

thought could be recognized, and devised a system for their classification. Approximately 35 *Galanthus* taxa were listed in Beck's account, which included four species: *G. nivalis*, *G. graecus*, *G. elwesii*, and *G. plicatus*. The Caucasian *G. latifolius* was omitted and *G. reginae-olgae* was reduced in rank to a forma of *G. nivalis*. Three varieties and 20 forms were recognized for *G. nivalis*, and it is in this part of the treatment that many of the horticultural names were incorporated.

A far more conservative enumeration of the genus was presented by Gottlieb-Tannenhain (1904), who recognized three species and eight subspecies in his account. All the subspecies were placed under *Galanthus nivalis*, including subsp. *nivalis*, subsp. *cilicicus*, subsp. *reginae-olgae*, subsp. *plicatus*, subsp. *allenii*, subsp. *elwesii*, subsp. *byzantinus*, and subsp. *graecus*. The other two species listed were *G. latifolius* and *G. fosteri*. This detailed and erudite study includes investigations of morphology and anatomy, distribution maps, specimen citations, and hypotheses of species evolution. In his key, two new characters were used for identification purposes: the number and position of the markings on the inner perianth segment and the type of vernation (either 'flat', 'enveloping', or 'reflexed'—now termed applanate, supervolute, and explicative, respectively). These features have been adopted in all subsequent treatments of the genus, in one way or another, but particularly by Stern (1956) who used leaf vernation as a character of primary importance for the subgeneric division of *Galanthus*.

During the first half of the twentieth century a number of new species were recognized from the Caucasus area, namely, *Galanthus alpinus* (Sosnowsky, 1911), *G. woronowii* (Losinskaya, 1935), *G. valentinae* (Grossheim, 1940), *G. lagodechianus* (Kemularia-Nathadze, 1947a), *G. ketzkhovelii* (Kemularia-Nathadze, 1947b), and *G. schaoricus* (Kemularia-Nathadze, 1941). A further two species, *G. caucasicus* (Grossheim, 1924) and *G. caspius* (Grossheim, 1940), were elevated from an infraspecific to a species rank.

In 1947 Kemularia-Nathadze (1947b) published a taxonomic review of *Galanthus* occurring in the Caucasus. In her treatment eight Caucasian species were enumerated: (1) *G. woronowii*, (2) *G. caspius*, (3) *G. valentinae*, (4) *G. latifolius*, (5) *G. lagodechianus*, (6) *G. ketzkhovelii*, (7) *G. caucasicus*, and (8) *G. schaoricus*. The genus, including those species occurring outside the Caucasus region, was subdivided into two sections, *Viridifolii* Kem.-Nath. and *Glaucaefolii* Kem.-Nath., and eight series.

Section *Viridifolii* contained the four series *Woronowii* Kem.-Nath. (including species nos. 1–3); *Latifoliae* Kem.-Nath. (species no. 4); *Fosteriae* Kem.-Nath. (not represented in the Caucasus); and *Angustifoliae* Kem.-Nath. (species nos. 5 and 6).

Section *Glaucaefolii* contained the four series *Nivales* Kem.-Nath. (including species no. 7); *Elwesiae* Kem.-Nath. (not represented in the Caucasus); *Plicatae* Kem.-Nath. (not represented in Caucasus); and *Schaoricae* Kem.-Nath. (species no. 8).

The main character used to distinguish the two sections was leaf colour: 'leaves not glaucous, green' for the *Viridifolii* and 'plants glaucous' for the *Glaucaefolii*. Other leaf features, such as shape, texture, and the shape of the apex, were employed to recognize the series.

A year after Kemularia-Nathadze's account appeared, Traub and Moldenke (1948) published a review of the tribe *Galantheae* (Herb. ex Baker) Hutchinson, which included the genera *Lapiedra*, *Leucojum*, and *Galanthus*. Their enumeration of *Galanthus* included 19 species, but did not include any of the new species described by Kemularia-Nathadze the year before. Traub and Moldenke arranged the species into two new subgenera, Subgenus *Eugalanthus* Traub & Moldenke and Subgenus *Plicatanthus* Traub & Moldenke. The former was characterized by 'Leaves simply channelled down the face', and the latter by the 'Edges of the leaf reduplicate [explicative]'. A combination of leaf features, flower and scape measurements, and flowering times were used in the key as subsidiary characters.

In 1956 Stern published *Snowdrops and Snowflakes*, a monograph of *Galanthus* and *Leucojum*, which became a standard reference work for these genera. Stern's classification of *Galanthus* is based primarily on leaf vernation, that is, how the leaves are folded in bud (after Gottlieb-Tannenhain, 1904). Three series were recognized: *Nivales* Beck, with leaves flat in vernation; *Plicati* Beck, leaves plicate (explicative) in vernation; and *Latifolii* Stern, leaves convolute (supervolute) in vernation. Stern also provided a key to the species, with special emphasis on the development of the leaves with respect to flowering time, perianth markings, and leaf colour (green versus glaucous). Twelve species, three subspecies, and one variety were recognized by Stern, of which two species, *Galanthus corcyrensis* and *G. rizehensis*, were described as new. Appendix 1 gives an outline of Stern's classification.

27

It is obvious from Stern's work that he was not aware of recent research that had been undertaken in the USSR by Kemularia-Nathadze (1947a, 1947b) and Koss (1951). In addition to the species described by Kemularia-Nathadze, Koss described three new species from the northern Caucasus: *Galanthus bortkewitschianus, G. angustifolius,* and *G. carbardensis.* A lack of material of other species from this area, particularly for *G. alpinus, G. transcaucasicus,* and *G. woronowii,* meant that these taxa could not be satisfactorily classified by Stern. His treatment of *Galanthus* was thus geo-politically biased, because it lacked information on those species occurring in the USSR.

Realizing the necessity of including taxa occurring outside Europe, Schwarz (1963) attempted to include many of the Caucasian species in a tentative key to the wild species of *Galanthus.* Contrary to Stern's classification, Schwarz divided *Galanthus* into two main sections based on leaf colour. Schwarz's work and the commentary attached to it (Stern, 1963; Parker, 1963) illustrate just how much taxonomic disagreement still existed at that time.

In 1965 Artjushenko published a taxonomic survey of all the known species of *Galanthus,* which, in contrast to the studies of Stern, concentrated on those species occurring in the Caucasus. Artjushenko started her work with a critique of all the major classifications of *Galanthus.* The general conclusion drawn from this exercise was that the classifications based on many of the traditionally used characters were artificial. According to Artjushenko the type of inner perianth mark, leaf vernation, and epidermal wax (green versus glaucous) were of minimal taxonomic importance on their own; she concluded that the division of *Galanthus* into taxonomic units should be based on the complex of all characters.

Artjushenko's study was the first to use anatomical features for the arrangement of *Galanthus* species into taxonomic groups. The presence or absence of air cavities (cavities in the mesophyll, viewed in transverse section) and the shape of the epidermal cells (as seen from epidermal peels) provided the necessary characters. Using these new data, in combination with other characters, Artjushenko found that she could quite successfully divide the genus into what she considered natural units. Furthermore, she found that her new classification was far more congruent with geography than previous treatments: species with rectangular epidermal cells were mainly confined to the Caucasus, and the species with more or less diamond-shaped (rhombic) cells were distributed in Europe and

Anatolia. Furthermore, the absence or presence of mesophyll cavities was also found to be in accordance with geography. Species occurring in central and southern Europe and most of the Caucasus had leaves with cavities, while groups of species from the western Caucasus were without this anatomical feature (*G. platyphyllus, G. woronowii, G. valentinae,* and *G. krasnovii*).

In further publications (1966, 1967, 1969, 1970) Artjushenko expanded and elaborated on her previous works, slightly modifying her classification and making some changes to the species enumerated. In her last paper covering all taxa (1970), seventeen species were recognized, with two subspecies for *G. nivalis* (subsp. *nivalis* and subsp. *angustifolius*). Appendix 3 summarizes Artjushenko's most recent classification.

Since Artjushenko's last monograph of *Galanthus,* published in *Amaryllidaceae SSSR* (1970), the genus has undergone no major revision, although quite a number of regional taxonomic reviews have been published. The first of these was undertaken by Artjushenko (1974) for the species occurring in Greece. This work is important because it included the investigation of material not seen during her previous studies, and she was able to reassess and clarify many of her original observations.

In preparation for *Flora Europaea,* Webb (1978) presented a well-balanced account of the taxonomic problems for the species of *Galanthus* occurring in Europe. This work also included one new combination, *G. plicatus* subsp. *byzantinus* (Baker) D.A. Webb, and one new subspecies, *G. elwesii* subsp. *minor* D.A. Webb.

Many of the questions raised by Webb's review received very careful attention by Kamari (1981, 1982), who undertook a detailed investigation of the species occurring in Greece. Cytological investigations (Kamari, 1981) were combined with morphological and morphometric studies (Kamari, 1982) to answer questions of species and infraspecific delimitation. On the basis of these studies Kamari made a number of new combinations and recognized a number of new infraspecific taxa. Three subspecies were recognized for *Galanthus reginae-olgae*: subsp. *reginae-olgae*, subsp. *corcyrensis* (Stern) Kamari, and subsp. *vernalis* Kamari. Two subspecies were recognized for *G. ikariae*: subsp. *ikariae* and subsp. *snogerupii* Kamari. And three varieties were recognized for *G. elwesii*: var. *elwesii*, var. *stenophyllus* Kamari, and var. *platyphyllus* Kamari. In total Kamari recognized nine taxa for Greece, belonging to four species.

Papanicolaou and Zacharof (1983) also undertook a cytological

29

investigation on Greek *Galanthus*, examining four species. This study concentrated on populations from northern Greece, and included karyotype analysis for *G. nivalis*, *G. elwesii*, and *G. elwesii* subsp. *minor*. Their study made no reference to the work of Kamari (1981, 1982).

The Turkish species were reviewed by Brickell (1984) in his treatment for the *Flora of Turkey*, which included discussion of specific taxonomic problems and highlighted issues needing further research. Eight species and three subspecies were recognized.

Based on herbarium studies of material held at local herbaria, Delipavlov (1971) gave a review of the genus *Galanthus* in Bulgaria. According to Delipavlov three species occur in Bulgaria: *G. nivalis*, *G. elwesii*, and *G. graecus*. The most widespread species is *G. graecus* (= *G. gracilis*, see page 154); *G. nivalis* is distributed along the coast of the Black Sea and in northwestern Bulgaria, and *G. elwesii* occurs in isolated localities throughout Bulgaria.

Four years after the treatment of *Galanthus* in *Flora of Turkey* (Brickell, 1984), Zeybek (1988) produced a new review of this genus in Turkey. In this treatment 14 new subspecies are described for seven species, giving a total of 24 taxa. For the delimitation and characterization of these taxa, special emphasis was placed on a number of characters previously considered to have little or no taxonomic significance, including the shape of the leaf apex, the shape of the anther apex, and the morphology of the stigmatic surface (the style apex). I attempted to use these characters, but found them too variable to be considered taxonomically informative, particularly the last two.

Following the above study, Zeybek and Sauer (1995) published a book on the *Galanthus* of Turkey, which includes an updated account totaling eight species, fifteen subspecies, and two varieties. Several species now known to occur in Turkey are absent from this work, including *G. caucasicus* (see Davis et al., 1988, and Erik and Demirkus, 1986), *G. koenenianus* (Lobin, Brickell, and Davis, 1993), *G. peshmenii* (Davis and Brickell, 1994) and, recently confirmed in northeastern Turkey, *G. krasnovii* (see page 185). In the taxonomic account, *G. elwesii* Hook. f. subsp. *melihae* (Zeybek, 1988) was recognized as a species, and a new variety was added for *G. fosteri*: var. *antepensis*.

Zeybek and Sauer's work provides much new and informative data on Turkish *Galanthus*, including many useful illustrations, maps, descriptions, and localities.

30

MORPHOLOGY

HABIT

All species of *Galanthus* are perennial herbaceous geophytes. The plants are either solitary or exist as small clumps formed by offsetting bulbs. The height of the plant is usually governed by the length of the scape, which varies from 2 to 20 cm depending on the species and stage of growth. If the scape is not fully developed, or if it is held at an angle, the leaves will be the tallest part of the plant. FIGURE 6 shows the general habit of *Galanthus*.

BULB AND SHOOT

The bulb is ovoid to almost spherical, and is covered by a thin, brown, papery tunic, which may be firmly attached and complete, or incomplete and only remaining in patches. The bulb is a 'true bulb', that is, it consists of the swollen leaf-bases of previous year's foliage. At the lower end of the bulb there is a flat area from which the roots originate and develop externally. In this region, but on the inside of the bulb, is the basal meristem where the various plant organs are initiated. During the start of the growing season, from the apex of the bulb, a shoot emerges covered by a cylindrical, translucent sheath. This sheath, another modified leaf, encases the young leaves and flower-bud and acts as protective structure for these parts as the shoot moves up through the soil.

Because the inflorescence of *Galanthus* has a terminal position, the structure of the bulb is sympodial (Müller-Doblies, 1971).

FOLIAGE

The leaves originate from the central area of the bulb, near the base. Normally, three leaves are produced each growing season: two (or infrequently three) become the foliage leaves and the third

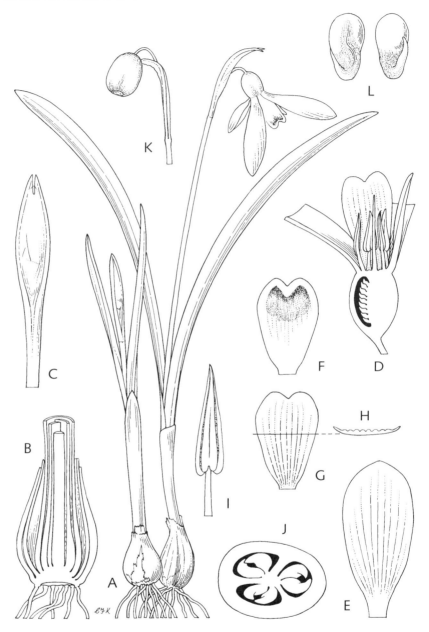

Figure 6. Habit and general morphology of *Galanthus.* **A** habit, ×1; **B** bulb, ×2; **C** bud, ×2;
D half flower, outer perianth segments removed, ×3; **E** outer perianth segment, adaxial
view, ×2; **F** inner perianth segment, adaxial view, ×3; **G** inner perianth segment, abaxial
view, ×3; **H** inner perianth segment, transverse section, ×3; **I** stamen, ×6; **J** ovary,
transverse section, ×6; **K** capsule, ×1; **L** seed, ×4. Drawn by Christabel King.

develops into the sheath described above. When the leaves appear above the ground they are opposite, with the adaxial (ventral or upper) surfaces facing each other.

At flowering time the leaves are either nearly fully developed (e.g. *Galanthus nivalis* and *G. plicatus*), only a few centimetres long (e.g. some variants of *G. reginae-olgae sensu lato*), or totally absent (e.g. *G. peshmenii* and the typical variant of *G. reginae-olgae* subsp. *reginae-olgae*). Full development of the foliage, usually a factor of length, does not occur until after flowering, at which stage the leaves tend to become recurved or nearly prostrate. At maturity the leaves are either linear to lorate or oblanceolate in outline. The leaves are held either nearly erect or prostrate, or at any angle in between.

The vernation of the leaves is of three main types: applanate, explicative, or supervolute. The terms *flat*, *plicate*, and *convolute* have been used, respectively, to describe these three types of vernation (e.g. Stern, 1956), but they should be dropped in favour of the more precise equivalents (Cullen, 1978). In *Galanthus*, applanate describes the type of vernation where the adaxial surfaces of the leaves are held flat against each other in bud (FIGURE 7A). Explicative vernation is similar to applanate, except that part of the leaf blade, near each of the margins, is reflexed sharply through nearly 180° (FIGURE 7B). Species with supervolute vernation (FIGURE 7C) have leaves that are curved upwards in bud (the margins are orientated towards the adaxial surface of the leaf) so that the one uppermost leaf is wrapped around the lower. At maturity the type of vernation can usually be determined by examining the base of the leaves at the point of attachment to the bulb, or, more conveniently, at the place where the leaves emerge from the ground; the position of one leaf to the other usually persists at maturity. This method is, however, not completely reliable for those taxa that have applanate

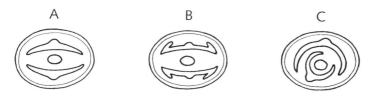

Figure 7. Types of vernation. Transverse sections through leaves at bud stage (shown larger than life size). **A** applanate vernation; **B** explicative vernation; **C** supervolute vernation. Drawn by Christabel King.

vernation, because as some species mature (e.g. *G. lagodechianus*) the margins of the leaves can curve slightly and appear almost supervolute.

The leaf surface is either plane, folded, or sulcate. In some species (e.g. *Galanthus woronowii* and *G. alpinus*) the adaxial surface often has two to four fine, longitudinal furrows that run along the length of the leaf. This usually causes the leaf to fold upwards. The abaxial (lower) leaf surface of *G. koenenianus* is conspicuously, longitudinally sulcate for the entire width of the leaf.

The texture of the leaf is usually smooth, but in some specimens it can be very finely striated or slightly puckered on the adaxial surface (e.g. *Galanthus krasnovii*).

A conspicuous midrib running along the abaxial surface of the leaf is common to most species, although in some the midrib is inconspicuous (e.g. *Galanthus platyphyllus*).

The leaf colour is green, green-matt, or glaucous. The adaxial and abaxial surfaces are either concolorous or discolorous. Dark or light green leaves are bright, shining, or dull. The glaucous-leafed taxa are greyish, grey-green, bluish, or somewhat silvery, and have either a matt or oily texture. In some species a pale median stripe is present (e.g. *Galanthus reginae-olgae*). Optimally, leaf colour should be assessed only on young living plants at or just before flowering time, as the true colour tends to fade rather rapidly after flowering.

The leaf margin is entire and flat, explicative, slightly revolute, or undulate (e.g. *Galanthus krasnovii*). The apex of the leaf is variable in outline, and may be acute, obtuse, or obtuse with a small apiculum (e.g. *G. platyphyllus*). The shape of the leaf apex is either flat (e.g. *G. nivalis*) or cucullate (e.g. *G. alpinus*).

INFLORESCENCE

The inflorescence consists of a single scape, which bears a single, erect flower-bud. The bud is enclosed by the spathe, which is composed of two spathe-valves (two modified leaves). These are positioned on either side of the flower. Between the two spathe-valves is a transparent, membranous tissue which completely covers the flower-bud. Upon expansion of the bud, which occurs just before anthesis, the membranous portion of the spathe ruptures on one side and the flower is exposed. The membranous part of the spathe will often, with time, split on both sides, freeing the two claw-like tips at the apex of the spathe. Initially the flower is held erect, but it soon becomes pendent and flexible on the filiform pedicel. The pedicel is either shorter or longer than the spathe, or roughly the same length. The scape is commonly concolorous with the leaves, and circular to oval in cross section. At flowering time the scape is held erect, or nearly so, becoming erecto-patent in fruit, then prostrate during dehiscence of the seed capsule.

FLOWER

The flowers of *Galanthus* are composed of six perianth segments, six anthers, one style, a receptacle, and a trilocular ovary. The flower is pendent and orientated through almost 180° from the true axis of the plant (in other words, it is upside-down). The perianth segments are free and arranged in two alternate whorls.

The outer perianth segments are conspicuously larger than the inner segments and deeply concave (rather like the bowl of a spoon). They are always white and faintly striated, although they can infrequently have small, green marks at the tips. The outline shape of the outer segments is commonly narrowly obovate to almost circular, with a narrow, unguiculate base. If the base is elongated then the segments are spathulate. The segments are motile, and can move towards or away from the axis depending on ambient air temperature; warmer temperatures cause the flowers to open, and colder ones make them close.

The inner segments are approximately half the dimensions of the outer segments, nearly straight to almost semi-circular, and are nearly always cuneate to obovate in outline (FIGURE 8). In the majority of species a small notch is present at the apex of each inner segment. In those taxa that lack this feature, the apex is either acute and somewhat pointed (e.g. *Galanthus krasnovii*) or obtuse (e.g. *G. platyphyllus*). On the outer face (adaxial surface) of each segment are green markings which, although highly variable, divide taxa into two types: (1) those taxa that have one mark at the apex, near the apical notch, and (2) those with two distinct marks, one apical and one basal. The apical mark of both types is usually either more or less ∧- to ∩-shaped or sometimes almost hippocrepiform to heart-shaped (inverted); occasionally it is split longitudinally into two smaller markings, one on either side of the apical notch (or if

35

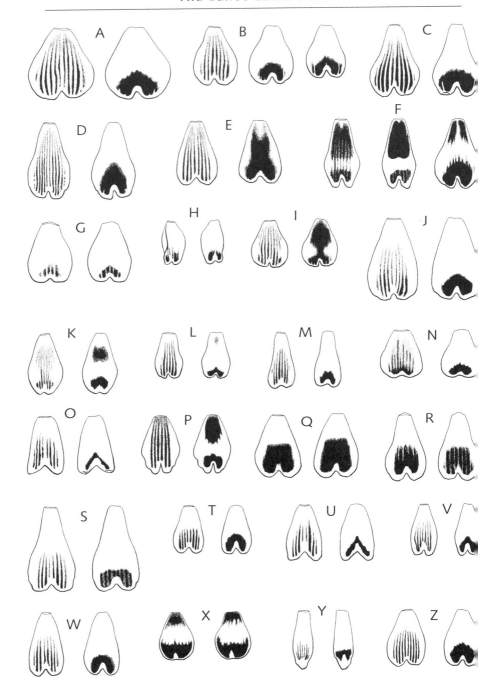

the notch is absent, in approximately the same place). The basal mark found in the two-marked types is usually represented by a more or less rectangular to oval patch, but it can sometimes be no more than a smudge or spot of light green or yellow. In some species the two marks may join to form one large more or less X-shaped mark (e.g. *G. elwesii, G. gracilis*). On the inner face (abaxial surface) are faint green marks composed of narrow, light green stripes. These markings are also variable, being either strictly apical or extending to the base of the segment. The markings either take the shape of those present on the outer surface (e.g. *G. ikariae*), or are much larger and not at all like the mark on the outer surface (e.g. *G. nivalis*). The inner surface is conspicuously ridged and furrowed, in contrast to the more or less smooth outer surface.

All *Galanthus* flowers are fragrant, although a scent usually cannot be detected unless the day is exceptionally warm or the flowers are held immediately underneath the nose. At room temperature, however, most species will produce a noticeable scent; most smell quite pleasant but others are rather acrid and unpleasant (such as *G. koenenianus*, which smells of urine).

STAMENS AND POLLEN (ANDROECIUM)

The stamens are attached to the flat receptacle and positioned in a ring around the style. All parts of the stamens are free, that is, they are not attached to each other or any other part of the flower except the receptacle. The anthers are introrse, non-versatile, yellow-orange, and basifixed to short, whitish filaments. The anthers do not extend beyond the ring of inner perianth segments. Each anther is lobed at the base and gradually tapers to an apiculum at the apex; this long, pointed tip is often slightly curved. In *Galanthus platyphyllus*, however, the apex is not pointed, but is instead either blunt (obtuse) or abruptly apiculate. Dehiscence occurs from ter-

Figure 8. **Inner perianth segments of *Galanthus*.** Inner surfaces to the left and outer surfaces to the right in each example. **A** *G. nivalis*; **B** *G. nivalis*; **C** *G. reginae-olgae* subsp. *reginae-olgae*; **D** *G. reginae-olgae* subsp. *vernalis*; **E** *G. plicatus* subsp. *plicatus*; **F** *G. plicatus* subsp. *byzantinus*; **G** *G. cilicicus*; **H** *G. peshmenii*; **I** *G. gracilis*; **J** *G. elwesii*; **K** *G. fosteri*; **L** *G. koenenianus*; **M** *G. angustifolius*; **N** *G. alpinus* var. *alpinus*; **O** *G. alpinus* var. *bortkewitschianus*; **P** *G. elwesii*; **Q** *G. ikariae*; **R** *G. ikariae*; **S** *G. woronowii*; **T** *G. rizehensis*; **U** *G. lagodechianus*; **V** *G. lagodechianus*; **W** *G. woronowii*; **X** *G. platyphyllus*; **Y** *G. krasnovii*; **Z** *G. transcaucasicus*. Drawn by Eleanor Catherine.

37

minal slits (pseudo-porandrous), which split further towards the base of the anther as anthesis progresses.

Galanthus pollen is orange-yellow and dust-like to the naked-eye. Investigation with an electron microscope reveals that each grain is heteropolar, monosulcate, and approximately 30 μm long (equatorial) by 15 μm wide (polar). The P/E ratio is c. 0.5. The exine is approximately 0.5 mm thick, and the tectum finely perforate. None of the species of *Galanthus* shows any significant differences in pollen morphology.

STYLE AND OVARY (GYNOECIUM)

The style is simple, slender, and slightly longer than the anthers. The stigmatic surface is rather small, and either acapitate, slightly capitate, or minutely three lobed. A transverse section through the style reveals a tri-radiate stylar canal, which continues throughout the length of the style to the placenta.

At the base of the style and filaments is the nectary, which, barely visible to the naked eye, consists of a small area of swollen tissue. The nectary secretes copious nectar, which covers the bases of the filaments and may even run down the inside of the inner perianth segments.

The ovary is inferior, and consists of three locules. Each locule contains numerous ovules, which are positioned on the central column of the ovary (axile placentation) in two rows, with three to six ovules in each row.

FRUIT AND SEED

The capsule, formed from the receptacle and ovary, is green and either oval or almost spherical. Despite its succulent nature the capsule is dehiscent. Dehiscence is confined to the upper half of the capsule, which splits into three along lines of dehiscence that lie roughly between the walls of each locule.

The seeds are ovoid, whitish, and furnished with a large, succulent, tail-like appendage, which is often hooked at the end. This conspicuous structure, which is about twice the length of the seed, is usually referred to as an elaiosome, because it consists of substances that are attractive to ants. Its composition and structure has not, I believe, been thoroughly examined. Later, when the seeds begin to dry, the appendage shrinks considerably and is far less obvious. When dry, the seeds are either pale brown, or mid- to dark brown, depending on the species. The main bulk of a seed consists of endosperm.

ANATOMY

The anatomy of *Galanthus* has been investigated with the aim of understanding the form and function of floral parts (Church, 1908) and for the purposes of providing information on the relationships between the various species (Gottlieb-Tannenhain, 1904; Artjushenko, 1965, 1966, 1970). Of these studies, the leaf-anatomical studies of Artjushenko provide the most important information relating to the systematic relationships of *Galanthus*.

According to Artjushenko (1965), two anatomical characters are particularly informative: the size of the air cavities in the leaf, as viewed in a transverse section, and the shape of the epidermal cells (observed in epidermal peels). Using these anatomical characters, Artjushenko divided *Galanthus* into two major groups: (1) the species from Europe and Asia Minor; and (2) those from the Caucasus. In combination with leaf vernation, a character used with some prominence by Gottlieb-Tannenhain (1904) and Stern (1956), the genus was further subdivided to give five groups, with no formal taxonomic rank. An overview of this arrangement of the species is given in Appendix 2.

Later, Artjushenko (1966) formally recognized the two main geographical groups as sections: Section 1 *Galanthus* and Section 2 *Viridifolii* Kem.-Nath. The shape of the epidermal cells and the geography of the species were the two main characters used to recognize these divisions. Appendix 3 shows the details of this classification. In her most recent account of *Galanthus*, Artjushenko (1970) retained this arrangement of the genus, and leaf colour was added as a supporting character for each of the sections: leaves glaucous for Sect. *Galanthus*, and leaves glaucous, green (shiny, matt, or dull green) for Sect. *Viridifolii* (see Appendix 3).

The leaf anatomy of *Galanthus* has been reassessed recently by Davis and Barnett (1997), with particular reference to the studies of Artjushenko. Full descriptions of the leaf anatomy of the genus and each of its species are given in this paper. In contrast to the work of Artjushenko (1965, 1966, 1970), this study indicates that epidermal cell shape (in surface view) is highly variable in *Galanthus* and of only minimal systematic value. This character is only useful for recognizing *G. plicatus*: the epidermal cells of the adaxial and abaxial epidermis are distinctly rhombic in outline. The epidermal cells of all other species of *Galanthus* are rectangular to narrowly rhombic (more or less rectangular, slightly tapering towards the ends of the cells), a variation that is evident within and between species. This study also shows that leaf cavities (air spaces) are not of critical systematic value. This character is variable within and between the species, and size classes are difficult to establish due to continuous variation. Unlike epidermal cell shape, however, this character does provide some useful systematic information, although it is highly variable within at least five species.

Other systematically informative characters identified by this study are the presence or absence of bulliform cells (enlarged, swollen cells) on the abaxial leaf surface; the presence or absence of a palisade layer; the presence or absence of a midrib; the position of the stomata within the epidermis; and the shape of the epidermal cells in transverse view (Davis and Barnett, 1997).

The Davis and Barnett investigation is comparable to the studies of Artjushenko (1965, 1966, 1970), because it identifies anatomical characters that are consistent with groupings based on either leaf colour and geographical distribution or distribution alone (as in the case of the two earlier papers of Artjushenko). The two authorities differ, however, on the particular characters identified as systematically informative. The 1997 study has also provided useful data at lower levels of taxonomic hierarchy, for example in the identification and circumscription of semi-cryptic species and in the understanding of taxonomic relationships that are not evident by investigation of morphology alone. Anatomical data has provided useful information for understanding the relationships between *Galanthus ikariae* and *G. woronowii*; *G. plicatus* and *G. woronowii*; *G. lagodechianus*, *G. rizehensis*, and *G. transcaucasicus*; and *G. nivalis* and *G. angustifolius* (formerly *G. nivalis* subsp. *angustifolius*). The details of this anatomical information, and other relevant discussions concerning anatomy, are given in the taxonomic part of this monograph.

CYTOLOGY

The majority of *Galanthus* have a chromosome number of 2n = 24. A number of records have counts of 2n = 36, but these have been recorded for species that also have counts of 2n = 24, such as *G. rizehensis* and *G. elwesii. Galanthus lagodechianus* is the exception for the genus, having a count of 2n = 72; this number of chromosomes has also been found in the species regarded here (see Taxonomy of *Galanthus*) as synonymous with *G. lagodechianus*, including *G. cabardensis, G. kemulariae,* and *G. ketzkhovelii.*

The cytology of *Galanthus* has been reviewed several times since the mid-1960s, and the reader who requires more information on this subject should refer to the following works. Species occurring in Armenia, Azerbaijan, Georgia, Russia, and Ukraine are covered in the works of Sveshnikova (1965, 1967, 1971a, 1971b, 1975) and Sveshnikova and Fodor (1983). An overview of the chromosome numbers for the species found in these countries is given in Agapova et al. (1990). The cytology of the Greek species has received careful attention from Kamari (1981, 1982) and Papanicolaou and Zacharof (1983).

No cytological data are available for the recently described *Galanthus koenenianus* and *G. peshmenii.* And for a few of the rarer species the cytology is insufficiently known.

POLLINATION

The flowers of *Galanthus* are adapted for pollination by insect vectors (entomophily), specifically for pollination by bees. These adaptations are both structural and dynamic, and compared with other members of the Amaryllidaceae represent quite a high degree of specialization. Indeed, the structure of the *Galanthus* flower is completely unique within the family, and has no parallel. A detailed account of the features and mechanisms of *Galanthus* pollination is given by Church (1908). However, a lot more work remains to be done on this subject, and detailed field studies are necessary to fully understand the complexities of pollination and gene exchange.

The pendulous orientation of the *Galanthus* flower protects the external parts of the androecium and gynoecium from damage by adverse weather conditions, particularly from rain. Further protection for the internal parts of the flower is afforded by the movement of the outer perianth segments, which enable the flower to 'open' and 'close' depending on the ambient air temperature. During warm weather the outer segments lift to reveal the inner whorl of segments, and during cold weather they move downwards to conceal them. According to Church, the flower does not open until the temperature reaches 10°C. At temperatures below 10°C the flowers close. These movements are totally dependent on temperature and are not effected by light. Flowers brought into a dark, warm room in the evening open within a short time (c. 30 minutes). Church states that this movement is caused by unequal rates of growth-extension in the basal area of each segment. Only a small amount of growth is necessary to cause recurvature of each segment. As the flower gets older this response slows. The growth of each flower, from when the bud first opens until it withers, is considerable, and the length of the outer segments can double (e.g. from 12 to 24 mm) during this period. This 'open and close' mechanism makes the flowers very efficient, because it ensures protection from the elements during periods when pollinator activity is negligible. When conditions are suitable the flower is fully functional.

The pendulous character of the flower means that the bee has to

43

hang almost upside-down to pollinate it. The morphology of the flower is, however, adapted for this purpose. The shape and position of the inner perianth segments are such that they form a loose tube around the anthers and style. This tube-like structure provides a place for the bee to alight while it visits the flower, so it can remove nectar with its proboscis. In this way the inner perianth segments are analogous to the corolla-tube or corona of other flower types. In many species of *Galanthus* the inner segments are curled upwards at the end, which makes the tube-like inner whorl almost campanulate. Church (1908) suggests that this makes the inner segments of *Galanthus* comparable with the flowers of *Polygonatum*, *Convallaria*, and *Endymion*, in which the bee holds on to the margins of the pendulous flower.

The type of coloration found on the inner segments of *Galanthus* is unusual in the Amaryllidaceae, and only in certain species of *Leucojum* (*L. aestivum* and *L. vernum*) is there anything similar. It is often assumed that the green marks play a role in the attraction of insect visitors, as 'honey guides' that indicate a nectar source, but this function has never been scientifically tested. At the apex of each inner perianth segment is a small notch, but the function of this notch, if indeed it has one, is also not clear. It may act as a guide for the pollinator, or perhaps it makes nectar and pollen removal easier, but these ideas are mere speculation. The inner perianth segments of *G. platyphyllus* and *G. krasnovii* lack the typical apical notch, for which the reason or functional significance is also unknown. I cannot even speculate as to the reason for this difference in morphology.

Dehiscence occurs from small slits at the apex of each anther, so the pollen is directed downwards onto the head of the bee as it moves towards the nectar source. *Galanthus* flowers are reported to be buzz-pollinated, meaning the movement of the bee, and specifically the vibrations caused by its wing movement, cause pollen to fall out of the anthers. I do not doubt that this mechanism occurs, but its significance in pollination could be overestimated. According to Church (1908) the pointed tips of the anthers also play a role in pollination, acting as 'triggers' that release pollen when they are touched.

Each anther contains numerous pollen grains which are yellow, very small, and dry. Any slight movement of the flower, such as tapping them slightly with a finger, will cause pollen to fall freely from the flower in small yellow clouds. This pollen release is particularly

44

noticeable when the flower is a few weeks old and the relative humidity is low. The amount of pollen falling into the immediate atmosphere is probably sufficient to cause pollination of other plants nearby, and I have noticed that plants growing close together (e.g. in a cold frame) set seed more frequently than widely spaced plants. It is not known how frequently wind pollination (anemophily) occurs in natural habitats, but it is probably negligible. The distance between individual plants in wild populations is usually too great for anemophily to be effective, as the pollen probably either falls to the ground or becomes dispersed by wind currents.

The structure of the *Galanthus* flower, and particularly its adaptation for entomophily, promotes effective out-crossing and minimizes self pollination. I suspect that *Galanthus* also possess self-incompatibility systems, but this has never been thoroughly tested. Many species of *Galanthus* are inter-fertile and produce viable seed when cross-pollinated with other species. No detailed crossing experiments have been undertaken, but hybrids between quite different species (e.g. *G. elwesii* and *G. plicatus*) have been produced.

In the British Isles, snowdrops are successfully pollinated by wild and hive bees, and in some years a good deal of fruit is set.

ECOLOGY

LIFE CYCLE

During so-called dormancy the constituent parts of the next season's shoot are actively developing. Examination of a bulb in July shows that the development of the flower-bud is already well advanced, and that all the necessary parts of the shoot are present. Nearer the time of flowering, two months or so before anthesis, the shoot elongates sufficiently to rupture the sheath, and shortly afterwards the tips of the leaves emerge through the soil. The flowering period of *Galanthus* occurs from October (e.g. *G. reginae-olgae*) all the way through to August (i.e., *G. platyphyllus*, but not in cultivation), although most species flower in the winter or early spring (January to April). If the conditions are favourable the shoot elongates with incredible speed. Conversely, if the habitat is cold, elongation is delayed. In the early stages of growth the leaves provide some protection for the flower-bud. In species with applanate and explicative vernation, the tips of the leaves are held tight over the bud. In the case of species with supervolute vernation, the leaves are tightly wrapped around the bud. Further elongation and development of the leaves exposes the flower-bud. The scape then continues to expand to its full length, although a further elongation does occur during flowering. At this stage the flower is more or less fully developed, erect, and enclosed within the transparent spathe. Eventually the flower expands and ruptures the membranous tissue of the spathe: the flower is now fully exposed to the environment. At first the flower remains erect, but after a short time the pedicel extends and orientates the flower through 180°. Experimentation by Church (1908) has shown that the flower is orientated by the pedicel independently of light or the effect of gravity. Shortly after this stage the flower is fully functional and is ready for pollination.

The time of flowering is more or less fixed for each species, although a shift in flowering time of up to six weeks is not uncommon. These shifts, factors of decreased or increased growth, are mostly governed by local climate. Increases in soil and air temperatures and amount of rainfall (or the availability of ground water) are the most important parameters. In the wild, flowering coincides with pollinator activity, which is at its greatest during warm, fair weather; although, flowering does not always occur during optimal conditions for pollination.

The flower lasts for an average of about one month, which is a long time compared with many other bulbous plants, even other members of the Amaryllidaceae, which can have rather ephemeral flowers. The flowers of *Hannonia* and *Lapiedra*, for example, often last only a matter of days. If the climate is unfavourable, due to very cold or very warm temperatures, the flower may not last more than three weeks, or less. But if the climate is favourable, the flowers may last up to six weeks, gradually fading as the capsule begins to develop. After flowering, parts of the flower, particularly the stamens, remain on the end of the capsule, but eventually they fall as fruit development continues. If the flower is not pollinated the capsule continues to expand, but eventually it turns yellowish, withers, and dies. The capsule of successfully pollinated flowers gradually increases in size and develops into an ovoid, berry-like fruit. At first, the developing fruit is held above the leaves by the scape, but as development progresses the scape becomes lax and lowers the capsule towards the ground. During fruit formation the leaves and scape continue to grow, but the height of the scape nearly always exceeds that of the leaves so that the fruit is held clear of the leaves. At maturity the scape becomes prostrate, and the fruit rests on the surface of the soil.

In the majority of species, that is, those flowering in February, the fruit ripens at the end of April or in June. During dehiscence the seeds remain in the capsule for some time, until they either fall out or are removed by ants. The fruit remains attached to the scape during and after dehiscence. If the fruits are removed from the scape before they are completely ripe, even shortly before dehiscence, they remain intact and do not shed their seeds. The seeds are dispersed by ants, which are attracted to the large, white, succulent appendage that covers the greater part of the seed (the elaiosome). Ants are capable of locating *Galanthus* seeds with incredible speed, and waste no time in emptying the capsules and taking the seeds to their nest. I assume that the advantage of this relationship for the plant is effective dispersal. Firstly, the seed is carried to

47

a suitable site, some distance from the parent plant and, secondly, it is placed in a favourable environment for germination and establishment. This scenario could be particularly important for species that grow in rocky areas, such as *G. peshmenii* and certain ecological variants of *G. woronowii*, where the placement of a seed into a suitable location for germination (e.g. a pocket of soil) is far more critical, because these species are sometimes surrounded by rocky, soil-less substrates.

After dehiscence, the aerial parts of the plant gradually fade and disappear. If germination is successful, the seedlings produce a small bulb and a single seed-leaf by the end of the next season. In the second season two leaves appear, and the bulb increases in size. In the third or fourth year the seedling matures and flowers, and has the potential to produce a new generation of plants.

PHYSICAL ECOLOGY

Galanthus occur principally in woodlands and forest. In locations where they do not grow in association with trees, the local environment is always cool and has plenty of water available during the seasons of growth and flowering. *Galanthus* do not occur in open, dry, sun-baked places, such as Mediterranean garrigue- or maquis-type vegetation, or on steppe. There are always exceptions, of course, but these generalizations serve to describe the basic ecological character of the genus.

The majority of species occur at altitudes above 1000 m, and several species are true alpine plants (above 1500–2000 m). At high altitudes, and in the more northerly latitudes, many species occur in areas that experience long and severe winters, remaining snow-covered for long periods. In such locations *Galanthus* do not flower until temperatures rise in the late winter or early spring, when deep snow has melted and the soil defrosted. In the southern part of its range, such as the southern Balkans and Mediterranean region, higher altitudes provide a more suitable environment than surrounding lowlands. Where the altitude is not that high (between 400 and 800 m), such as on many of the Aegean Islands, refugia-type habitats offer suitable niches for existence: steep-sided river and stream valleys provide cool, moist, and shady micro-environments. Populations that occur further north, such as central Europe and areas of the northern Balkans, exist either in mountainous areas or in the lowlands. In these regions, cooler and wetter conditions prevail, enabling populations to exist at lower altitudes.

Galanthus are usually found in areas of reasonably high seasonal rainfall, or where plenty of water is available from other seasonal sources, such as melting snow (hence the common association with mountains). Water also affects the local distribution of populations and individuals. *Galanthus* are often encountered near streams, rivers, lakes, in river valleys, and in steep-sided gorges. The amount of water needed for optimum growth and survival is different for each species. Some species exist in quite dry places; others need far more moisture. *Galanthus cilicicus* and *G. peshmenii* exist in the Mediterranean region, which has a modest annual precipitation, whereas *G. platyphyllus*, for example, frequently occurs in very wet places, such as in pools of water produced from melting snow. However, no species grow in permanently wet or boggy conditions.

Undisturbed deciduous woodland is by far the most frequent habitat for *Galanthus*. Broad-leafed evergreen woodland and coniferous woodland also provide environments for many species. In broad-leafed evergreen woodland the trees are widely spaced or interspersed with shrubs and smaller trees, so enough light reaches the herb layer where *Galanthus* exist. In most cases, this means that only primary or long-established evergreen forest can support populations of *Galanthus*. In the case of woodlands that contain a high percentage of coniferous species, such as *Abies* and *Pinus*, it is more usual to find *Galanthus* occurring at the edges or in clearings. Mixed woodland composed of either deciduous species or a mixture of deciduous and evergreen species is also a frequent habitat.

Galanthus occasionally occur in areas of grass or grassland, but this is usually only in areas of higher altitude, at about 1000 m or above. *Galanthus platyphyllus* is found almost exclusively in subalpine to alpine meadows. In many subalpine grassland habitats, woodland is usually not far away, and populations may either occur exclusively in the grassland or extend across both habitats. Alpine grasslands are above the tree-line and are thus devoid of trees. In both types of grassland habitat, the turf is always short immediately before and during the flowering period.

Slope and aspect are also important factors affecting local distribution. *Galanthus* very often occur in places where there is an appreciable incline, and many populations grow on steep slopes. The greatest exception to this rule are populations that grow alongside rivers and streams, but even in these locations, the sloping sides of the river bank are also frequent habitats. In regions that experience long, dry summers, such as the southern part of the distribution range, many populations occur on hillsides, mountains, and cliffs that have a north-facing aspect. This position provides a considerably cooler and moister environment than the south-facing side. Even in cooler and wetter areas, however, many populations still occur in places that are north-facing.

Soil is another important factor influencing distribution. *Galanthus* occur most frequently on base-rich soils, or at least, on soils overlying basic rocks, such as limestone or other calcareous substrates. The majority of the populations that I have visited occur on areas of limestone, and if soil or substrate is recorded on herbarium specimens, it is nearly always noted as calcareous. Not all *Galanthus* occur on basic soils, however, and some species are commonly found on neutral to acid soils overlying volcanic and metamorphic rocks, including *G. plicatus*, *G. krasnovii*, and *G. rizehensis*.

Galanthus are sometimes found in most unlikely habitats. *Galanthus peshmenii* stands out as one such exception, because it occurs in places remarkably atypical for the genus, particularly in its locations on the island of Kastellorhizo. On this island, *G. peshmenii* occurs almost exclusively on limestone cliffs and rock outcrops, eking out a tenacious existence in crevices and hollows. The species exists there in the relatively cool conditions of the north-facing, shady rocks and boulders. The bulbs occur deep within the rocks, which provide protection from desiccation and grazing animals. *Galanthus peshmenii* grows at very low altitudes, as low as 5 m above sea level, and sometimes as little as 10 m from the seashore.

Galanthus cilicicus and some populations of *G. reginae-olgae* also occur at low altitudes (c. 300 m) in Mediterranean maquis vegetation. In these habitats, individual plants are often found in more open places, in grassy areas and between rocks or shrubs. *Galanthus cilicicus* sometimes occurs on low limestone rocks, which are not too dissimilar from the limestone pavements of northern England and Scotland.

At the other end of the extreme is *Galanthus platyphyllus*, which, as I have already mentioned, grows in alpine meadows. This species is a true alpine, growing up to c. 2600 m in the high Caucasus. The season here is very late, and the winter snow does not clear until July or August, the period when *G. platyphyllus* flowers.

In the eastern area of distribution, in the Caucasus and surrounding regions between the Black and Caspian seas, *Galanthus* occur either in the high central Caucasus or in high altitude, high rainfall areas around the sea coasts. *Galanthus alpinus, G. platyphyllus*, and *G. lagodechianus* are examples of high altitude species mainly confined to the central Caucasus. *Galanthus woronowii, G. rizehensis*, and *G. krasnovii* are found almost exclusively in the mountainous areas around the eastern coast of the Black Sea, and *G. transcaucasicus* occurs in the mountains that run along the southern part of the Caspian Sea. There are, of course, exceptions to these distributions, and some species occur in both in regions.

In the coastal region around the Black Sea, the position and height of the Pontus mountains and western Transcaucasian ranges, coupled with their proximity to the sea, give rise to an area of high rainfall. The forests and woodlands in this region are luxuriant, particularly in the foothills of the mountains, supporting large numbers of herbaceous plants. *Galanthus* occur here in relatively large numbers, in mixed deciduous woodland (*Fagus orientalis, Alnus* spp., *Carpinus* spp., *Quercus* spp.) and evergreen woodland (*Abies* spp., *Pinus* spp., *Taxus baccata, Buxus colchica*). In areas of particularly high rainfall, *G. woronowii* grows in very meagre soils on limestone scree and on the rock ledges of steep-sided river gorges.

In most regions of the central Caucasus the winters are long and severe, and the snow cover remains for long periods. The geophyte flora, including *Galanthus*, does not flower until temperatures rise and the deep snow has melted, which may be months after the flowering period of the populations near the coast. In common with the other species, the most frequent habitat is mixed deciduous woodlands, followed by coniferous woodland. As in other mountain habitats, populations can also be located at the margins of woodlands, in clearings, and in other open areas.

Habitats for individual species are described in more detail in the Taxonomy of *Galanthus*.

CONSERVATION

The survival of many *Galanthus* species is threatened in nature due to the pressures of humankind. The two main threats are the ever-increasing demands for land (e.g. forestry, agriculture, and settlement), which are diminishing the natural habitat available, and the collecting of *Galanthus* for the horticultural bulb trade, which is decreasing natural populations. *Galanthus* is the most heavily traded wild-collected bulb genus in the world. Damage to natural populations from over-collecting by bulb enthusiasts can also cause the decline of species.

In most countries it is forbidden to remove *Galanthus* from the wild, as they are usually protected by local law. Trade or export of bulbs is controlled by the Convention on International Trade in Endangered Species of Wild Fauna and Flora (CITES). *Galanthus* are placed on Appendix II of CITES, an action that requires members of the treaty to regulate imports and exports through a system of permits. For persons without a CITES permit, the trade, or import and export, of any quantity of bulbs is illegal. This legislation thus effectively prevents anyone (without a permit) from moving any quantity of *Galanthus* across the borders of the countries within the CITES treaty. Permits are obtained from the CITES management offices of the export and import countries involved.

The threat to *Galanthus* from habitat destruction is a complicated issue involving many factors, and considerable effort is needed to reduce or curtail this pressure. Damage to populations caused by over-collecting is, however, far easier to reduce and we, as consumers, gardeners, and horticulturists, should take the responsibility to ensure that it is kept to an absolute minimum. This is not a difficult goal to achieve: by buying or trading only in nursery-raised stock or plants produced from other sustainable sources, and by not collecting *Galanthus* in the wild, we can reduce the threat to each species.

Galanthus elwesii is by far the most common wild-collected species in commerce. Trade in this species has existed since the turn of the century, and accelerated in intensity up to the 1990s. During the last few decades millions of bulbs of *G. elwesii* have been exported from Turkey and sold in European garden centres and supermarkets. It has been estimated that during a five-year period, between the late 1980s and early 1990s, about 175 million bulbs of *G. elwesii* (probably also including other *Galanthus* species) were exported from Turkey to The Netherlands. A large number of these bulbs have survived in European gardens, but the majority have perished because of the unsuitability of this species (and others) to the climate. The natural distribution of this species is quite vast, probably being one of the most widespread species after *G. nivalis.* In its various localities the habitats are very variable, and certain populations, most notably those of southern Turkey, are almost certainly not suitable for many of the cold, wet gardens of northern Europe. The unsuitable climate, however, is probably not the main reason why wild traded *G. elwesii* has not fared so well in cultivation. The more likely cause is that the majority of imported plants are sold as dry, dormant bulbs. Unlike many other bulbous plants such as *Narcissus*, dry bulbs do not establish very well and often perish soon after planting.

When buying bulbs of *Galanthus elwesii*, or any other snowdrop for that matter, it is better to purchase stock of a reliable clone or horticultural variety, preferably when it is sold 'in the green' (i.e., still with its leaves); and, once again, always check to be sure the bulbs you are offered have been propagated from legitimate nursery stock or sustainable wild sources. Snowdrops offered by specialist snowdrop nurseries are almost certain to make first class garden plants; those collected directly from the wild are not.

It is encouraging to see that many of the larger bulb companies are selling good quality, home-produced *Galanthus* bulbs, including *G. elwesii*. These stocks are raised from selected, reliable clones. Schemes for the cultivation of *Galanthus* in Turkey, not involving the collection of wild bulbs, are now also producing favourable results, both for the local growers and the environment. Turkey has adopted a system of quotas to significantly reduce the number of wild-collected *Galanthus* bulbs in the trade. Collection sites are monitored to measure the effect of trade on natural populations.

For those requiring more information about gardening and plant conservation I can recommend *The Gardener's Guide to Plant Conservation*, an excellent and concise book by Marshall (1993).

CULTIVATION

OUTDOOR CULTIVATION

Most *Galanthus* are easy to grow in the open garden, provided some forethought is given when selecting a site and some care is given when planting. Once the basic requirements are satisfied, only minimal aftercare is necessary. All the species are hardy, to a greater or lesser degree, and many can withstand very cold winters.

In the wild, most species of *Galanthus* occur in deciduous woodlands, and as a general rule, the practice is to emulate these conditions in cultivation. Deciduous woodlands offer plenty of light during autumn and winter, because the trees are leafless, and in summer the herb-layer of the woodland floor is shaded by the leaves of the trees. In the garden, *Galanthus* should therefore be planted in a position that receives good light during their growing season (autumn to spring), with cool conditions during the resting period (the summer). This is a gross oversimplification, but it serves to establish the basic requirements for the genus in cultivation. Most species benefit from either good light or direct sunlight (while in flower), but areas in semi- or dappled-shade are also suitable. Locations in deep shade should be avoided.

During the growing season, *Galanthus* need to be in a situation that receives sufficient water, although the soil should never become waterlogged, or the surrounding air too humid. Even in the resting period the planting site should not become sun-baked, although one or two species will tolerate drier conditions (such as *G. elwesii* and *G. fosteri*).

Galanthus are not particularly fussy about the soil, but a rather heavy, fertile loam, with a neutral or slightly alkaline pH is usually considered the most suitable. Good results are achieved on a wide variety of soils, however, including those on sand and clay. Highly alkaline soils, such as those on chalk or limestone, also suit the majority of species. A few prefer slightly more acidic, woodland-type soils, such as those consisting of large quantities of decomposed leaf litter or other humus-rich material. If the soil is not satisfactory then it can be improved by adding either loam, grit, or humus, as required. Impoverished soils lacking in organic matter can be improved by top-dressing or digging in well-rotted leaf litter or other humus-rich material, although I have heard it said that *Galanthus* do not like to be given rich organic material, such as mushroom compost and well-rotted horse manure. Stern (1956, p. 78) had a very clear opinion on this matter and wrote: 'Animal manure is poison to snowdrops and nothing will kill them more quickly'. While I dare not advocate the use of animal manure, it is my experience that most *Galanthus* are not harmed by it. I have used well-rotted animal manure and mushroom-compost on my own collection to no ill effect, and found that they benefit from it. Indeed, I know of one galanthophile who top-dresses his collection with a very liberal covering of well-rotted horse manure each year, or thereabouts.

If the basic requirements of the individual species can be satisfied, then it is up to personal taste and imagination where *Galanthus* are planted. The woodland garden is, naturally, one of the best places to locate them, and many species do very well in this garden habitat. The rock garden is suitable for many species, and it can provide suitable niches for species that are a little more demanding, such as those requiring extra drainage or protection from cold winds. Top dressing with gravel, as commonly used on rock gardens and alpine beds, is beneficial because it keeps the plants clean, deters weeds, and provides some protection from slugs and snails. Ornamental bark mulch, however, does not seem to be compatible with *Galanthus* and is best avoided.

Planting in grass is a useful option for the more robust types, including *Galanthus nivalis*, *G. plicatus*, the larger clones of *G. elwesii*, and many of the garden cultivars. The grass must not be too thick or vigorous, otherwise the *Galanthus* will not be able to compete for space, moisture, and later, light. Grassy areas in half or dappled shade are likely to be the most suitable, because the grass is often thinner and weaker in these places. As with other bulbs growing through grass, the plants must be left to die back before the grass is cut. *Galanthus nivalis* can be grown in grassy areas that contain substantial numbers of herbs, so the grass mixtures containing meadow and wild-flower seeds are suitable. Flower beds, perennial beds, and mixed borders can also be suitable homes, provided that the ground is not disturbed by digging or rigorous weeding. In such situations *Galanthus* can be used to add life to parts of the garden that would otherwise be dull and uninteresting during the winter and early spring. Labelling plants properly will reduce the risk of damage when undertaking weeding or similar activities.

For those wishing to grow a larger collection of plants together in one place, the raised-bed method probably offers the best solution. This method has been used with good results by many growers of snowdrops and other bulbous plants. This structure is simply an area of raised soil held in by a surround of wood or bricks. The size of the bed is up to personal taste or, perhaps, the amount of available space, but ideally it should not be less than approximately 1 × 2 m. The sides of the frame need only be about 10–15 cm high but a little higher, up to 30 cm, is better; it should be deep enough to provide an improved depth of soil and better drainage than the surrounding ground. In most cases wood is the preferred building material, but bricks are also suitable. Railway sleepers are admirably suited to the building of such a frame, being sturdy, long lasting, and attractive. Once constructed, the ground is lightly dug within the frame and filled with soil. The type of soil used depends on what species are going to be grown, but ordinary garden soil with a good quantity (one-third to one-half by volume) of well-rotted compost, leaf mould, or other bulky humus-rich material is suitable for most species; for thin soils that lack substance, plenty of loam should be added. After construction a period of at least a few weeks is allowed for the soil to consolidate, but on no account should it be firmed down hard at any stage. After this the bed can be planted. Individual bulbs or clumps need plenty of space between, approximately 15–30 cm for mature plants and 5–10 cm for seedlings and young bulblets from twin-scales. This decreases the chances of disease, and provides some measure of isolation should one plant or part of the collection become diseased or infested with pests. The exact planting scheme will depend on personal requirements, taste, and purpose. Other bulbous plants, perennials or small shrubs can also be planted in the frame, if desired. A bed incorporating a few other types of plant is likely to provide a healthier environment. Each accession should be permanently labelled, and it is also good practice to make a sketch of the position of each plant or group of propagules in the frame, just in case the labels are lost or inadvertently moved.

Galanthus often look their best in the wild-garden, or in parks and larger estates where large numbers of bulbs are planted. Large drifts of any bulbous plant are an impressive and magical sight, and *Galanthus* is certainly no exception. Even within the confines of a modest town garden the effect of mass planting can be recreated by planting one or two of the faster spreading species or their cultivars. *Galanthus nivalis*, and many of its multitude of cultivars, is eminently suitable for this purpose; this species is inexpensive, well-suited to a cool temperate climate, robust, and rapidly reproductive.

Most species of *Galanthus* are perfectly hardy in the British Isles, Europe, and much of North America and will survive even the harshest of winters. However, many of the species from more southerly latitudes, such as the southern Balkans, the Mediterranean region, and southern Turkey, sometimes require a little more protection and slightly drier conditions. These species include *G. elwesii*, *G. gracilis*, *G. reginae-olgae*, *G. cilicicus*, *G. fosteri*, and *G. peshmenii*; the last three may need to be cultivated under glass in some areas (see below for a discussion of this method). These six species should be grown in situations that receive plenty of sun through their growing season: winter and spring for *G. elwesii*, *G. gracilis*, and *G. fosteri*, and autumn to spring for the autumn-flowering species, *G. peshmenii* and *G. reginae-olgae*, and for *G. cilicicus*, which flowers slightly later. These species, excluding some variants of *G. elwesii* and *G. gracilis*, require moderate to good drainage. If necessary, the soil can be improved by adding either coarse grit or sharp sand, or the plants can be grown in a raised bed or on the rock garden. Planting underneath established deciduous trees is another alternative, for the soil there is usually drier than in other places in the open garden. In the summer these species can tolerate direct sunlight on the soil, but it must not become dust-dry; in this matter the type of soil plays an important role, because some types, such as sand and clay soils, can dry out very quickly. Loam soils and those on limestone or chalk retain moisture, and even if they appear dry on the surface are often moist and cool several centimetres below.

In his very useful book *Seven Gardens*, Anderson (1973, p. 116) tells us that he planted *Galanthus elwesii* and *G. reginae-olgae* on a 'fiercely drained' dry stone wall, at Lower Slaughter in the Cotswolds: 'Strange as it may seem, *Galanthus elwesii* is at home as also *G. reginae-olgae*'.

Some *Galanthus* species have wide distributions, and populations can occur in quite different habitats and climates. Plants adapt to their environment, and so, within one species, the ecology is often slightly, or even quite considerably, variable. This has a bearing on cultivation, as the requirements of some clones will be different from others, even within the same species. For example, most clones of *G. elwesii* will grow just about anywhere in the garden, whereas others appear to be more demanding, unless the grower is familiar with that particular variant. In some cases it is a matter of trial and error, and one must keep a close watch on new acquisitions. Clones of species that have been in cultivation for several years or decades tend to fare better than plants of recent wild origin; second generation seedlings of wild-collected plants usually make much better garden plants than their parent(s).

With plants that are proving difficult to keep, it is usually better to move them to another part of the garden to see if they improve in a different situation, rather than watch them decline where they are. If one is fortunate to receive a large number of plants of a single clone, then it is probably best to try them in different parts of the garden to see where they do best.

Galanthus bulbs are often sold dry, when they are in their dormant phase. This method of merchandizing is suitable for many of the Mediterranean bulbous plants that do not suffer from drying, such as *Narcissus*, *Crocus*, *Hyacinthus*, and *Scilla*, but it is inappropriate for many woodland plants, such as *Galanthus* and *Cyclamen*. Bulbs of snowdrops left for months or even just weeks in warm, dry supermarkets and garden centres will not produce very good plants the following season, if they survive at all. It is therefore always best to purchase *Galanthus* when they are in leaf and the bulbs fully turgid, a state which is often referred to as 'in the green'. Specialist *Galanthus* suppliers nearly always sell their bulbs in this way, despatching plants soon after they have finished flowering. It is advantageous if the underground parts of the plant are covered with some moist peat, or another sterile, moisture-retentive medium, as this will reduce desiccation of the bulb and roots. Plants bought in this way will usually flower in the next season and will suffer only a small check in their growth.

Planting *Galanthus* is a simple task, and if the soil is suitable it will need little or no preparation. For small numbers of plants the hole can be dug with a trowel; for larger quantities, or where the soil is difficult to dig, a small spade will be needed. The hole should be at least deep enough to accommodate the plant at its original planting depth, which is usually the distance from the roots to the top of the sheath. It is best to make the hole slightly deeper and loosen the soil at the bottom, and add good top-soil or sterile potting compost to give the roots a good start. Many growers place a handful of sharp sand at the bottom of the hole and place the bulbs directly on top of this. I am not sure of the exact purpose of this practice, but it may serve to keep the basal region of the bulb clean until roots are formed in the next season, thus preventing disease. The hole can then be filled with new soil, the original soil, or soil that has been improved by adding loam, leaf-mould, grit, and so forth. The soil around the plant should be firmed but not so hard that it becomes compacted. Each plant should be planted at its original planting depth, which is approximately at the demarcation line between the green (above ground) and white or yellow (below ground) parts. If it is difficult to ascertain the original planting depth level the soil at the top of the sheath. Dry bulbs should be planted at a depth of approximately two to three times the height of the bulb. The amount of care taken when planting often depends on the rarity of the species or cultivar being planted. A roughly dug hole and a heel-in with a boot is suitable for mass plantings of G. *nivalis* or strong-growing cultivars, whereas some of the trickier species benefit from extra care and attention.

Particularly rare or slow-growing species, or ones that are needed for show and display, can be grown in lattice pots. The lattice pots used for aquatic pond plants, which have plastic mesh sides, are the most suitable. The size of the mesh should be sufficient to let the roots emerge from the pot into the soil, but small enough to stop the bulbs and bulblets from falling out. These pots are filled with a good loam-based potting medium and then planted in the ground so the rim is just below the surface. The labels should be placed either within the pot or tied directly to it, to aid location. This system combines the advantages of growing plants in conventional pots and out in the open ground. When the plants have outgrown their containers they can be lifted and divided.

AFTERCARE

Generally speaking, *Galanthus* do not require a great deal of after-care and can be left undisturbed for many years. It is commonly stated that clumps need to be lifted and divided every three years to increase the number of plants and prevent die-back from congestion. This rule is a useful yardstick, but is not universally applicable to all species or cultivars and dividing this frequently can be detrimental to plant health. After division, many plants take a year or so to settle down, and so disturbing them in the third year means that they never get a chance to become properly established, and thus they are never at their best. Even some of the more vigorous types will come to no harm if left for five to seven years, or longer. Moreover, some clones have the greatest impact when growing in tight colonies. Like many other aspects of gardening, a careful and sensitive judgement is more useful than any rule or generalization.

In most gardens with average to good soil, feeding is not necessary, especially if top dressing with organic material is undertaken. An application of general purpose fertilizer at the standard recommended rate, once a year or every other year, will suffice for gardens on poorer soils. For gardens on very poor soils the amount should be increased, or one of the modern slow release fertilizers (also recommended for plants in pots) can be substituted. Personally I prefer organic fertilizers, such as fish, blood, and bone, but usually I find feeding unnecessary. Feeding *Galanthus* can have a significant effect on plant size, and I know a few growers who like to increase the stature of their plants by giving them a generous feeding regime.

During December and January it is often worth keeping an eye open for emerging shoots and flower-buds, so that if there is anything likely to obstruct the growth of emerging plants it can be removed or cut back.

If the ground in which *Galanthus* are growing becomes dry during the growing season it may be necessary to water them. This is particularly important for those species that originate from areas of high rainfall or that experience wet conditions during growth, such as *G. platyphyllus* and *G. krasnovii*. In most cases, however, watering is not necessary.

COMPANION PLANTING

Very rarely is one so fortunate as to have unlimited space in which to grow all the plants one would like. For this reason it is often necessary to grow different types of plants together, so that the limited space is optimized. For some growers this is a problem, but for others it is an opportunity to make the best of their plants by combining them together, or planting in such a way that each area of the garden is of interest throughout the year.

Ground cover such as herbaceous plants, many types of ferns, and woody creepers can be successfully planted with *Galanthus*. Of the herbaceous types, many of the woodland or shade tolerant geraniums (*Geranium* spp.) are ideal because their rhizomatous stems do not penetrate too far into the soil, or they cover a large area of soil from a relatively small root space. *Geranium* 'Kashmir White', *G. pyrenaicum*, and *G. lambertii* are three species amongst many that do this job particularly well. Some of the stronger-growing, more invasive varieties such as *Geranium* 'Buxton's Blue' are not so useful, since they tend to cover the soil too densely. The advantage with many geraniums is that they can be pulled away from emerging *Galanthus* shoots in the winter, yet still put on plenty of new growth and give a good show later in the year.

Deciduous ferns are also very good companion plants because they provide a good amount of soil coverage without taking up too much root space, but the stoloniferous varieties, such as *Matteuccia struthiopteris* (ostrich fern), are best avoided. Many of the garden ferns come into leaf after the leaves of *Galanthus* have died down, and so competition for light and space is not a problem. Species and cultivars of *Dryopteris* and *Polystichum* are very well suited for this purpose.

Ivy (*Hedera* spp.) is classically associated with *Galanthus*; they are often seen together in flower arrangements and on Christmas cards. In the garden, *Hedera* are sometimes considered a bit of a nuisance, because they are often invasive and rather coarse, but they can be used to good effect. The combination of *Galanthus* flowers with the deep green backing of *Hedera* leaves offers something particularly pleasing, which probably explains the popularity of this common combination. In the living garden, however, only the more robust species of *Galanthus*, including *G. nivalis* and the larger forms of *G. elwesii*, are suitable for growing through *Hedera*, as ivy is inclined to be too vigorous for many species. To some, *Hedera* is unattractive and 'thuggy', but it does provide an effective ground cover, and many different species and cultivars are of horticultural value.

Cyclamen make good companion plants for *Galanthus*, as their leaves provide a neat, green backdrop, not unlike the effect of *Hedera*. Indeed, the foliage of *Cyclamen* is remarkably similar to that of *Hedera*, especially *C. hederifolium*, which as the specific epithet suggests, has ivy-like leaves. *Cyclamen* are first-class garden subjects in their own right, and will out-stage *Galanthus* at certain times of the year. With careful planning, however, both can be planted to provide an area of beauty throughout their respective growing seasons;

for example, plant *C. hederifolium*, an autumn-flowering species, with spring-flowering *Galanthus*, or plant *C. coum*, a spring-flowering species, with autumnal or late-spring-flowering *Galanthus*. *Cyclamen* are particularly good 'bed-partners' because they are not invasive, yet can still provide some measure of ground cover. Furthermore, the leaves of most species remain attractive for a good many months and do not become overbearing or leggy after flowering. For those interested in creating a more natural look in their garden, *Cyclamen* are good candidates for companion planting schemes; they are commonly found growing side-by-side with *Galanthus* in the wild.

In the same league as *Cyclamen*, and with many similar attributes, are hellebores (*Helleborus* spp.). Again, these are excellent garden subjects on their own, but they can be used in combination with *Galanthus* to create areas of impact in the late winter and early spring garden. Most of the garden-worthy hellebores flower at the same time of year, or slightly later, than many of the *Galanthus* species and require very similar growing conditions. Hellebore species with leaves that persist through the summer and winter months, such as *H. orientalis*, have the advantage that they provide some measure of ground cover. *Galanthus* can be planted quite close to hellebores with no ill effect, although it may be necessary to cut back the old leaves when they cover emerging *Galanthus* buds.

CULTIVATION IN POTS

Galanthus are generally not suitable plants for growing in pots, but with care a measure of success can be achieved. In some circumstances culture in pots is unavoidable, such as during alterations to the garden or when growing plants for display or for shows. In some cold districts it is likely that a few species will need to be grown under glass, which could mean that they need to be accommodated in pots.

The first consideration is choice of container. For reasons that will become apparent in the following paragraphs, it is preferable to grow *Galanthus* in good quality, porous, clay pots. These should be of the taller variety, so that the roots have an undisturbed, cool, deep root-run. The width of the pot is also important. As a general guide three to five bulbs can be accommodated in a 10 cm pot and six to ten in a 15 cm one, depending on the size of the bulbs. And the pots should be clean.

The next consideration is the choice of a suitable growing medium. I always prefer a loam-based soil for pot-grown plants, which is undoubtedly the best type for *Galanthus*. For mature plants, a standard potting soil mix is suitable, to which one quarter by volume of small (c. 3 mm) grit should be added. For species that require a slightly lighter soil, such as *G. plicatus*, include well-rotted, good quality leaf-mould (or peat if there is no suitable alternative). Before potting, place a circular piece of plastic gauze at the bottom of the pot. This serves to keep the soil in the pot and prevents worms, woodlice, etc., from burrowing into the potting medium— a tip passed on to me by Tony Hall at Kew. Thick, small-meshed greenhouse shading material can also be used for this purpose.

Galanthus potted in the green should be planted at the same depth they were before being removed from the ground or from their last pot. Dormant bulbs should be planted at least two to three times as deep as the height of the bulb. If the pot cannot accommodate at least 5–7 cm of soil above and below the bulb, a deeper one should be used. Fill the pot to within a few centimetres of the rim, and top-dress with gravel or grit if preferred. If the plant still has its foliage, water it thoroughly; dry, dormant bulbs need only be given a light watering. If temperatures near or below freezing are imminent, delay watering until warmer weather arrives.

Whatever the location in which the pots are finally situated, it is strongly recommended that they be plunged into a bed of sand. The plunge-bed method has two great advantages. Firstly, the pots are more likely to maintain the correct level of moisture, which is important because *Galanthus* do not like to dry out. Secondly, plants are less prone to fluctuations in temperature. The porous quality of the clay pot enables it to draw water from the sand and release water when the pot is too wet. The deep pots and surrounding moist sand will ensure that the bulbs are kept at a temperature comparable to those planted in the garden. In the summer this means that the bulbs are more likely to remain cool. In winter, this system reduces the risk of plants freezing in their pots, since they are not exposed to the elements like free-standing pots. Soil in a wet pot can easily turn into a block of ice in very cold weather, damaging underground parts, and ultimately causing the death of a plant. Each pot should be plunged deeply, so that the level of the soil corresponds roughly to the level of the sand. After plunging, water the sand surrounding the pot; if the soil in the pot is dry water this too.

In summer, the sand in the plunge-bed will not normally need watering, but as a guideline the sides of the pots should be slightly moist and cool to the touch, particularly at the base where the bulbs are situated. If for any reason the bed dries out too much, give it a light watering, and then after a few days check it again. If the sand does dry out for a short period, say a week or so, the plants should suffer no harm. However, during August and September take more care with the watering regime, as many species will have started into growth by then. In winter and spring, the main growing period, keep the sand evenly moist at all times but never wet or water-logged.

It is essential to repot *Galanthus* at least every second year, although it is much better to repot annually. After one season's growth the condition of the soil deteriorates and loses many of its important qualities. At the very least, the soil becomes exhausted of nutrients, but the structure and texture of the soil also changes, to the extent where plants suffer. The best time for repotting is after flowering, whilst plants are still in the green. Alternatively, repot in the early stages of dormancy, shortly after the foliage has died back

By now readers may have come to the conclusion that it is much easier to grow plants in the open garden, rather than in pots.

CULTIVATION UNDER GLASS

When it is necessary to protect plants from the combination of low temperatures and excessive moisture, growing 'under glass' is a suitable option. In the British Isles, only three species need normally be considered for growing under glass: *Galanthus peshmenii*, *G. fosteri*, and *G. cilicicus*. All of these species can be successfully grown outdoors, particularly in milder districts, but in a few locations it is preferable to give some protection. In some gardens *G. reginae-olgae* will also benefit from the extra protection of growing under glass.

Galanthus can be grown in cold frames, unheated glasshouses, and even in polythene tunnels (poly-tunnels). These structures should receive plenty of light during winter and have some provision for shading during the summer; good ventilation is essential at all times of the year. If the plants are grown in pots they are best plunged into a bed of sand, as discussed above. *Galanthus* can also be planted directly into the soil of the greenhouse or frame, which has several advantages over the plunge method, not least of which is the fact that it saves the hard work involved in maintaining a collection in pots. Whatever method is used, care should be taken to avoid the plants' becoming too dry or too hot

During the growing period carefully monitor the moisture content of the soil in the plunge-bed or glasshouse, since even those species requiring cultivation under glass need plenty of moisture during growth. A good circulation of air is also very important, and every effort should be made to ensure that plenty of ventilation is provided. For cultivation in frames this is achieved by removing the frame-lights, or even the frame itself, during fair weather. In the glasshouse, leave the vents, windows, and door open at all times except for the very coldest periods. It is important to remember that even the aforementioned species do not require a great deal of protection. Temperatures below freezing (to −10°C) will not do much harm, unless the cold period lasts for several days or the soil is very wet.

In the summer months the soil should not dry out completely, although *Galanthus fosteri* can tolerate a few months of dry conditions (after the foliage has died down). If necessary use shading to reduce the internal temperature of the greenhouse. If using cold frames, remove the lights in the summer and replace them if the plants need protection during extended periods of rainfall. If the frame still gets excessive sun in the summer, place a few layers of shade-netting over the frame or directly over the plants.

Galanthus grown under glass flower considerably earlier than plants in the open garden, and a difference of one month is not exceptional.

PROPAGATION

Division, seed, and twin-scaling or chipping are the three main methods of propagating *Galanthus*. Division is by far the easiest and most frequently used method, because most species and cultivars readily produce new bulbs from the mother plant.

In contrast to division, growing from seed is not very popular, mainly because it is considered to be a rather slow, time consuming, and inconsistent method. For those interested in hybrids and cultivars this method is inappropriate because genetically identical plants (clones) are not produced. But for the grower of species and the plant breeder, propagation by seed offers many possibilities. Moreover, growing from seed is in fact easy and often rewarding.

Since the early 1980s, twin-scaling or chipping has become very popular. This vegetative technique is very useful for propagating plants that do not reproduce very quickly by offsets, such as many of the choicer cultivars and some species. Once a successful protocol has been established this method is very productive, repaying any extra investment in time and effort.

PROPAGATION BY DIVISION

This method is by far the easiest, requiring no special skills or equipment. The best time for division is at the end of the growing season, after the plants have finished flowering and when the leaves start to die back. Colonies can be divided during or just after flowering, but they may suffer some check in their growth in the next year, because *Galanthus* keep growing for some months after the flowers have faded as the leaves continue to produce storage products for the bulb.

The colony selected for division should be carefully dug up, preferably with a garden fork, so that the bulbs are not damaged. It is advisable, particularly with rare plants, to lay down a sheet of plastic or an old compost bag so that none of the bulbs are lost or inadvertently trodden on. Remove the bulk of soil from the bulbs,

66

and then carefully tease the clump apart with the fingers. Before planting it is advisable to check for any signs of disease or infestation. If plants show any signs of health problems, treat them at this stage using appropriate means (see the Pests and Diseases chapter). If the bulbs are healthy, plant them out in their new position or give them to friends. If the plants are going back to their original site it is beneficial to add some new soil, organic matter, or a little coarse sand or grit to the planting area. If for any reason the bulbs are unhealthy, or the soil might possibility be harbouring pests or diseases, select a new site and do not plant the original area with *Galanthus* for a few years.

It is important to provide adequate space between the newly divided bulbs. In most cases about 5 cm is sufficient, but this distance can be doubled if required. Once the clump has been divided, either water it in lightly or give it a more generous amount of water if the soil is dry. Do not water when frost or low temperatures are imminent.

PROPAGATION BY TWIN-SCALING AND CHIPPING

by Dr Ronald Mackenzie

Twin-scaling is not a new technique for the propagation of bulbous plants. In 1935 H.P. Travis described in detail the propagation of *Hippeastrum* by a very similar method. Today this technique is used by commercial growers to propagate *Narcissus* and *Nerine*, which are very well suited to twin-scaling because they have a large number of bulb-scales. In comparison, *Galanthus* have fewer scales, thus the increase per bulb is never as great.

The twin-scaling technique takes advantage of the meristematic nature of the bulb base-plate. This dome-shaped structure is actually a shortened stem, to which the thick, fleshy bulb-scales (modified leaves) are attached. The method involves the removal of the main growing point of the bulb, which eliminates apical dominance, and allows the basal plate to divide and form bulblets.

1. Preparation of the Bulb

Select the plants needed for twin-scaling and dig up the bulbs when the leaves die down in late spring or early summer. If possible select

67

a large, flowering-sized bulb. It should be round, have a single nose (growing point or shoot), and be free from disease or infestation. A round bulb is best because it is the easiest to divide. Remove any remains of the outer tunic (the papery, brown tissue covering the bulb) with the fingers, and then remove all of the roots and outer crust of the basal plate with a scalpel. Cut the top third of the bulb to create a flat surface. Dividing the basal plate will be much easier with this flat surface on which to stand the bulb.

2. Dividing the Bulb

At this stage, surface-sterilize the bulb. Wearing fine rubber gloves (medical quality) and using a tissue soaked in industrial spirit (70% ethanol), swab the surface of the bulb thoroughly but quickly. The bulb is now ready for division. Stand it on its new flat surface and, using a scalpel, divide the basal plate into 2, 4, 8, 16, and then 32 radial sections. If the bulb is small it may not allow for this many pieces. After dividing the basal plate, extend the incisions through the bulb to produce wedges (known as chips). This technique is known as chipping. If sufficient basal plate and scales are left on each chip, cut them again (between the scales) to produce twin-scales. For all but the very largest bulbs division should stop here since the size of the twin-scale should not be too small, otherwise bulblet production will be slow and the twin-scale may fail.

Propagation can be undertaken from the larger chips, using the same method as for twin-scales. Of course, the number of propagules will be far less; on the other hand propagation will usually be faster and in some cases more successful.

Treat the scales with a systemic fungicide applied at the standard dilution recommended by the manufacturer. Soak the scales for 30 minutes (or according to the manufacturer's instructions), then wash with distilled water with the aid of a clean sieve.

3. Storage and Incubation

Add 40 mls of water to 500 mls of Vermiculite™, then place the Vermiculite into a small (10 cm × 7 cm) polythene bag; 120 gauge or less is recommended to allow for some air circulation. On contact with water Vermiculite gives off heat, so leave it to cool for approximately 15 minutes before adding the scales. Place the twin-scales into the Vermiculite and seal the bag with an elastic band. Allow just one or two bulbs per bag, depending on the size of the bulb, so that each chip or twin-scale is in contact with plenty of Vermiculite. This will aid the development of the bulbils and limit cross infection (because the amount of contact between each piece of bulb will be reduced).

Store the bags of twin-scales in a warm, dark cupboard. If possible, keep the temperature at about 20°C; at higher temperatures fungal infection increases. Observe the bags on a regular basis for signs of fungal infection. If infection does occur remove the twin-scales and treat with fungicide again. *Penicillium* spp. and *Rhizopus* spp. have been observed on twin-scales.

In late summer, after approximately 12 weeks of incubation, pea-sized bulblets should have developed on the chips or twin-scales. At this stage they are ready for planting into soil. Planting should commence before the bulblets have produced any small roots. Transferring the bulblets at a later stage is difficult because the delicate roots are likely to be damaged during potting.

4. Planting the Bulblets and Growing

Plant the chips or twin-scales into pots containing a loam-based potting medium of the type suitable for plantlets and seedlings amended with one-third (by volume) of sharp grit or small diameter pea gravel to insure good drainage. The size of the container will depend on the number of twin-scales, but generally a pan 20–22 cm in diameter will accommodate between 30 and 40 twin-scales. Pans (short, wide pots) are preferable to ordinary pots for this purpose because they are better drained; furthermore, the bulblets produced by this method do not need the soil depth provided by a conventional pot. Clay pots are preferable to plastic.

The pans can either be situated in a cold greenhouse, a cold frame, or in a raised bed. As with growing mature plants, the plunge-bed method is highly recommended for pans containing twin-scales. The above sections Cultivation in Pots and Cultivation Under Glass provide details on these growing techniques. The twin-scales of most species are remarkably frost hardy and do not require a great deal of protection from low temperatures. On balance, however, a greenhouse or cold frame is preferable, as the extra warmth will speed up growth and assist in the survival of the less robust species. Once planted and situated, keep a keen eye on the moisture level of the potting compost, which should be evenly moist but never completely dry or waterlogged.

Depending on the species, a single leaf should appear within four months of potting. *Galanthus reginae-olgae* and other autumn-flowering species often appear in late autumn, and the others soon after, staying on through the winter and early spring. Keep the young bulbs in the same location and under the same conditions until they become dormant in the following spring or summer. Once the leaf has died down, transfer the small bulbs to the open ground. If the species or cultivar is rare or highly valued then it can be given better treatment by planting into a raised bed or into mesh pots (see the section Outdoor Cultivation); but in most cases an ordinary site will suffice.

The important requisites of successful twin-scaling are hygienic conditions when cutting the bulb, care when dividing the bulb into either chips or twin-scales, and treatment with a suitable fungicide.

PROPAGATION BY SEED

Galanthus seed should be harvested when fresh, which is when the seed capsules rupture and expose their seeds at the end of the growing season. It is important to keep a careful eye on the ripening capsules because the seeds are highly attractive to ants and can be removed within a matter of days or even hours. Removal of the capsules from the scapes before they are ripe is not an option because the seeds will not develop fully once they are detached from the plant.

Once harvested the seeds can be sown immediately, or they can be left for a few weeks in a cool place before sowing. As with many other plants, higher yields and quicker germination rates are effected when fresh seeds are sown. However, if the seeds are stored properly in cool and dry conditions they can also be sown in the early autumn. Older seeds, stored for about one year, are still viable and are worth sowing if they have not dried out too much.

Conventional pots or pans can be used for sowing, provided they are clean and in good condition. Again, I prefer to use clay pots and plunge them into sand, but this is not critical and other methods are often just as successful. The choice of potting mixture is more important, and again I prefer to use a loam-based seed-sowing

70

medium. Approximately one-fourth by volume of sharp sand or sharp grit should be added to the mixture to increase the drainage. Fill the pots right to the top, but only very loosely, and then firm down with the bottom of another pot so that there is a space of about 1.5–2 cm between the top of the soil and the rim of the pot. Sow the seeds thinly by placing them on the top of the potting mixture and then cover them lightly with more of the mixture (c. 0.5 cm). Finish by covering with small diameter pea gravel (5 mm or less) or stone chippings of a similar diameter so that the potting mixture is no longer visible. Water the pots either using a watering can with a very fine rose attached or by capillary action (i.e., by placing the pots in a tray of water). After watering place the pots in a cold frame located in a cool, shady spot. An elaborate frame is not required and one without lights is suitable for most species. The pots do not need very much attention after sowing; give them a light watering if they dry out in the summer and keep them evenly moist during the period of expected germination (autumn and winter) and when the first seed leaves appear.

After germination the seedlings can either be left in their pots for another year, or potted-on into larger containers if quicker growth is required. The former option is often preferred, as two-year-old seedlings are more robust and thus more suitable for transplanting. Undertake repotting as soon as the seedlings start to die down, just before they go dormant in the late spring or early summer. The seedlings should be potted into large pans or deep trays, or planted in raised beds. From the third year onwards the seedlings can be planted in the open garden.

Most seedlings will flower in their third year, but others may take four. It is possible to produce flowering specimens in two years from seed, but the growing regime has to be very intense to achieve these results.

PESTS AND DISEASES

Galanthus are not particularly susceptible to pests and diseases, particularly if they are well grown according to good garden practices. In most cases the root cause of many such problems is poor or inappropriate growing conditions, and it is this aspect of cultivation that needs to be addressed if pests and diseases are to be kept to a minimum. Following this logic, I have directed this section of the book to deal with the underlying causes of pests and diseases, i.e., how and where the plants are grown. In many cases, however, problems do occur for no good or apparent reason. For the control of pests and diseases, I prefer physical rather than chemical methods of treatment. I am hesitant to suggest or recommend any particular pesticides or other chemical treatments; furthermore, as I never resort to chemicals, I am in no position to offer any advice on this subject. If the problem is particularly acute then one should seek the advice of a qualified person at a good nursery, garden centre, horticultural society, or other such authority. For more detailed information on pests and diseases, a number of useful publications are available. In the United Kingdom, refer to the MAFF (Ministry of Agriculture, Fisheries, and Food) guides: *Bulb Pests* (RB 51), *Diseases of Bulbs* (RB 117), and *Bulb and Corm Production* (RB 62).

PESTS

The large narcissus fly (*Merodon equestris*) is one of the worst pests, although it is not always the most damaging and it is often easily controlled. This pest is manifest as a single, large maggot, found either within the bulb, eating the scales, or between two or more bulbs. It is often only detected when the bulbs are dug up and closely inspected, but if the grower is keenly observant he may notice symptoms such as poor growth, lack of flowers, or the death of offsets and small bulbs. The most simple treatment is to remove the maggot by hand and dispose of it, after which the bulbs should be thoroughly inspected for signs of damage and secondary infections.

Damaged bulbs should be removed and discarded from the rest of the clump, and it is advisable to incinerate all infected plant tissue. If the bulb is particularly rare or desirable, then the damaged parts should be removed with a sharp knife and the remaining bulb treated with a fungicide and replanted in a position where it will not come into contact with other stock. If the bulb is healthy then it should recover within a year or two, even if it was reduced to approximately half of its original size with the removal of its damaged areas.

Large narcissus fly is a particular problem when *Galanthus* are grown in pots, or in frames situated in warm, sheltered situations. If this problem persists then provide cooler conditions by either increasing the amount of shade or by relocating to a more favourable site in the garden. For pot-grown plants, the simple solution is to plant them out in the garden. But if this is not an option, then improve conditions in which the pots are maintained by keeping them as cool as possible (see the above sections Cultivation in Pots and Cultivation Under Glass). If growing *Galanthus* in pots, it is good practice to inspect the bulbs for infestation each time repotting is undertaken.

The small narcissus fly (*Eumerus strigatus, E. tuberculatus*) is sometimes found within or on the outside of *Galanthus* bulbs, but it is usually a secondary pest and not the main cause of ill health. As the name suggests, it is smaller than the large narcissus fly, often allowing for several maggots to each bulb; in this case the bulb is usually so badly damaged that the only course of action is to remove all the soft bulbs and burn them. Both types of narcissus fly can be encountered at almost any time through the year.

Another group of pests that attack the underground parts of *Galanthus* are bulb mites (*Rhizoglyphus echinops, Steneotarsonemus laticeps*). The mites are very small, 1 or 2 mm long, and either white or greenish. They are quite active and can be seen moving on the surface of the bulb or between the scales. Symptoms are not often seen on the foliage, and usually the plant looks healthy. The infestation is often only detected by examination of the bulb, which shows that certain areas of the bulb are brown, chaffy, or scarred; closer inspection should reveal the mites themselves. Treatment should be undertaken immediately by using approved pesticides, but badly infected bulbs should be burnt. Bulb mites are most often found on plants that have already been weakened by some other agent or physical damage. Inappropriate growing conditions are often the primary cause, however, and bulb mites seem to be prevalent in gardens where *Galanthus* are grown in considerable numbers.

In rare circumstances, *Galanthus* bulbs are eaten by rodents. This is, fortunately, never a great problem, particularly when compared with other bulbous plants that can suffer considerable damage from rodents, such as crocuses. Mice are usually the biggest problem, burrowing underground or through raised beds to eat the bulbs from below. If this problem is only minor, or if the grower does not want to use baiting or trapping, one way to protect the most valued plants is to grow them in lattice pots (see the above section Outdoor Cultivation). Lattice pots will deter burrowing rodents, particularly mice, as it affords a physical barrier between mouse and bulb. Further protection can be given by covering the top of the lattice pot with wide-gauge wire netting or chicken-wire, as this will prevent entry from the top.

The leaves of *Galanthus* are rarely attacked by any pests, due to the toxic alkaloids present in them. Aphids, for example, are seldom a problem but they do sometimes attack young foliage and the juvenile flower. Once again, this problem is far more common when plants are grown in warm, sheltered spots or in glasshouses and frames, in which cases the foliage is likely to be 'soft'. In the short term, infestations of aphids can be controlled by removal with the fingertips or by washing them over with a jet of water from a hose or spray; the addition of soap or detergent to the water helps in their removal. In the long term, the growing environment of the plants should be altered so that they are grown 'harder', that is, under greater influence of the environment. Aphid control is important not because they are a great pest in themselves, but because they have the potential to spread viruses via their method of feeding.

Occasionally *Galanthus* are attacked by slugs and snails. Immature foliage and young flower parts are most frequently eaten; weak and recently propagated plants are always most at risk. Plants grown under glass are susceptible because they are often not growing as strongly as those outdoors. Plants in pots are also at greater risk, because snails and slugs frequently hide between and under the pots. The most effective methods of control are by physical removal or by baiting with poisons. Maintaining a clean and tidy garden or growing area is a good means of reducing the numbers of these pests, as it gives them fewer places in which to hide. For those growers with a little more time on their hands, and with small areas to

74

keep in check, removal by hand during the hours of darkness (when activity of slugs and snails is at its greatest) is often successful.

DISEASES

Fortunately *Galanthus* are not prone to viruses and even in those cases that are diagnosed as such, the real cause of the malady is often debatable. Some argue that the very light-green-leafed cultivars are in fact infected with a virus. This has not been proved, however, and the vigour and health of these cultivars does not seem to be noticeably different from that of others.

Viral diseases are usually manifest as a mottling or striping of the leaves, followed by, or in association with, loss of vigour. If these symptoms are evident, the affected plants should be removed from the ground and inspected for other signs of pests and diseases. If no other cause of illness is apparent then a virus may be the cause of malformity and loss of vigour. In these cases the plant should be incinerated immediately. It is also good practice to remove any remaining *Galanthus* from the site and relocate then in another part of the garden, but preferably not in close contact with other stock. If a virus infection is suspected or identified with certainty, then it is best to be as thorough as possible and dispose of all the infected plants. It is always sad to lose a coveted species or cultivar, but leaving infected plants in the garden will increase the risk of spread to others.

Fungal diseases can affect plants in the garden and those under propagation (e.g. twin-scales). For plants that are actively growing, *Botrytis* is the most likely cause of fungal infection. A grey, furry covering on the plant, particularly on newly emergent flowers and foliage, is the most obvious symptom. If unchecked, the furry covering is followed by softening of the plant tissues and ultimately the death of the plant. *Botrytis* is usually caused by too much watering leading to waterlogging, or by excessively humid conditions. It can be a particular problem when *Galanthus* are cultivated under glass, in cold frames, and in glasshouses. In these conditions the chances of fungal infection are minimized by improving air circulation and by being careful with the watering. Soil condition is also important here, as a poor, depleted, or inappropriate soil will increase the chances of waterlogging. The distance between plants is also a consideration; reducing the planting density will not only improve air circulation but will also reduce the likelihood of the fungus moving from plant to plant. For potted plants, the risk of fungal infection is greatly increased if the soil is not changed every year.

If the symptoms of *Botrytis* are recognized at an early stage, the plant, or the majority of the plants within a clump, can be saved. If *Botrytis* is detected the plants should be dug up or removed from their pots immediately, and the bulbs inspected for signs of softness. All soft bulbs should be removed and burnt. Those remaining need to be treated with a fungicide dip, left to dry, and then replanted in good soil. If the year is a particularly wet and humid one, a spray of fungicide is a good measure for plants grown under glass. This precautionary treatment must not, however, become a routine practice as it can induce the fungus to acquire a resistance to the fungicide.

Bulb rot (*Penicillium* spp.) and soft rot (*Rhizopus* spp.) can occur on stock that is undergoing twin-scaling or other forms of propagation. Softened plant tissue and patches of a white fungus covering indicate that the material is infected. The control of these fungi is outlined in the section covering twin-scaling.

TAXONOMY OF *GALANTHUS*

GENERIC DESCRIPTION

Galanthus *L*. [Syst. Nat. edn. 1, in Hexandria Monogynia (1735); L., Hort. Cliff.: 134 (1737); L., Gen. Pl. edn. 2: 137 (1742)]; L., Sp. Pl. 1: 288 (1753); Mill., Gard. Dict. edn. 7: (1759); Ludw., Defin. Gen. Pl. edn. 3: 366 (no. 909) (1760); Knorr, Thes. rei Herb. 1(2): 18, pl. S. 15 [lower fig.] (1770); Juss., Gen. Pl.: 55 (1789); J.F. Gmel., Syst. Veg. (Syst. Nat. edn. 3) 1: 523 (no. 401) (1796); F. Heyne, Term. Bot. 1: t. 3 (1799); J. St.-Hil., Exposit. Fam. Naturel. 1: 159 (1805); Mouton-Font., Syst. Pl. 2: 12 (no. 433) (1805); Pers., Syn. Pl. 1: 349 (no. 776) (1805); Léman, Nouv. Dict. Hist. Nat. edn. 2, 12: 356 (1817); T. Nees, Gen. Pl. Fl. Germ. 2: t. 50 (1835); Endl., Gen. Pl. 3: 174 (no. 1265) (1837); D. Dietr., Syn. Pl. 2: 1174 (1840); Benth. & Hook. f., Gen. Pl. 3: 719 (1883); Pax in Engl. & Prantl., Nat. Pflanzenfam. div. 2, 5: 105 (1887); T. Durand, Index Gen. Phan.: 416 (no. 7823) (1888); Baill., Hist. Pl. 13: 42 (1895); Pax & K. Hoffm. in Engl. Nat. Pflanzenfam. edn. 2, 15a: 403 (1930). Type: *G. nivalis* L.
Acrocorion Adans., Fam. Pl. 2: 57 (1763).
Galactanthus Lem. in Orb., Dict. Univ. Hist. Nat. 6: 250 (1845), *in syn.*
Chianthemum Siegesb. ex Kuntze, Rev. Gen. Pl. 2: 703 (1891), *nom. illeg.*

DESCRIPTION. Bulbous, scapose perennial. *Bulb* ± spherical or ovoid to obclavate, whitish; tunic thin, brown, sometimes absent. *Sheath* tube-like, sheathing the leaf bud, membranous, whitish, minutely striped. *Leaves* basal, two, rarely three or more; vernation either applanate, supervolute, or explicative, leaves usually remaining flat, curved, or folded at maturity according to the type of vernation; linear to oblanceolate, either absent, shorter, or longer than scape at flowering time and usually developing in length and width after flowering; erect or recurving at maturity; adaxial surface either smooth, explicative (leaves folding distinctly towards the abaxial surface), or with two to four fine, longitudinal furrows that run along the length of each leaf (leaves folding either slightly upwards or downwards, particularly common on non-flowering plants); abaxial surface either smooth, folded, furrowed (see adaxial), or distinctly sulcate; either green, glaucescent (green with overlying glaucous tones, becoming glaucous), or glaucous, sometimes with a glaucescent or glaucous median stripe, abaxial and adaxial surfaces either concolorous or discolorous; midrib conspicuous or inconspicuous; margins either flat, slightly undulating, or slightly revolute; apex acute to obtuse, or acuminate, flat to cucullate, often with a small whitish area at the very apex. *Scape* one or infrequently two, green to glaucous, circular to oval in cross section; erect to erecto-patent in flower, prostrate in fruit. *Spathe* one, of two connate valves, 2–3 cm × 0.3–0.5 cm, adaxial side green, lateral-abaxial sides whitish, membranous, apices cucullate, curved forward at anthesis. *Pedicel* one, circular in cross section, 0.5–1 mm in diameter, shorter or longer than the scape at anthesis, pendent at flowering time. *Flower* one, pendent, mainly white, usually fragrant. *Perianth segments* six, unequal, in two whorls, free. *Outer perianth segments* (outer whorl) three, white, erecto-patent in bud, narrowly obovate to almost circular in outline, concave to deeply concave, cochleariform, longitudinally striated, slightly unguiculate to distinctly unguiculate (segment then becoming spathulate). *Inner perianth segments* (inner whorl) three, smaller than outer perianth segments, mostly white, erect in bud, slightly concave, ± cuneate to oblanceolate in outline, emarginate (with a distinct apical notch) or marginate (without an apical notch: apex either obtuse or acute), longitudinally striated; adaxial (outer) surface with variable green markings; abaxial (inner) surface also with variable green markings, not as distinct or as well defined as on the adaxial face, composed of faint green stripes. *Stamens* six, free, inserted on the receptacle, shorter than inner perianth segments, c. 6–7 mm long, basifixed; *filaments* short, c. 1 mm long, whitish. *Anthers* yellow, lobed at the base, tapering to a distinct apiculum, or anthers obtuse without a distinct apiculum, c. 5–6 mm × 1.2 mm, dehiscing from a terminal slit and splitting towards the base slightly during anthesis; *pollen* yellow, dust-like. *Style* slender, exceeding the length of the anthers, c. 8 mm long; *stigma* small, acapitate to capitate, or sometimes minutely three-lobed. *Ovary* inferior, 4–6 mm × 2–4 mm, obovoid to oval or almost spherical, triloculate, placentation axile.

Capsule oval to almost spherical, dehiscent, green. *Seeds* oval to almost spherical, pale brown to dark brown, with a prominent, white appendage.

FLOWERING PERIOD. Autumn to spring (October–April), with one species flowering in the spring and early summer (April–August).

HABITAT. Occurring in various habitats but mainly in temperate deciduous woodlands from sea level to alpine altitudes.

DISTRIBUTION. Throughout Europe and Asia Minor. Occurring eastwards from the Pyrenees to the southern coast of the Caspian Sea, and southwards from Germany and Poland to Lebanon and Israel. Doubtfully native above 50°N latitude; frequently introduced and naturalized in northern Europe.

INFRAGENERIC CLASSIFICATION

Many systems of infrageneric classification have been proposed for *Galanthus*, including those of Boissier (1882), Baker (1888), Beck (1894), Gottlieb-Tannenhain (1904), Kemularia-Nathadze (1947b), Traub and Moldenke (1948), Stern (1956), Artjushenko (1965, 1966, 1969, 1970), and Khokhrjakov (1966). The details of the various classifications are given in the Taxonomic History of the Genus, and summaries of the most recent classifications by Stern and Artjushenko are given in Appendix 1 and Appendix 3. In my opinion the most workable and accurate subgeneric classification, to date, is that of Artjushenko (1970), published in her work *Amaryllidaceae SSSR*. This classification is based upon a sound knowledge of the genus, particularly of the Caucasian species. Despite Artjushenko's work, the subgeneric classification in Stern's *Snowdrops and Snowflakes* is still widely used, particularly in the British Isles, because Stern's classification is physically accessible, straightforward, and easy to use. It does not, however, represent the natural history of this group, namely, the genealogical relationships between the component species.

In this monograph I propose a new classification for *Galanthus*. It is similar to the classification by Artjushenko (1970), and to a lesser extent Stern (1956), but it makes some significant amendments to the positions (and hence relationships) of some species within each of the groups. I have adopted the use of series and subseries, instead of sections or subgenera, because the morphological characteristics on which this classification is based are not sufficient to warrant any higher taxonomic rank, even when compared with many other genera in the *Amaryllidaceae*. This new classification is based on the analysis of all the systematic information available for this genus, including morphology, anatomy, and molecular data (Davis, 1994; Davis and Barnett, 1997). It is not within the bounds of this current volume to go into the details of a systematic analysis of *Galanthus*, the results of which will be published separately (Davis et al., in prep.).

SYNOPSIS OF THE GENUS *GALANTHUS*

1. Series *Galanthus*
   1. *G. nivalis* L.
   2a. *G. reginae-olgae* Orph. subsp. *reginae-olgae*
   2b. *G. reginae-olgae* Orph. subsp. *vernalis* Kamari
   3a. *G. plicatus* M. Bieb. subsp. *plicatus*
   3b. *G. plicatus* M. Bieb. subsp. *byzantinus* (Baker) D.A. Webb
2. Series *Latifolii* Kem.-Nath.
   I Subseries *Glaucaefolii* (Kem.-Nath.) A.P. Davis
   4a. *G. alpinus* Sosn. var. *alpinus*
   4b. *G. alpinus* Sosn. var. *bortkewitschianus* (Koss) A.P. Davis
   5. *G. angustifolius* Koss
   6. *G. cilicicus* Baker
   7. *G. peshmenii* A.P. Davis & C.D. Brickell
   8. *G. koenenianus* Lobin, C.D. Brickell & A.P. Davis
   9. *G. elwesii* Hook. f.
   10. *G. gracilis* Čelak.
   II Subseries *Viridifolii* (Kem.-Nath.) A.P. Davis
   11. *G. fosteri* Baker
   12. *G. ikariae* Baker
   13. *G. woronowii* Losinsk.
   14. *G. transcaucasicus* Fomin
   15. *G. lagodechianus* Kem.-Nath.
   16. *G. rizehensis* Stern
   17. *G. krasnovii* A.P. Khokhr.
   18. *G. platyphyllus* Traub & Moldenke

Plate 1

Galanthus nivalis

CHRISTABEL KING

Plate 2

Galanthus reginae-olgae subsp. *reginae-olgae*

CHRISTABEL KING

Plate 3

Galanthus plicatus subsp. *plicatus* (at early stage of flowering) CHRISTABEL KING

Plate 4

Galanthus gracilis (with variation in leaf, flower markings, and receptacle colour)

Plate 4 *continued*

Plate 5

Galanthus cilicicus

CHRISTABEL KING

Plate 6

Galanthus peshmenii

CHRISTABEL KING

Plate 7

Galanthus elwesii

Plate 8

Galanthus elwesii (variant with one mark
on each inner perianth segment)

CHRISTABEL KING

Plate 9

Galanthus alpinus var. *alpinus* (upper) at early stage of
flowering; *Galanthus alpinus* var. *bortkewitschianus* (lower)

CHRISTABEL KING

Plate 10

Galanthus koenenianus   CHRISTABEL KING

Plate 11

Galanthus angustifolius

CHRISTABEL KING

Plate 12

Galanthus fosteri

CHRISTABEL KING

Plate 13

Galanthus ikariae

CHRISTABEL KING

Plate 14

Galanthus woronowii

CHRISTABEL KING

Plate 15

Galanthus transcaucasicus

Plate 16

Galanthus rizehensis

CHRISTABEL KING

Plate 17

Galanthus lagodechianus

CHRISTABEL KING

Plate 18

Galanthus krasnovii

CHRISTABEL KING

Plate 19

Galanthus platyphyllus

CHRISTABEL KING

KEY TO THE SERIES AND SUBSERIES OF *GALANTHUS*

1. Leaves applanate or explicative in vernation, if applanate, leaves always glaucescent (semi-glaucous), never glaucous or green; mainly confined to Europe .. 1. series **Galanthus**
1. Leaves applanate or supervolute in vernation, if applanate, leaves glaucous or green, only infrequently glaucescent; mainly confined to Turkey and the Caucasus . . . .
. . . . 2. series **Latifolii** (2)
2. Leaves glaucous . . . . I subseries **Glaucaefolii**
3. Leaves green . . . . II subseries **Viridifolii**

KEY TO THE SPECIES OF *GALANTHUS*

1. Leaves bright to dark green or very slightly matt green **2**
1. Leaves glaucous or glaucescent **9**

2. Inner perianth segments marginate (without an apical notch)
. . . . **3**
2. Inner perianth segments emarginate (with an apical notch) .
. . . . **4**

3. Anthers blunt; inner perianth segments obtuse at the apex ..
. . . . **18. platyphyllus**
3. Anthers apiculate; inner perianth segments acute at the apex
. . . . **17. krasnovii**

4. Leaves applanate in vernation **5**
4. Leaves supervolute in vernation **6**

5. Leaves usually bright, shining green or infrequently matt green, lacking a median stripe . . . . **15. lagodechianus**
5. Leaves usually matt green, often with a faint median stripe . . .
. . . . **16. rizehensis**

6. Inner perianth segments with two green marks (one apical, one basal) . . . . **11. fosteri**
6. Inner perianth segments with one green mark (apical only) ..
. . . . **7**

81

7. Inner perianth mark up to, but never greater than, half the length of the segment; leaves green or matt green; Caucasus and northeastern Turkey **8**
7. Inner perianth mark at least half the length of the segment, and usually greater; leaves rather matt green; the Aegean islands of Greece . . . . **12. ikariae**

8. Inner perianth mark ± ∧ to ∩-shaped, rounded at the apex; leaves matt green; eastern Caucasus and northern Iran . . . . **14. transcaucasicus**
8. Inner perianth mark ± ∩-shaped, usually flat-topped at the apex; leaves bright green or glossy green; western and central Caucasus and northeastern Turkey . . . . . **13. woronowii**

9. Leaves either glaucescent or leaf surfaces discolorous **10**
9. Leaves distinctly glaucous, leaf surfaces concolorous **13**

10. Leaves explicative (2–4 folded) in vernation; leaf-lamina folded towards the abaxial surface of the leaf . . . . **3. plicatus**
10. Leaves applanate in vernation; leaf-lamina not folded **11**

11. Upper leaf surface with a prominent glaucous median stripe, on a green or glaucescent background, abaxial and adaxial leaf surfaces discolorous . . . . **2. reginae-olgae**
11. Upper leaf surface glaucescent, without a distinct glaucous median stripe, abaxial and adaxial leaf surfaces concolorous **12**

12. Leaves absent or distinctly shorter than scape at flowering time; autumn flowering . . . . **7. peshmenii**
12. Leaves well developed, slightly shorter to longer than the scape at flowering time; winter to spring flowering . . . . . **1. nivalis**

13. Inner perianth segments with two separate green marks, one apical and the other basal, or one large ± X-shaped mark **14**
13. Inner perianth segments with one green mark at the apex, or rarely a very faint yellow or green coloration near the base **15**

82

14. Leaves supervolute in vernation, 0.6–2.5(–3.5) cm wide . . . . .
. . . . **9. elwesii**
14. Leaves applanate in vernation, 0.3–1.2(–2.2) cm wide . . . .
. . . . **10. gracilis**

15. Abaxial leaf surface with distinct longitudinal furrows; inner
perianth segments often with a very faint yellowish or green
patch near the base . . . . **8. koenenianus**
15. Abaxial leaf surface ± smooth, without longitudinal furrows;
inner perianth segments without a yellow or green col-
oration at the base **16**

16. Leaves supervolute in vernation, usually more than 1 cm wide
. . . . **18**
16. Leaves applanate in vernation, less than 1 cm wide **17**

17. Leaves usually more than 0.6 cm wide; autumn to winter flowering; southern Turkey . . . . **6. cilicicus**
17. Leaves less than 0.5 cm wide; spring flowering; northern Cau-
casus . . . . **5. angustifolius**

18. Inner perianth segments with apical markings only (i.e., one
mark on each inner perianth segment), basal markings absent (i.e., always only one mark on each inner perianth segment); leaves usually narrow c. 1–2 cm wide; Caucasus, Transcaucasus, and northeastern Turkey . . . . **4. alpinus**
18. Inner perianth segments with apical and basal markings (i.e.,
two marks on each inner perianth segment), basal markings
sometimes absent (i.e., with one mark on each inner perianth segment); leaves usually broad c. 2–3.5 cm wide; south-
eastern Europe, the Balkans, and Turkey . . . . **9. elwesii**

NOTES ON THE TAXONOMY OF *GALANTHUS*

The herbarium material consulted for this study is not cited here. A
complete list is held at the Library, Royal Botanic Gardens, Kew.

Ind. loc., used here as an abbreviation for 'indication of locality', represents quotes or information given in the protologue
which have been used to track down the type specimens for each
name. In more recent publications where the author has explicitly

and precisely cited the type, the indications of locality are not given.

Galanthus has a considerable number of synonyms. In this chapter I have attempted to account for all the names that I believe to represent plants of wild origin or those that are relevant within a botanical framework. A list of synonyms representing mostly horticultural entities is given in Appendix 5.

To ease the retrieval of taxonomic and bibliographical data from this monograph, standard abbreviations have been used where possible for authors of plant names (Brummitt and Powell, 1992), journals (Lawrence, 1968; Bridson and Smith, 1991), and books (Stafleu and Cowan, 1966–1978).

Appended to this book is a glossary of abbreviations, terms, and Latin.

In the taxonomic works of Zeybek (1988) and Zeybek and Sauer (1995) the designation of type specimens is inconsistent. For example, the number of the type specimen is often different and sometimes the whole specimen citation has been changed. I have identified these inconsistencies and noted them in the text. The designation of the type in the original publication, that is, where the name was first described, should not be altered or replaced unless there are good reasons for doing so (see ICBN).

1. SERIES GALANTHUS

Galanthus series **Galanthus**
Type of series: *G. nivalis* L.
Galanthus Reihe [series] *Nivales* Beck in Wiener Ill. Gart.-Zeitung 19: 47 (1894), *pro parte*; Stern, Snowdr. & Snowfl.: 20 (1956) [as series *Nivales* Beck], *pro parte*.
Galanthus series *Nivales* Kem.-Nath. in Trudy Tbilissk Bot. Inst. ser. 2, 11: 182 (1947), *pro parte*.; A.P. Khokhr. in Bull. Glavn. Bot. Sada Akad. Nauk SSSR 62: 61 (1966), *pro parte*.
Galanthus subgenus *Eugalanthus* Traub & Moldenke in Herbertia 14: 104 (1947), *nom. illeg., pro parte*.
Galanthus section *Galanthus* Artjush. in Bot. Zhurn. (Moscow & Leningrad) 51(10): 1442 (1966), *pro parte*; Artjush., Amaryllidaceae SSSR: 74 (1970), *pro parte*; A.P. Khokhr. in Bull. Glavn. Bot. Sada Akad. Nauk SSSR 62: 61 (1966), *pro parte*.
Galanthus subgenus *Galanthus* A.P. Khokhr. in Bull. Glavn. Bot. Sada Akad. Nauk SSSR 62: 60 (1966).

Galanthus Reihe [series] *Plicati* Beck in Wiener Ill. Gart.-Zeitung
19: 56 (1894), *pro parte*, Stern, Snowdr. & Snowfl.: 20 (1956) [as
series *Plicatii* Beck] *pro parte excl. G. woronowii.*
Galanthus series *Plicatae* Kem.-Nath. in Trudy Tbilissk Bot. Inst. ser.
2, 11: 167 (1947) *nom. nud.*
Galanthus subgenus *Plicatanthus* Traub & Moldenke in Herbertia
14: 112 (1947). Lectotype: *G. plicatus* M. Bieb. [designated by
Traub and Moldenke (1947)].
Galanthus section *Plicatus* (Beck) A.P. Khokhr. in Bull. Glavn. Bot.
Sada Akad. Nauk SSSR 62: 61 (1966). Type: *G. plicatus* M. Bieb.

DESCRIPTION. As above in the Key to the Series and Subseries of
Galanthus.

1. GALANTHUS NIVALIS

Galanthus nivalis is the common snowdrop of woodlands and gardens in the British Isles. It is one of the most popular of all cultivated bulbous plants, as it is an endearing subject and easy to grow,
being well-suited to a cool temperate climate. *Galanthus nivalis* is
ubiquitous in cultivation, and many thousands are sold each year in
the horticultural trade. Once planted it will persist and increase
freely, often producing large and impressive drifts where space permits. It is very popular with keen gardeners and especially snowdrop enthusiasts, because of the large number of cultivars and
clones available.

Galanthus nivalis was described by Linnaeus in his *Species Plantarum* (1753), which provided a scientific, binomial name for the
snowdrop, a plant found naturally in the woods and mountains of
central Europe. The distribution of this species was given by Linnaeus as: *'Habitat ad radices Alpinum Veronae, Tridenti, Viennae'*, three
localities defining an area of northern Italy and Austria.

This is a variable species and throughout its distribution a number of taxa have been named in an attempt to record this variation,
for example: *Galanthus montana* Schur, from Germany; *G. nivalis*
var. *minus* Ten., from Italy; *G. imperati* Bertol. from southern Italy; *G.
nivalis* var. *carpaticus* Fodor, from the Ukraine; and *G. nivalis* subsp.
humboldtii N. Zeybek, from European Turkey. Furthermore, because of its long history in cultivation, a large number of taxa and
cultivars have been recognized, leading to an even greater prolif-

85

eration of names associated with the *nivalis* epithet. A review of the horticultural literature, such as *The Gardeners' Chronicle, The Journal of the Royal Horticultural Society,* and *The Garden (London),* shows that these cultivated plants have varied origins. Some are wild-collected plants, but most have arisen in cultivation as man-made hybrids, chance crosses, or from selections made from individual plants showing peculiar aberrations. A perusal of the synonymy for *G. nivalis* (see below and Appendix 5) gives some idea of just how many names are associated with this species. Moreover, before many of the other species had been described, most *Galanthus* were referred to or associated with *G. nivalis,* including many of those located in the Caucasus, Turkey, and the Balkans. Also, early treatments of *Galanthus* usually associated infraspecific taxa with *G. nivalis,* probably because it was the best known and most ubiquitous species. Gottlieb-Tannenhain (1904), for example, placed almost all the known species (seven of nine) as subspecies of *G. nivalis.* This treatment was viewed by later authors as very conservative, and most of these subspecies have since been recognized as species. However, two of these subspecies have been used with some frequency. These are *G. nivalis* subsp. *cilicicus* (see Stern, 1956; Kamari, 1982; Brickell, 1984, 1986) and *G. nivalis* subsp. *reginae-olgae* (see Stern, 1956; Webb, 1978). Later in this monograph, however, we shall see that these two subspecies should be recognized at the rank of species.

The distribution of *Galanthus nivalis* extends from the Pyrenees in the west to the Ukraine in the east. The northern limit of distribution is difficult, if not impossible, to ascertain because of naturalization, although it has been suggested that *G. nivalis* is not a native species north of Paris (Webb, 1978). In the British Isles, despite common belief, *G. nivalis* is almost certainly not a native species, as it usually occurs near habitation and simply does not behave like an indigenous species. The range of variation of *G. nivalis* in the British Isles does not correspond with the main populations that occur in central and eastern Europe. It is possible to find variants of *G. nivalis* that resemble those collected from all parts Europe; therefore, the patterns of variation evident in natural distributions do not exist in the British Isles. Often, so-called wild populations of *G. nivalis* are represented by sterile clones or horticultural varieties. Furthermore, other species, such as *G. elwesii, G. woronowii,* and *G. plicatus,* are sometimes naturalized in Britain, species that are totally outside their natural, and often very discrete, distributions. The southern-most limit of distribution is also difficult to pinpoint ex-

86

actly but lies somewhere in southern Italy and Albania. *Galanthus nivalis* does not extend into Asian Turkey or the Caucasus but occurs with some frequency in European Turkey and the Ukraine (Andriyenko et al., 1992).

At the edges of its distribution *Galanthus nivalis* becomes rather atypical, particularly in areas where it overlaps with other species. Specifically, two regions have obscure species boundaries: European Turkey, where *G. nivalis* meets *G. plicatus sensu lato*, and the southern half of the former Yugoslavia where *G. nivalis* overlaps with *G. reginae-olgae*.

In the *Flora of Turkey*, Brickell (1984) suggests that hybridization could have occurred between *Galanthus plicatus* subsp. *byzantinus* and *G. nivalis* in European Turkey (near Istanbul in the area of Kemerburgaz Forest). No definite records exist for subsp. *byzantinus* on this side of the Bosporus (see discussion of *G. plicatus* subsp. *byzantinus*, page 107), although *Galanthus* specimens have been found in this area (*Warburg s.n.*; *Baytop, Brickell & Mathew* 8543; and personal observation) with an additional green mark at the base of each inner perianth segment, a character indicative of *G. plicatus* subsp. *byzantinus*. These individuals are intermediate between *G. nivalis* and *G. plicatus* subsp. *byzantinus*, displaying varying combinations of characters from both taxa. Some plants, for example, have leaves similar to *G. nivalis* (margins flat, not explicative) with a second, but rather weak, inner perianth mark, like subsp. *byzantinus*; and some plants have leaves that are very slightly explicative (and thus similar to *G. plicatus*), with one or two inner perianth marks. These populations also contain plants with aberrant flowers, including plants with disfigured perianth segments and semidouble flowers, features that sometimes occur when plants are hybridized in cultivation. A plausible explanation for the origin of these populations is, therefore, that hybridization has occurred between *G. nivalis* and *G. plicatus* subsp. *byzantinus*, as suggested by Brickell (1984). The fact that both putative hybrid parents are found in close proximity to these populations, and no other species, adds weight to a theory of hybrid origin. Moving away from Istanbul Province one can find 'pure' *G. nivalis* in Thrace, and *G. plicatus* subsp. *byzantinus* is found in Asiatic Turkey to the east.

In the southern part of its range *Galanthus nivalis* tends to display certain characteristics that are not typical for the species. In parts of southern Italy, for example, populations display some characters indicative of *G. reginae-olgae*, a species distributed adjacently in

Greece. Specifically, the leaves often display a median glaucous or semi-glaucous stripe on the adaxial surface, a characteristic feature of *G. reginae-olgae*. These plants are also generally larger in all parts. None of these characters are particularly stable, however. A variation is noticeable between populations, and no definite dividing line can be drawn between the distribution of 'true' *G. nivalis* and these intermediates. In all other features, these populations represent *G. nivalis* and not *G. reginae-olgae*. *Galanthus reginae-olgae* flowers in the autumn and has leaves either absent or much shorter than the scape at flowering time; *G. nivalis* flowers in the spring and has leaves usually well developed at flowering time. *Galanthus imperati* (Bertoloni, 1839), a species collected in the district of Naples, has often been associated with these large nivalis-like plants. This name is widely used, particularly in the horticultural literature (see page 219), because it was commonly cultivated in gardens. *Galanthus imperati* has been considered a subspecies of *G. nivalis* (Baker, 1888; Traub and Moldenke, 1948) and a variety of *G. nivalis*. The question is: Do these populations merit any taxonomic recognition? On morphological evidence, a separate species cannot be recognized, and it is debatable whether the difference is sufficient to merit recognition at any infraspecific level. Morphometric characters, such as the size of the leaf and flower, are, on inspection, far too variable to be considered as useful distinguishing characters. Moreover, in other parts of Europe, such as European Turkey, one can find equally large plants as those found in southern Italy, which are just as far removed from typical *G. nivalis*. To start naming all these regional variants would cause chaos and instability in the classification, and in my opinion it is best not to recognize such variation in a formal taxonomic manner.

Intermediates between *Galanthus nivalis* and *G. reginae-olgae*, similar to those found in southern Italy, also occur in the southern half of the former Yugoslavia and probably Albania. As one moves further south, from Montenegro and northern Greece, *G. nivalis* is replaced by *G. reginae-olgae*. This replacement is not a gradual change, however, and the patterns of variation are sometimes complex. *Galanthus reginae-olgae* subsp. *vernalis* (Kamari, 1982) represents an intermediate between *G. nivalis* and *G. reginae-olgae*. Like *G. nivalis*, it flowers in the spring and has well-developed leaves at flowering time, but like *G. reginae-olgae*, it possesses a distinct glaucous median stripe on the upper surface of the leaf.

Despite these variations, *Galanthus nivalis* is easy to recognize.

The leaves are always applanate (flat) in vernation, glaucescent (slightly glaucous, with green undertones), and never folded or furrowed; the inner perianth segments possess one green mark at the apex of each inner perianth segment; the flowering season is in winter (January, February, and sometimes early March).

If one is still unsure as to the identification of *G. nivalis*, closer inspection of the inner perianth markings can usually provide further diagnostic characters. On the external face of each inner perianth segment the ∩- or ∧-shaped mark is usually slightly to markedly enlarged at the tips, on either side of the apical notch (see FIGURE 8). And on the internal face of each inner perianth segment the green markings run all the way to the base of the segment. These features are found in other species of *Galanthus*, such as *G. reginae-olgae*, but this extra information may help to provide a positive identification in cases where it is difficult to accurately assess leaf colour.

CULTIVATION. *Galanthus nivalis* is the easiest of all snowdrops to grow in the British Isles, northern Europe, and the cooler parts of North America. It is very frost-hardy, suitable for a wide range of growing conditions and soils, and, providing the basic growing requirements are satisfied, it will persist and multiply the first year or two after planting. The many millions of naturalized plants in woodlands and the fine displays in gardens are testimony to the suitability of this species to our climate. In *The Flower-Garden Displayed*, Furber (1732) went as far to say: 'They will grow any where, and in any soil'. This statement might be a slight exaggeration, but it is fair to say that *G. nivalis* is by far the easiest species to cultivate. It will grow in all but the worst of soils and in any position that is not deeply shaded, waterlogged, or excessively dry. It is remarkably robust and will survive strong winds and very cold temperatures. It can also compete with the more vigorous plants in the garden, and endures the bullying of many tough herbaceous neighbours. Colonies of *G. nivalis* can withstand being covered-over with herbaceous plants in the summer as long as the ground is clear during the winter.

Being a woodland plant in nature, *Galanthus nivalis* is particularly happy when grown underneath deciduous trees. This situation provides a cool environment in the summer, and in the winter the leafless trees allow plenty of light.

The more vigorous clones of *Galanthus nivalis* benefit from division. This task should be undertaken when colonies become congested, which can occur in as little as two or three years. If division is not undertaken then die-back and loss of vigour can occur, although in good soils even neglected and tightly packed colonies usually increase in size and do not suffer. A few clones will push their bulbs to the soil surface, even when growing in small clumps. These natural offerings can either be removed from around the parent plants and replanted, or left to disperse randomly around the garden. Avoid dividing any *Galanthus* too often, as it usually takes at least two years for newly divided clumps to settle down and perform at their best.

Galanthus nivalis *L.*, Sp. Pl. 1: 288 (1753); Jacq., Fl. Austriac. 4: 7, t. 313 (1776); Huds., Fl. Anglica edn. 2, 1: 140 (c. 1778); Lam., Fl. Franç. edn. 1, 3: 500 (1778); Lam., Dict. Encycl. Meth. Botan. 2: 590 (1788); Sowerby & Sm., English Botany edn. 1, 1: t. 19 (1790); Sturm, Deutschl. Fl. 1(6): t. 1 (1798); Willd., Sp. Pl. 2(1): 29 (1799); Roem., Fl. Eur. 5: [no page numbers], incl. fig. (1800); Sm., Fl. Brit. 1: 352 (1800); Redouté, Liliac. 4: t. 200 (1808); Bohl, Tent. Fl. Bohem. 2: 5 (1815); Spreng., Syst. Veg. 2: 48 (1825); Wimm. & Grab., Fl. Siles. 1: 309 (1827); Gaudin, Fl. Helv. 2: 471 (1828); Rchb., Fl. Germ. Excurs. 1: 87 (1830); Schult. & Schult.f., Syst. Veg. 7(2): 781 (1830); Bertol., Fl. Ital. 4: 4 (1834); Herb., Amaryllidaceae 330 (1837); J.W. Loudon, Ladies' Flower-Gard. bulb. pl.: 180 (1841); Griseb., Spic. Fl. Rumel.: 2: 375 (1844); Neilr., Fl. Wien 1: 871 (1846); Rchb., Icon. Fl. Germ. Helv. 9: 363, t. 807 (1847); Kunth, Enum. Pl. 5: 470 (1850); Ledeb., Fl. Rossica 4: 113 (1853), *pro parte*; J.W. Loudon, Brit. Wild Flowers: 293–294 (1859); Neilr., Aufz. Ungarn Slavon. Gefässpfl.: 61 (1866); Schur, Enum. Pl. Transsilv.: 658 (1866); Schloss., Fl. Croatia: 1065 (1869); Zangh., Fl. Ital. 1: 871 (1876); Boiss., Fl. Orient. 5: 144 (1882); D. Brândzâ, Prodr. Fl. Románe: 452 (1879–1883); Baker, Handb. Amaryll.: 16 (1888); Velen., Fl. Bulg.: 539 (1891); Velen., Fl. Bulg. supp. 1: 265 (1893); Siebert & Voss, Vilm. Blumengärt. edn. 3, 1: 1006 (1895); Gottl.- Tann. in Abh. K. K. Zool.-Bot. Ges. Wien 2(4): 29 (1904); Rouy, Fl. France 13: 20 (1912); Fiori, Nuov. Fl. Analit. Italia 1: 285 (1923); Hayek in Fedde, Prodr. Fl. Penins. Balcan. 30(1): 101 (1932); Losinsk. in Kom., Fl. SSSR 4: 479 (1935); Rech.f., Fl. Aegaea: 735 (1943); Traub & Moldenke in Herbertia 14: 104 (1948); Stern, Snowdr. & Snowfl.: 25 (1956); Artjush. in Bot. Zhurn. (Moscow & Leningrad) 50(10): 1446 (1965); Artjush. in Bot. Zhurn. (Moscow & Leningrad) 51(10): 1443 (1966); Artjush. in Daffodil Tulip Year Book: 82 (1967); Artjush. in Pl. Life 25(2–4): 143 (1969); Artjush., Amaryllidaceae SSSR: 74 (1970); Delip. in Izv. Bot. Inst.

21: 165 (1971); Beldie, Fl. Român. 2: 270 (1979); D.A. Webb in Tutin et al. (eds.), Fl. Europ. 5: 77 (1980); Kamari in Bot. Jahrb. Syst. 103(1): 111 (1982); Papan. & Zacharof in Israel J. Bot. 32: 27 (1983); C.D. Brickell in P.H. Davis et al. (eds.), Fl. Turkey 8: 370, map 55 (1984); C.D. Brickell in Walters et al. (eds.), Europ. Gard. Fl. 1: 318 (1986); Dostál, Nová Kvetena CSSR 2: 1226 (1989); P. Schönfelder & Bresinsky et al., Verbreitungsatlas Farn Blütenpfl. Bayerns: 601, map. 2083 (1990); N. Zeybek & E. Sauer, Türk. Kardelenleri 1: 39, fig. 5 (1995). Ind. loc.: Habitat ad radices Alpinum Veronae, Tridenti, Vienae. Type: Herb. Linn. No. 409.1 (lectotyope LINN!, selected by A.P. Davis in C.E. Jarvis et al. 1993).
Chianthemum nivale (L.) Kuntze, Rev. Gen. Pl. 2: 703 (1891), *nom. illeg.*

G. nivalis L. var. (a) *majus* [*sic*] Ten., Fl. Napol. 1: 140 (1811–1815); Kunth, Enum. Pl. 5: 470 (1850); Parl., Fl. Ital. 3: 75 (1858), *in syn.*; Beck in Wiener Ill. Gart.-Zeitung 19: 52, fig. 1, 8 and 9 (1894). Type: type not known.

G. nivalis L. var. (b) *minus* Ten., Fl. Napol. 1: 140 (1811–1815); Fiori, Nouv. Fl. Analit. Italia 1: 285 (1923); Hayek in Fedde, Prodr. Fl. Penins. Balcan. 30(1): 101 (1932). Type: type not known.

G. nivalis L. var. *grandior* Schult. & Schult. f., Syst. Veg. 7(2): 781 (1830).

G. imperati Bertol., Fl. Ital. 4: 4 (1834); Bertol., Fl. Ital. 4: 5 (1839); Kunth, Enum. Pl. 5: 470 (1850); Burb. in Garden (London) 11: 194, incl. fig. (1877); Harpur-Crewe in Gard. Chron. new ser., 11: 237, fig. 32a (1879); J. Allen in Garden (London) 29: 75 (1886); Ewbank in Garden (London) 39: 272 (1891). Ind. loc.: Ital. Bucaneve maggiore. Perenn. Habui ex regno Neapolitano ab Eq. Prof. Tenorio. Floret Aprili, Majo. Type: not traced.
G. nivalis L. subsp. *imperati* (Bertol.) Baker, Handb. Amaryll.: 17 (1888); Traub & Moldenke in Herbertia 14: 105 (1948).
G. nivalis L. var. *imperati* (Casp.) Mallett in Garden (London) 67: 87 (1905), *comb. invalid.*

G. nivalis L. γ [var.] *hortensis* Herb., Amaryllidaceae: 330 (1837); Kunth, Enum. Pl. 5: 470 (1850). Type: a living plant assumed not to have been preserved.

91

G. nivalis L. var. *europaeus* Beck forma *hortensis* (Herb.) Beck in Wiener Ill. Gart.-Zeitung 19: 50 (1894).

G. montana [*sic*] Schur, Enum. Pl. Transsilv.: 658 (1866).

G. nivalis L. σ [var.] *montanus* (Schur) Rouy, Fl. France 13: 21 (1912); Zahar. in Savul. & Nyár., Fl. Republ. Social. Romania 11: 408 (1966). Ind. loc.: In feuchten hainen der Gebirge, auf dem Götzenberg bei heltau, Glimmerschiefer; um Krondstadt; 2000' bis 3000', Kalksubstrat. April, Mai., *Baumgarten*. Type: not traced.

G. nivalis L. var. *scharlockii* Casp. in Schriften Königl. Phys.-Ökon. Ges. Königsberg [3 Jan. 1868]: 18 (1868); Mallett in Garden (London) 67: 87 (1905); Harpur-Crewe in Gard. Chron. new ser., 11: 342, fig. 48 (1879), as *G. nivalis* L. var. *shaylockii* [*sic*]. Type: type not known.

G. shaylockii [*sic*] (Casp.) J. Allen in Garden (London) 29: 75 (1886), *comb. invalid.*

G. scharlockii (Casp.) Baker, Handb. Amaryll.: 17 (1888); Correvon in Le Jardin 32: 140 (1888); Burb. in Gard. Chron. ser. 3, 7: 268, fig. 43 (1890); J. Allen in J. Roy. Hort. Soc. 13(2): 182 (1891); Burb. in J. Roy. Hort. Soc. 13(2): 208 (1891); Ewbank in Garden (London) 39: 273 (1891); J. Allen in Garden (London) 40: 272 (1891).

G. nivalis L. var. *europaeus* Beck forma *scharloki* [*sic*] (Casp.) Beck in Wiener Ill. Gart.-Zeitung 19: 52, fig. 1,7 (1894).

?*G. atkinsi* [*sic*] hort. Barr [possibly offered in a catologue under this name, see J. Allen in Garden (London) 40: 272 (1891)] (1875), *nom. nud.*

G. nivalis L. [var.] *atkinsi* [*sic*] J. Allen in Garden (London) 40: 272 (1891), *nom. nud.*

G. nivalis L. var. *atkinsii* Mallett in Garden (London) 67: 87 (1905). Type: a living plant assumed not to have been preserved.

G. nivalis L.var. *hololeucus* Čelak. in Abh. Königl. Böhm. Ges. Wiss.: 198 (1891). Type: type not known.

G. nivalis L. var. *europaeus* Beck forma *hololeucus* (Čelak.) Beck in Wiener Ill. Gart.-Zeitung 19: 50 (1894).

G. alexandrii Porcius, Anal. Acad. Române 14: 274 (1893). Type: type not known.

G. nivalis L. forma *pictus* Maly in Verh. Zool.-Bot. Ges. Wien 54: 302 (1904). Type: type not known.

G. nivalis L. α [var.] *typicus* Rouy, Fl. France 13: 20 (1912), *nom. invalid.*

G. nivalis L. var. *carpaticus* Fodor in Ukrajins'k. Bot. Zhurn. 40(5): 32, fig. 1 (1983). Ind. loc.: Hab. in montibus vulcaneis Transcarpathiae (Antalovecka Polijana) IV-V. Type: in Herbaria Universitatis Ushorodiensis URSS 1956 (UU, holotype).

G. nivalis L. subsp. *humboldtii* N. Zeybek in Doga. Tu. J. Botany 12(1): 97 (1988); N. Zeybek & E. Sauer, Türk. Kardelenleri 1: 42, fig. 7 (1995). Type: A1 Kirklareli: İğneada, Eski Orman Kampı, 1–2m, 19.2.1982, *M.A.Önür* (holotype IZEF 906 [IZEF 1836 in 1995 account], isotype ISTE). Note (1): In Zeybek (1988) and Zeybek and Sauer (1995) the holotype cited for this taxon is not the same; the number of the second designation is given here but not the full citation. Note (2): Examination of herbarium specimens collected near this locality suggests that populations represented by this taxon are probably an extension of the hybrid *G. nivalis* × *G. plicatus* subsp. *byzantinus* found in Istanbul Province. Some specimens have slight green markings at the base of each inner perianth segment, indicating that introgression has occurred between *G. nivalis* and *G. plicatus* subsp. *byzantinus*, or between *G. nivalis* and the hybrid *G. nivalis* × *G. plicatus* subsp. *byzantinus*.

G. plicatus M. Bieb. subsp. *subplicatus* N. Zeybek in Doga. Tu. J. Botany 12(1): 99 (1988).Type: A2 Istanbul: Bahçeköy, Belgrat Ormanı, Kurt Kemeri, Carpinus betulus ağaçları altı, 31.3.1980, *N. Zeybek* (holotype IZEF 406 [IZEF 1833 in 1995 account], isotype ISTE).

G. nivalis L. subsp. *subplicatus* (N. Zeybek) N. Zeybek & E. Sauer, Türk. Kardelenleri 1: 47, fig. 9 (1995). Note: This taxon represents entities of *G. nivalis* from the Belgrad forest near Istanbul. In this locality, it seems likely that *G. nivalis* has hybridized with *G. plicatus* (probably *G. plicatus* subsp. *byzantinus*), because the leaves are very slightly explicative (the leaves are distinctly explicative in both subspecies of *G. plicatus*), and sometimes the inner perianth segments have weak basal marking (a feature of *G. plicatus* subsp. *byzantinus*).

G. nivalis L. forma *pleniflorus* P.D. Sell in P.D. Sell & G. Murrell, Fl. Gr. Brit. and Irel. 5: 363 (1996). Type: Abundant in old copse, by Shepreth churchyard, Cambs., v.c. 29, 52/393475, 19 Feb. 1994, P.D. Sell 94/26 (holotype CGE) [see *Galanthus nivalis* 'Flore Pleno' in the Cultivars chapter].

[*G. plicatus sensu* Guss., Pl. Rar.: 140 (1826), *non* Salisb., *non* M. Bieb., *non* Hohen.]

[*G. reflexus auct. non* Herb. ex Lindl.: Baker, Handb. Amaryll.: 17 (1888); Harpur-Crewe in Gard. Chron. n.s., 11: 237 (1879); Burb. in J. Roy. Hort. Soc. 13(2): 208 (1891); J. Allen in J. Roy. Hort. Soc. 13: 185 (1891); Stern, Snowdr. & Snowfl.: 75 (1956).]

[*G. nivalis* L. β [var.] *major sensu* Fiori, Nouv. Fl. Analit. Italia 1: 286 (1923), *non* Redouté.]

DESCRIPTION. *Bulb* ± spherical to ovoid, (1.5–)2–2.2 cm × 1.1–1.5(–2) cm. *Sheath* 3.5–6 cm × 0.5–0.6 cm. *Leaves* applanate in vernation; ± linear but usually slightly broader in the middle to upper third, at flowering (4.5–)5–15(–26) cm × (0.3–)0.4–0.8(–1.4) cm, after flowering developing slightly in length and width, erect or somewhat recurved at maturity; surfaces concolorous, glaucescent (semi-glaucous), or infrequently glaucous; leaf surfaces smooth; midrib conspicuous; margins flat or slightly revolute near the base; apex obtuse to acute, flat. *Scape* (2–)7–15(–18) cm long, green. *Pedicel* 1.2–3 cm long. *Outer perianth segments* obovate to broadly obovate, 1.5–2(–2.5) cm × 0.6–1.1 cm, slightly unguiculate. *Inner perianth segments* ± obovate to cuneate, 0.7–1.2 cm × 0.4–0.6 cm, emarginate; each segment with a variable, ± ∩- to ∧-shaped mark, the ends of each mark usually slightly to markedly enlarged, located on the adaxial surface above the apical notch; abaxial surface with a mark extending to the base of each segment. *Anthers* tapering to an apiculum. *Capsule* almost spherical, c. 1–1.2 cm in diameter. *Seeds* pale brown, c. 0.4 cm long.

ILLUSTRATIONS. Sowerby & Sm., English Botany edn. 1, 1: t. 19 (1790); Redouté, Liliac. 4: t. 200 (1808); Rchb., Icon. Fl. Germ. Helv. 9: 363, t. 807 (1847); Ross-Craig, Drawings Brit. Pl. 24: pl. 7 (1972); Rix & R. Phillips, Bulb Book: 13, fig h. (1981); N. Zeybek & E. Sauer, Turk. Kardelenleri 1: 43, fig. 7 (1995). PLATES 1, 20, 21.

FLOWERING PERIOD. Winter to spring (January to May).

HABITAT. Most frequently occurring in deciduous woodland (*Fagus silvatica, Quercus* spp., *Carpinus* spp., etc.), and occasionally in coniferous woodland (*Abies* spp.). Also occurring in meadows, pasture, amongst scrub, near rivers and on stony slopes, particularly on calcareous soils. At an altitude of 100–1400 m but more commonly at c. 300–600 m.

DISTRIBUTION. Throughout Europe: eastwards from the Pyrenees to the Ukraine, and southwards from Germany and Poland to southern Italy, Albania, and northern Greece. Doubtfully native above 50°N latitude. Frequently introduced and naturalized in The United Kingdom of Great Britain and Northern Ireland, The Netherlands, and other countries of northern Europe. MAP 1, page 96.

2A. GALANTHUS REGINAE-OLGAE
SUBSP. REGINAE-OLGAE

Galanthus reginae-olgae was first collected in Greece on Mt Taygetus in the Peloponnese. It was described by Orphanides (1876), who named it in honour of the queen of Greece.

Galanthus reginae-olgae is usually a rather distinctive species. The leaves are fairly narrow (c. 5 mm), linear, and each has a prominent glaucous median stripe on the upper surface. Flowering occurs predominately in the autumn, at which stage the leaves are either absent, just emergent, or only partially developed. This latter feature gives this species a very characteristic appearance (see PLATE 2), which is seen in only one other species in the genus, namely *G. peshmenii*. After flowering the leaves elongate and attain a length similar to that of other species; the width also often increases. The vernation is always applanate. A large flower size has often been attributed as an ancillary character, but this is by no means universal or characteristic for this species.

The morphology of *Galanthus reginae-olgae* suggests that it is well adapted to its environment. A central glaucous stripe on the leaf, the production of a flowering scape without leaves, the presence

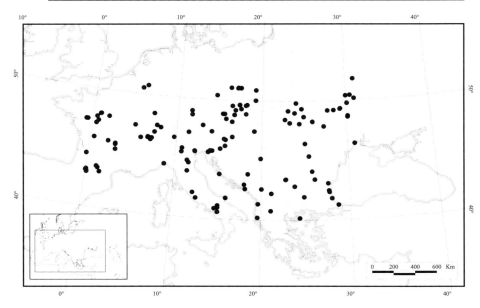

Map 1. Distribution of *Galanthus nivalis.*

of a palisade mesophyll (an anatomical character, seen in transverse sections of the leaf), and an autumn flowering period are all characters found in other members of the Amaryllidaceae that grow in hot and dry environments (e.g. *Lapiedra martinezii, Leucojum* spp., *Sternbergia* spp.).

Despite its rather unique appearance, *Galanthus reginae-olgae* is sometimes not recognized at the rank of species. The characters used to define *G. reginae-olgae* are often misinterpreted, and it is sometimes thought that there is a more or less continuous range of variation between *G. nivalis* and *G. reginae-olgae*. For these reasons, many authors have treated *G. reginae-olgae* as a subspecies of *G. nivalis* (Gottlieb-Tannenhain, 1904; Stern, 1956; Webb, 1978). Stern (1956) did not state explicitly why he considered *G. reginae-olgae* and *G. nivalis* as one species. In his key, *G. reginae-olgae* subsp. *reginae-olgae* is separated from subsp. *nivalis* by flowering time, and whether the flowers appear before or with the leaves. Webb (1978) went into some detail when considering the status of *G. reginae-olgae* and gave a quite lengthy discussion on the variability of the critical characteristics of this species. He also considered the presence of morphological intermediates between *G. reginae-olgae* and

96

G. nivalis that exist in southern Europe (see discussion on page 87) to be an important factor. According to Webb, the degree of leaf development (whether the leaves are absent or present at flowering time), was a variable character and of little taxonomic value. In his discussion he quotes a specimen collected by Brickell and Mathew (*Brickell & Mathew* 8102), commenting, 'But the excellent material . . . shows some plants with leaves already protruding several centimetres from the sheath [as in *G. nivalis*] while others are quite leafless [as in *G. reginae-olgae*]'. This observation is correct, and similar examples are found when examining other material. Kamari (1982) argues, however, that in nature *G. reginae-olgae* nearly always has leaves that are either absent or just emergent at flowering time; after field observation and cultivation experiments she showed that leaf emergence of even 1–2 cm was a rare phenomenon.

Kamari (1982) also stresses the importance of leaf colour as a character to separate *Galanthus reginae-olgae* from other species, and particularly from *G. nivalis*. Stern (1956) did not give great weight to the colour of the leaves, although he did recognize them as being different for each species: in his description of *G. nivalis* subsp. *reginae-olgae* the leaf colour is given as 'green . . . with a glaucous central stripe', and *G. nivalis* subsp. *nivalis* as 'green, glaucous'. In my opinion leaf colour is an important character and can nearly always be used to separate *G. nivalis* from *G. reginae-olgae*, in agreement with Kamari.

Previously, populations of *Galanthus* from Corfu and Sicily were recognized as a subspecies of *G. reginae-olgae* and *G. nivalis*, or as a distinct species. The most well-known and commonly used names for these populations include the epithet *corcyrensis*. Beck (1894) described *G. nivalis* var. *europaeus* forma *corcyrensis*. Later, Halácsy (1904) changed the rank to variety, and then Stern (1956) recognized the taxon as a species: *G. corcyrensis* (Beck) Stern. According to Stern's (1956) concept, *G. corcyrensis* was most closely related to *G. nivalis*, but was different from that species with respect to flowering time, shape of the inner perianth mark, and in the timing of leaf development; he describes the leaves as 'green, glaucous', like those of *G. nivalis*. The distribution of *G. corcyrensis* is given as Corfu and Sicily. Investigation of living plants and herbarium material by Kamari (1982) clearly showed that the affinities of *G. corcyrensis* are with *G. reginae-olgae* and not *G. nivalis*. She reported that the leaves of *G. corcyrensis* are characteristic of *G. reginae-olgae*, that is, the leaves have a median glaucous central band and are not fully developed at flowering time. Based on these observations Kamari changed the combination and status of this taxon to *G. reginae-olgae* subsp. *corcyrensis* (Beck) Kamari. Using cultivation experiments, Kamari showed that the Corfu populations produced leaves and flowering scapes almost simultaneously, unlike *G. reginae-olgae* subsp. *reginae-olgae* which usually flowers without the leaves. Other minor characters, of less taxonomic significance, were the larger size of the inner perianth mark, the narrower inner and outer segments (up to 10 mm broad as opposed to more than 10 mm broad in subsp. *reginae-olgae*), and the pedicel was said to be shorter than the spathe. In Kamari's account, *G. reginae-olgae* subsp. *corcyrensis* is given as occurring on Corfu and in Albania, although it seems that no specimens were investigated from the latter. According to Kamari (1982), populations of *G. reginae-olgae* from Sicily did not belong to subsp. *corcyrensis*.

In the treatment of *Galanthus* presented here, I have not recognized *G. reginae-olgae* subsp. *corcyrensis*, as I believe that it is not sufficiently different from the typical species to warrant recognition. Investigation of herbarium and living material of *G. reginae-olgae*, collected from Corfu (*Marr* 289; *Rix* 462; *Marr* 1200; *Sønderhousen* 999), shows that plants from this island exhibit a very similar leaf development pattern to plants occurring on the Greek mainland. These individuals can have leaves that are either absent at flowering time, emergent by a few centimetres, or several centimetres long. Furthermore, the sizes of the inner perianth mark and inner perianth segments are variable, and do not consistently conform with the description of subsp. *corcyrensis* (see Kamari, 1982).

Galanthus reginae-olgae occurs predominately in Greece, and is most frequent in the south, particularly in the Peloponnese. It also occurs on the Ionian island of Corfu, on Sicily, and in the southern part of the former Yugoslavia. Records of *G. reginae-olgae* from southern Turkey (e.g. Zeybek and Sauer, 1995) are erroneous, as populations from this area have been recognized as *G. peshmenii*, a new species for Turkey and the Eastern Aegean (Davis and Brickell, 1994).

Galanthus reginae-olgae is found in a variety of habitats, such as stunted woodland, deciduous woodland, amongst rocks and scrub, near streams on sloping ground, and in river valleys and gorges. It is most abundant at higher altitudes, around 1000 m. Like other species from southern Europe, most of these habitats provide suitable micro-environments in areas otherwise unsuitable for a pre-dominately woodland plant.

2B. GALANTHUS REGINAE-OLGAE
SUBSP. VERNALIS

In her treatment of the Greek species of *Galanthus*, Kamari (1982) named one new subspecies for *G. reginae-olgae*, a spring-flowering variant called *G. reginae-olgae* subsp. *vernalis*. This was set apart from the other subspecies of *G. reginae-olgae* (see key in Kamari, 1982: p. 113) by its spring-flowering habit; from subsp. *reginae-olgae* by the leaves which develop during flowering; and from subsp. *corcyrensis* by the size of the outer perianth segments (usually more then 10 mm in subsp. *vernalis*). The distribution of subsp. *vernalis* is given as the Peloponnese, Ispiros (mainland Greece), and, tentatively, as southern Italy and Sicily.

During the course of my investigations I have seen subsp. *vernalis* in the southern part of the former Yugoslavia, and have examined living plants collected on Sicily. Individuals seen in the former Yugoslavia match perfectly with the description of subsp. *vernalis*: the leaves were almost fully developed (as in *G. nivalis*) and each possessed a central glaucous median stripe on the upper surface; and they were flowering in the early, Balkan, spring (21 February). Plants from Sicily, however, do not universally display these characteristics. Leaf development is variable (as in populations from mainland Greece) and flowering can occur from autumn (e.g. 31 October 1970, *Sønderhousen* 57, K!) to spring (14–20 February 1982, *Whitehead* 15, K!; 22 March 1935, *Bórgsen s.n.*, C!). Once again, the size of the outer perianth segments is a variable, which may be more, or less, than the specified measurement (10 mm) for this subspecies (Kamari, 1982). I have recognized *Galanthus reginae-olgae* subsp. *vernalis* in this taxonomic treatment, but this subspecies must be regarded as rather imperfectly differentiated, because none of its distinguishing characters is completely discontinuous.

CULTIVATION. *Galanthus reginae-olgae* is a useful snowdrop for the garden because of its early-flowering habit and ability to grow in places where other species might fail. An additional attribute, but one that is not typical for this species, is the possession of large flowers. *Galanthus reginae-olgae* is usually the first snowdrop to flower in the garden, and is only very occasionally later than the autumn-flowering cultivars of *G. elwesii*, such as 'Earliest of All'. The earliest flowering variants of *G. reginae-olgae* produce their flowers in early to mid-October. Following this, others flower in November and December, at which time the earliest types will already have started to produce their seed capsules and have leaves that have developed to several centimetres. From late December and into early January *G. reginae-olgae* subsp. *vernalis* takes over, flowering up to the time of the first *G. nivalis*.

Galanthus reginae-olgae is more or less hardy but does best in situations that do not become too wet and cold during the growing season. It often grows well under a large tree, where the ground is slightly drier than the open garden. The species is also admirably suited to cultivation on rock gardens, and in other places where it is possible to provide extra drainage and protection from the most severe weather. It requires rather more sun than most, and should not be planted in situations that do not receive the sun in winter.

Galanthus reginae-olgae *Orph.* in Atti Congr. Intern. Botan. Firenze: 214 (1876); Burb. in Garden (London) 39: 243 (1891); Halácsy, Consp. Fl. Graec. 3(1): 206(1904); Artjush. in Bot. Zhurn. (Moscow & Leningrad) SSSR 50(10): 1446 (1965); Artjush. in Bot. Zhurn. (Moscow & Leningrad) 51 (10): 1443 (1966); Artjush. in Daffodil Tulip Year Book: 82 (1967); Artjush. in Pl. Life 25(2–4): 144 (1969); Artjush., Amaryllidaceae SSSR: 76 (1970); Artjush. in Ann. Mus. Goulandris 2: 13, fig. 2a (1974); Kamari in Bot. Chron. 1(2): 67 (1981); Kamari in Bot. Jahrb. Syst. 103(1): 113 (1982); C.D. Brickell in Walters et al. (eds)., Europ. Gard. Fl. 1: 317 (1986). Type: in regione abietina Mt Taygetos Laconiae prope Gaitza 1872, Psarides *s.n.* (ATHU, W). [after Kamari, 1982]

G. olgae Orph. ex Boiss., Fl. Orient. 5: 146 (1882); Baker, Handb. Amaryll.: 18 (1888); Burb. in J. Roy. Hort. Soc. 13(2): 206 (1891); Burb. in Garden (London) 39: 243 (1891); Siebert & Voss, Vilm. Blumengärt. edn. 3, 1: 1006 (1895); Traub & Moldenke in Herbertia 14: 106 (1948).

G. nivalis L. var. *europaeus* Beck forma *olgae* (Orph. ex Boiss.) Beck in Wiener Ill.Gart.-Zeitung 19: 51, fig.1,5 (1894).

G. nivalis L. subsp. *reginae-olgae* (Orph.) Gottl.-Tann. in Abh. K. K. Zool.-Bot. Ges. Wien 2(4): 32 (1904); Hayek, Prodr. Fl. Penins. Balcan. 3: 101 (1932); Stern, Snowdr. & Snowfl.: 31, pl. 4 (1956); D.A. Webb in Tutin et al. (eds.), Fl. Europ. 5: 77 (1980); Rix & R. Phillips, Bulb Book: 183, fig. o (1981).

G. nivalis L. var. *reginae-olgae* (Orph.) Fiori, Nouv. Fl. Analit. Italia 1: 286 (1923).

Chianthemum olgae (Orph. ex Boiss.) Kuntze, Rev. Gen. Pl. 2: 703 (1891), *nom. illeg.*

DESCRIPTION. *Bulb* ± spherical to ovoid, 1.2–2.2 cm × 1–1.6 cm. *Sheath* 2.5–8 × 0.4–0.6 cm. *Leaves* applanate in vernation; ± linear but usually broader in the middle to upper third, at flowering either absent, much shorter than scape or about as long as the scape, 0–20(–24) cm × (0.4–)0.5–1(–1.4) cm, after flowering developing to 8–18(–24) cm × 0.5–0.8 cm, recurving at maturity; adaxial surface green to glaucescent, with a prominent glaucous median stripe; abaxial surface glaucous; surfaces smooth; midrib conspicuous; margins flat or slightly revolute near the base; apex acute to obtuse, flat. *Scape* (7–)8–13(–15) cm long, green. *Pedicel* 2–3 cm long. *Outer perianth segments* ± obovate to narrowly obovate, 1.9–2.5(–3) cm × 0.7–1.2(–1.8) cm, slightly unguiculate. *Inner perianth segments* ± cuneate to obovate, 1–1.2 cm × 0.4–0.6 cm, emarginate; each segment with a variable ± ∩- to ∧-shaped mark, the ends of each mark sometimes slightly to markedly enlarged, located on the adaxial surface above the apical notch; abaxial surface with a mark extending to the base of each segment. *Anthers* tapering to an apiculum. *Capsule* almost spherical, c. 1 cm in diameter. *Seeds* pale brown, c. 0.5 cm long.

KEY TO SUBSPECIES OF *GALANTHUS REGINAE-OLGAE*

1. Leaves absent or distinctly shorter than scape at flowering; autumn flowering (September to December) ....
 .... a. subsp. **reginae-olgae**
1. Leaves never absent, always well developed at flowering; winter to spring flowering (January to March) .. b. subsp. **vernalis**

a. Galanthus reginae-olgae *Orph.* subsp. **reginae-olgae**
G. corcynensis [*sic*] T. Shortt in Gard. Chron. new ser., 20: 728 (1883), *nom. nud.*
G. corcyrensis J. Allen in Garden (London) 29: 75 (1886), *nom. nud.*
G. nivalis L. [var.] *corcyrensis* hort. ex Leichtlin in Gard. & Forest 1: 499 (1888), *nom. nud.*

G. corcyrensis Leichtlin ex Correvon in Le Jardin 2: 139 (1888), *nom. nud.*

G. corcyrensis (*praecox*) hort. ex Baker, Handb. Amaryll.: 17 (1888), *nom. nud.*

G. corcyrensis Burb. in J. Roy. Hort. Soc. 13(2): 201 (1891), *nom. nud.*

G. nivalis L. var. *europaeus* Beck forma *corcyrensis* hort. ex Beck in Wiener Ill. Gart.-Zeitung 19: 51, fig. 1,6 (1894). Type: a living plant assumed not to have been preserved.

G. nivalis L. β [var.] *corcyrensis* (Beck) Halácsy, Consp. Fl. Graec. 3: 206 (1904).

G. corcyrensis (Beck) Stern, Snowdr. & Snowfl.: 34; fig. 7 (p. 35) (1956); Artjush. in Bot. Zhurn. (Moscow & Leningrad) 50(10): 1446 (1965); Artjush. in Bot. Zhurn. (Moscow & Leningrad) 51 (10): 1443 (1966); Artjush. in Pl. Life 25(2–4):145 (1969); Artjush., Amaryllidaceae SSSR: 76 (1970). Ind. loc.: lectus ex Hort. Highdown, Sussex, F.C.Stern, II. XI, 1950. Type: neotype (designated by Stern) from garden of F.C.Stern, Goring-by-sea, Sussex, I February 1946, *Stern* cult. (BM!).

G. reginae-olgae Orph. subsp. *corcyrensis* (Beck) Kamari in Bot. Chron. 1(2): 68 (1981), *comb. invalid.;* Kamari in Bot. Jahrb. Syst. 103(1): 115 (1982), *descr.*

G. octobrensis T. Shortt in Gard. Chron. new ser., 20: 728 (1883), *nom. tant.*

G. octobrensis J. Allen in Garden (London) 29: 75 (1886), *nom. nud.*

G. octobriensis hort. ex Baker, Handb. Amaryll.: 17 (1888), *nom. nud.*

G. octobrensis Leichtlin ex Correvon in Le Jardin 2: 139 (1888), *nom. nud.*

G. octobrensis Burb. in Gard. Chron. ser. 3, 7: 268 (1890), *nom. tant.*

G. octobrensis J. Allen in J. Roy. Hort. Soc. 13(2): 179 (1891), *nom. nud.*

G. octobrensis Ewbank in Garden (London) 39: 272 (1891); *nom. nud.*

G. octrobrensis hort. ex Burb. in J. Roy. Hort. Soc. 13(2): 206 (1891), *nom. nud.*

G. octobrensis Burb. in Garden (London) 39: 243 (1891), *nom. nud.*

G. nivalis L. forma *octobrinus* hort. ex Voss in Siebert and Voss in Vilm. Blumengärt. edn. 3, 1: 1006 (1895). Type: a living plant assumed not to have been preserved.

G. nivalis L. var. *octobrensis* Mallett in Garden (London) 67: 87 (1905), *comb. invalid.* Note: According to Allen (1886) this plant was originally introduced by Lord Walsingham, from Scrofitza, or Conchi, in Albania, some 80 or 97 km north of Corfu.

G. praecox J. Allen in Garden (London) 29: 75 (1886), *nom. nud.*

G. praecox Burb. in J. Roy. Hort. Soc. 13(2): 207 (1891), *nom. tant.*

G. praecox Burb. in Garden (London) 39: 243 (1891), *nom. nud.*

G. nivalis L. var. *praecox* Mallett in Garden (London) 67: 87 (1905), *comb. invalid.* Note: Grown in gardens from c. 1886–1905, said to have originated from Corfu, (Allen, 1886).

G. olgae reginae [*sic*] hort. ex Leichtlin in Gard. and Forest 1: 499 (1888), *nom. nud.*

G. rachelae Burb. in Gard. Chron. ser. 3, 7: 268 (1890), *nom. tant.*

G. rachelae J. Allen in J. Roy. Hort. Soc. 13(2): 180 (1891), *nom. nud.*

G. rachelae Ewbank in Garden (London) 39: 272 (1891), *nom. tant.*

G. rachelae Burb. in J. Roy. Hort. Soc. 13(2): 207 (1891), *nom. nud.*

G. rachelae Burb. in Garden (London) 39: 243 (1891). Note: Introduced into cultivation at The University College gardens in Dublin, in 1884, from Mount Hymettus in Greece. Type: a living plant assumed not to have been preserved.

G. nivalis var. *rachelae* Mallett in Garden (London) 67: 87 (1905), *comb. invalid.*

G. elsae Burb. in Gard. Chron. ser. 3, 7: 268 (1890), *nom. tant.*

G. elsae J. Allen in J. Roy. Hort. Soc. 13(2): 181 (1891[March 10th]), *nom. nud.*

G. elsae Burb. in Garden (London) 39: 243 (1891[March 14th]). Note: There is sufficient detail in this article to constitute effective publication; this may, however, not have been the intention of the author. Type: a living plant assumed not to have been preserved.

G. elsae Ewbank Garden (London) 39: 272 (1891), *nom. tant.*

G. nivalis L. var. *elsae* Mallett in Garden (London) 67: 87 (1905), *comb. invalid.* Note: Grown in gardens from c. 1889–1905. The original plants were said (Allen, 1891) to have beeen collected by Dr Mahaffy on Mount Athos, in Greece in April 1889.

G. imperati Bertol. forma *australis* Zodda in Fl. Ital. Exsicc.: num. 762 (1904), *in sched.* Type: prope Messanam (Messina) in nemoribus frigidus montanus prope S. Lucia del Mela loco Issala nec

103

non prope S. Pier Niceto loco Bocche d'aqua, × 1904, *Zodda* 762(K!, BM!, OXF!, LE!, LI!).

DESCRIPTION. *Bulb* 1.5–2.2 cm × 1–1.6 cm. *Sheath* 3–4 cm × 0.4–0.5 cm. *Leaves* either absent or shorter than the scape at flowering, never well developed during flowering, 0–10(–14) cm × 0.5–0.7 cm after flowering, developing to 8–18(–24) cm × 0.5–0.8 cm. *Scape* 8–12 cm long. *Outer perianth segments* 1.9–2.5(–3) cm × 0.7–1.2(–1.8) cm.

ILLUSTRATIONS. Stern, Snowdr. & Snowfl.: 31, pl. 4; 35, fig. 7(1956); Artjush. in Ann. Mus. Goulandris 2: 12, 2a (1974); Rix & R. Phillips, Bulb Book: 183, fig. o (1981); Kamari in Bot. Jahrb. Syst. 103(1): 116, fig. 2 (1982); Kamari in Bot. Jahrb. Syst. 103(1): 117, fig. 3 (1982). PLATES 2, 24, 25.

FLOWERING PERIOD. Autumn (September–December).

HABITAT. Woods (*Platanus orientalis, Pinus nigra*), scrub, and turf, frequently moist and shady areas (river banks and gorges) on calcareous soils. Usually on north-facing aspects at an altitude of 20–1200 m, commonly at altitudes of 600–1000 m.

DISTRIBUTION. Mainland Greece, and particularly the Peloponnese; the Ionian island of Corfu, and Sicily. MAP 2.

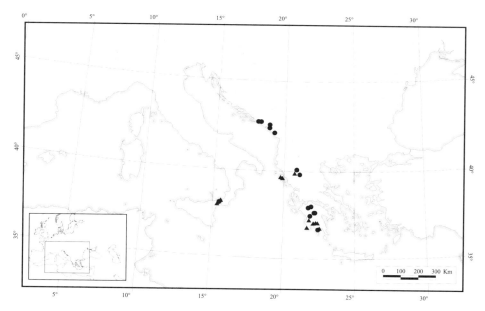

Map 2. Distribution of *Galanthus reginae-olgae* subsp. *reginae-olgae* [▲] and subsp. *vernalis* [•].

b. Galanthus reginae-olgae *Orph.* subsp. **vernalis** Kamari in Bot. Chron. 1(2): 68 (1981), *nom. nud.*; Kamari in Bot. Jahrb. Syst. 103 (1):116 (1982), *descr*; C.D. Brickell in Walters et al. (eds.), Europ. Gard. Fl. 1: 317 (1986). Type: Achaia, montes Erymanthos, supra pagum Kaletzi, alt. c. 1200 m, *Phitos & Kamari* 15826 (Holotype UPA!).

DESCRIPTION. *Bulb* 1.2–2.2 cm × 1–1.6 cm. *Sheath* 2.5–8 cm × 0.4–0.6 cm. *Leaves* almost fully developed at flowering, 5–20(–24) cm × (0.4–)0.5–1(–1.4) cm, after flowering developing slightly in length and width, 8–12(–24) cm × 0.5–1 cm. *Scape* (7–)9–13(–15) cm long. *Outer perianth segments* 1.9–2.5(–3) cm × 0.7–1.2 cm.

ILLUSTRATIONS. Kamari in Bot. Jahrb. Syst. 103(1): 118, fig. 4 (1982). PLATES 22, 23.

FLOWERING PERIOD. Spring (January–March).

HABITAT. Occurring in similar habitats to *G. reginae-olgae*, including deciduous woodland (*Fagus silvatica, Quercus* spp., *Carpinus* spp. etc.), and occasionally in coniferous woodland (*Abies* spp.), 750–1300 m.

DISTRIBUTION. Mainland Greece, and particularly the Peloponnese; Sicily, the southern part of former Yugoslavia and possibly Albania. MAP 2.

3A. GALANTHUS PLICATUS SUBSP. PLICATUS

Galanthus plicatus has been in cultivation since at least the sixteenth century, and is recorded in the literature of this period. Clusius informs us, in his *Rariorum aliquot stirpium, per Pannonian, Austriam & vicinas . . . historia* (1583), that he received a single bulb from Constantinople from Madame de Heysentein, and he remarks that the flower is as equally fragrant as those of *Leucojum vernum*, but in his opinion more agreeable. There was obviously a close association between this species and Clusius, as it has been referred to as Clusius's snowdrop (Somerus, 1820) and *G. clusii* (see Steud, 1840).

According to Loudon (1841) *G. plicatus* was first introduced into British gardens in the late sixteenth century, as she states: 'It is a native of Russia, and though it was first brought to England in 1592, it is very rarely in British gardens; probably from the flowers being less showy than that of the common kind'.

In the pre-Linnaean literature (before 1753), including those titles listed above, *Galanthus plicatus* is most often called *Leucoium bulbosum praecox byzantinum*. It seems, however, that this name was not used exclusively for *G. plicatus*, and sometimes it is employed for the larger forms of *G. nivalis*. In *Historia Plantarum*, Ray (1688) used this name for the robust variant of *G. nivalis* from Italy, often known as *G. imperati*. Ray cited the following provenance for *Leucoium bulbosum praecox byzantinum*: 'Neapoli etiam à Fer. Imperato, è monte Virgineo erutus', a locality for *G. nivalis* and not *G. plicatus*. In these early references it is, therefore, often difficult to say with any certainty if the epithet *byzantinus* refers to *G. plicatus* or *G. nivalis*. The illustrations accompanying these texts offer no solution here, because they are rather stylized and do not show the critical diagnostic features of either species.

It was Marschall von Bieberstein (1819) who provided the legitimate binomial name of *Galanthus plicatus*, based on material collected in the Crimean peninsula. *Galanthus plicatus* was so named because of its distinctive leaf morphology. In mature plants the leaf margins are folded sharply downwards towards the underside of the leaf, usually 90° to almost 180° from the horizontal. When in bud the margins are folded flat against the lower surface of the leaf (see FIGURE 7). The epithet *plicatus* is not the most accurate term for describing this type of leaf morphology, the correct one being explicative (Cullen, 1978). The leaves and other features of this species are clearly depicted in *Curtis's Botanical Magazine* tab. 2162 (Somerus, 1820), a plate which also shows that this plant has a single, bold apical mark on each inner perianth segment.

The leaf colour of *G. plicatus* is quite variable, particularly on the upper surface. The leaves can either be bright green, matt green, or semi-glaucous. Many specimens have a broad, diffuse, semi-glaucous median band or stripe running along the length of the upper leaf surface. Sometimes this band is rather weak, and it is often absent altogether. The undersurface of the leaf is nearly always whitish glaucous, with the green of the leaf often showing through the wax coating.

Galanthus plicatus is often associated in literature with *G. woronowii*, because both species have leaves with folds in them. Stern (1956) and Traub and Moldenke (1948) placed *G. woronowii* into divisions of the genus containing *G. plicatus* (series *Plicati* and subgenus *Plicatanthus*, respectively) because the leaves of both species were considered as 'plicate' or 'reduplicate' (explicative). This association is erroneous, however, because the folds in the leaf of *G.*

106

woronowii are not homologous with those of *G. plicatus*. In *G. woronowii* the leaf has two to four fine, longitudinal grooves on the upper surface, causing the leaves to fold slightly upwards or downwards, whereas the leaves of *G. plicatus* are exclusively explicative (see PLATE 3). The origin and cause of the folding is different in each case, and this is clearly seen when the leaves are observed in transverse section. The leaf folding of *G. plicatus* is caused by two longitudinal rows of enlarged (bulliform) cells in the lower epidermis, and in *G. woronowii* the leaf folding is caused by longitudinal rows of enlarged cells in the upper mesophyll of the leaf (Davis and Barnett, 1997). These features are clearly visible when transverse sections of the leaves are made into anatomical preparations, and examined using the light microscope.

Galanthus plicatus has a well-defined distribution, restricted principally to an area around the western part of the Black Sea. It occurs in the Crimea, Romania, and in northwestern Turkey. It is not ubiquitous throughout this range, however, and is found in large numbers in only a few, restricted, localities.

3B. GALANTHUS PLICATUS SUBSP. BYZANTINUS

Baker (1983b) described *Galanthus byzantinus* from cultivated material sent to him by James Allen, which had been collected from Constantinople (now Istanbul). In his diagnosis, Baker considered this species to be intermediate between *G. plicatus* and *G. elwesii*, having the explicative leaves of the former species and the glaucous leaves of the latter. The inner perianth segments were described as being like those of *G. elwesii*, that is, with apical and basal markings. Unfortunately, the type specimen of *G. byzantinus* is not very complete, and consists only of a single flowering scape, without leaves or bulb. This does not present too great a problem, however, because Baker was explicit in his description: 'the margins [of the leaf] as in the Crimean Snowdrop distinctly and permanently recurved' (Baker, 1893b). This allows us to characterize Baker's *G. byzantinus* as a plant with explicative vernation, like *G. plicatus*, and with flowers that have two marks on each inner perianth segment (one apical and one basal).

Many authors have recognized the strong affinity between *Galanthus byzantinus* and *G. plicatus*. Beck (1894) considered these two species as conspecific, and made *G. byzantinus* a variety of *G. plicatus*; Stern (1956) placed *G. byzantinus* and *G. plicatus* in their own series, with *G. woronowii*; and Webb (1978) considered *G. byzantinus* to be a subspecies of *G. plicatus*. Webb (1978) presented a thoughtful and concise discussion on the taxonomy of *G. byzantinus*, and his treatment of this taxon has held favour with later authors (e.g. Brickell, 1984, 1986). Webb concluded that the only difference between *G. plicatus* subsp. *plicatus* and subsp. *byzantinus* was the number of green marks on each inner perianth; *G. plicatus* subsp. *byzantinus* was characterized by two marks on each perianth segment, and subsp. *plicatus* by one mark. However, in his discussion, Webb stated that the number of marks were of limited taxonomic value, because of the random occurrence of this character in populations of subsp. *plicatus*. This assumption was based on study of a specimen from Babadag in Romania (Flora Romaniae Exsiccata, No. 225, *leg. Borza-Sintenis s.n.*), which Webb believed to possess a similar mark to subsp. *byzantinus*. Study of this herbarium specimen, however, and one other from Romania (e.g. 24 ii 1873, *Sintenis s.n.*) shows that the inner perianth mark is not like that of subsp. *byzantinus*. Referring back to the description of *G. byzantinus*, Baker (1893b) states that the perianth has: 'a green horseshoe-shaped mark round the sinus, . . . and another green blotch covering the lower part of [its] back'. Or in other words, the perianth has two separate marks, one at the apex and one at the base. The specimens from Romania do not have marks like this, as theirs are always single. In some specimens from Romania the mark is large and can extend almost to the base of the segment, but they never have two separate marks. A similar confusion has occurred with Turkish material of subsp. *plicatus*, and in particular collections made in the Lake Abant area (Bolu Province), which have been referred to as subsp. *byzantinus*. Like the Romanian populations, plants from Bolu can possess a very large single mark, but they never have two separate marks.

Defined in this way, which is in accordance with the original concept for this species, *Galanthus plicatus* subsp. *plicatus* is found in the Crimea, Romania, and northern Turkey (e.g. Bolu and Zonguldak provinces). But this distribution begs the question, where does *G. plicatus* subsp. *byzantinus* come from? In the discussion that follows the description of *G. byzantinus* (Baker, 1893b), Constantinople is indicated as the type locality. Reference to the type specimen (2 ii 1893, *Allen s.n.*, K!) does not add further detail to its locality, but accompanying this specimen is the correspondence between Baker and Allen. Their letters provide more information about the localities for *G. byzantinus*, but still leave the reader unsure about the true origin of the type collection. A letter dated 17 January 1893 indicates plants from Turkey in Asia Minor, but later correspondence of 29 April 1893 gives details of plants collected in the European part of Turkey. It becomes clear from these letters, however, that Allen is suggesting that two distinct variants come from Constantinople, one from the European and one from the Asiatic side of Turkey (both from Istanbul Province). In situ examination of populations in Istanbul Province confirms this observation. *Galanthus plicatus* subsp. *byzantinus* is found in the Asiatic part of Istanbul Province, whereas in European Turkey it is evident that hybridization has occurred between *G. nivalis* and *G. plicatus* subsp. *byzantinus* (see page 87). Individuals in this locality are comparable to plants described by Allen in his letters, which share the characteristics of both species. This confirms Webb's suspicion: 'records from the European side of the Bosporus seem to be erroneous' (Webb, 1978: p. 310). A number of records support subsp. *byzantinus* occurring in European Turkey, but these need to be confirmed by field study.

Galanthus plicatus is one of the finest snowdrops for the garden, being easy to cultivate, robust, and floriferous. For the enthusiast it is particularly valuable, because it is available in a variety of forms and has many named cultivars, including: 'Three Ships', an early-flowering clone; 'Wendy's Gold', which has a yellow ovary and inner perianth markings; and 'Trym', which is most extraordinary because the external perianth segments have been replaced by what appear to be large internal segments (which have a marking like that found on the inner segments). The most well-known of all the *G. plicatus* cultivars is 'Warham'. According to Lady Beatrix Stanley (1939), this plant was introduced from the Crimea during the Crimean War, about 1855.

Many of the best garden cultivars have been produced as a result of crossing with *Galanthus plicatus*, as the 'blood' of this species seems to increase the vigour and substance of the progeny. *Galanthus plicatus* has been most frequently hybridized with *G. nivalis*, or chance cross-pollinations have occurred between these species. Some of the best cultivars, however, are the outcome of cross-pollination with *G. elwesii*, such as the cultivar 'John Gray'.

CULTIVATION. Successful cultivation of *G. plicatus* requires no special methods, and it will grow happily if it receives the basic requirements for cultivation. Its variability does, however, mean that some clones are more suitable to certain conditions, and a watchful eye should be kept on new plants to make sure that they are suitably placed. *Galanthus plicatus* does well under trees, in the rock garden, and even naturalized in grass. In its natural environment it is mainly a plant of woodlands, although it is also frequently found in the open, near streams and small rivers, and amongst scrub. It does have a reputation for dying for no good reason, and the sudden loss of specimens does occur. On the whole, however, I think these reports are exaggerated. In cultivation *G. plicatus* often produces large numbers of seedlings, unlike many other species.

Galanthus plicatus *M. Bieb.*, Fl. Taur.-Caucas. 3: 255 (1819); Somerus in Bot. Mag. 47: tab. 2162 (1820); Edward's Bot. Reg. 7: tab. 545 (1821); Spreng., Syst. Veg. 2: 48 (1825); Schult. & Schult.f., Syst. Veg. 7(2): 782 (1830); Herb., Amaryllidaceae: 330. (1837); D. Dietr., Syn. Pl. 2: 1174 (1840); J.W. Loudon, Ladies' Flower-Gard. bulb. pl.: 180 (1841); Kunth, Enum. Pl. 5: 471 (1850); Ledeb., Fl. Rossica 4: 114 (1853), *pro parte*; Rupr. in Regel, Gartenflora 12: 178, t. 400, fig. 3 (1863); Gard. Chron new ser., 2: 237, fig. 31a (1879); Boiss., Fl. Orient. 5: 145 (1882); Baker, Handb. Amaryll.: 18 (1888); Dykes in Gard. Chron. ser. 3, 65: 187, fig. 85a (1919); Lozinsk. in Kom., Fl. SSSR 4: 479, pl. 30, fig. 7, a, b, c (1935); Traub & Moldenke in Herbertia 14: 113 (1948); Stern, Snowdr. & Snowfl.: 42, fig. 10 (1956); Artjush. in Bot. Zhurn. (Moscow & Leningrad) 50(10): 1446 (1965); Artjush. in Bot. Zhurn. (Moscow & Leningrad) 51(10): 1445 (1966); Artjush. in Daffodil Tulip Year Book: 82 (1967); Artjush. in Pl. Life 25(2–4): 146 (1969); Artjush. in Amaryllidaceae SSSR: 77 (1970); Beldie, Fl. Român. 2: 270 (1979); D.A. Webb in Tutin et al. (eds.), Fl. Europ. 5: 77 (1980); Rix & R. Phillips, Bulb Book: 13, fig. a (p. 12) (1981); C.D. Brickell in Walters et al. (eds.), Europ. Gard. Fl. 1: 317 (1986). Type: ex Tauria, 1808, *Bieberstein s.n.* (holotype LE!).
G. nivalis L. subsp. *plicatus* (M. Bieb.) Gottl.-Tann. in Abh. K. K. Zool.-Bot. Ges. Wien 2(4): 35 (1904).
Chianthemum plicatum (M. Bieb.) Kuntze, Rev. Gen. Pl. 2: 703 (1891), *nom. illeg.*

DESCRIPTION. *Bulb* ± spherical to ovoid, 2–4.5 cm × 2–2.8 cm. *Sheath* 2.5–8 cm × 0.5–0.9 cm. *Leaves* explicative in vernation; ± lin-

ear to lorate, often narrowed at the base, longer or shorter than
scape at flowering (3.6–)4.5–20(–25) cm × 0.6–1.6 cm, after flowering developing to 8–21(–27) cm × 0.6–1.6 cm, frequently recurved at maturity; adaxial surface green to glaucescent or almost
glaucous, with or without a glaucescent, broad, median stripe; abaxial surface commonly whitish glaucous; surfaces smooth apart from
the 2–4 longitudinal folds at the margins, or at maturity the folding
is often either side of the midrib; midrib conspicuous; margins with
2–4 longitudinal folds, folded downwards towards the abaxial surface, flat to undulate; apex obtuse to acute, flat. *Scape* (5–)7–15
(–18) cm long, green. *Pedicel* 2–3 cm long. *Outer perianth segments*
obovate to broadly obovate, or ± rhomboid, 1.5–2.4 cm × 0.9–1.4
cm, slightly unguiculate. *Inner perianth segments* ± obovate to cuneate, 0.8–1.2 cm × 0.5–0.7 cm, emarginate; each segment with a very
variable, bold ± ∧-shaped to ∩-shaped mark on the adaxial surface
above the apical notch, or sometimes the mark is much larger and
extends from the apex up to nearly the base of the segment, when
it is often ± X-shaped; or each segment with two marks, apical and
basal: the second mark near the base of the segment and covering
up to half its length, usually ± rectangular; abaxial surface with a
mark extending up to half the length of the segment or extending
to the base. *Anthers* tapering to an apiculum. *Capsule* almost spherical to ellipsoid, 1–1.4 cm in diameter. *Seeds* mid- to dark brown, c.
0.5 cm long.

KEY TO SUBSPECIES OF *GALANTHUS PLICATUS*

1. Inner perianth segments with one green mark (apical) . . . . . .
. . . . a. subsp. **plicatus**
1. Inner perianth segments with two green marks (apical and
basal) . . . . b. subsp. **byzantinus**

a. Galanthus plicatus *M. Bieb.* subsp. **plicatus**
G. latifolius Salisb., Gen. Pl.: 95 (1866), *nom. illeg.*

G. plicatus M. Bieb. var. *genuinus* Beck forma *typicus* Beck in Wiener
Ill. Gart.-Zeitung 19: 57, fig. 2, 18 (1894), *nom. invalid.*

G. plicatus M. Bieb. var. *genuinus* Beck forma *excelsior* Beck in Wiener
Ill. Gart.-Zeitung 19: 57, fig. 2,19 (1894), *nom. invalid.*

G. plicatus M. Bieb. var. *genuinus* Beck forma *maximus* Beck in Wiener Ill. Gart.-Zeitung19: 57 (1894), *nom. invalid.*

G. byzantinus Baker subsp. *brauneri* N. Zeybek in Doga. Tu. J. Botany 12(1): 101 (1988), '*braunerii*'; N. Zeybek & E. Sauer, Türk. Kardelenleri 1: 80, fig. 30 (1995). Type: (1) designated in 1988: A3 Bolu: Abant Gölü Orman Bölge Şefliği Tomruk Deposu çevresi, 1400 m, *Zeybek* (holotype IZEF 942, isotype ISTE). (2) designated in 1995: A3 Bolu, Abant Gölü kenardlarindaki sirtar, c. 1350 m, 9 April 1983, *A. Baytop & T. Baytop* (holotype ISTE 5017, isotype IZEF 1821).

?*G. plicatus* M. Bieb. subsp. *gueneri* N. Zeybek in Doga. Tu. J. Botany 12(1): 99 (1988) '*guenerii*'. Type: A8 Artvin: Arhavi Dikyamac Köyü üstü Alnus orman alti, 850 m, 16 Feb.1977, *M. Coşkun* 231 (holotype AE 5765, isotype IZEF).

G. plicatus M. Bieb. subsp. *karamanoghluensis* N. Zeybek in Doga. Tu. J. Botany 12(1): 100 (1988). Type: A4 Ankara: Kızılcahamam, Akyarma Geçidi, 1550 m, 15 April 1973, *K. Karamanoğlu & M. Koyuncu* (holotype AE 4708, isotype IZEF).

G. byzantinus Baker subsp. *saueri* N. Zeybek in Doga. Tu. J. Botany 12(1): 101 (1988), '*saueri*'; N. Zeybek & E. Sauer, Türk. Kardelenleri 1: 79, fig. 29 (1995). Type: A3 Bolu: Abant Gölü yolu, 1250 m, 12 April 1978, *E. Sauer* (holotype BRD. Saarland Univ. Herb. [SAAR] 18643, isotype IZEF 1823).

G. byzantinus Baker subsp. *tughrulii* N. Zeybek in Doga. Tu. J. Botany 12(1): 100 (1988); N. Zeybek & E. Sauer, Türk. Kardelenleri 1: 78, fig. 28 (1995). Type: A2 İzmit: Keltepe, 1050 m, 8 February 1985, *L. Tuğrul* (holotype IZEF 926 [IZEF 1820 in 1995 account], isotype ISTE).

?*G. plicatus* M. Bieb. subsp. *vardarii* N. Zeybek in Doga. Tu. J. Botany 12(1): 100 (1988). Type: C8 Trabzon: Sürmene, Arpalı Köy 4 March 1983, *N. Zeybek* (holotype IZEF 917).

G. plicatus M. Bieb. subsp. *plicatus* var. *viridifolius* P.D. Sell in P.D. Sell & G. Murrell, Fl. Gr. Brit. and Irel. 5: 363 (1996). Type: Sawston churchyard, Cambs., v.c. 29, 52/487493, 16 Feb. 1995, *P.D. Sell & J.G. Murrell* (holotype CGE).

112

Plate 20. *Galanthus nivalis* in cultivation, Surrey, England. Photo by R. Hyam.

Plate 21. A glaucous-leafed variant of *Galanthus nivalis*, European Turkey, 24 March 1991. Photo by A.P. Davis.

Plate 22. *Galanthus reginae-olgae* subsp. *vernalis* in a shady rock crevice with *Cyclamen hederifolium*. Photographed near Kotor in Montenegro, 21 February 1991. Photo by A.P. Davis.

Plate 23. *Galanthus reginae-olgae* subsp. *vernalis* in Montenegro. Photo by B. Mathew.

Plate 24. Habitat of *Galanthus reginae-olgae* subsp. *reginae-olgae*, Mt. Taygetus, Peleponnese, Greece. Photo by J. Marr.

Plate 25. *Galanthus reginae-olgae* subsp. *reginae-olgae* in cultivation, October 1994. Photo by J. Fielding.

Plate 26. *Galanthus plicatus* subsp. *plicatus* with *Cyclamen coum*, near Lake Abant, northwest Turkey, 19 March 1991. Photo by A.P. Davis.

Plate 27. Variant of *Galanthus plicatus* subsp. *plicatus* with large green mark on the inner perianth segments, near Lake Abant, northwest Turkey, 19 March 1991. Photo by A.P. Davis.

Plate 28. Flower of *Galanthus plicatus* subsp. *byzantinus*, near Istanbul, northwest Turkey. Photo by T. Baytop.

Plate 29. *Galanthus cilicicus*, near Mersin, Içel Province, southern Turkey. Photo by O. Sønderhousen.

Plate 30. *Galanthus gracilis* in cultivation, Kent, England. Photo by A.P. Davis.

Plate 31. Habitat of *Galanthus gracilis*, Mt. Vertiskos, northern Greece. Photo by A.P. Davis.

Plate 32. *Galanthus gracilis* in *Paliurus spina-christi* scrub in northwest Turkey, 21 February 1999. Photo by A.P. Davis.

Plate 33. Habitat of *Galanthus elwesii*, Mt. Vermion, northern Greece, 25 March 1991. Photo by A.P. Davis.

Plate 34. *Galanthus elwesii* in cultivation, Surrey, England. Photo by R. Hyam.

Plate 35. A fine group of *Galanthus elwesii* in a Surrey garden, England. Photo by B. Mathew.

[*G. clusii* Fisch. ex Steud., Nomencl. Bot. edn. 2, 1: 653 (1840), *in syn.*]

DESCRIPTION. *Inner perianth segments* with one mark on the adaxial surface of each segment, apical only: the apical mark either ± ∧- to ∩-shaped or larger and extending towards the base of the segment for up to 2/3 of its length, positioned above the apical notch.

ILLUSTRATIONS. Somerus in Bot. Mag. 47: tab. 2162 (1820); Rupr. in Regel, Gartenflora 12: tab. 400, fig. 3 (1863); Lozinsk. in Kom., Fl. SSSR 4: 479, pl. 30, fig. 7, a, b, c (1935); Stern, Snowdr. & Snowfl.: 43, fig. 10 (1956); Rix & R. Phillips, Bulb Book: 12, fig. a; 15, inset photo [as *G. byzantinus*] (1981); T. Baytop & B. Mathew, Bulb. Pl. Turkey: 23, fig. 2 (1984); N. Zeybek & E. Sauer, Türk. Kardelenleri 1: 79, fig. 29; 81, fig. 30 (1995). PLATES 3, 26, 27.

FLOWERING PERIOD. Spring (February–April).

HABITAT. Occurring in or at the margins of mixed deciduous forests (*Fagus silvatica, Quercus* spp., *Tilia argentea, T. platyphylla, Carpinus betulus, Sorbus tormentalis, Ulmus* spp., etc.) and coniferous forest (*Juniperus altari, Abies* spp.). Found on calcareous and acidic soils; soil often rich and leafy soils but also occurring on heavier soils. Often on sloping ground. From 80–1350 m, but most frequently at c. 1000–1300 m.

DISTRIBUTION. Romania, northern Turkey, and the Crimea. MAP 3.

b. Galanthus plicatus M. *Bieb.* subsp. **byzantinus** *(Baker) D.A. Webb* in Bot. J. Linn. Soc. 76(4): 310 (1978); C.D. Brickell in P.H. Davis et al. (eds.), Fl. Turkey 8: 367, map 54 (1984); C.D. Brickell in Walters et al. (eds.), Europ. Gard. Fl. 1: 318 (1986). Ind. loc.: 'This spring I have had good specimens sent by Mr James Allen . . .'. Type: Constantinople, 2 ii 1893, *Allen s.n.*, cultivated material from T.S. Ware at Tottenham (England), 17 ii 1893 (K!).

G. byzantinus Baker in Gard. Chron. ser. 3, 13: 226 (1893); Bowles in J. Roy. Hort. Soc. 43: 35, fig. 16 (1918); Stern, Snowdr. & Snowfl.: 46, fig. 47 (1956); Artjush., Amaryllidaceae SSSR: 77 (1970); 1970; D.A. Webb in Tutin et al. (eds.), Fl. Europ. 5: 78 (1980); Rix & R. Phillips, Bulb Book: 15, fig. d (p. 14) (1981); T. Baytop & B. Mathew, Bulb. Pl. Turkey: 23, [excl. pl. = *G. plicatus* subsp. *plicatus*] (1984); N. Zeybek & E. Sauer, Türk. Kardelenleri 1: 74, fig. 26 (1995).

G. plicatus M. Bieb. var. *byzantinus* (Baker) Beck in Wiener Ill. Gart.-Zeitung 19: 57 (1894).

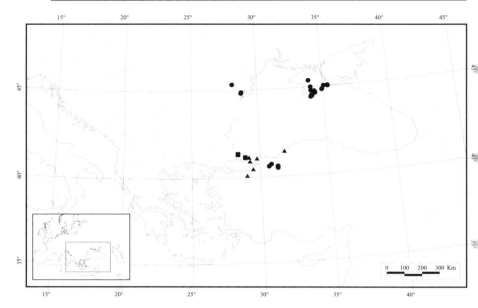

Map 3. Distribution of *Galanthus plicatus* subsp. *plicatus* [●]; subsp. *byzantinus* [▲]; and *Galanthus plicatus* subsp. *byzantinus* × *Galanthus nivalis* [■].

G. nivalis L. subsp. *byzantinus* (Baker) Gottl.-Tann. in Abh. K. K. Zool.-Bot. Ges. Wien 2(4):41 (1904).

DESCRIPTION. *Inner perianth segments* with two marks on the adaxial surface of each segment, apical and basal: the apical mark ± ∧- to ∩-shaped, positioned above the apical notch; the basal mark near the base and covering up to about half the basal area of each segment.

ILLUSTRATIONS. Stern, Snowdr. & Snowfl.: 47, fig. 47 (1956); Rix & R. Phillips, Bulb Book: 14, fig. e (1981); N. Zeybek & E. Sauer, Türk. Kardelenleri 1: 75, fig. 26 (1995). PLATE 28.

FLOWERING PERIOD. Spring (February–April).

HABITAT. Occurring in mixed deciduous forest (*Fagus silvatica, Quercus* spp., etc.) and scrub, often near streams and small rivers. Found on rich and leafy soils, but also on clay and sandy soils. From 100–300 m.

DISTRIBUTION. Northwestern Turkey. MAP 3.

114

2. SERIES LATIFOLII

Galanthus series **Latifolii** ['Latifoliae'] *Kem.-Nath.* in Trudy Tbilissk Bot. Inst. ser. 2, 11: 179 (1947), **emend.** A.P. Davis.
Type of series: *G. platyphyllus* Traub & Moldenke (= *G. latifolius* Rupr.)

Galanthus series *Latifolii* Stern, Snowdr. & Snowfl.: 20 (1956), *nom. illeg.* Type: *G. ikariae* Baker subsp. *latifolius* Stern [a mixed element containing three species].

Galanthus series *Latifolii* A.P. Khokhr. in Bull. Glavn. Bot. Sada Akad. Nauk SSSR 62: 60 (1966), *pro parte, nom. illeg.*

I SUBSERIES GLAUCAEFOLII

Galanthus subseries **Glaucaefolii** *(Kem.-Nath.)* **comb. nov. et emend**. A.P. Davis.
Lectotype of subseries: *G. caucasicus* (Baker) Grossh. [designated by A.P. Khokhr. (1966)].
Galanthus section *Glaucaefolii* Kem.-Nath. in Trudy Tbilissk Bot. Inst. ser. 2, 11: 182 (1947), *pro parte.*
Galanthus subsection *Glaucifolii* (Kem.-Nath.) A.P. Khokhr. in Bull. Glavn. Bot. Sada SSSR 62: 61 (1966).

Galanthus series *Elwesiae* Kem.-Nath. in Trudy Tbilissk Bot. Inst. ser. 2, 11: 167 (1947), *nom. nud.*
Galanthus series *Elwesiani* Kem.-Nath. ex A.P. Khokhr. in Bull. Glavn. Bot. Sada Akad. Nauk SSSR 62: 61 (1966). Type: *G. elwesii* Hook. f.

Galanthus series *Schaoricae* Kem.-Nath. in Trudy Tbilissk Bot. Inst. ser. 2, 11: 183 (1947). Type: *G. schaoricus* Kem.-Nath.

Galanthus series *Alleniani* A.P. Khokhr. in Bull. Glavn. Bot. Sada Akad. Nauk SSSR 62: 61 (1966), *nom. illeg.*—series *Schaoricae* Kem.-Nath., *in syn.*

Galanthus series *Caucasici* A.P. Khokhr. in Bull. Glavn. Bot. Sada

Akad. Nauk SSSR 62: 61 (1966). Type: *G. caucasicus* (Baker) Grossh.

Galanthus section *Graeci* A.P. Khokhr. in Bull. Glavn. Bot. Sada Akad. Nauk SSSR 62: 61 (1966), *pro min. parte.* Type: not stated, section containg several species.

DESCRIPTION. As in the Key to the Series and Subseries of *Galanthus.*

4A. GALANTHUS ALPINUS VAR. ALPINUS

The name *Galanthus alpinus* should now be used to represent the glaucous-leafed snowdrop of the Caucasus. In a recent paper (Davis, Mordak, and Jury, 1996), *G. alpinus*, *G. bortkewitschianus* Koss., and *G. caucasicus* (Baker) Grossh. are considered to represent a single species.

Galanthus caucasicus
In an attempt to provide a stable name for the 'common Snowdrop of the Caucasus', Baker (1887) described a new subspecies, namely *G. nivalis* L. subsp. *caucasicus*. This subspecies is clearly described as a glaucous-leafed plant, with leaves 11 mm wide, and with a flower possessing a single green mark on each inner perianth segment. Some years later, Grossheim (in Grossheim and Schischkin, 1924) changed the status of this plant to the rank of species.

Galanthus caucasicus occurs throughout the Caucasus range in Russia and Georgia and in northeastern Turkey (Lazistan). Grossheim (1940; see Map 223) included Dagestan and Azerbaijan (including Karabakh) as part of the range of *G. caucasicus*, but this was contested by Artjushenko (1970), who thought these were records for *G. lagodechianus*. An expedition to Russia and Abkhasia by H. Mordak et al. in 1987 (pers. comm.), has confirmed that *G. caucasicus* occurs in the western Transcaucasus, in agreement with Grossheim (Map 223).

The Typification of *Galanthus caucasicus*
When Baker (1887) described *Galanthus nivalis* subsp. *caucasicus* he did so from living material, grown at the Royal Botanic Gar-

116

dens, Kew. Unfortunately, none of these plants has survived to the present day, and there is no material (e.g. a herbarium specimen or plate) preserved in the herbarium or archives at Kew that can act as type material. In the protologue that accompanies the description of subsp. *caucasicus*, however, Baker states that he saw six different collections of *G. plicatus*, identifying them as belonging to his new subspecies. None of these specimens were signed, initialled, or annotated by Baker.

Recognizing that there was no type for *Galanthus caucasicus*, Stern (1956) decided to choose one of Baker's six 'plicatus' specimens to act as a lectotype, selecting a specimen collected by Hohenacker in Azerbaijan ('In sylvis prope Lankoran [Lenkoran], iii 1836', *Hohenacker s.n.*). There are three duplicates of this collection at Kew, but only one of them has any material of *G. caucasicus*, and this is mixed with *G. transcaucasicus*, a species that is more commonly found in this area and from where the type collection of this species was made. For these reasons the lectotypification by Stern has been rejected (Davis et al., 1996) because it is ambiguous.

The specimen best matching Baker's description of *Galanthus caucasicus*, and one that is included in the original set that he saw at Kew (i.e., one of the 'six plicatus specimens') is the collection of Szovits, from Tbilisi (Tiflis, *Szovits s.n.*). This collection was considered as the most suitable choice for a new lectotype, and has been designated for this purpose.

Galanthus alpinus

In 1911 Sosnowsky described *G. alpinus* from material collected by himself in the alpine zone of Mount Lomis-mta in the district of Borzhomi (near Bakuriani) in Georgia. According to Sosnowsky, the leaves of *G. alpinus* are glaucous like those of *G. nivalis*, but wider like *G. latifolius* Rupr. (now *G. platyphyllus*), which are usually 2–4 cm wide (2 cm wide in Sosnowsky's description). *Galanthus alpinus* has been included in the majority of Floras for the Caucasus area (Grossheim, 1928; Losinskaya, 1935; Kemularia-Nathadze, 1941), and in the monographs of Artjushenko (1965, 1966, 1970), as a species occurring in Georgia. Artjushenko (1970) united *G. alpinus* with *G. schaoricus* Kem.-Nath., a species described from the Ratscha district of western Georgia, which increases the range of *G. alpinus* by adding many specimens from Adzhariya. Recently, *G. alpinus* has been found in northern Armenia, in the lower montane zone (Gabrieljan and Tamanian, 1982), although the populations are few and each is small (Gabrieljan, 1988).

Stern (1956) tentatively placed *Galanthus alpinus* into the synonymy of *G. allenii*, a decision he based on a comparison of the description of this species in the Flora of the URSS (Losinskaya, 1935) with Baker's original description of *G. allenii*. On the basis of this written evidence, Stern's conclusion seems reasonable, but comparison of living plants readily indicates the clear differences between the two species.

Galanthus bortkewitschianus
Galanthus bortkewitschianus was described by Koss (1951), from material collected in the northern Caucasus. This species was set apart from *G. alpinus* by its larger leaves (12–13 cm long, 1.2–1.4 cm wide at anthesis, and up to 35 cm long and 3.5 cm wide when in fruit), lack of plication ('*plicatis destitutis*'), and mucronate anthers ('*anthers omnibus mucronatis*'). It is a rather curious species, known from only one restricted locality in Karbardino-Balcaria (Russia) near the river Kamenka, where it is said to form a single, vegetatively propagating population of 5–6 hectares (Artjushenko, 1967). Artjushenko (1967) also reports that it is sterile, a fact that is supported by a triploid chromosome count of 3n = 36 (Sveshnikova, 1965, 1971, 1975). Sveshnikova (1971a) states that *G. bortkewitschianus* is a typical autopolyploid of *G. alpinus*.

According to Artjushenko (1970) *Galanthus caucasicus*, *G. alpinus*, and *G. bortkewitschianus* form a taxonomic group, defined by the unique combination of supervolute vernation, glaucous leaves, and a single green mark on each of the inner perianth segments. Two anatomical characters are also used to group these species: (1) 'leaves with hollows' (mesophyll cavities, as seen in transverse section) and (2) right-angled (oblong) epidermal cells (Artjushenko, 1966, 1967). Artjushenko separated each of these species from the other mainly on the basis of morphometric characters. In her key, for example (see Artjushenko, 1969), *G. caucasicus* and *G. alpinus* are separated by leaf width (1–1.6 cm and 2–2.5 cm, respectively), and *G. alpinus* and *G. bortkewitschianus* are separated by flower size (1.5 cm and 1.5–2 cm long, respectively) and by the fact that mature fruits are not known to develop in the latter species.

Study of *Galanthus alpinus*, particularly from specimens housed

118

in the Tbilisi herbarium (TBI) and including the type (1911, *Sosnowsky s.n.* holotype TBI), shows that this species has strong morphological affinities with *G. caucasicus,* in agreement with Artjushenko (1965, 1966, 1970). Moreover, it appears that no morphological characters, quantitative or qualitative, distinguish *G. alpinus* from *G. caucasicus.* Leaf width is not a reliable character for the separation of these two species, as measurement of herbarium specimens from localities throughout the Caucasus shows that this character is highly variable. The average leaf width of *G. caucasicus* is 1.26 cm (range 0.45–2.8 cm), and 1.46 cm (range 0.65–2.9 cm) for *G. alpinus.* Most specimens of *G. alpinus* have leaves that are usually less than 2 cm, and only very rarely as wide as 2.5 cm, i.e., the size quoted in Artjushenko's key (Artjushenko, 1969); even Artjushenko (1967) stated: 'But there are examples [of *G. caucasicus*] with broad enough leaves, like *G. alpinus*'. The type specimen of *G. alpinus* has a maximum leaf width of 1.5 cm.

The type material of *Galanthus bortkewitschianus* (iii 1947, *Koss s.n.,* isotype LE!), and living specimens collected from the *locus classicus* clearly show the main features of this species, as given by Koss (1951). The average leaf width of these specimens is 2.4 cm, which, although slightly wider than the average for *G. alpinus* and *G. caucasicus,* falls well within the range of variation for these species. None of the specimens seen for this study have leaves as wide as those described by Koss (1951) when in the fruiting stage (the fruit swells but does not fully develop), given as 3.5 cm wide. Flower size is also variable, within and between these three species, and many specimens have outer perianth segments spanning the size range given by Artjushenko (1969).

From our studies (Davis, Mordak, and Jury, 1996) we concluded that *Galanthus caucasicus, G. alpinus,* and *G. bortkewitschianus* do not exhibit sufficient morphological differences to warrant their recognition at the level of species. However, *G. bortkewitschianus* was recognized at the rank of variety, to account for its somewhat distinctive appearance and different chromosome number.

When the above three species are brought together under *G. alpinus,* the distribution range of this taxon includes the Caucasus and Transcaucasus (within the limits of Russia, Georgia, Armenia, and Azerbaijan), northeastern Turkey (Lazistan), and possibly northern Iran.

As *Galanthus alpinus* is the earliest described taxon of the three species under discussion, this name becomes operative for reasons of priority. In the interests of nomenclatural stability, a proposal to conserve *G. caucasicus* could have been made, as this is the most widely used and commonly accepted name. This idea, however, was rejected (Davis et al., 1996) because the name *G. caucasicus* is a source of confusion and ambiguity: the epithet *caucasicus* has been widely used for *G. elwesii*, and the typification of *G. caucasicus* is problematic (see above). The first of these points, the confusion over the use of the name *G. caucasicus*, is discussed in more detail below (from Davis et al., 1996).

The confusion between *G. caucasicus* (i.e., *G. alpinus*) and *G. elwesii*

Galanthus caucasicus (now *G. alpinus,* see above) has often been closely associated with *G. elwesii* Hook. f., a species from the Balkans and Anatolia. Both these species possess glaucous leaves and supervolute vernation, but they can be separated by the number of green marks on each inner perianth segment. Each inner perianth segment of *G. elwesii* has two marks (apical and basal, which may join together to form one large ± X-shaped mark), but each inner segment of *G. alpinus* has only one mark (apical). Confusion between these species has occurred because there are a number of clones of *G. elwesii* in cultivation with single apical marks, and these plants superficially resemble *G. caucasicus.* In nature, these variants of *G. elwesii* are either very rare or perhaps do not occur at all, and therefore do not cause difficulties with the circumscription of these two species; furthermore, their distributions do not overlap. It seems, however, that the aforementioned peculiarity has caused a problem in the use of the name *G. caucasicus,* as there is convincing evidence that all plants called *G. caucasicus* in cultivation represent the variant of *G. elwesii* with a single mark on each inner perianth segment.

Wyatt (1967) was probably the first author to cast doubt on the identity of cultivated *Galanthus caucasicus,* and suggested that specimens grown under this name represented *G. elwesii.* Wyatt stated: 'In a letter written in 1942 to me, Mr E.A. Bowles said that the name *"caucasicus"* had been given to plants imported forty years previously, and sold under the name of *"cilicicus"* or *"elwesii"* . . . If this is correct, the plants which we know as *"caucasicus"* must have come from the Taurus Mountains; and if Baker [probably referring to Baker, 1887] is right that *caucasicus* comes only from the Caucasus, our plants have no right to be called *"caucasicus"* '. A comment by Parker (1963, p. 141) is also worth quoting here: 'Up to about thirty years ago importations of *G. elwesii* sometimes contained a number of plants in which there was a variation in flower detail, the main distinction being the absence of basal green markings on the inner segment. These plants have since appeared from other sources and some are said to have some differences in foliage, though this does not appear to be a constant feature. *G. elwesii* varies considerably in its period of flowering, covering the same period as the plant (*G. caucasicus*) described by Stern.'

Observations on cultivated material of *Galanthus elwesii* collected in southern Turkey, particularly from populations in the eastern part of its range, show that the type of perianth markings can vary greatly. Within a sample of 20 individuals the markings can vary from those typical of *G. elwesii* to that indicative of *G. caucasicus*. It is likely that individuals with single inner perianth marks have been selected, propagated, and distributed erroneously as *G. caucasicus*.

The use of *Galanthus caucasicus* in recent literature, including Stern (1956), is restricted to forms of *G. elwesii* with a single inner perianth mark.

I have stated above that the number of inner perianth marks is, despite the odd aberrant individual, a reliable character for the separation of *Galanthus alpinus* (including *G. caucasicus* and *G. bortkewitschianus*) and *G. elwesii* in the wild. True *G. alpinus* can also be separated from *G. elwesii* by other morphological differences, although these are less decisive than the number of marks on the inner perianth segment: *G. alpinus* is often smaller in overall dimensions than *G. elwesii*; the average leaf width of *G. alpinus* (see figures quoted above) is less than the variants of *G. elwesii* with a single apical mark on the inner segment (average 2.52 cm; range 2–3.6 cm); the leaves of *G. alpinus* are always straight, whereas those of *G. elwesii* can be twisted; *G. alpinus* often flowers when the leaves are very short and not fully developed, unlike the leaves of *G. elwesii*, which are mostly well developed at anthesis.

If one excludes all the specimens formerly and erroneously known as *Galanthus caucasicus* (i.e., *G. elwesii*), *G. alpinus* is a rare plant in cultivation, presently grown only in limited numbers in a few gardens. Most of the specimens I have seen were received as *G. alpinus* from botanical gardens in Russia. Of the few plants that are in cultivation, most of them are usually rather diminutive; they have quite narrow leaves (c. 0.6–1.5 cm wide) that are often not fully developed at flowering time, having reached only a few centimetres long, which is much shorter than the flowering scape. Most specimens that I have seen possess an inner perianth mark that is rather narrow and angular (see FIGURE 8).

In the wild *Galanthus alpinus* is found from the foothills of the low mountain belt (c. 270 m) up to the subalpine zone (c. 2200 m). It occurs in deciduous forests, or their margins and clearings, amongst scrub, and in river valleys, most frequently on soils overlying calcareous rocks. In the eastern and western parts of its distribution this species is only found as small isolated populations (Helen Mordak, pers. comm.).

CULTIVATION. I have seen *Galanthus alpinus* growing really well on two occasions. The first was in 1992 when I was overwhelmed by the sight of a sizeable drift of *G. alpinus* var. *alpinus* growing in the lawns of the botanic gardens at the Komarov Institute in St. Petersburg, where it seems to thrive perhaps because the winter and spring temperatures in St Petersburg closely match those of the Caucasus. Secondly, I have seen *Galanthus alpinus* var. *bortkewitschianus* growing very well on the rock garden at Kew. It is planted in one of the cooler areas, with some shade and protection provided by surrounding plantings and rocks. The soil is approximately neutral pH. Kew is well known for its mild microclimate, a sharp contrast to St. Petersburg where the winters are bitterly cold. Given this sharp contrast in growing conditions it is likely that *G. alpinus* has the potential to be successful in various environments, and may thus prove, in time, to be a successful garden subject.

4B. GALANTHUS ALPINUS VAR. BORTKEWITSCHIANUS

Galanthus alpinus var. *bortkewitschianus* differs from var. *alpinus* in its rounded flowers, squat habit (leaves considerably shorter than the scape during flowering), linear to narrowly oblanceolate leaves, and yellowish bulb; the diploid chromosome number of var. *bortkewitschianus* is 2n = 36, and var. *alpinus* 2n = 24. No great biological significance is attached to this variety, however, and I believe that this represents nothing more than a single aberrant population of

122

G. alpinus that has maintained a somewhat distinctive morphology through vegetative propagation.

A historical overview of *Galanthus alpinus* var. *bortkewitschianus* is given under the discussion for *G. alpinus* var. *alpinus*, above.

Galanthus alpinus *Sosn.* in Vestn. Tiflissk. Bot. Sada 19: 26 (1911); Grossh., Fl. Caucas. 1: 244 (1928); Losinsk. in Kom., Fl. SSSR 4: 479 (1935); Grossh., Fl. Caucas. edn. 2, 2: 193, map 224 (1940); Kem.-Nath. in Makaschv. et al., Fl. Georgia 2: 526 (1941); Kem.-Nath. in Trudy Tbilissk Bot. Inst. ser. 2, 11: 182 (1947); Traub & Moldenke in Herbertia 14: 112 (1948); Artjush. in Alp. Gard. Soc. Gr. Brit. 30(2): 124 (1962); Artjush. in Bot. Zhurn. (Moscow & Leningrad) 50(10): 1445 (1965); Artjush. in Bot. Zhurn. (Moscow & Leningrad) 51(10): 1447 (1966); Artjush. in Daffodil Tulip Year Book: 81 (1967); Artjush. in Pl. Life 25(2–4): 148 (1969); Artjush., Amaryllidaceae SSSR: 79, fig. 49 (1970); Gabrielyan & Tamanian in Biol. Zhurn. Armenii 35(5): 410 (1982); Dimitr. in Opred. rast. Adzh. izd. 2, 2: 151 (1990); A.P. Davis, Mordak & Jury in Kew Bull. 51(4): 746 (1996). Ind. loc.: Legi in monte Lomis-mta prope Borshom in regione alpina (7200'). Type: in regione montis Lomis-mta prope Borshom (culta in sectione caucasica), 1911, *Sosnowsky s.n.* (holotype TBI!).

DESCRIPTION. *Bulb* ovoid to ± spherical, 2.1–2.6(–3) cm × 1.5–2.1 cm, whitish or yellowish. *Sheath* 2.5–5.5 cm × 0.4–0.7 cm. *Leaves* supervolute in vernation; ± linear or very narrowly oblanceolate, at flowering 2.5–20(–25) cm × (0.45–)0.6–2.2(–2.5) cm, after flowering developing to 13–23 (–35) cm × 0.6–2.5 cm, recurving or erect at maturity; glaucous, adaxial and abaxial surfaces concolorous; surfaces smooth or with two to four fine, longitudinal furrows; midrib conspicuous; margins flat; apex acute to obtuse, flat to cucullate. *Scape* 9–16 cm long, glaucescent to glaucous. *Pedicel* 1.5–3 cm long. *Outer perianth segments*, 1.5–2 cm × 0.8–1.1 cm, broadly obovate to rounded, slightly unguiculate. *Inner perianth segments* ± obovate to cuneate, 0.7–1 cm × 0.4–0.5 cm, emarginate; each segment with a variable, narrow ± ∧- to ∩-shaped mark on the adaxial surface above the apical notch; abaxial surface with a mark extending halfway to two-thirds up the segment from the apex. *Anthers* tapering to an apiculum. *Capsule* almost spherical, 0.6–1 cm in diameter. *Seeds* pale brown, c. 0.3–0.5 cm long.

KEY TO THE VARIETIES OF
GALANTHUS ALPINUS

1. Bulb-scales whitish; flowers either ellipsoid or globose; seed capsules developing to maturity (fertile); widespread in the Caucasus (Russia, Georgia, Armenia) and neighbouring areas (northeastern Turkey); 2n = 24 . . . . **a. var. alpinus**

1. Bulb-scales yellowish; flowers globose; seed capsules not known to develop to maturity (sterile); found in only one site in district Chegem, upper Kamenka region, Karbardino-Balcaria (western Caucasus, Russia); 3n = 36 . . . .

. . . . **b. var. bortkewitschianus**

a. var. alpinus

G. nivalis L. var. *redoutei* Rupr. ex Regel, Gartenflora 12: 177, pl. 400, fig. 2 (1863); Regel, Gartenflora 23: 202, (1874), *in adnot.*; Boiss., Fl. Orient. 5: 144 (1882), *pro parte excl. G. nivalis* var. *caspius* Rupr. [= *G. transcaucasicus* Fomin], et *G. nivalis sensu* Redouté, Liliac. 4: tab. 200 [= *G. nivalis* L.]. Ind. loc.: 'welche vom Herrn Academiker von Ruprecht im Caucasus gesammelt und der Petersburger Gartembau-Gesellschaft als *G. Redoutei* aus dem Caucasus eingesendet ward.' Type: Iberia caucasia pr. Tiflis, copios ad rivul, Kodshori, 390 hex., 7, 22 March 1861, *Ruprecht* 1 (LE!).

G. redoutei (Rupr. ex Regel) Regel, Gartenflora 23: 202 (1874) ['not accepted' by Regel].

G. nivalis L. ß [var.] *major* Redouté (*in descr.* Redouté, Liliac. 4: tab. 200) ex Rupr. in Regel, Gartenflora 17: 131 (1868) [! descr. tab. 200 = *G. nivalis* L.], ? *nom. illeg.* ?Ind. loc. 'Ich fand sie oft und häufig bei Tiflis in der Kodshori Schult, . . .'. ?Type: Iberia caucasia pr. Tiflis, copios ad rivul, Kodshori, 390 hex., 7, 22 March 1861, *Ruprecht* 1 (LE!). Nomenclatural note: It is not clear whether Ruprecht intended to make var. *major* distinct from var. *redoutei*, or was in fact describing the same entity, because in both cases he refers to the same herbarium material.

G. grandis Burb. in J. Roy. Hort. Soc. 13(2): 203 (1891), *nom. nud.*

G. nivalis L. subsp. *caucasicus* Baker in Gard. Chron. ser. 3, 13: 313 (1887); Baker, Handb. Amaryll.: 17 (1888). Ind. loc.: 'We have in the Kew Herbarium specimens from six different collectors, and in every case it [*G. nivalis* subsp. *caucasicus*] is called 'plicatus' on

the label . . . As it is flowering at the present time in the herbaceous ground at Kew I take the opportunity of placing on record a diagnosis and description made from living specimens'.
Type: description made from living material, type assumed not to
have been preserved. Stern's lectotypification is rejected as his
designation of type is ambiguous (see page 116). Lectotype: Tiflis [1828–1830], *Szovits s.n.* (lectotype K!; isolectotype LE! selected by A.P. Davis et al., 1996).

G. caucasicus (Baker) Burb. in J. Roy. Hort. Soc. 13(2): 200 (1891)
['not accepted' by Burb.].

G. nivalis L. var. *caucasicus* (Baker) Beck in Wiener Ill. Gart.-Zei-
tung: 19 (1894).

G. nivalis L. var. *caucasicus* (Baker) Fomin in Fomin & Woronow,
Opred. Rast. Caucas. Krym. 1: 280 (1909), *nom. illeg.*

G. nivalis L. var. *caucasicus* (Baker) J. Phillippow in Kuzn. et al.
(eds.), Fl. Caucas. Critic. 2.5: 5 (1916), *nom. illeg.*

G. caucasicus (Baker) Grossh. in Grossh. & Schischk., Pl. Orient.
Exsic. fasc. 1: 4, no. 6 (1924); Grossh., Fl. Caucas. 1: 244 (1928);
Losinsk. in Kom., Fl. SSSR 4: 478 (1935); Grossh., Fl. Caucas.
edn. 2, 2: 192, tab. 24, fig. 5, map 223 (1940); Kem.-Nath. in
Makaschv. et al., Fl. Georgia 2: 525 (1941); Kem.-Nath. in Trudy
Tbilissk Bot. Inst. ser. 2, 11: 182 (1947); Traub & Moldenke in
Herbertia 14: 107 (1948); Artjush. in Bot. Zhurn. (Moscow &
Leningrad) 50(10): 1445 (1965); Artjush. in Bot. Zhurn. (Moscow & Leningrad) 51(10): 1446, fig. 4 (1966); Artjush. in Daffodil Tulip Year Book: 73, fig. 21 (1967); Artjush. in Pl. Life 25(2–
4): 147, fig. 30 (1969); Artjush., Amaryllidaceae SSSR: 78, fig. 47
(1970); Artjush. in Spisok rast. Herb. Fl. SSSR 19: 26, No. 5159
(1972); Galushko, Fl. N. Caucas. 1: 172 (1978); Kolak., Fl. Abkhas. 4: 111 (1986); P.H. Davis et al. (eds.), Fl. Turkey 10: 226
(1988).

G. cilicicus Baker subsp. *caucasicus* (Baker) O. Schwarz in Bull. Alp.
Gard. Soc. Gr. Brit. 31: 134 (1963), *comb. invalid.*

G. schaoricus Kem.-Nath. in Makaschv. et al., Fl. Georgia 2: 526
(1941), *nom.nud.*; Kem.-Nath. in Zametki Sist. Geogr. Rast. 13: 6
(1947), *nom. illeg.* (*G. caucasicus* (Baker) Grossh., *in syn.*); Kem.-
Nath. in Trudy Tbilissk Bot. Inst. ser. 2, 11: 183 (1947). Ind. loc.:
Georgia occid. Inter frutices regionis sylvaticae mediae in cal-
careis. Prov. Kutais, distr. Ratscha (Radja). Fauces fl. Schaora
'lacum Tschelischis-Udabno' prope pagum Nikorzminda. 2. V.

1926 fr. L. Kemularia-Nathadze 22. IV. 36. fr. et fl. M.Sochadze; locus Charistwali. 22. IV. 36. fr. et fl. M. Sochadze. Type: Georgia, Prov. Kutais, distr Ratscha Schaora, in frutices inter p. Nikorzminda et locus Charistwali, 20 April 1938, *Sochadze s.n.* (holotype TBI!).

[*G. nivalis sensu* Ledeb., Fl. Rossica 4: 113 (1853), *pro parte.*]

DESCRIPTION. *Leaves* at flowering 4–20(–28) cm × (0.45–)0.6–2.2 (–2.5) cm, after flowering developing to 13–23(–35) cm × 0.6–2.5 cm. *Outer perianth segments* obovate to ± elliptic, 1.5–2 cm × 0.8–1.1 cm, slightly unguiculate. *Capsule* almost spherical, 0.6–1 cm in diameter. *Seeds* c. 0.4 cm long.

ILLUSTRATIONS. Grossh., Fl. Caucas. edn. 2, 2: 192, tab. 24, fig. 5 (1940); Artjush. in Bot. Zhurn. (Moscow & Leningrad) 51(10): 1446, fig. 4 (1966); Artjush. in Daffodil Tulip Year Book: 73, fig. 21 (1967); Artjush. in Pl. Life 25(2–4): 147, fig. 30 (1969); Artjush. Amaryllidaceae SSSR: 78, fig. 47 (1970). PLATES 9, 37.

FLOWERING PERIOD. Spring (February–May).

HABITAT. From the foothills and the low mountain zone to the subalpine zone, 270–2200 m. Occurring in deciduous forests, forest margins, and clearings; in river valleys and infrequently on thin soil on rocks. Associated with calcareous soils.

DISTRIBUTION. Caucasus and Transcaucasus (within the limits of Russia, Georgia, Armenia, and Azerbaijan), in the neighbouring area of Lazistan (in northeastern Turkey), and possibly in northern Iran. MAP 4.

b. var. **bortkewitschianus** *(Koss) A.P. Davis* in A.P. Davis, Mordak & Jury in Kew Bull. 51(4): 750 (1996).

G. bortkewitschianus Koss in Bot. Mater. Herb. Inst. Kom. Akad. Nauk SSSR 14: 130, fig. 1 (1951); Artjush. in Bot. Zhurn. (Moscow & Leningrad) 50(10): 1445 (1965); Artjush. in Bot. Zhurn. (Moscow & Leningrad) 51(10): 1447 (1966); Artjush. in Daffodil Tulip Year Book: 73 (1967); Artjush. in Pl. Life 25(2–4): 148, fig. 30 (1969); Artjush., Amaryllidaceae SSSR: 79, fig. 50 (1970); Galushko, Fl. N. Caucas. 1: 172, fig. 39c (1978); C.D. Brickell in Walters et al. (eds.), Europ. Gard. Fl. 1: 318 (1986). Ind. loc.: Caucasus septentrionalis, republica autonoma Cabardensis, in Fageto, iii 1947, G. Koss; in Herb. Univ. Mosq. conservatur. Type: Northern Caucasus, Kabardah, near the river Kamenka, distr.

126

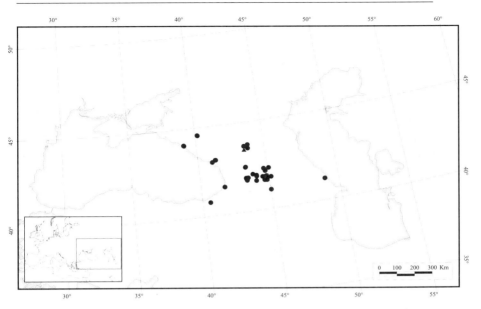

Map 4. Distribution of *Galanthus alpinus* var. *alpinus* [●] and var. *bortkewitschianus* [▲].

Chegem, east side of hill, 1200–1500 m, March 1947, *Koss s.n.* (holotype, *non vidi*; isotype LE!).

DESCRIPTION. *Leaves* at flowering 2.5–11(–16) cm × 1.5–2.4 cm, after flowering developing to 13–23(–25) cm × 1.8–2.5 cm, apex acute, cucullate. *Outer perianth segments* obovate, 1.5–1.7 cm × 1–1.2 cm, abrubtly unguiculate. Capsules not known to develop to maturity.

ILLUSTRATIONS. Koss in Bot. Mater. Herb. Inst. Kom. Akad. Nauk SSSR 14: 130, fig. 1 (1951); Artjush. in Pl. Life 25(2–4): 148, fig. 30 (1969); Artjush., Amaryllidaceae SSSR: 79, fig. 50 (1970); Galushko, Fl. N. Caucas. 1: 172, fig. 39c (1978); A.P. Davis, Mordak & Jury in Kew. Bull. 51(4): 751, fig. 1 (1996). PLATES 9, 38.

FLOWERING PERIOD. Spring (March–April).

HABITAT. A species occurring at the middle mountain zone in forest (*Fagus* spp.), often near streams, 1200–1500 m.

DISTRIBUTION. Known only from the type locality. MAP 4.

5. GALANTHUS ANGUSTIFOLIUS

Galanthus angustifolius was described by Koss (1951), from the Republic of Karbardino-Balcaria in the northern Caucasus. The identity of this species was founded on two main characteristics: very narrow leaves (2–5 mm) and large flowers. According to Koss (1951) the affinities of *G. angustifolius* lie with *G. caucasicus* (now a synonym of *G. alpinus*), presumably on the basis that both of these species have linear glaucous leaves and a single apical mark on each inner perianth segment.

Artjushenko (1967) was well aquainted with this species, and cultivated *G. angustifolius* at the Komarov Institute in St. Petersburg. She stated that the leaves were glaucous, applanate in vernation, and had a leaf anatomy that was similar, if not identical, to *G. nivalis*: '[*G. angustifolius*] has no differences from specimens of *G. nivalis* gathered near Kiev (Belaya Tserkov)'. Based on this assessment, Artjushenko placed *G. angustifolius* into the synonymy of *G. nivalis* because she found no distinguishing features between these two species. Later, Artjushenko (1966, 1969, 1970) made *G. angustifolius* a subspecies of *G. nivalis* (*G. nivalis* subsp. *angustifolius* (Koss) Artjush.), separated from subsp. *nivalis* by its lesser dimensions.

In 1991 I visited Nalchik Botanic Gardens and Nalchik University Gardens in Karbardino-Balcaria, where I had the opportunity to examine living examples of *G. angustifolius* that had been collected from natural locations in the northern Caucasus. These plants displayed all the characteristics of the species and were easy to identify by their narrow, glaucous leaves and applanate vernation. The leaves were distinctly glaucous, not partly glaucous (glaucescent) as in *G. nivalis*, and the width of the leaves ranged from 3 to 5 mm, which is narrower than the smallest variants of *G. nivalis*. Anatomical investigations (Davis and Barnett, 1997) show that leaf anatomy of *G. angustifolius* is not like *G. nivalis*, in contrast to the findings of Artjushenko (1965). On this evidence, which is backed by molecular studies (Davis et al., in prep.), I conclude that *G. angustifolius* is a distinct species and shares an affinity with *G. alpinus*, in agreement with Koss (1951). This assumption is logically consistent with geographical distribution, since *G. nivalis* occurs mainly in central Europe and its eastern-most distribution is in the Ukraine near Kiev (MAP 1, page 96). *Galanthus angustifolius* occurs in the northern Caucasus (MAP 5, page 130), and *G. alpinus* (MAP 4, page 127)

128

throughout the Caucasus (concentrated in central Georgia) and Transcaucasus.

CULTIVATION. Apart from a small number of collections in larger botanic gardens, true *Galanthus angustifolius* is probably not in cultivation in the British Isles. Garden specimens grown as *G. angustifolius*, at least all the examples that I have seen, represent narrow-leafed forms of *G. nivalis*. If *G. angustifolius* is introduced into cultivation it would probably be best to give it the same treatment as *G. alpinus*. In its native habitat *G. angustifolius* grows in deciduous forest, in areas of the Caucasus that receive considerably colder winters than most parts of the British Isles.

Galanthus angustifolius *Koss* in Bot. Mater. Gerb. Inst. Kom. a Akad. Nauk SSSR 14: 134, fig. 3 (1951). Ind. loc.: Respublica [*sic*] Cabardensis, in silvis mixtis, III 1947, G. Koss (Herb. Univ. Mosq.). Type: N Caucasus, Karbarda. In mixed forest, on the north side of the hills, at the altitude of 700–750 m, iii 1947, *Koss s.n.* (holotype ?MHA, isotype LE!).
G. nivalis L. subsp. *angustifolius* (Koss) Artjush. in Bot. Zhurn. (Moscow & Leningrad) 51(10): 1443, fig. 3 (1966); Artjush. in Pl. Life 25(2–4): 144, fig. 24 (1969); Artjush., Amaryllidaceae SSSR: 75, fig. 44 (1970).

DESCRIPTION. *Bulb* ± spherical to ovoid, small, 1.0–2 cm × 0.7–1 cm. *Leaves* applanate in vernation; linear, very narrow, at flowering (3.5–)5.5–8 cm × (0.2–)0.35–0.5 cm, after flowering developing to 8–16 cm × (0.2–)0.35–0.7 cm, usually erect at maturity and often characteristically curved, to give a ± wine-glass shape in outline; glaucous, abaxial and adaxial surfaces concolorous; surfaces smooth; margins flat; apex obtuse, flat to cucullate. *Scape* 7–14 cm long, glaucescent to glaucous. *Pedicel* 1.8–3 cm long. *Outer perianth segments* obovate, 1–2(–2.3) cm × 0.4–0.7 cm, slightly unguiculate. *Inner perianth segments* ± obovate to cuneate, 0.7–1 cm × 0.4–0.5 cm, emarginate; each segment with a variable ± ∧-shaped mark on the adaxial surface above the apical notch; abaxial surface with a mark extending to either half or almost the entire length of the segment. *Anthers* tapering to an apiculum. *Capsule* almost spherical, 0.6–1 cm in diameter. *Seeds* pale brown, c. 0.4 cm long.

ILLUSTRATIONS. Koss in Bot. Mater. Gerb. Inst. Kom. a Akad. Nauk SSSR 14: 134, fig. 3 (1951). PLATES 11, 39.

FLOWERING PERIOD. Spring (March–May).

129

HABITAT. Occurring in deciduous and mixed deciduous forest (*Carpinus* spp., *Acer* spp., etc.), and scrub (*Corylus* sp.), in leafy soils, and often near rivers and streams, 700–1000 m.

DISTRIBUTION. Northern Caucasus: within the limits of Russia (Dagestan, Karbardino-Balcaria, and Severo-Osetinskaya). MAP 5.

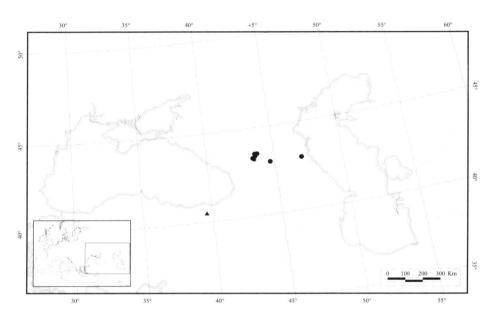

Map 5. Distribution of *Galanthus angustifolius* [●] and *Galanthus koenenianus* [▲].

6. GALANTHUS CILICICUS

In 1897 Baker received some dried specimens of *Galanthus* from W. Siehe (9 i 1896, *Siehe s.n.*) collected in southern Turkey in the Cilician Taurus, at an elevation of 560 m. In the same year he received from T.S. Ware some living specimens from the same locality, from which he drew up the description for *G. cilicicus*. Initially, the plants presented by Ware were determined as *G. fosteri* but Baker decided that they represented something new and unique. According to Baker these two new collections were set apart from *G. fosteri* by the following features: 'less robust habit, much narrower leaves, narrowed gradually from the middle to a very narrow base, and by the want of the large green blotch over the lower half [apex]

130

of the perianth'. Other important characteristic were the 'bright green' leaves, and a flowering time from November to March. This combination of characters, coupled with the fact that this species has always been exceptionally rare in the wild and in cultivation, has lead subsequent authors to affiliate *G. cilicicus* with other species, particularly *G. nivalis*. According to Gottlieb-Tannenhain (1904), *G. cilicicus* was closely related to *G. nivalis* and he therefore recognized it as subspecies of the latter, a treatment that has been followed by other authors (Stern, 1956; Brickell, 1984).

Upon examining the type specimen and living material of *Galanthus cilicicus*, Stern (1956) challenged Baker's description of this species by giving the colour of the leaves as glaucous and not bright green. Stern proposed that *G. cilicicus* was a geographical variant of *G. nivalis*, introduced to the eastern Mediterranean by man, a theory that he thought would explain its geographical disjunction from the main distribution range of *G. nivalis*.

Artjushenko's (1969) opinion differed entirely from Stern's and followed Baker's description of *G. cilicicus* by giving the leaves of this species as: 'dark green, matt surfaced, but without glaucous bloom', or as: 'green and opaque, but not glaucous' (Artjushenko, 1974). *Galanthus cilicicus* was accordingly placed in section *Viridifolii* by Artjushenko (1966, 1969, 1970), a taxonomic grouping characterized by species with green leaves, which occur predominately in the Caucasus area. *Galanthus cilicicus* was compared directly with *G. rizehensis*, a species with dark green leaves that occurs around the eastern part of the Black Sea coast in northern Turkey, southern Russia, and western Georgia.

Recently, *Galanthus cilicicus* has been recollected in the Province of Içel in southern Turkey (*Nutt 17/87, Sønderhousen* 1992), enabling the examination of authentic wild source material. Investigation of this material and of the type specimen indicates that the leaf colour is glaucous, like *G. elwesii*; examination also confirms that the vernation is applanate. This morphological evidence clearly points towards a relationship with species that have glaucous leaves, namely *G. gracilis* and *G. peshmenii*, and not *G. nivalis* or *G. rizehensis*, which have glaucescent and green leaves, respectively. Furthermore, *G. cilicicus* occurs in southern Turkey, like the aforementioned glaucous-leafed species; *G. nivalis* is not known to occur in Asia, and has certainly never been recorded in southern Anatolia.

Galanthus cilicicus is probably most closely allied to *G. peshmenii* because both these species have applanate vernation, one mark on

131

each inner perianth segment, and an autumn to winter flowering period (November to February). Differences in leaf morphology and leaf anatomy distinguish these two species (see discussion for *G. peshmenii*). *Galanthus cilicicus* is also quite similar to *G. gracilis* because it has glaucous leaves and applanate vernation. These species are easily separated, however, because *G. gracilis* has two marks on each inner perianth segment (or occasionally these are fused to form one large more or less X-shaped mark) and the leaves are often twisted, two features not found in *G. cilicicus*.

In the wild, *Galanthus cilicicus* seems to be an exceptionally rare species, occurring in only a few localities in southern Turkey. It is also infrequent in cultivation and at the present time is known in the British Isles only from the collection made by Richard Nutt (*Nutt* 17/87).

The ecology of this species is rather similar to *Galanthus peshmenii*. According to Ole Sønderhousen's field notes, it occurs on limestone areas amongst grass and maquis, at the edges of fields or woodland margins. In some locations the limestone is flat and more or less horizontal, with frequent, straight gullies and furrows, not unlike the limestone pavements of Britain; in other locations it occurs on rock outcrops and small cliffs. In both types of habitat, *G. cilicicus* occurs either in small pockets of soil, or amongst other plants in larger expanses of soil.

CULTIVATION. *Galanthus cilicicus* is not a particularly valuable garden plant, because it is less robust than many other snowdrops and does not seem to propagate fast enough to produce attractive clumps or drifts. It does, however, have a certain charm, and it will, of course, be of interest to those who like to grow the rarer species. Furthermore, its late autumn to early winter flowering period provides some interest at a time of year when most other snowdrops are not yet in leaf or flower.

As with other snowdrop species that are poorly represented in cultivation, *Galanthus cilicicus* probably needs to be tried in a number of situations before the best method of cultivation is discovered. Richard Nutt grows it against the wall of his house where the soil is probably better drained that the open garden and where it is protected from the worst of the weather. It is likely that the species will prefer gardens that are situated on alkaline soils, because of its association with limestone in its natural habitat. Gardens in warmer or drier areas may also be more suitable. Experiments with growing *G. cilicicus* in pots, plunged in frames, have not met with a measurable amount of success; they survive and often flower but increase very slowly.

Galanthus cilicicus *Baker* in Gard. Chron. ser. 3, 21: 214 (1897); Dammer in Gard. Chron. ser. 3. 23: 79, fig. 29 (1898); Traub & Moldenke in Herbertia 14: 111 (1948); P.H. Davis in Kew Bull. 1: 112 (1949); T. Baytop & B. Mathew, Bulb. Pl. Turkey: 22 (1984); Artjush. in Ann. Mus. Goulandris 2: 18, fig. 5 (1974), *pro parte*. Ind. loc.: 'collected by Herr Walter Siehe on the Cilician Taurus in 1896, at an elevation of 560 meters above sea level'. Type: Cilicia [Cilician Taurus], 560 m., 9 i 1896, *Siehe s.n.* (holotype K!).

G. *nivalis* L. subsp. *cilicicus* (Baker) Gottl.-Tann. in Abh. K. K. Zool.-Bot. Ges. Wien 2(4): 33 (1904); Stern, Snowdr. & Snowfl.: 28, fig. 5 (p. 29) (1956); C.D. Brickell in Walters et al. (eds.), Europ. Gard. Fl. 1: 318 (1986), *pro parte*; N. Zeybek & E. Sauer, Türk. Kardelenleri I/ Beitr. Kennt. Türk. Schneeglöckhen I: 40, fig. 6 (1995).

DESCRIPTION. *Bulb* ± spherical to ovoid, 1.4–2.2 cm × 1.3–1.5 cm. *Sheath* 2.5–5 × 0.3–0.5 cm. *Leaves* applanate in vernation; linear, at flowering (7–)11–15 cm × 0.5–0.7 cm; after flowering developing to 15–18(–25) cm × 0.5–0.8 cm, erect to recurved at maturity; glaucous, surfaces concolorous; apex obtuse to acute, flat. *Scape* 10–18 cm long, green to glaucous. *Pedicel* 1.5–2.5 cm long. *Outer perianth segments* obovate to broadly obovate, 1.8–2.2 cm × 0.6–1 cm, slightly unguiculate. *Inner perianth segments* ± obovate to cuneate, 0.9–1.1 cm × 0.4 cm, emarginate; each perianth segment with a variable, narrow ± ∧- to ∩-shaped mark on the adaxial surface above the apical notch; abaxial surface with a mark similar in shape and size to the adaxial mark. *Anthers* tapering to an apiculum. *Capsule* almost spherical, 0.5–1 cm in diameter. *Seeds* pale brown, c. 0.4 cm long.

ILLUSTRATIONS. Dammer in Gard. Chron. ser. 3, 23: 79, fig. 29 (1898); Stern, Snowdr. & Snowfl.: 28, fig. 5 (1956); (1974); N. Zeybek & E. Sauer, Türk. Kardelenleri 1: 41, fig. 6 (1995). PLATES 5, 29.

FLOWERING PERIOD. Winter (November–January).

HABITAT. On outcrops of limestone rocks, amongst grass and shrubs, c. 500 m.

DISTRIBUTION. Southern Turkey. MAP 6.

133

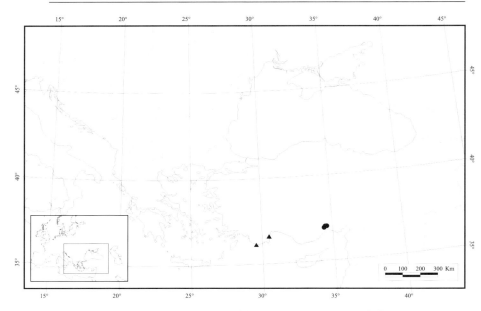

Map 6. Distribution of *Galanthus cilicicus* [•] and *Galanthus peshmenii* [▲].

7. GALANTHUS PESHMENII

Galanthus peshmenii is a recently described species (Davis and Brickell, 1994), named in honour of the late Dr H. Peşmen. It has a very restricted distribution in the wild and is known from only a small area in Antalya Province of southern Turkey and the nearby Greek island of Kastellorhizo (Megisti). According to data from herbarium specimens, this species was first collected in 1973 on Kastellorhizo by the Greek botanist Stamatiadou (*Stamatiadou* 19259). This was followed by a collection made on the Turkish mainland in 1978, by Peşmen, Yildiz, and Günes, which was used as the type material for this species (*Peşmen, Yildiz, & Günes* 4125). Originally, collections from Kastellorhizo were believed to represent *G. cilicicus* Baker (Artjushenko, 1974) or *G. nivalis* subsp. *cilicicus* (Baker) Gottl.-Tann. (Kamari, 1982; Brickell, 1984), and collections made on the Turkish mainland have also been placed under *G. reginae-olgae* Orph. (Brickell, 1984). These determinations were not far off the mark, however, as *Galanthus peshmenii* shares many of the features of the above species.

Galanthus peshmenii is an autumn-flowering plant that produces

134

its flowering scapes before the leaves emerge from the surface of the soil. Occasionally, the leaves are present at flowering time but even in these instances they are very short and not fully developed (see fig. 1 in Davis and Brickell, 1994; and PLATE 6). The vernation of the leaves is applanate.

In flowering time and growth habit *Galanthus peshmenii* closely matches *G. reginae-olgae*, a species from Greece, Sicily, and the southern part of the former Yugoslavia. These two species are, however, easily distinguished from one another by the colour and dimensions of the leaves, and the shape of the inner perianth mark. *Galanthus reginae-olgae* has a glaucous median stripe on the adaxial surface of the leaves on a background of green; *G. peshmenii* possesses leaves that are glaucescent (green with glaucous undertones) to glaucous, with or without a slight underlying median stripe. The leaves of *G. peshmenii* are usually narrower and longer than those of *G. reginae-olgae*, and have a distinctly flaccid appearance when fully developed. The inner perianth mark of *G. reginae-olgae* is very similar to that of *G. nivalis* and is usually represented by a bold ∧- to ∩-shaped mark; and on the inside of the inner perianth segment the green mark runs from the apex to the base of the segment (see FIGURE 8). The markings on the inner segments of *G. peshmenii* are quite different. The outer mark is narrow and shaped like a ∧, and on the inside of the segment the mark is small and covers only approximately half the length of the segment. In terms of flower markings, leaf characteristics (including vernation), and flowering time, *G. peshmenii* is very much like *G. cilicicus*, but differs from this species in its leafless, or near-leafless, flowering habit and long, narrow leaves.

Davis and Brickell (1984) considered *Galanthus peshmenii* to be closely related to *G. reginae-olgae*. After a more in-depth assessment of *G. peshmenii*, however, I am now of the opinion that the species has its closest affinity with *G. cilicicus*. Molecular data from an analysis of chloroplast and ribosome DNA (Davis et al., in prep.) clearly shows that *G. cilicicus* is the single most closely related species to *G. peshmenii*. In the same study *Galanthus reginae-olgae* is shown to be allied to *G. nivalis* and *G. plicatus*, and not to *G. peshmenii*. These results are logical in a geographical context, as both *G. peshmenii* and *G. cilicicus* occur in the Mediterranean coastal area of southern Turkey. It seems that the leafless flowering habit and autumn flowering time of *G. reginae-olgae* and *G. peshmenii* are characteristics that have evolved independently (i.e., in different lineages) in *Galanthus*, in response to environmental factors: both species occur in rather more arid conditions than most other *Galanthus* species. Other species of Amaryllidaceae also share the above two features, such as *Leucojum autumnale, Lapiedra martinezii,* and *Sternbergia clusiana,* three species which occur in similar habitats to *G. peshmenii* and *G. reginae-olgae.*

The leaf anatomy of *Galanthus peshmenii* is unique because it has a well-defined palisade layer, a feature clearly seen when transverse sections of the leaf are observed using a light microscope. The well-defined palisade layer, usually an adaptation to high light levels, is present in many other members of the Amaryllidaceae, including those genera mentioned above. *Galanthus reginae-olgae* also has a palisade layer, but it is not as well developed as that of *G. peshmenii.*

The morphological and anatomical features of *Galanthus peshmenii* are put into context when populations of this species are examined in situ. On the island of Kastellorhizo, a typical hot, dry Mediterranean island, *G. peshmenii* grows almost exclusively as a chasmophyte on low-altitude, north-facing cliffs and rock outcrops. It is also found very close to the sea, sometimes just 10 m from the seashore, and as little as 5 m above sea level. Pockets of soil in rock fissures, hollows, and holes provide micro-habitats for its existence, affording protection from the extremes of temperature and climate. *Galanthus peshmenii* is often found at a height or position that is out of reach of grazing animals, especially goats. Indeed, possibly the reason this species is found so frequently growing on rocks is that it has been eaten out of existence elsewhere on the island.

On the Turkish mainland *Galanthus peshmenii* is not found in such extreme habitats as those of Kastellorhizo, but even here the location of populations is still rather atypical for the genus. In Antalya Province the species grows in low altitude *Pinus* forest, in rocky places, in maquis, and in scrubby areas below cliffs.

CULTIVATION. *Galanthus peshmenii* was first introduced into cultivation in this country by Dr Martyn Rix from collections he made on Kastellorhizo in 1974 (*Rix* 4010). He cultivated these collections in pots in an unheated glasshouse, where they grew quite happily, and have survived to the present day. In 1991 I was given some bulbs of this collection, which I kept in a pot, situated in a cold frame. The pots were plunged in sand, and the lights of the cold frame were placed over the bed only during cold, wet periods. This was quite successful during the autumn months but in the winter, after a few days of temperatures constantly below freezing, the plants did

136

not fare so favourably, and eventually I resorted to growing them in the glasshouse during the winter. This is not to say that *G. peshmenii* is not hardy in the British Isles but rather that growing in pots may not be entirely satisfactory, probably because the bulbs and roots are too easily frozen. At Kew, Tony Hall grows it with much greater success, which may be because he uses deeper pots with a more freely draining compost. Other growers have followed a similar cultivation regime and report that their plants are growing well and are increasing. In warmer districts, if one can spare material for experimentation, it is worth trying *G. peshmenii* in the garden. Encouraging results have been achieved in raised beds and stone troughs that contain well-drained, friable soil, although the bulbs should not receive too much heat in the summer months. As with other snowdrops, sunshine is beneficial during the growing and flowering period.

Galanthus peshmenii *A.P. Davis & C.D. Brickell* in The New Plantsman 1: 14, fig. 1 (1994). Type: Turkey. Prov. Antalya. Kemer Kesmeboğazı—Gedelma köyü arası, c. 300 m, 3 xi 1978, *Peşmen, Yildiz, & Günes* 4125 (holotype HUB!, isotype E!).

[*G. cilicicus non* Baker, *pro parte*, Artjush. in Ann. Mus. Goulandris 2: 18, fig. 5 [? = *G. peshmenii*] (1974).]

[*G. nivalis* L. subsp. *cilicicus auct. non* (Baker) Gottl.-Tann., *pro parte*, Kamari in Bot. Jahrb. Syst. 103(1): 111 (1982); C.D. Brickell in P.H. Davis et al. (eds.), Fl. of Turkey 8: 370, map 55 (1984).]

[*G. reginae-olgae auct. non* Orph.: C.D. Brickell in P.H. Davis et al. (eds.), Fl. Turkey 8: 367, map 54 (1984); N. Zeybek & E. Sauer, Türk. Kardelenleri 1: 45, fig. 8 (1995).]

DESCRIPTION. *Bulb* ± spherical to ovoid, 2–2.5(–4.7) cm × 1.7–2.3 cm. *Sheath* 1.5–3 × 0.3–0.5 cm. *Leaves* applanate in vernation; linear, either absent during flowering or only partially developed, (0–)1.7–8 cm × 0.2–0.4 cm, after flowering developing to 10–25(–30) cm × 0.25–0.4 cm, recurving at maturity, and becoming prostrate-flaccid in terricolous forms to pendent in chasmophytes; adaxial surface glaucescent with a faint underlying median stripe, abaxial surface glaucous; surfaces smooth; midrib conspicuous; margins flat or slightly revolute near the base; apex obtuse, flat. *Scape* 9–12.5

137

cm long, green. Pedicel 2–3 cm. *Outer perianth segments* narrowly obovate, 1.6–2.3 cm × 0.8–1 cm, slightly unguiculate. *Inner perianth segments* ± elliptic to cuneate, 0.7–0.8 cm × 0.4–0.5 cm emarginate; each perianth segment with a variable, often diffuse, ± ∩- to ∧-shaped mark, on the adaxial surface above the apical notch; abaxial surface with a mark nearly extending to the base of each segment. *Anthers* tapering to an apiculum. *Capsule* spherical to ellipsoid, c. 1 cm in diameter. *Seeds* pale brown, c. 0.5 cm long.

ILLUSTRATIONS. A.P. Davis & C.D. Brickell in The New Plantsman 1: 14, fig. 1 (1994); N. Zeybek & E. Sauer, Türk. Kardelenleri 1: 46, fig. 8 (1995). PLATES 6, 36.

FLOWERING PERIOD. Flowering in autumn (October–November).

HABITAT. A low altitude species, from 5–300 m, occurring in maquis or at the base of north-facing, rocky, limestone bluffs. On the island of Kastellorhizo almost exclusively found in solution hollows and crevices in limestone rocks, in places where plants cannot be grazed by goats.

DISTRIBUTION. The eastern Mediterranean Greek island of Kastellorhizo and adjacently in southwestern Turkey. MAP 6, page 134.

8. GALANTHUS KOENENIANUS

Galanthus koenenianus was discovered in the late 1980s in northeastern Turkey, and named in honour of its collector, Manfred Koenen (Lobin, Brickell, and Davis, 1993). It is a unique species, due to the presence of a distinctly furrowed abaxial leaf surface. The deep furrows are particularly dramatic when the leaf is cut in transverse section and compared against leaf sections taken from other species (Davis and Barnett, 1997). The presence of a small, yellow or light green mark near the base of each inner perianth segment is another unusual feature, although some specimens do not have this mark.

The first collections of this species were represented by very small plants, not more than 7 cm high, although more recent collections show that *Galanthus koenenianus* can attain the dimensions of closely related species, such as *G. alpinus*.

Galanthus koenenianus has a limited distribution in the wild, being found only in the Gümüshane Province in northeastern Turkey. Here, in the Pontus Mountains, it occurs at subalpine altitude of around 1500 m. The height and situation of the Pontus range, and

138

its close proximity to the Black Sea, ensures that the vegetation here receives a high rainfall for most of the year, and the winter often brings heavy snowfall. According to field observations (Manfred Koenen pers. comm.), *G. koenenianus* grows in mixed woodland, mainly amongst deciduous trees (*Acer campestre* subsp. *lepicarpa, Sambucus edulus, S. nigra,* and *Sorbus torminalis*); *Picea orientalis* and *Fagus orientalis* represent the dominant vegetation. The soil here is volcanic, and has a pH of around 7 or lower. According to Manfred Koenen the strongest plants are found underneath or near *Coryllus avellana.* The reason for this is not known, but perhaps the *Corylus* provides some measure of protection against grazing animals, or perhaps the leaves produce a favourable soil. In these sites *G. koenenianus* is often accompanied by *Cyclamen parviflorum.*

In terms of general morphology, *Galanthus koenenianus* is similar to *G. alpinus,* as both species possesses glaucous leaves, supervolute vernation, and a single mark at the apex of each inner perianth segment. The distribution of these two species is more or less contiguous, as the western-most populations of *G. alpinus* occur in the mountains around the eastern end of the Black Sea coast. It is also possible that *G. koenenianus* is closely related to *G. elwesii,* another species with glaucous leaves and supervolute vernation but possessing two separate marks on each inner perianth segment. The small green or yellow spot on the inner segment of *G. koenenianus* could be the remains of a second, separate marking, which if still present would make this species more like *G. elwesii* than *G. alpinus.*

CULTIVATION. Manfred Koenen has successfully cultivated *Galanthus koenenianus* for some years. He grows it in ordinary garden soil, enriched with well-rotted leaf-mould (approximately three years old). His plants are situated in a bed that receives plenty of winter sun and summer shade from a nearby tree.

Galanthus koenenianus *Lobin, C.D. Brickell & A.P. Davis* in Kew Bull. 48(1): 161, fig. 1 (1993). Type: Northeastern Turkey, Gümüshane Province, Soganli Dagi, between Yagmudere and Araliya, 1550 m, 8 Sept. 1988 (Cult. Bonn. fl.: March 1991; fr.: June 1991; seed: 1 July 1991), *Koenen* 30*88*Tr*KP (holotype K!).

DESCRIPTION. *Bulb* ± spherical to ovoid, c. 2 cm × 1.1 cm. *Sheath* 2–2.2 cm × 0.4–0.5 cm. *Leaves* supervolute in vernation; linear to very narrowly oblanceolate, at flowering c. 2.5 cm × 0.5 cm, after flowering developing to 12–22.8 cm × 0.5–1.2 cm, and becoming broader in the upper third, usually erect at maturity; glaucous with an oily sheen, surfaces concolorous; adaxial surface smooth, abaxial surface distinctly sulcate; midrib conspicuous; margins flat; apex obtuse to acute, cucullate. *Scape* c. 5.5 cm long, glaucous. *Flower* smelling of urine. *Outer perianth segments* narrowly obovate, 1.5–1.7 cm × 0.6–0.8 cm, slightly unguiculate. *Inner perianth segments* ± obovate to cuneate, 0.7–0.8 cm × 0.4–0.5 cm, emarginate; each perianth segment with a variable, narrow, ± ∧-shaped mark on the abaxial surface above the apical notch, and often with a faint yellowish patch near the base of each segment; adaxial surface with a mark extending to the base of each segment. *Anthers* tapering to a short apiculum. *Capsule* spherical to ellipsoid, c. 1 cm in diameter. *Seeds* not seen.

ILLUSTRATIONS. Lobin, C.D. Brickell & A.P. Davis in Kew Bull. 48(1): 161, fig. 1 (1993). PLATES 10, 40, 41.

FLOWERING PERIOD. Spring (February–March).

HABITAT. A subalpine species occurring in the characteristic high precipitation area of the north-facing Pontus mountain range (c. 1550 m).

DISTRIBUTION. Northeastern Turkey. MAP 5, page 130.

9. GALANTHUS ELWESII

In many works, *Galanthus elwesii* has been associated with a number of other species that have glaucous leaves and two marks on each inner perianth segment, namely *G. gracilis* Čelak., *G. graecus* Orph. ex Boiss., and *G. maximus* Velen. For this group, Stern (1956) recognized two species and one variety: *G. elwesii* var. *elwesii*, *G. elwesii* var. *maximus* (Velen.) Beck, and *G. graecus*. According to Stern, *G. graecus* is a species with narrow twisted leaves, applanate vernation, and inner perianth segments that are straight (not flared) and 7 mm wide; *G. elwesii* var. *elwesii* is described as having erect leaves, which are straight and not twisted, with hooded (cucullate) apices; *G. elwesii* var. *maximus* differs from the latter only by its slightly twisted leaves. The descriptive line drawings in Stern's monograph illustrate his concepts of these taxa.

Stern's treatment of these species is criticized by Webb (1978). Webb states that Stern had a 'reckless disregard for the type concept' because he did not examine the types of *G. graecus* or *G. elwesii* var. *maximus*, and did not adhere to the authors' original con-

140

cepts for these species. For example, the original descriptions and type specimens for *G. elwesii* (Hooker, 1875) and *G. graecus* (Boissier, 1882) do not match Stern's descriptions and drawings of these species. Because Stern did not refer to the type specimens, or follow the authors' original concepts of these species, his treatment of these species is not meaningful and the taxa should be regarded as *G. elwesii sensu* Stern and *G. graecus sensu* Stern. Unfortunately, Stern's concepts of *G. graecus* and *G. elwesii* have been, and still are, frequently used in literature and in horticulture.

According to Webb (1978) *Galanthus graecus sensu* Stern and *G. elwesii sensu* Stern are very closely related, and represent 'two extremes of variation within the complex', a complex, he states, that contains 'a continuous range of variation from one taxon to the other'. Furthering this idea, he suggests that the intermediates are more common than either of the extremes. Webb considers that *G. elwesii* var. *maximus* is not distinguishable from *G. elwesii* and does not represent any of the aforementioned extremes. Owing to the ambiguity over the use of *G. graecus*, but wishing to recognize a subspecies for one end of this range of variation (i.e., *G. graecus sensu* Stern), Webb created *G. elwesii* subsp. *minor*. The two subspecies of *G. elwesii* were separated as follows: for subsp. *minor*, 'Leaves usually 5–12 mm wide, twisted with involute [applanate] vernation. Outer perianth segments nearly flat, 7–1 mm wide'; and *G. elwesii* subsp. *elwesii*, 'Leaves usually 14–22 mm wide, rarely up to 30 mm, twisted or straight with convolute [supervolute] vernation. Outer perianth segments convex, 11–15 mm wide'.

In her investigations on the Greek snowdrops, Kamari (1981, 1982) reduced *Galanthus gracilis*, *G. graecus*, and *G. maximus* to a single variable species under *G. elwesii*. Then, to recognize the great variability of *G. elwesii*, she enumerated three new varieties for this species: var. *elwesii*, var. *stenophyllus*, and var. *platyphyllus*. From the descriptions given by Kamari (1982), it can be inferred that these varieties are equivalent to *G. elwesii* Hook. f., *G. graecus sensu* Stern (*G. gracilis*), and *G. elwesii* var. *elwesii sensu* Stern, respectively.

Later, Brickell (1984) clarified matters by examining the type material of *Galanthus graecus* Orph. ex Boiss., a species that he considered to be synonymous with *G. elwesii*. This conclusion agrees with a comment made by Greuter (in a footnote to Artjushenko, 1974), who pointed out that *G. elwesii* appears to coexist (according to Artjushenko's specimen citations) with *G. graecus* on the Aegean island of Khios, which, incidentally, is the *locus classicus* of the latter

141

species. With *G. graecus* placed into the synonymy of *G. elwesii*, Brickell (1984, 1986) used *G. gracilis* to represent the second entity of this species complex, equivalent to *G. elwesii* subsp. *minor*, and *G. graecus sensu* Stern. Thus, in Brickell's treatment, *G. elwesii* is the name for the populations with supervolute vernation and broad leaves, and *G. gracilis* for those with applanate vernation and narrow leaves.

Recently, Zeybek (1988) has described a number of subspecies for *Galanthus elwesii* in a taxonomic investigation of *Galanthus* in Turkey. He named four new subspecies for *G. elwesii*: subsp. *tuebitaki*, subsp. *melihae*, subsp. *yayintaschii*, and subsp. *akmanii*. In a later treatment for Turkish *Galanthus*, Zeybek and Sauer (1995) elevated *G. elwesii* subsp. *melihae* to *G. melihae*.

After some considerable time spent studying *Galanthus elwesii*, I am convinced that two species are involved in this complex—*G. elwesii* and *G. gracilis*—in agreement with Brickell (1984, 1986). For my investigations I visited a number of localities in Turkey, Greece, and the Aegean Islands, to observe variation *in situ*. Confirming the findings of Webb (1978) and Kamari (1981, 1982), these studies found that populations can be either one of the extreme types (recorded as subspecies and varieties by these authors, respectively, or as species by Brickell 1984, 1986) or of an intermediate type. Populations encountered on mainland Greece, for example, display a skewed pattern of variation, biased towards one of the extreme variation types. These observations were comparable to those made by Kamari (1982, 1982), who stated, 'One of these varieties [the extremes of variation or the intermediates] may slightly to markedly predominate in any one population'. In southwestern Turkey some populations are typical of those described by Webb (1978), which are between the two extremes of variation. Despite this pattern of variation, however, discrete populations are usually found, and it is easy to identify them as either *G. elwesii* or *G. gracilis*. One can speculate that hybridization has occurred in populations containing complex patterns of variation.

Field studies also agree with the suggestion made by Webb (1978) that the leaf width correlates with the type of vernation. Broad-leafed plants tend to have supervolute vernation (*Galanthus elwesii*), and narrow-leafed plants usually have applanate vernation (*G. gracilis*). Generally this idea holds true, although sometimes narrow-leafed individuals of *G. elwesii* are found, such as those in northern Greece, and broad-leafed specimens of *G. gracilis* occur, such as those in western Turkey. No statistical assessment of this phenomenon has been made.

The distribution of *Galanthus elwesii* and *G. gracilis* is generally sympatric (see MAP 7, page 152, and MAP 8, page 156). Frequently both taxa have been recorded in the same locality (Artjushenko, 1974) and possibly even in the same populations (Kamari, 1982). However, the characters used to separate *G. elwesii* and *G. gracilis*, namely vernation and leaf width (Webb, 1978), are stable and not influenced by the environment: in common-garden experiments the integrity of these two species is maintained, and they can nearly always be unambiguously identified. Molecular data, from the chloroplast genome (cpDNA) and ribosomal DNA (rbDNA), support the recognition of two separate species in that *G. elwesii* and *G. gracilis* can be easily identified by discrete molecular 'markers'. These markers, which are represented as visualized pieces of DNA on an electrophoretic gel, are characteristic for each species regardless of geographical distribution. The level of molecular diversity observed in these studies is comparable with other species, such as *G. nivalis* and *G. plicatus*, which are far more morphologically distinct.

The variants of *Galanthus elwesii* with one mark at the apex of each inner perianth segment have often been confused with *G. caucasicus* (now known as *G. alpinus*), and it seems that nearly all the plants known in cultivation today as *G. caucasicus* are in fact *G. elwesii* with a single mark. The true *G. alpinus* is not like the plant we know in gardens under the name of *G. caucasicus*, and should not cause confusion with single-marked variants of *G. elwesii* (see page 120). Furthermore, it seems that the single-marked variants of *G. elwesii* are not known in the wild, and herein lies a very strange phenomenon. I have observed two collections of *G. elwesii*, of known wild provenance, that have changed from having two marks on each inner perianth segment to one! Both these plants were in cultivation for several years before changing in this way; each was collected in a different part of southern Turkey; and each was growing in a different location (in the same garden). It remains to be seen if the mutation is stable but this phenomenon could explain the existence of the single-marked variant. Of all the wild collected specimens of *G. elwesii* that I have examined, which is several hundred, I have not found one with a single apical mark. A collection made in southern Turkey, near Alanya, by Brian Mathew (*Mathew* 11063—for which no herbarium specimen was made at the time of collection) has a single mark (see PLATE 8); however, this collection was not taken directly from the wild but from the nursery bed of a local bulb grower, although it may have originally came from a wild source.

Sell (1996) has formally recognized the aforementioned variant of *Galanthus elwesii* at the rank of variety, calling it *G. elwesii* var. *monostictus*. The holotype of this variety was collected in the botanic garden at Cambridge. This variety has not been recognized in the taxonomic account presented here, because at the present time I believe that this entity is a plant of horticulture. If single-marked variants of *G. elwesii* were found in the wild, however, var. *monostictus* should be upheld.

Finally, it is necessary to discuss an important nomenclatural matter concerning *Galanthus elwesii*. I have left this discussion to the end because I believe that if it had been included with the above historical overview it would have added considerable confusion to that discussion. It has recently come to my attention that the type of *G. elwesii* (Manisa Dağ, 1874, cult. Miserdine, 25 ii 1875, *Elwes s.n.* (holotype K!)) does not match the current and long-standing concept of this species. Conversely, this specimen, and the description for *G. elwesii* Hooker (1875), are equivalent to *G. gracilis* Čelak. (1891).

In the discussion above I have said how *Galanthus gracilis* differs from *G. elwesii*, but to recapitulate, these species are most easily separated by one critical feature: the former possesses applanate vernation of the leaves, and the latter supervolute vernation. In the description of *G. elwesii* (Hooker, 1875) the leaves are described as 'not being folded within the sheath, but twisted'; no mention is made of the leaves being folded one around the other (i.e., supervolute). In the figure accompanying the description in *Curtis's Botanical Magazine* (tab. 6166) the leaves are clearly applanate, as are the leaves of the type specimen. Furthermore, each of the inner perianth segments is reflexed at the very apex, a character that has been associated with *G. gracilis* by Brickell (1984: p. 370): 'The inner perianth segments are often distinctly flared . . . whereas flared inner perianth segments are not known to occur in *G. elwesii*'.

Collections of glaucous-leafed *Galanthus* species made from stations close to the type locality represent the original concept of *G. elwesii*, that is to say, *G. gracilis*. For example the figure of *G. elwesii* subsp. *elwesii* in Zeybek and Sauer (1995, fig. 15, p. 57) collected on Yamanlar Dağ (close to Manisa Dağ), depicts a photograph of a living plant with applanate vernation. Living material collected from

Yamanlar Dağ (*Colin Mason s.n.*) agrees in almost every detail with the illustration of *G. elwesii* in *Curtis's Botanical Magazine* (tab. 6166). Although Yamanlar Dağ is not the exact type locality for *G. elwesii*, Hooker states: '*Galanthus elwesii* is a native of the summits of Yamanlar Dağ north of the Gulf of Smyrna [now Izmir], where it was discovered by M. Balansa in 1854'. In 1874, H. Elwes collected more material from Manisa Dağ (near Smyrna, *Elwes s.n.*), and cultivated it in his garden at Miserdine in England. At that time this species was distributed under the name of *G. plicatus*, until Elwes, having a good knowledge of the genus, pointed out its unique character. Hooker (1875) agreed with his opinion and described these collections as a new species, in honour of Elwes.

To summarize, it appears that the plant traditionally known as *Galanthus elwesii*, as recognized by the majority of authors of this century (including myself), is not the same plant as that described by Hooker (1875). Conversely, it represents a large variant of *G. gracilis*, which is sometimes referred to as the cultivar 'Cassaba'. Quite clearly, to change the name and concept of this well-known plant is disadvantageous, and I have thus proposed to conserve the name *G. elwesii*, with a conserved type that matches its traditional usage (Davis, 1997).

CULTIVATION. *Galanthus elwesii* is common in cultivation and has been grown in gardens for more than 100 years. It is usually represented in cultivation by large, bold plants that have broad leaves and substantial flowers. One or two clones are real monsters. Recently a plant was given to me by Harry Hay: it was 30 cm tall and had leaves 3–3.5 cm wide, four leaves per bulb, two flowering scapes per bulb, and a large almost narcissus-like bulb. Other varieties are known for their bold or curious perianth markings, such as the hybrids 'Merlin' and 'Colesborne' which are favoured because of their nearly all green inner perianth segments. A number of other *G. elwesii* hybrids also make very good snowdrops. 'John Gray' and 'Robin Hood', probably hybrids between *G. elwesii* and *G. plicatus*, are magnificent plants. 'John Gray' has very large flowers distinctively marked on the inner segments with a large green X, and 'Robin Hood' is a well-proportioned plant with a satisfying, erect habit.

Trade in wild-collected *Galanthus elwesii* has been, and still is, very common, but once again it should be stressed that imported bulbs will probably not be as successful in the garden as home-grown plants from nurseries and bulb specialists. Particularly more diffi-

145

cult to grow will be plants that have been sold as dry, dormant bulbs, rather than those sold 'in the green'. Moreover, tried and tested clones usually do better in the garden than bulbs imported from the wild, as garden-worthiness of the latter is unknown. Recent practices have, however, moved away from the older method of simply digging up bulbs from the wild and exporting them. In Turkey, plants are starting to be cultivated as a sustainable crop, and some of the larger bulb growers in Europe are vegetatively propagating reliable clones to provide marketable stock. Wild-collected *G. elwesii* is, however, still available in commerce.

Owing to the wide range of habitats in which *Galanthus elwesii* grows in the wild, it is not so easy to give hard and fast rules for the best method of cultivation. Most clones do very well when planted in the same way as any other snowdrop, and will thrive in the open garden. This is particularly true of the larger forms of *G. elwesii* (often sold as *G. caucasicus*), which make very good garden plants. Others, however, and particularly those with a more recent wild origin may need rather different requirements for successful cultivation. The cold, wet weather of some districts does not favour the cultivation of a species that predominately occurs in a markedly warmer and drier climate. Many populations of *G. elwesii* grow in districts where the winters are not too cold, and where the rainfall is rather modest, such as the islands of the eastern Aegean Sea and Mediterranean Turkey. With this in mind, in the case of some of the more difficult clones, it is worth trying them in drier, more sheltered parts of the garden, and where the soil does not become excessively wet. Other populations, however, do grow in cooler and wetter areas, such as the mountainous areas of central and northern Turkey, and will therefore be better suited to the cooler, damper climates found in Britain and in some parts of Europe and North America.

Many clones of *Galanthus elwesii* are suitable for the rock garden or raised bed and benefit from the increased drainage and shelter afforded here. In my garden, I grow a number of clones in a south-facing gravel bed, which receives full sunlight for most of the year, and where the ground becomes rather hot in the summer. This bed is situated at ground level, and lies a few feet above a solid base of chalk. Here the soil is very alkaline and inclined to set rather hard when dry, although I improve it by mixing one-third of the top soil with one-third grit and one-third well rotted leaf-mould. Although most snowdrops prefer to be kept in much cooler conditions, some

146

clones of *G. elwesii* (and *G. gracilis*) flourish in this bed. As a rough guide to what these conditions are like, I grow *Agapanthus* sp., *Agave* spp., *Allium akaka, Arum creticum, Arum concinnatum, Crassula sarco-caulis* 'Ken Aslet', *Helichrysum coralloides, Origanum* 'Kent Beauty', *Prostanthera cuneata,* and *Sedum crassularia* in the same bed. It is important, however, that the soil does not dry out completely, and in the summer the soil should always be cool and slightly moist several centimetres below the surface (e.g. the depth of a trowel). Growing snowdrops in positions such as this can have many advantages, extending the area in which you can grow snowdrops and providing interest at a time of year when little else is in flower.

Galanthus elwesii *Hook.* f. in Bot. Mag. 101: tab. 6166 (1875), *nom. cons. prop.* (see Davis, 1997); Harpur-Crewe in Gard. Chron. new ser., 2: 237, fig. 31b (1879); Boiss., Fl. Orient. 5: 145 (1882); Baker, Handb. Amaryll.: 17 (1888); Burb. in J. Roy. Hort. Soc. 13: 201, fig. 26 (1891); Ewbank in Garden (London) 39: 272 (1891); Beck in Wiener Ill. Gart.-Zeitung 19: 54, fig. 2, 12–14 (1894); Bowles in J. Roy. Hort. Soc. 43: 35, fig. 14, 15 (1918); Dykes in Gard. Chron. ser. 3, 65: 187, fig. 85b (1919); Elwes, Memoirs: 65 (1930); Rech. f., Fl. Aegaea: 735 (1943); Traub & Moldenke in Herbertia 14: 106 (1947); Stern, Snowdr. & Snowfl.: 58, fig.15 (1956); Artjush. in Bot. Zhurn. (Moscow & Leningrad) 51(10): 1445 (1966); Stoj., Stev. & Kitan., Fl. Bulg. edn. 4, 1: 237 (1966); Artjush. in Pl. Life 25(2–4): 146 (1969); Artjush., Amaryllidaceae SSSR: 77 (1970); Delip. in Izv. Bot. Inst. 21: 167 (1971); Artjush. in Ann. Mus. Goulandris 2: 15, fig. 3a. (1974); D.A. Webb in Bot. J. Linn. Soc., 76(4): 312 (1978); D.A. Webb in Tutin et al. (eds.), Fl. Europ. 5: 78 (1980); Rix & R. Phillips, Bulb Book: 13, 15, fig. c (p. 12), fig. e (p. 13), fig. e (p. 14) (1981); Kamari in Bot. Jahrb. Syst. 103(1): 119 (1982); Papan. & Zacharof in Israel J. Bot. (32): 25 (1983); T. Baytop & B. Mathew, Bulb. Pl. Turkey: 22 (1984); C.D. Brickell in P.H. Davis et al. (eds.), Fl. Turkey 8: 368, map 54 (1984); C.D. Brickell in Walters et al. (eds.), Europ. Gard. Fl. 1: 318 (1986); N. Zeybek in Doga. Tu. J. Botany 12(1): 98–99 (1988); N. Zeybek & E. Sauer, Türk. Kardelenleri 1: 57, fig. 15 (1995). Ind. loc.: '*Galanthus Elwesii* is a native of the summits of Yamanlar dagh mountains, north of the Gulf of Smyrna, where it was discovered by M. Balansa in 1854 . . . Mr Elwes collected the specimens here figured on the mountains near Smyrna in 1874, and cultivated them in his garden in Miserdine.' Rejected type: Manisa Dagh (mons Sipylus of the ancients) [near

Smyrna], 610–914 m 1874 (cult. Miserdine, 25 ii 1875), *Elwes s.n.* (holotype K!). Conserved type: Turkey, Adana Prov., north part of Giaour Dagh [near Adana], 610 m, 18 v 1879, *Danford s.n.* (K!).

G. nivalis L. subsp. *elwesii* (Hook. f.) Gottl.-Tann. in Abh. K. K. Zool.-Bot. Ges. Wien 2(4): 39 (1904).

Chianthemum elwesii (Hook. f.) Kuntze, Rev. Gen. Pl. 2: 703 (1891), *nom. illeg.*

G. graecus Orph. ex Boiss., Fl. Orient. 5: 145 (1882); Baker, Handb. Amaryll.: 18 (1888); Velen., Fl. Bulg. supp. 1: 265 (1898); Traub & Moldenke in Herbertia 14: 106 (1948); Zahar. in Savul. & Nyár., Fl. Republ. Social. Romania 11: 412, pl. 63, fig. 3 (1966); Beldie, Fl. Român. 2: 270 (1979). Ind. loc.: 'in regione superiori montis Pellinos insulae Chios alt. 3800' (Orph!) Fl. Aprili. Type: seen by Brickell (1984): 'The type of *G. graecus* (G!) is taken from plants cultivated in Athens by Orphanides and collected by him on Khios'.

G. nivalis L. subsp. *graecus* (Orph. ex Boiss.) Gottl.-Tann. in Abh. K. K. Zool.-Bot. Ges. Wien 2(4): 40 (1904), *pro parte.*

Chianthemum graecum (Orph. ex Boiss.) Kuntze, Rev. Gen. Pl. 2: 703 (1891), *nom. illegit.*

G. elwesii Hook. f. [var.] *major* Anon. in Garden (London) 25: 371, incl. fig. (1884). Type: original material a living plant assumed not to have been preserved.

G. globosus Wilks in Garden (London) 31: 393 (1887), *nom. nud.*

G. elwesii Hook. f. [var.] *globosus* Ewbank in The Garden (London) 39: 272 (1891), *nom. nud.*

G. globosus Burb. in J. Roy. Hort. Soc. 13: 203, fig. 28 (1891). Type: original material a living plant assumed not to have been preserved.

G. bulgaricus Velen., Fl. Bulg. 539 (1891), *nom. nud.*

G. maximus Velen., Fl. Bulg. 540 (1891); Velen., Fl. Bulg. supp. 1: 266 (1893). Ind. loc.: In regione submontana ad urbem Orhanie a. 1891. detexit amic. *Mclichar*, ad Silven leg. amic. *Skorpil.* Type: not traced.

G. elwesii Hook. f. var. *maximus* (Velen.) Beck in Wiener Ill. Gart.-Zeitung 19: 55 fig. 2, 14 (1894); Watt in Gard. Chron. 3: 101, 103,

148

fig. 41 (1937); Stern, Snowdr. & Snowfl.: 61 (1956); Artjush. in Ann. Mus. Goulandris 2: 16, fig. 3b (1974).

G. nivalis L. var. *maximus* (Velen.) Stoj. & Stevanov, Fl. Bulg. 4: 257 (1923).

G. graecus Orph. ex Boiss. β [var.] *maximus* (Velen.) Hayek in Fedde, Prodr. Fl. Penins. Balcan. 30(1): 102 (1932).

G. graceus Orph. ex Boiss. forma *maximus* (Velen.) Zahar. in Savul. & Nyár., Fl. Republ. Social. Romania 11: 413 (1966).

G. elwesii Hook. f. var. *robustus* Baker in Gard. Chron. ser. 3, 13: 226 (1893). Type: original material a living plant assumed not to have been preserved.

G. elwesii Hook. f. var. *whittallii* S. Arn. ex Moon in Garden (London) 57: 44 (1900); W. Irving in Garden (London) 59: 262 (1901).

G. elwesii Hook. f. var. *whittallii* S. Arn. in Gard. Chron. ser. 3, 24(2): 466 (1898), *nom. provis.* Ind. loc.: 'It is worthy of bearing the name of its discoverer, who has recently benefited the gardens of this country by distributing many bulbs and new plants from Asia Minor' [with a painting by Miss Alice West]. Type: hort. Elwes, 13 Feb. 1901, (K!).

G. caucasicus (Baker) Grossh. var. *hiemalis* Stern in J. Roy. Hort. Soc. 86(7): 324 (1961), *nom. invalid.*; Stern in Bull. Alp. Gard. Soc. Gr. Brit. 31(2): 137 (1963), *nom. invalid.*

G. elwesii Hook. f. var. *platyphyllus* Kamari in Bot. Jahrb. Syst. 122 (1): 122, fig. 6 (1982). Type: Lesvos, mons Olympos, 3 km a loco versus pagum Magalochorion, alt. 800–900 m; in frutcticetosis, *Kamari & Christodolakis* 15834 (UPA!).

G. elwesii Hook. f. subsp. *wagenitzii* N. Zeybek in Doga. Tu. J. Botany 12(1): 98 (1988); N. Zeybek & E. Sauer, Türk. Kardelenleri 1: 63, fig. 19 (1995). Type: C5 Mersin: Yavca Köyü, 1250 m, elma bahçeleri, 11.2.1982, *N. Zeybek* (holotype IZEF 905 [IZEF 1782 in 1995 account], isotype ISTE). See note page 84.

G. elwesii Hook. f. subsp. *tuebitaki* N. Zeybek in Doga. Tu. J. Botany 12(1): 98 (1988). N. Zeybek & E. Sauer, Türk. Kardelenleri 1: 64, fig. 20 (1995). Type: A4 Ankara: Kızılcahamam Milli Park, 1350 m, 16.3.1983, *N. Zeybek* (holotype IZEF 912 [IZEF 1785 in 1995 account], isotype ISTE). See note page 84.

G. elwesii Hook. f. subsp. *yayintaschii* N. Zeybek in Doga. Tu. J. Botany 12(1): 98 (1988); N. Zeybek & E. Sauer, Türk. Kardelenleri 1: 66, fig. 21 (1995). Type: B2 Manisa: Demrci-Simav (Kütahya) yolu, 4–5 km de tarla içleri, 5.3.1979, *A. Yayintaş* (holotype IZEF 401 [IZEF 1781 in 1995 account], isotype ISTE). See note page 84.

G. elwesii Hook. f. subsp. *akmanii* N. Zeybek in Doga. Tu. J. Botany 12(1): 99 (1988); N. Zeybek & E. Sauer, Türk. Kardelenleri 1: 68, fig. 22 (1995). Type: A4 Ankara: Urus, Örencik Köyü, kayalık step yamaçlar, 1500 m,7.3.1981, *N. Zeybek-M.Koyuncu-M. Aydogdu* (holotype IZEF 409 [IZEF 1783 in 1995 account], isotype ISTE). See note page 84.

G. elwesii Hook. f. subsp. *melihae* N. Zeybek in Doga. Tu. J. Botany 12 (1): 98 (1988).
G. melihae (N. Zeybek) N. Zeybek & E. Sauer, Türk. Kardelenleri 1: 54, fig. 12 [bottom left], 13, 14 (1995). Type: A3 Kokaeli: Kaynarca civarı, tarla kenarları, 5.2.1983, *N. Zeybek* (holotype IZEF 944 [IZEF 1784 in 1995 account], isotype ISTE). See note page 84.

G. gracilis Čelak. subsp. *baytopii* N. Zeybek in Doga. Tu. J. Botany 12 (1): 96 (1988).
G. elwesii Hook. f. subsp. *baytopii* (N. Zeybek) N. Zeybek & E. Sauer, Türk. Kardelenleri 1: 60, fig. 17, 18 (1995). Type: C3 Antalya: Akeski, Çimi Köyü Yaylası, Toptaş, 1400 m, 6.2.1984, *N. Zeybek* (holotype IZEF 922 [IZEF 1810 in 1995 account], isotype ISTE). See note page 84.

G. elwesii Hook. f. var. *monostictus* P.D. Sell in P.D. Sell & G. Murrell, Fl. Gr. Brit. and Irel. 5: 363(1996). Type: Grassland Botanic Garden, Cambridge, 54/452572, 17 Feb. 1994, P.D. Sell 94/14 (holotype CGE).

[*G. caucasicus* hort.—*sensu auct.*: Stern, Snowdr. & Snowfl.: 137, fig. 14 (1956), *non* (Baker) Grossh.]

DESCRIPTION. *Bulb* ± spherical to ovoid, 2.1–2.7(–3.2) cm × (1.5–) 1.8–2.1 cm. *Sheath* 3–6 cm × 0.5–0.8 cm. *Leaves* supervolute in vernation; ± linear to very narrowly oblanceolate, at flowering (4.8–)

5.5–25(–28) cm × (0.5–)0.6–3.1(–3.5) cm, after flowering developing to 10–26 (–32) cm × 0.7–3.2(–3.6) cm, usually erect at maturity and infrequently slightly twisted; glaucous, or very infrequently matt green, surfaces concolorous; adaxial surface smooth or with two to four fine, longitudinal furrows; midrib conspicuous; margins flat; apex obtuse, flat to cucullate. *Scape* 9–18 cm long, glaucous. *Pedicel* 1.5–3 cm long. *Outer perianth segments* obovate to broadly obovate or almost circular, 1.8–2.3(–2.6) cm × 1–1.5(–1.7) cm, slightly unguiculate to unguiculate. *Inner perianth segments* ± obovate to cuneate, or ± rhomboidal, 1–1.2 cm × 0.6–0.7 cm, emarginate, apex flat; each perianth segment with two distinct marks on the adaxial surface, one apical and one basal, the apical mark just above the apical notch, a variable ± ∧- to ∩-shaped mark or an inverted ± heart-shaped mark, the basal mark covering up to half the basal area of the segment, infrequently this mark is divided into two, longitudinally; the inner perianth markings may sometimes join together to form one large ± X-shaped mark, or sometimes only the apical mark is present (cultivated material); abaxial surface of the inner segment with a similar mark to the adaxial face. *Anthers* tapering to an apiculum. *Capsule* almost spherical, 1–2 cm in diameter. *Seeds* pale brown, c. 0.4 cm long.

ILLUSTRATIONS. Harpur-Crewe in Gard. Chron. new ser., 2: 237, fig. 31b (1879); Burb. in J. Roy. Hort. Soc. 13: 201, fig. 26 (1891); Bowles in J. Roy. Hort. Soc. 43: 35, fig. 14, 15 (1918); Dykes in Gard. Chron. ser. 3, 65: 187, fig. 85b (1919); Stern, Snowdr. & Snowfl.: 59, fig.14, 15 [p. 56, as *G. caucasicus* early form and *G. caucasicus* late form] (1956); Artjush. in Ann. Mus. Goulandris 2: 17, fig. 3a (1974); Rix & R. Phillips, Bulb Book: 12, fig. c; 13, fig. e; 14, fig. e (1981); Kamari in Bot. Chron. 1(2): 61, photo 61 (1981); Kamari in Bot. Jahrb. Syst. 103(1): 121, fig. 5 (1982); N. Zeybek & E. Sauer, Türk. Kardelenleri 1: 51, fig. 17; 56, fig. 13, 14; 58, fig. 15; 62, fig. 18; 63, fig. 19; 65, fig. 20; 67, fig. 21; 69, fig. 22 (1995). PLATES 8, 33, 34, 35.

FLOWERING PERIOD. Spring (February–May).

HABITAT. A species occurring in a variety of habitats: found in forest (*Quercus* spp., *Fagus* spp., *Pinus* spp., etc.), scrub (*Quercus coccifera, Pteridium aquilinum*), and in forest clearings, subalpine pastures, and amongst rocks, 100–1600 m but most commonly at 800–1000 m.

DISTRIBUTION. Bulgaria, northeastern Greece, and the eastern Aegean Islands (Khios, Lesvos, Samos, Thassos), southern Ukraine, Turkey, eastern Yugoslavia (former). MAP 7.

151

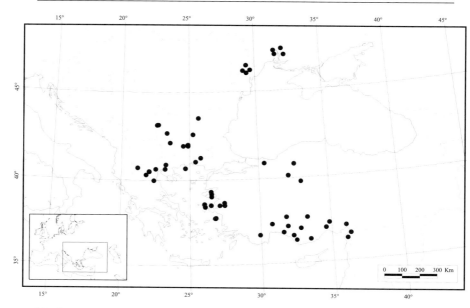

Map 7. Distribution of *Galanthus elwesii*.

10. GALANTHUS GRACILIS

This glaucous-leafed species is commonly associated with a number of other taxa, but particularly *Galanthus graecus* and *G. elwesii*. Some authors (e.g. Stern 1956; Artjushenko 1966, 1969, 1970, 1974; Deli-pavlov, 1971) have placed *G. gracilis* into the synonymy of *G. graecus*, while others have considered it synonymous with *G. elwesii* (Kamari, 1981). In this monograph, however, I have recognized *G. gracilis* as a distinct species (see also previous discussion under *G. elwesii*). *Galanthus gracilis* and *G. elwesii* are undoubtedly closely related, but they can be easily distinguished from one another by the type of vernation, which is applanate and supervolute, respectively. Other distinguishing characteristics, which are reliable but not totally discrete for each species, are the width of the leaves and the general dimensions of the plant: *G. gracilis* usually has narrow leaves and is generally of smaller dimensions than *G. elwesii*. The leaves of *G. gracilis* are more frequently twisted than *G. elwesii* but both species can also be straight. According to Brickell (1984, 1986), the apices of the inner perianth segments are flared (slightly reflexed), a feature which he uses as an ancillary character for separating this species from *G. elwesii*.

152

The distribution of *Galanthus gracilis* overlaps with *G. elwesii*, and populations of each species are often found growing in close proximity. However, the patterns of distribution for these species are different. In Turkey *G. gracilis* occupies a more westerly distribution, whereas *G. elwesii* is found further to the east; the former is more common in western Turkey, particularly in the southwest, but does not extend very far into south-central Turkey, where *G. elwesii* occurs with some frequency. In Bulgaria (Delipavlov, 1971) and other countries around the northwestern coast of the Black Sea, *G. gracilis* is more common than *G. elwesii*.

Galanthus gracilis is usually a plant of mountainous habitats, most frequently occurring at altitudes above 1000 m although it can occur near sea level. At higher altitudes it seems to favour open situations and is often located at the edge of forests and in clearings. In Greece and Turkey I have encountered it growing in large clearings in short grass.

CULTIVATION. A number of clones of this species are now available from nurseries that specialize in snowdrops. Some of the best clones are very small plants, which possess very narrow, upright, twisted, almost grass-like leaves. Despite their small size, these variants are robust, long-lived, and quickly multiplying (from offsetting bulbs). *Galanthus gracilis* 'Highdown' is a cultivar with these characters, but there are other similar clones without cultivar names.

The cultivation requirements of *Galanthus gracilis* are much the same as those of *G. elwesii*, and much of the information on the latter species is applicable here. Because *G. gracilis* is usually a rather small species it is probably a good idea to situate it where it will not be overlooked or forgotten, such as in a rock garden or alpine bed. Being a plant that is often found above 1000 m, and because of its rather small size, *G. gracilis* is a plant that is not incongruous amongst alpines or other small plants placed in the alpine category.

Galanthus gracilis *Čelak.* in Sitzungsber. Königl. Böhm. Ges. Wiss. Prag. Math.-Naturwiss. Cl.: 195 (1891) *nom. cons. prop.*; Velen., Fl. Bulg.: 539 (1891); Traub & Moldenke in Herbertia 14: 105 (1948); T. Baytop & B. Mathew, Bulb. Pl. Turkey: 22 (1984); C.D. Brickell in P.H. Davis et al. (eds.), Fl. Turkey 8: 369, map 55 (1984); C.D. Brickell in Walters et al. (eds.), Europ. Gard. Fl. 1: 318 (1986); N. Zeybek & E. Sauer, Türk. Kardelenleri 1: 51, fig. 11, 12 [top right] (1995). Ind. loc.: In Bulgarien und Ostrumelien, und zwar bei Schumla

153

(Milde!). Type: Bulgaria, prope Sumla [Schmula] (Sumen) frequens, Marte 1890, *Milde s.n.* (holotype PR!).

G. graceus Orph. ex Boiss. forma *gracilis* (Čelak.) Zahar. in Savul. & Nyár., Fl. Republ. Social. Romania 11: 413 (1966).

G. reflexus Herb. ex Lindl. in Edward's Bot. Reg. 31: 35, misc. 44 (1845), *nom. rej. prop.*; Kunth, Enum. Pl. 5: 471 (1850). Ind. loc.: Mr Lauder found this snowdrop on Mt. Gargarus [Kaz Dağ, Gurgen Dağ] and sent it with crocus corms to the Dean of Manchester. Type. Probably a living plant, assumed not preserved. Note: *G. reflexus* represents an overlooked, earlier name for *G. gracilis*. I propose to conserve the name *G. gracilis* against *G. reflexus*.

G. elwesii Hook. f. var. *reflexus* (Herb. ex Lindl.) Beck in Wiener Ill. Gart.-Zeitung 19: 55 (1894).

G. elwesii Hook. f. subsp. *minor* D.A. Webb in Bot. J. Linn. Soc. 76(4): 312 (1978); D.A. Webb in Tutin et al. (eds.), Fl. Europ. 5: 78 (1980); Rix & R. Phillips, Bulb Book: 13, fig. f (1981); Papan. & Zacharof in Israel J. Bot. (32): 25 (1983). Type: Flora Bulgarica austr.: prope Stanimaka, 23 iii 1895, *Stribrny s.n.* (holotype K! isotype LE!).

G. elwesii Hook. f. var. *stenophyllus* Kamari in Bot. Jahrb. Syst. 122 (1): 122 (1982). Type: Prov. Thessaloniki, montes Vertiskos, in cacumine Megali Harváta, 1103 m, in apertis silvae Fagi, *Phitos* 15832a (holotype UPA!).

[*G. graecus auct. non* Orph. ex Boiss.: P.H. Davis in Kew Bull. 1: 113 (1949).]

[*G. graecus auct. non* Orph. ex Boiss., *pro parte*: Stern, Snowdr. & Snowfl.: 40, fig. 9 (1956); Artjush. in Pl. Life 25(2–4): 146 (1969); Artjush., Amaryllidaceae SSSR: 76 (1970); Delip. in Izv. Bot. Inst. 21: 163 (1971); Artjush. in Ann. Mus. Goulandris 2: 14, fig. 2b (1974).]

DESCRIPTION. *Bulb* ± spherical to ovoid, 1.4–2 cm × 1–1.5 cm. *Sheath* 1.5–3 cm × 0.4–0.5 cm. *Leaves* applanate in vernation; ± linear, at flowering (2.3–)5.5–16(–24) cm × (0.25–)0.3–0.9(–1.2–2.2) cm, after flowering developing to 5.5–16(–24) cm × 0.3–0.9(–1.2–2.3) cm, commonly erecto-patent to erect at maturity, usually twisted, glaucous or infrequently green to glaucescent, surfaces ±

154

concolorous; adaxial surface smooth or infrequently with two to four fine, longitudinal furrows; midrib conspicuous; apex obtuse to acute, flat. *Scape* 6–10(–12) cm long, glaucous. *Pedicel* 1–3 cm long. *Outer perianth segments* obovate to broadly obovate, 1.8–2.3 (–2.6) cm × 0.8–1.4 cm, slightly unguiculate. *Inner perianth segments* ± obovate to cuneate, or ± rhomboidal, oblong, 1–1.2 cm × 0.6–0.7 cm, emarginate, apex frequently reflexed; each perianth segment with two distinct marks on the adaxial surface, one apical and one basal, the apical mark just above the apical notch, a variable ± ∧- to ∩-shaped mark or an inverted ± heart-shaped mark, the basal mark covering up to half the basal area of the segment, infrequently this mark is divided into two, longitudinally; the inner perianth markings may sometimes join together to form one large ± X-shaped mark; abaxial surface of the inner segment with a similar mark to the adaxial face. *Anthers* tapering to an apiculum. *Capsule* almost spherical, 1–1.4 cm in diameter. *Seeds* pale brown, c. 0.4 cm long.

ILLUSTRATIONS. Stern, Snowdr. & Snowfl.: 41, fig. 9 (1956); Bulb Book: 13, fig. f (1981); N. Zeybek & E. Sauer, Türk. Kardelenleri 1: 52, fig. 11; 55, fig. 12 [top right] (1995). PLATES 4, 30, 31, 32.

FLOWERING PERIOD. Spring (February–May).

HABITAT. A species occurring in a variety of habitats, such as forest (*Pinus brutia*, *Pinus* spp., *Pinus pallasiana*, *Quercus* spp., *Fagus* spp., *Cedrus* spp., *Ulmus* spp., etc.), scrub, and clearings within vegetation. Found at altitudes from 10–1600 m, and up to 2000 m. At higher altitudes, of 1000 m or more, also common in grass, pastures (short turf), and amongst rocks. Common on sloping ground, and often found on calcareous substrates.

DISTRIBUTION. Bulgaria, northeastern Greece, and the islands of the eastern Aegean (Samos, ?Lesvos), Romania, southern Ukraine, and western Turkey. MAP 8, page 156.

II SUBSERIES VIRIDIFOLII

Galanthus subseries **Viridifolii** *(Kem.-Nath.)*, **comb. nov. et emend.** A.P. Davis.
Lectotype of subseries: *G. platyphyllus* Traub & Moldenke [designated by Artjush. (1966)].
Galanthus section *Viridifolii* Kem.-Nath. in Trudy Tbilissk Bot. Inst. ser. 2, 11: 177 (1947), *pro min. parte*. Type: not stated.
Galanthus section *Viridifolii* Kem.-Nath. *emend.* Artjush. in Bot.

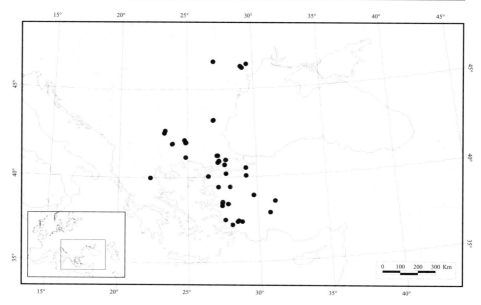

Map 8. Distribution of *Galanthus gracilis*.

Zhurn. (Moscow & Leningrad) 51(10): 1445 (1966), *pro parte*; Artjush. in Amaryllidaceae SSSR: 74(1970), *pro parte*.

Galanthus subsection *Viridifolii* (Kem.-Nath.) A.P. Khokhr. in Bull. Glavn. Bot. Sada Akad. Nauk SSSR 62: 60 (1966). Type: *G. woronowii* Losinsk.

Galanthus series *Woronowii* Kem.-Nath. in Trudy Tbilissk Bot. Inst. ser. 2, 11: 177 (1947); *emend* A.P. Khokhr. in Bull. Glavn. Bot. Sada Akad. Nauk SSSR 62: 61 (1966) [as series *Woronowiani*]. Type: *G. woronowii* Losinsk.

Galanthus series *Fosteriae* Kem.-Nath. in Trudy Tbilissk Bot. Inst. ser. 2, 11: 167 (1947), *nom. nud.*
Galanthus series *Fosteriani* Kem.-Nath. ex A.P. Khokhr. in Bull. Glavn. Bot. Sada Akad. Nauk SSSR 62: 60 (1966). Type: not stated.

Galanthus series *Angustifoliae* Kem.-Nath. in Trudy Tbilissk Bot. Inst. ser. 2, 11: 180 (1947). Type: not stated.

156

Galanthus subgenus *Crinoides* A. P. Khokhr. in Bull. Glavn. Bot. Sada Akad. Nauk SSSR 62: 60 (1966). Type: *G. krasnovii* A.P. Khokhr.

Galanthus series *Krasnoviani* A.P. Khokhr. in Bull. Glavn. Bot. Sada Akad. Nauk SSSR 62: 60 (1966). Type: *G. krasnovii* A.P. Khokhr.

Galanthus section *Platyphyllus* A.P. Khokhr. in Bull. Glavn. Bot. Sada Akad. Nauk SSSR 62: 60 (1966). Type: *G. woronowii* Losinsk.

Galanthus series *Caspi* A.P. Khokhr. in Bull. Glavn. Bot. Sada Akad. Nauk SSSR 62: 61 (1966), *nom. illeg.*

DESCRIPTION. As in the Key to the Series and Subseries of *Galanthus*.

11. GALANTHUS FOSTERI

Galanthus fosteri was named by Baker (1889) in honour of M. Foster, who imported bulbs of this species from the neighbourhood of Amasia (Amasya Province) in northern Turkey. According to Baker, *G. fosteri* has leaves that are like those of *G. latifolius* Rupr. (now *G. platyphyllus*): 'broad and bright green', and with flowers akin to *G. elwesii*, with 'a large green blotch on the lower part [base] of the segments'. Because of this unique combination of characteristics, *G. fosteri* has very rarely been mistaken for, or closely associated with, other taxa in the genus, a fact that is illustrated by the uncomplicated synonymy given in the taxonomic accounts for this species.

The leaves of *Galanthus fosteri* are either shiny or slightly matt on the adaxial surface, and the vernation is always supervolute. Anatomical and morphological investigation of living material and herbarium specimens shows that the leaves of this species are more like *G. woronowii* and *G. transcaucasicus* than *G. platyphyllus*, in contrast to Baker's protologue. Each inner perianth segment of *G. fosteri* has two distinct marks, one apical and one basal. These markings are similar to those of *G. elwesii* and *G. gracilis* but I have not seen any examples of *G. fosteri* where the two marks are joined to form a single, large, more or less X-shaped mark, as in *G. elwesii* and *G. gracilis*.

Galanthus fosteri mainly occurs in south- and north-central Turkey (in the provinces of Amasya, Kayseri, Gaziantep, and Ordu) and in Syria and Lebanon. These areas are much further east than populations of *G. elwesii*, and much further south than either *G. woronowii* or *G. transcaucasicus.*

Despite its mainly southern distribution *Galanthus fosteri* is like the majority of other *Galanthus* species in that it occurs in cool, shady habitats. In Lebanon, for example, Davis and Stern (1949) record this species growing on the ledges of shady limestone rocks with *Scilla cernua*, in *Quercus calliprinos* and *Pistachia palaestina* maquis. The association of limestone rocks and shade is a frequently recorded habitat feature. *Galanthus fosteri* is usually located at altitudes from 1000 m to 1600 m.

CULTIVATION. This is another species that is not at all common in cultivation, which is quite surprising as it was introduced at least 100 years ago and is not as difficult to grow as some of the more demanding species. The clone commonly grown is the Davis and Hedge collection (*Davis & Hedge* 26830) from Turkey (Dumanli Dağ, above Haruniye, in the province of Adana), which is often offered by specialist nurseries. This clone has proved to be quite durable, but it is not a particularly good garden plant and is not very free flowering. First and second generation progeny of this clone have now been produced, however, and these are much better plants than the parent. More recent introductions, including some collections from Syria, are proving to be even more promising.

Galanthus fosteri is usually situated in the more sheltered and often drier parts of gardens, because it is commonly thought to be a tender species. Recently though, I have seen specimens placed in far more exposed situations where they appear to do very well and often look much better than those grown with more protection.

Galanthus fosteri is often grown in pots and under glass, as some growers find it difficult in the garden. Fortunately, unlike many other *Galanthus*, this species is more tolerant of this method of cultivation, and it is possible to produce a large pan of healthy growing bulbs using this method.

The bulbs of *Galanthus fosteri* can be left dry and unplanted for several weeks in the summer without harm, provided they are kept cool.

Galanthus fosteri *Baker* in Gard. Chron. ser. 3, 5: 458 (1889); Burb. in Gard. Chron. ser. 3, 7: 268 (1890); Burb. in J. Roy. Hort. Soc. 13: 203, fig. 28 (1891); Ewbank in Garden (London) 39: 272 (1891); J. Allen in J. Roy. Hort. Soc. 13: 176 (1891); Ewbank in Garden (London) 45: 125 (1894); Gottl.- Tann. in Abh. K. K. Zool.-Bot. Ges.

Wien 2(4): 43 (1904); Bowles in J. Roy. Hort. Soc. London 43: 34, fig. 13 (1918); Post & Dinsm., Fl. Syria, Palest. Sinai 2: 605 (1933); Traub and Moldenke in Herbertia 14: 111 (1947); P.H. Davis in Kew Bull. 1: 113 (1949). Stern, Snowdr. & Snowfl.: 53 (1956); Artjush. in Bot. Zhurn. (Moscow & Leningrad) 51(10): 1449 (1966); Artjush. in Pl. Life 25(2–4): 150 (1969); Artjush., Amaryllidaceae SSSR: 81 (1970); Rix & R. Phillips, Bulb Book: 17, fig. b (p. 16) (1981); T. Baytop & B. Mathew, Bulb. Pl. Turkey: 22 (1984); C.D. Brickell in Davis et al. (eds.), Fl. Turkey 8: 371, map 55 (1984); C.D. Brickell in Walters et al. (eds.), Europ. Gard. Fl. 1: 318 (1986); N. Zeybek & E. Sauer, Türk. Kardelenleri 1: 70, fig. 23, 24 (1995). Ind. loc.: 'imported by Professor M. Foster, from the neighbourhood of Amasia, in the province of Sirwas, in North Central Asia Minor'. Type: central Asia Minor, Amasia, 1889, *Foster s.n.* (holotype K!; isotype OXF!, E!).

G. latifolius Rupr. forma *fosteri* (Baker) Beck in Wiener Ill. Gart.-Zeitung 19: 57, fig. 2, 17 (1894).

G. fosteri Baker var. *antepensis* N. Zeybek & E. Sauer, Türk. Kardelenleri 1: 72, fig. 25 (1995), *nom. nud.* Type: C6 Gaziantep: Gaziantep-Bahçe, Gaziantep'ten 30 km uzatka, Acarobası Köyü makilikeri, kalker kayalar arasında humuslu topraklarda, c. 1200 m, 16.02.1994, *N. Zeybek* (holotype IZEF 2155).

DESCRIPTION. *Bulb* ± spherical to ovoid, 2–2.5 cm × 1.8–2 cm. *Sheath* 2–5 cm × 0.4–0.6 cm. *Leaves* supervolute in vernation; ± linear to lorate, slightly narrowed at the base; at flowering (4–)8–14(–17) cm × (0.6–)1–1.5(–2.4) cm, after flowering developing in length and width; erect to recurving at maturity; bright to dark green, shining or matt, or infrequently glaucescent; surfaces ± concolorous; adaxial surface smooth or with two to four fine, longitudinal furrows; midrib conspicuous; margins flat; apex acute to obtuse, flat to cucullate. *Scape* 8–16 cm long, green. *Pedicel* 1–2.5 cm long. *Outer perianth segments* narrowly obovate, 1.8–2.6 cm × 1–1.5 cm, slightly unguiculate. *Inner perianth segments* ± obovate to cuneate, or ± rhomboidal, 1.2–1.4 cm × 0.6–0.8 cm, emarginate; each segment with two marks on the adaxial surface, one apical and one basal; the apical mark a variable ± ∧- to ∩-shaped mark or ± hippocrepiform, positioned above the apical notch; the basal mark covering an area at the base of the segment, rectangular to oval or sometimes only a diffuse, light green patch; abaxial surface mark similar to the adaxial markings. *Anthers* tapering to an apiculum. *Capsule* spherical, 1–1.5 cm in diameter. *Seeds* brown, c. 0.5 cm long.

ILLUSTRATIONS. Burb. in J. Roy. Hort. Soc. 13: 203, fig. 28 (1891); Bowles in J. Roy. Hort. Soc. London 43: 34, fig. 13 (1918); Rix & R. Phillips, Bulb Book: 16, fig. b (1981); N. Zeybek & E. Sauer, Türk. Kardelenleri 1: 70, fig. 23; 71, fig. 24; 73, fig. 25 (1995). PLATES 12, 42.

FLOWERING PERIOD. Spring (January–April).

HABITAT. Occurring amongst limestone rocks and near cliffs, at the edge of forest (*Fagus* spp., *Quercus* spp., etc.), in maquis, and under or nearby small trees and shrubs. Usually found growing in shade. A species of subalpine altitudes, 1000–1600 m.

DISTRIBUTION. ?Israel, Jordan, Lebanon, Syria, and Turkey. MAP 9.

12. GALANTHUS IKARIAE

Galanthus ikariae was originally described from material gathered on the Aegean island of Ikaria, by collectors sent out by E. Whittall in 1893. According to Baker's description (1893a), the salient features of *G. ikariae* are bright green, broad leaves and a single mark on each inner perianth segment. These features are clearly depicted in an illustration accompanying a description by Turrill (1937) in the *Curtis's Botanical Magazine* (tab. 9474). This plate also shows that each inner perianth segment has a large, heavy marking that is longer than half the total length of the segment (see also FIGURE 8).

Galanthus ikariae is frequently confused with other green-leafed snowdrops, particularly *G. woronowii* (see the discussion for *G. woronowii*). Although it is true that these species can appear to be very alike, there is no real reason for confusion. The inner perianth mark of *G. ikariae* is very large and bold, as stated above, and even when the mark is a similar shape to that of *G. woronowii* (see below) it still usually covers a larger area of the segment. *Galanthus ikariae* also has leaves that are dark matt green, and not bright green like those of *G. woronowii*. A further means of telling these species apart is by looking at transverse sections of the leaves, since the leaf anatomy of each species is quite different. When a leaf of *G. ikariae* is sectioned and examined under a microscope, large air spaces are evident across the width of the leaf, and the mesophyll cells (the cells making up the bulk of the leaf tissue) are loosely arranged

160

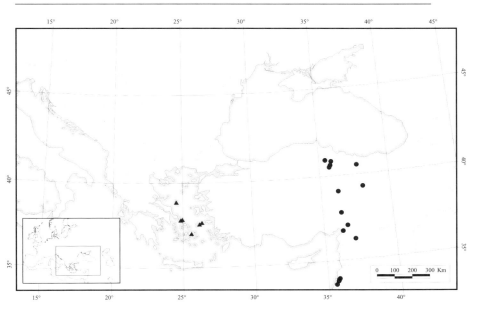

Map 9. Distribution of *Galanthus fosteri* [●] and *Galanthus ikariae* [▲].

with spaces between them. The large air spaces can be clearly seen with either the naked eye or a ×10 hand lens when the leaf is cut in half with a knife or pair of scissors. The leaves of *G. woronowii*, and all other broad-, green-leafed snowdrops, do not display this feature, but instead the leaf blade has very small air spaces that are either invisible or barely discernible to the naked eye. As a rule-of-thumb test, it is possible to fit a dress maker's pin into the air spaces of *G. ikariae* with little or no difficulty.

In the wild, *Galanthus ikariae* is mainly confined to wet, shady places at altitudes above 600 m, where it escapes the severity of the hot, dry Aegean summer. Populations of *G. ikariae* are commonly found in close proximity to a water source, usually in deep shade on sloping ground. Small river gorges with rather luxuriant vegetation, including deciduous trees, are a frequent habitat. In these locations *Galanthus ikariae* is often found growing through ivy (*Hedera helix*) or with *Cyclamen hederifolium*. Sometimes *G. ikariae* is found on flat, wet areas in deep soil at the bottom of gorges, where it attains a much larger size than normal. I have seen plants growing in such situations in Andros, and have recorded leaves of up to 3 cm wide and 50 cm long. *Galanthus ikariae* is not totally confined to river

161

gorges, however, and I have seen plants growing in and at the edge of scrub and woodland. In this habitat, the size of the plants is considerably reduced, and the leaves are a darker green.

Since its discovery on the island of Ikaria, *Galanthus ikariae* has been collected from at least three other Aegean islands, including Andros, Naxos, and Skyros; further collections have also been made on Ikaria. These records have expanded our knowledge of the range of variation for *G. ikariae*, including the variability of plant size, leaf texture, perianth marking, and flowering time. To account for this type of variation, Kamari (1982) recognized two subspecies for *G. ikariae*, describing subsp. *snogerupii* as new. According to Kamari, three main characters distinguish subsp. *snogerupii* from subsp. *ikariae*: 'the leaves are bright glossy green [deep green in subsp. *ikariae*], slightly undulate and much broader; the size of the green spot on the inner perigon segments is smaller than or, at most, equal to half the length of these segments'. In Kamari's treatment, subsp. *ikariae* is confined to Ikaria, and subspecies *snogerupii* to Skyros, Andros, and Naxos. Kamari notes from her description that subsp. *snogerupii* approaches *G. woronowii*, particularly in the size and shape of the inner perianth mark (cf. Artjushenko, 1974). In Kamari's view, the perianth marks of *G. ikariae* subsp. *snogerupii* and *G. woronowii* are both less than half the total length of the segment itself and are characteristically flat topped, i.e., the end of the mark furthest from the apex of the segment is distinctly blunt and not curved as in most other taxa (see FIGURE 8, Q). Kamari also notes that the leaves of these two taxa are very similar in colour, size, and form.

I have had the opportunity to study populations on Andros and Ikaria and found that the morphological characters used to distinguish between *Galanthus ikariae* subsp. *ikariae* and subsp. *snogerupii* are highly variable. Plants studied on Andros revealed that populations present on this island conform to both subsp. *ikariae* and subsp. *snogerupii*; and on the island of Ikaria, there are populations that represent intermediates between the two subspecies. Study of herbarium specimens from Naxos (*Runemark* R. 348; *Runemark & Bentzer* R. & B. 24011; *Runemark & Snogerup* R. & S. 4666; and *Runemark* R. 705) show that plants found on this island conform to the description of *G. ikariae* subsp. *ikariae* and not subsp. *snogerupii*, as recorded by Kamari (who considered subsp. *ikariae* to be an endemic of Ikaria). Based on this evidence, and considering the type of variation found within other species, it is my opinion that these subspecies are not sufficiently distinct and as such they have therefore not been recognized in this account.

Although the inner perianth markings of some *Galanthus ikariae* resemble those of *G. woronowii,* such as those recognized as subsp. *snogerupii,* the size is different for these two species. In *G. ikariae* these markings are always rather large and cover a considerable surface area of each inner perianth segment, whereas the markings of *G. woronowii* are smaller, and in extreme cases, when they are greatly reduced, they can become divided into two marks, one on either side of the apical notch.

CULTIVATION. During the first half of this century *Galanthus ikariae* seems to have been fairly well known in cultivation; Burbidge (1893), Bowles (1918, p. 34), Dykes (1919), and Turrill (1937) were all familiar with this plant. In the late 1950s it was offered for sale by the Giant Snowdrop Company (L.W.H. Mathias), and so it must have been grown in at least a few gardens. The number of *G. ikariae* in cultivation today, however, is remarkably small, and one should remember that many of the plants growing in gardens under this name are in fact *G. woronowii.* The reason for the scarcity of this species in cultivation is not clear. Nutt (1974) comments that: 'it has rarely been collected but it seeds so easily in gardens that it should be far more common than it is'. This is certainly true, and I have seen large groups of *G. ikariae* (up to 500 bulbs) that have apparently grown to their present size on account of propagation by seed. One possible explanation for the scarcity of this species is that it is not very frost tolerant, being killed or damaged during severe winters. In places where *G. ikariae* grows successfully and has persisted for some years, the micro-environment or local climate is markedly milder than in other areas. It grows well at Kew, for example, where it is located under deciduous trees in a rather friable, light soil.

Perseverance with the cultivation of this species is certainly worth the effort, as this is surely one of the most beautiful of all snowdrop species. *Galanthus ikariae* is well proportioned, it has bold, neat, clean leaves, and the flower is large and attractively marked. Because it is one of the last species to flower in cultivation, it provides a good finish to the snowdrop season.

The most common form of *Galanthus ikariae* in cultivation today is one that resembles the plant illustrated in tab. 9474 of *Curtis's Botanical Magazine* and in Rix and Phillips (1981, p. 14, fig. c). This variant, or something very similar to it, has been referred to as 'Butt's Variety', although this name is not frequently used.

Galanthus ikariae *Baker* in Gard. Chron. ser. 3, 13: 506 (1893); Burb. in Garden (London) 49: 330 (1896); Bowles in J. Roy. Hort. Soc. London 43: 34 (1918); Dykes in Gard. Chron. ser. 3, 65: 188 (1919); Turrill in Bot. Mag. 160: tab. 9474 (1937); Rech. f., Fl. Aegea: 735 (1943); Traub & Moldenke in Herbertia 14: 112 (1948); Stern, Snowdr. & Snowfl.: 48, fig. 12 (1956); Artjush. in Ann. Mus. Goulandris 2: 16, fig. 4 (1974); Nutt in J. Roy. Hort. Soc. 99(1): 22, fig. 19 (1974); D.A. Webb in Tutin et al. (eds.), Fl. Europ. 5: 78 (1980); Rix & R. Phillips, Bulb Book: 15, 17, fig. b and c (p. 14), inset photo (p. 17) (1981); Kamari in Bot. Jahrb. Syst. 103(1): 125, fig. 7 (1982). Ind. loc.: 'discovered in the island of Nikaria (the classical Icaria) . . . by the collectors sent out by Mr Whittall, of Smyrna'. Type: from the island of Nikaria, anciently called Ikaria, 1893, *Whittall* 38 (holotype K!).

> *G. ikariae* Baker subsp. *snogerupii* Kamari in Bot. Chron. 1(2): 76 (1981), *nom. nud.*; Kamari in Bot. Jahrb. Syst. 103(1): 124, 126; fig. 8 (1982), *descr.*, Type: Andros. Mt Kouvara, on the ridge 1 km NE of the top, 850–920 m, *Snogerup & Bothmer* 38774 (holotype LD).

DESCRIPTION. *Bulb* ± spherical to ovoid, 2–2.8 cm × 1.5–2.5 cm. *Sheath* 4.5–7 cm × 0.5–0.7 cm. *Leaves* supervolute in vernation; lorate, slightly narrowed at the base, at flowering (7–)11–35(–50) cm × (1–)1.5–2.5 (–3) cm, after flowering developing in length and width, usually recurving at maturity; bright to dark green, often matt or infrequently very slightly glaucescent, surfaces ± concolorous; adaxial surface smooth or with two to four fine, longitudinal furrows; midrib conspicuous; margins flat to slightly undulate; apex obtuse, flat. *Scape* 6–20 cm long, green. *Pedicel* 1.5–2.5 cm long. *Outer perianth segments* narrowly obovate, 1.8–3(–3.2) cm × 1.1–1.6 cm, slightly unguiculate. *Inner perianth segments* ± obovate to cuneate, 1–1.4 cm × 0.5–0.8 cm, emarginate; each segment with a variable, very bold, ± ∩-shaped mark, sometimes with a flat top, extending from half to two-thirds the length of the segment, found on the adaxial surface above the apical notch; mark on the abaxial surface similar in shape and size to the adaxial mark. *Anthers* tapering to an apiculum. *Capsule* spherical, 1–1.5 cm in diameter. *Seeds* brown, c. 0.5 cm long.

ILLUSTRATIONS. Turrill in Bot. Mag. 160: tab. 9474 (1937); Stern, Snowdr. & Snowfl.: 49, fig. 12 (1956); Artjush. in Ann. Mus. Goulandris 2: 19, fig. 4 (1974); Nutt in J. Roy. Hort. Soc. 99(1): 19–22, fig. 19 (1974); Rix & R. Phillips, Bulb Book: 14, fig b and c; 17, inset photo (1981); Kamari in Bot. Chron. 1(2): 61, photo 1 (1981); Kamari in Bot. Jahrb. Syst. 103(1): 125, 126, fig. 7, 8 (1982). PLATES 13, 50, 51.

FLOWERING PERIOD. Spring (January–April).

HABITAT. Occurring in wet and shady places, in river gorges and by streams, in deciduous woodland (*Acer sempervirens*, etc.), amongst low herbaceous, woodland vegetation (*Hedera helix, Cyclamen hederifolium*, etc.). Also recorded in drier places, such as on rocky limestone, under trees, and amongst scrub. On limestone and schist formations, 600–750 m.

DISTRIBUTION. The Aegean Islands of Greece (Andros, Ikaria, Naxos, Skyros). MAP 9, page 161.

13. GALANTHUS WORONOWII

The naming of this snowdrop has caused great confusion, and even today the correct name is seldom used. In the past it has been known erroneously as *Galanthus latifolius* (*sensu* Masters, 1881; Stern and Gilmour, 1946), *G. ikariae* subsp. *latifolius* Stern (Stern, 1956) or as a *G. ikariae* (*sensu* Artjushenko, 1965, 1966, 1970; Brickell, 1984, 1986). The following paragraphs explain in detail the taxonomic history of *G. woronowii*, because it is imperative that the confusion over the use of the name be resolved.

The beginning of this confusion can probably be traced back to an article by Stern and Gilmour (1946) on *Galanthus latifolius* (*Curtis's Botanical Magazine*, tab. 9669). According to these authors all green-leafed snowdrops known at that time were forms of *G. latifolius*, including *G. ikariae, G. fosteri*, and *G. rizehensis* (as *G. latifolius* var. *rizehensis*). However, the plant illustrated in tab. 9669 is not *G. latifolius* of Ruprecht (1868). *Galanthus latifolius* (now known as *G. platyphyllus*, see page 189) is an alpine plant of the central Caucasus with characteristics very different from the plant illustrated in *Curtis's Botanical Magazine*. It is likely that Stern and Gilmour did not examine the type material of *G. latifolius* in the herbarium at St. Petersburg (8 v 1860, *Bayern s.n.*), or other authentic material of this species, such as that held at Kew (16 vii 1881, *Brotherus s.n.*). Some 10 years later, in *Snowdrops and Snowflakes*, Stern (1956) regarded *G. latifolius* Rupr. (including *G. platyphyllus*) as a synonym of *G. ikariae*, a species formerly known only from the Aegean island of Ikaria. Two

165

subspecies were recognized in Stern's monograph: *G. ikariae* subsp. *ikariae*, for the broad, green-leafed snowdrop of the Aegean and *G. ikariae* subsp. *latifolius* for all the similar looking counterparts found in northern Turkey and the Caucasus. Therefore, *G. woronowii* is now frequently, but incorrectly, called *G. ikariae* subsp. *latifolius*.

Stern included *Galanthus woronowii* in *Snowdrops and Snowflakes*, but did not consider it to be related to any of the other broad, green-leafed snowdrops from the Caucasus, or to *G. ikariae*. Instead, *G. woronowii* was recognized as a distinct species 'nearly related to *G. plicatus*'. Stern made the association with *G. plicatus* because he considered both species to possess plicate [replicate] leaves.

Artjushenko (1966), who had the opportunity to examine living material of *Galanthus woronowii* from the Caucasus, added a considerable degree of clarity to the taxonomy of these green-leafed snowdrops. She recognized that *G. platyphyllus* (the name replacing *G. latifolius* Rupr.) was distinct from *G. ikariae*, and showed that *G. woronowii* was not associated with *G. plicatus*. Artjushenko also demonstrated that Stern's assessment of *G. woronowii* was incorrect, by showing that the leaves of *G. woronowii* were not like those of *G. plicatus*; in *G. woronowii* the leaves fold towards the upper surface (as in the original description of this species by Losina-Losinskaya [1935]) and not to the lower, like *G. plicatus* (see also discussion on page 106).

In contrast to Stern, Artjushenko (1965) associated *Galanthus woronowii* with *G. ikariae*, and went as far as to consider these two species as synonymous. Furthermore, Artjushenko (1965, 1966, 1970) did not recognize separate subspecies for the Aegean and Transcaucasian populations, and treated *G. ikariae* as one widely distributed, variable, species. Many contemporary authors followed this treatment for *G. ikariae* (see page 169); thus *G. woronowii* remained in synonymy for many years. In a later paper on the Greek species of *Galanthus*, however, Artjushenko (1974) redefined her concept of *G. ikariae* based on material from Ikaria, the *locus classicus* (all the material she previously examined was probably from northeastern Turkey and the western Caucasus). She concluded, on the basis of morphological and cytological data, that *G. ikariae* was a distinct species and quite separate from *G. woronowii*. According to Artjushenko, *G. ikariae* was set apart from *G. woronowii* by possessing dull green leaves (bright green and glossy in *G. woronowii*), and an inner perianth mark that was at least half the total length of the segment itself (the perianth mark being considerably

166

smaller in *G. woronowii*). The cytological data came from a paper by Sveshnikova (1971b), which shows that *G. ikariae* and *G. woronowii* differ in the details of chromosomes 4 and 6 and in the size of the satellite chromosomes.

Under Artjushenko's emended treatment, *Galanthus ikariae* is seen as an endemic of the Aegean, and *G. woronowii* (equal to *G. ikariae* subsp. *latifolius* Stern, *pro parte*) is the valid name for the broad-, green-leafed plants of northeastern Turkey and the western Caucasus (Colchis and Lazistan, respectively). I have studied populations near Sochi (Russia) and examined the plentiful herbarium material housed at the Komarov Institute (LE) and can confirm that this species is distinct from *G. ikariae* and *G. plicatus*.

Galanthus woronowii most closely resembles *G. ikariae*. Both of these species have broad, green leaves and supervolute vernation, but unlike *G. ikariae* the leaves of *G. woronowii* are usually light green and only occasionally matt (covered with a slight wax coating). The foliage of *G. woronowii* often has two to four fine, longitudinal furrows on the upper surface of the leaf, a feature of many other species with broad leaves, such as *G. ikariae, G. elwesii*, and *G. fosteri*. The flowers of *G. woronowii* possess a single, variable green mark at the apex of each inner perianth segment. This mark is variable but is most often represented by one of two rather distinct shapes. The first is the common, more or less ∩-shaped mark; the second type of mark is larger and has a flat top, shaped rather like a small stone bridge (FIGURE 8, s). This second mark (FIGURE 8, w) is similar to that found in some populations of *G. ikariae* (see page 164), but it is never as large; in *G. ikariae* the perianth marks are nearly always longer than half the length of the inner segment. Frequently, this second type of mark is quite small, and sometimes it is reduced to only two small green spots at the apex of the segment, one in each lobe. I have never seen any specimens of *G. ikariae* with this marking. On the inside of the inner perianth segment, the green mark is usually about twice the size of that on the outside.

For situations in which a positive identification of *G. woronowii* cannot be made using the above features, the anatomy of the leaves can be relied upon to establish the identity of this species (see page 160).

As with many other *Galanthus* species, *G. woronowii* is often highly variable, particularly with respect to size. In the Black Sea coast area of Russia, where this species occurs with some frequency, the morphology seems to be correlated to habitat. For this reason, Svesh-

167

nikova and Lebedeva (Lebedeva, pers. comm.) have recognized three ecological forms for *G. woronowii* (of no formal taxonomic status). The two most easily recognized of these are the woodland and rocky forms. The first of these, as the name suggests, occurs in woodland and is recognized by having rather dark green leaves that lie flat to the ground and a scape that is longer than the leaves at flowering time. The 'rocky form' is found on limestone rock ledges, scree, and even fallen trees; it may either grow on thin soils or be rooted in moss. It is characterized by its light green, erect leaves that are as long as, or longer than, the scape at flowering time. Plants of this form can be very large and have leaves up to 35 cm long and 3 cm wide, approaching the dimensions of *G. platyphyllus*. Common-garden growing experiments carried out in Sochi (Lebedeva, unpublished results), show that these features persist in cultivation and are not affected by environmental factors. It could be argued that these forms need taxonomic recognition. However, the range of variation of these forms seems to be far more complicated when morphological intermediates and plants of different habitats are examined. Clearly, this in an interesting species that requires further study.

CULTIVATION. *Galanthus woronowii* has probably been cultivated in gardens for more than a century, but in almost all instances it has been called *G. latifolius*, *G. ikariae* subsp. *latifolius*, or *G. ikariae*, as discussed above. Under the guise of these names, *G. woronowii* is well represented in cultivation and is commonly offered for sale by specialist nurseries and some of the larger commercial firms. It can be a very attractive and useful garden plant, if a good, reliable clone is selected and it is given the right conditions. Even a small clump of *G. woronowii* is an attractive sight and can be a welcome contrast to the more commonly cultivated narrow-, glaucous-leafed snowdrops. The leaves are often a fresh green colour, which gives a satisfying background to the pure white flowers. After flowering the leaves stay fresh looking, and because they are held rather close to the soil, they provide a neat groundcover. *Galanthus woronowii* is thus particularly useful in areas of the garden where other foliage plants have not yet emerged from the ground.

Galanthus woronowii thrives in a number of situations in the garden and is fairly tolerant of a range of climatic conditions. In the wild it occurs in areas with a high annual rainfall, and accordingly should not be planted in areas of the garden where it will dry out or become sun-baked during the summer. The bulbs should not, however, be grown in areas that become waterlogged. In its natural habitat this species is found only in freely draining soils and other porous substrates. In the Caucasus I have seen plants growing in limestone scree, pockets of soil on steep cliff ledges, in thin soils on top of large rocks, and even on mossy tree trunks; in deciduous woodlands, a common habitat for this species, it mostly occurs on sloping ground or on ridges.

A deep, friable, humus-rich soil seems to suit *Galanthus woronowii*, and time spent preparing the ground before planting is beneficial for the establishment of new stock. This species grows particularly well under deciduous trees and, if provided with a little shade in the summer, also in raised beds and larger rock gardens.

Galanthus woronowii *Losinsk.* in Kom., Fl. URSS 4: in addenda, 749 (1935); Grossh., Fl. Caucas. edn. 2, 2: 193, map. 225 (1940); Kem.-Nath. in Trudy Tbilissk Bot. Inst. ser. 2, 11: 177 (1947); Kolak., Fl. Abkhas. 4: 112 (1986); Dimitr. in Opred. rast. Adzh. izd. 2(2): 152 (1990). Ind. loc.: Culta in Horto Botanico Academiae Scient. URSS, misit Steup anno 1928 e Krassnaja Polyana. Type in Herb. Inst. Bot. Ac. Sc. URSS. Type: this species was cultivated in the Department of Systematics (LE) and was received by Steup in 1928 from Sochi, Krasnaya-Polyana, iv 1934 (holotype LE!).

G. ikariae Baker subsp. *latifolius* Stern, Snowdr. & Snowfl.: 50 fig. 13 (1947), *pro parte excl. G. platyphyllus* Traub & Moldenke (= *G. latifolius* Rupr.).

[*G. plicatus sensu* Ledeb., Fl. Rossica 4: 114 (1853), *pro parte.*]

[*G. latifolius auct. non* Rupr.: Masters in Gard. Chron. new ser., 15: 404 (1881); Stern & Gilmour in Bot. Mag. 164: tab. 9669 (1946).]

[*G. ikariae auct. non* Baker *pro parte.* Artjush. in Bot. Zhurn. (Moscow & Leningrad) 50(10): 1445 (1965); Artjush. in Bot. Zhurn. (Moscow & Leningrad) 51(10): 1448, fig. 5 (1966); Artjush. in Daffodil Tulip Year Book: 70, fig. 5, map 20 (1967); Artjush. in Pl. Life 25(2–4): 148, fig. 30 (1969); Artjush., Amaryllidaceae SSSR: 76 (1970); C.D. Brickell in P.H. Davis et al. (eds.), Fl. Turkey 8: 372, map 55 (1984); C.D. Brickell in Walters et al. (eds.), Europ. Gard. Fl. 1: 319 (1986); Mordak in Spisok rast. Gerb. flory SSSR 27(92): No. 7107 (1990).]

169

[*G. ikariae auct. non* Baker: Baytop & Mathew, Bulb. Pl. Turkey: 22 (1984).]

DESCRIPTION. *Bulb* ± spherical to ovoid, 2–2.5 cm × 1.5–1.7 cm. *Sheath* 4.5–7 cm × 0.5–0.7 cm. *Leaves* supervolute in vernation; lorate to narrowly oblanceolate, at flowering (5–)8–20(–32.5) cm × (0.85–)1.1–2(–3) cm, after flowering developing to 13–25(–41) cm × (0.9–)1.3 cm × 2.1(–3) cm, recurving or erecto-patent at maturity; bright to dark green, shining, or infrequently very slightly glaucescent, surfaces ± concolorous; adaxial surface ± smooth or with two to four fine, longitudinal furrows; margins flat to slightly undulate; apex obtuse, flat. *Scape* 4–19 cm long, green. *Pedicel* 1.5–2.5 cm long. *Outer perianth segments* narrowly obovate, 1.6–2.4(–2.8) × 0.7–1.3(–1.6) cm, slightly unguiculate. *Inner perianth segments* ± obovate to cuneate, 0.7–1.2 cm × 0.4–0.6 cm, emarginate; each segment with a variable, narrow to broad, ± ∩-shaped mark, sometimes with a flat top and occasionally split longitudinally into two small, spot-like, marks, mark located on the adaxial surface above the apical notch; abaxial mark similar in shape and size to the adaxial mark. *Anthers* tapering to an apiculum. *Capsule* spherical, 1–1.5 cm in diameter. *Seeds* brown, c. 0.5 cm long.

ILLUSTRATIONS. Stern & Gilmour in Bot. Mag. 164: tab. 9669 (1946); Artjush. in Bot. Zhurn. (Moscow & Leningrad) 51(10): 1448, fig. 5 (1966); Artjush. in Daffodil Tulip Year Book: 70, fig. 5 (1967); Artjush. in Pl. Life 25(2–4): 148, fig. 30 (1969). PLATES 14, 49.

FLOWERING PERIOD. Spring (January–April).

HABITAT. Occurring in deciduous and mixed deciduous forest (*Carpinus* spp., *Quercus* spp., *Fagus* spp., etc.), coniferous forest (*Taxus baccata*, *Pinus* spp., and *Abies* spp.), and mixed deciduous-coniferous forest (in the Caucasus region typically *Taxus baccata* and *Buxus colchica*). Frequently occurring in stoney and rocky places: on calcareous rocks, in gorges, on stony slopes, and on scree. Also found on river banks, in scrub (*Corylus* spp.) and at the margins of forest. In moist and shady gorges it can also occur as an epiphyte or on fallen tree trunks, rooting in moss. Occurring at 70–1400 m.

DISTRIBUTION. Caucasus and Transcaucasus, in southern Russia (mainly in the Krasnodar region), Georgia (mainly Abkhazia and Adzhariya), and northeastern Turkey. Primarily found around the eastern Black Sea coast area in the ancient provinces of Colchis and Lazistan (The Euxine Province). MAP 10.

170

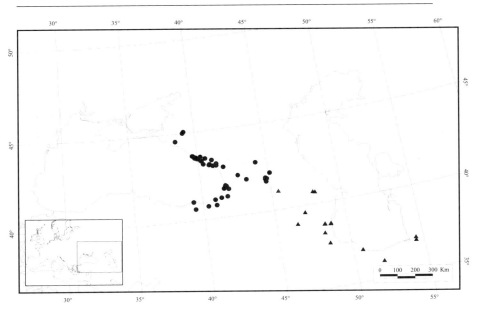

Map 10. Distribution of *Galanthus woronowii* [•] and *Galanthus transcaucasicus* [▲].

14. GALANTHUS TRANSCAUCASICUS

Galanthus transcaucasicus was described from the Talysh mountains in Azerbaijan, by Fomin, in an *Identification Key to the Plants of the Caucasus and Crimea* (Fomin and Woronow, 1909). Due to the nature of this publication, an annotated key, the description of *G. transcaucasicus* is brief, and it is difficult to get a real idea of the characteristic features of this species. The short description, translated from the Russian, is as follows: 'Leaves green, without greasy/oily shine, linear, 1.5 cm wide, obtuse, slightly grooved [furrowed], carinate below, a little shorter than flower stalk. Flowers large; outer tepals [perianth segments] 2–2.5 cm long, obovate; inner tepals [perianth segments] one-third shorter than outer ones, emarginate, with a semicircular, green spot, which is diffluent [i.e., ± ∧-shaped] below; anthers with a subulate appendage at the apex. Perennial. Talysh, in lowland/ lower belt forests'. The type specimen of *G. transcaucasicus* (24 ii 1910, *Kowig s.n.*) is also not particularly informative, and as with many other herbarium specimens of *Galanthus* it does not clearly show all the salient features of the living plant. For these reasons, and because of the comparatively small

171

amount of collecting and field work undertaken in Azerbaijan and Iran, *G. transcaucasicus* has remained a poorly known species.

Stern (1956), for example, relied on the description given in the *Flora of the USSR* for his information on this species, on the assumption that no material was available for study in the herbaria that he had consulted. It was not enumerated in Stern's work, but instead placed into *Species non satis notae* (Stern, 1956, p. 24).

Artjushenko (1967) compared *Galanthus transcaucasicus* with *G. rizehensis* and *G. lagodechianus*, two other green-leafed taxa that occur in the Caucasus. According to Artjushenko *G. transcaucasicus* has leaves that are directly comparable with *G. rizehensis*, i.e., they are dark green with a matt coloration on the adaxial surface. On the basis of this evidence she united these species, making *G. rizehensis* a synonym of *G. transcaucasicus*. In a later assessment of these species, Artjushenko (1969) re-evaluated her previous taxonomy and recognized *G. transcaucasicus* as a separate species from *G. rizehensis* (instead, *G. rizehensis* was made a synonym of *G. cilicicus* Baker), but still considered them to be closely related.

Upon examination of herbarium material, and by reference to the various descriptions of taxa from the Talysh, Kemularia-Nathadze (1977) considered that two species occurred in Iran and Azerbaijan: *Galanthus transcaucasicus* and *G. caspius* (Rupr.) Grossh. This idea is in contrast to the views of her contemporaries, who had always assumed that only one species grew in this area, and that *G. caspius* was a synonym of *G. transcaucasicus*. According to Kemularia-Nathadze, however, the descriptions and herbarium material showed large differences between these two species, particularly regarding leaf width and colour.

During the course of my investigations I have examined the type material of *Galanthus transcaucasicus* and other herbarium material from Azerbaijan, Armenia, and Iran. I have also, very fortunately, had the opportunity to examine and study living plants from throughout the range of this species, including material recently collected from the *locus classicus*. The morphology of specimens collected from the type localities of *G. transcaucasicus* and *G. caspius* (both collected near the village Lerik near Lenkoran, by the Caspian Sea) are in general agreement with the descriptions of these taxa. An important feature, however, and one that has not previously been recorded to my knowledge, is that the vernation is supervolute and not applanate as supposed by Artjushenko (1967). Other living plants collected in northern Iran, around the Caspian

172

Sea coast, also possess this character. From these observations I conclude that the distinguishing features of *G. transcaucasicus* are deep green, moderately wide leaves (1–1.5 cm, up to 2.3–2.5 cm) with two to four fine, longitudinal grooves on the upper surface (as in *G. woronowii*, etc.; often causing an upward folding of the leaves); the colour of the upper leaf surface is green-matt (green but very slightly glaucous), the vernation is supervolute, and the flowers have a single apical mark on each inner perianth segment. This description does not contradict Fomin's description of this species.

In terms of morphology, therefore, *Galanthus transcaucasicus* is similar to *G. woronowii*, which also has rather broad, green leaves and supervolute vernation.

In contrast to Artjushenko's observations (Artjushenko, 1967), it appears that *Galanthus transcaucasicus* is not closely related to, or comparable with, *G. rizehensis* or *G. lagodechianus*, because the latter species have rather narrow, linear leaves and applanate vernation. The leaf anatomy of *G. transcaucasicus* is also quite different from that of *G. rizehensis* and *G. lagodechianus* (Davis and Barnett, 1997), as the latter species have large air spaces in their leaves (small and narrow in *G. transcaucasicus*) and no bulliform cells in the upper epidermis (features seen in transverse section using a microscope). A study of *Galanthus* from Armenia and northern Azerbaijan, however, shows that *G. lagodechianus* does occur in these countries; therefore, it is possible that these specimens could have been taken to represent *G. transcaucasicus*, which would explain the confusion with *G. rizehensis* and *G. lagodechianus*.

Examination of the above material also shows that *Galanthus transcaucasicus* and *G. nivalis* var. *caspius* are conspecific, in accord with the view of Grossheim (1940), Artjushenko (1966, 1967, 1969) and Wendelbo (1970). Ruprecht (1868) described *G. nivalis* var. *caspius* from the Talysh area, in Lenkoran, that is, from the same type locality as *G. transcaucasicus*. According to Ruprecht, var. *caspius* resembles *G. latifolius* (which he described in the same publication), but had leaves that were not as broad. After reference to Ruprecht's diagnosis, and the type material of *G. nivalis* var. *caspius*, it is quite clear that this taxon is synonymous with *G. transcaucasicus*.

CULTIVATION. This species was reintroduced into cultivation in the British Isles during the early 1990s. As I have had very little experience in growing this species, and know of no one else who cultivates it, I cannot offer any hard and fast advice on cultivation. From my limited experience of *G. transcaucasicus*, I would assume

173

that it is probably best to treat it as one would *G. woronowii* or *G. lagodechianus*. It is perfectly hardy and should be planted outside.

Galanthus transcaucasicus *Fomin* in Fomin & Woronow, Opred. Rast. Caucas. Krym. 1: 281 (1909); J. Philippow, Fl. Caucas. Critic. 29(5): 4 (1916); Grossh., Fl. Caucas. 1: 244 (1928); Losinsk. in Kom., Fl. SSSR 4: 478 (1935); Traub & Moldenke in Herbertia 14: 110 (1948); Stern, Snowdr. & Snowfl.: 24, in *Species non satis notae* (1956); Artjush. in Bot. Zhurn. (Moscow & Leningrad) 50(10): 1445 (1965); Artjush. in Bot. Zhurn. (Moscow & Leningrad) 51(10): 1449 (1966); Artjush. in Daffodil Tulip Year Book: 76, 81 (1967); Artjush. in Pl. Life 25(2–4): 150 (1969); Artjush., Amaryllidaceae SSSR: 81 (1970); Wendelbo in Rech. f., Fl. Iran. (67): 7 (1970). Kem.-Nath. in Zametki Sist. Geogr. Rast. 34: 34 (1977); Wendelbo, Tulips & Irises Iran: 54, fig. 57 (1977). Ind. loc.: Talysh in lower forest zone. Type: Prov. Baku. Prop. pag. Lenkoran, culta in sectio caucas, 24 ii 1910, *Kowig s.n.* (holotype TBI!).

G. *nivalis* L. var. *caspius* Rupr. in Gartenflora 17: 132 (1868). Ind. loc.: [translated] In the lower woods by the Caspian Sea. Lenkoran (Hohenacker); 'flowering from November to February (Buhse) and Ghilon, from where there are several characteristic specimens, dating from the journey of S.G. Gmelin, and gathered from Enzeli to Abeknar by Hablitzel, flowering in January, already faded in mid-February with almost ripe seedpods (Gmelin's Reise and Hablitzlmss. 1771, 1774 n. 46)'. Type: lectotype (selected here by H. Mordak): In Waldung um Lenkoran, v, *Hohenacker s.n.* (LE!).

G. *caspius* (Rupr.) Grossh., Fl. Caucas. edn. 2, 2: 193, tab. 24, fig. 6, map. 223 (1940) *nom. illeg.*, *G. transcaucasicus in syn.*; Kem.-Nath. in Trudy Tbilissk Bot. Inst. ser. 2, 11: 178 (1947).

[*G. nivalis sensu* Ledeb., Fl. Rossica 4: 113 (1853), *pro parte.*]

[*G. plicatus non.* M. Bieb *sensu* Hohen., Enum. Pl. Elisazethp.: 228 (1883).]

[*G. nivalis non* L. *sensu* Barsa, Fl. Iran 5: 158, fig. 71 (1950).]

DESCRIPTION. *Bulb* ± spherical to ovoid, 1.5–3 cm × 1–3.1(–3.5) cm. *Sheath* 3–7 cm × 0.5–0.7 cm. *Leaves* supervolute in vernation;

174

linear to lorate, to narrowly oblanceolate, at flowering 7–20(–27) cm × (0.5–)0.6–1.7–2(–2.3) cm, after flowering developing to 10–18 cm × 0.6 cm × 1.7–2.3(–2.5) cm, recurving at maturity; bright to dark green, frequently matt or very slightly glaucescent, surfaces ± concolorous or brighter on the abaxial surface; adaxial surface ± smooth or with two to four fine, longitudinal furrows; midrib conspicuous; margins flat; apex obtuse to acute, flat. *Scape* (2.5–)4–12(–17) cm long, green. *Pedicel* 1.5–3 cm long. *Outer perianth segments* narrowly obovate, 1.5–2.5(–3) cm × 0.7–1.1 cm, slightly unguiculate. *Inner perianth segments* ± obovate to cuneate, 0.7–1.2 cm × 0.4–0.6 cm, emarginate; each segment with a variable ± ∩- to ∧-shaped mark, on the adaxial surface above the apical notch; abaxial mark similar in shape and size. *Anthers* tapering to an apiculum. *Capsule* almost spherical to globose, 1–1.5 cm in diameter. *Seeds* unknown. Note: Examination of populations *in situ* and study of specimens in local herbaria in Azerbaijan and Iran may significantly alter some of the dimensions given in this description (particularly leaf width).

ILLUSTRATIONS. Wendelbo, Tulips & Irises Iran: fig. 57 (1977). PLATES 15, 47, 48.

FLOWERING PERIOD. Winter to spring (December–April).

HABITAT. Occurring in and at the edge of forests. Ecology imperfectly known but recorded on sandy slopes, and on moist soils, apparently up to an altitude of 2000 m.

DISTRIBUTION. Armenia, Azerbaijan, and northern Iran, particularly around the southern coast of the Caspian Sea. MAP 10, page 171.

15. GALANTHUS LAGODECHIANUS

During a 16-year period, from 1947 to 1963, four species with very similar characteristics were described from the Caucasus, namely *Galanthus lagodechianus* (Kemularia-Nathadze, 1947a), *G. ketzkhovelii* (Kemularia-Nathadze, 1947b) *G. cabardensis* (Koss, 1951), and *G. kemulariae* (Kuthaladze, 1963). These species all have linear green leaves, applanate vernation, and a single apical mark on each inner perianth segment. The type specimens of *G. lagodechianus*, *G. ketzkhovelii*, and *G. kemulariae* were all collected from areas near Tbilisi, in the south-central Caucasus. The first two species were both located in the Lagodechy Reserve, near Tbilisi. *Galanthus cabardensis*

175

was collected from the northern Caucasus, in the Russian state of Karbardino-Balcaria.

Artjushenko (1965) carefully studied these four species and concluded that the minor differences in leaf dimensions, colour, texture, and size—characters formerly used to recognize these species —could not be used for the recognition of separate taxa. The cytological investigations of Sveshnikova (1965) concur with Artjushenko's findings by showing that these four species share a chromosome number of 2n = 72. All other species of *Galanthus* have a chromosome number of 2n = 24, or 2n = 36. Accordingly, Artjushenko (1965, 1966) united *G. lagodechianus, G. ketzkhovelii, G. cabardensis,* and *G. kemulariae* under one species—*G. lagodechianus*—a treatment that has not been challenged by subsequent workers.

As detailed in the discussion for *Galanthus rizehensis, G. lagodechianus* is closely allied to this species, since both possess a combination of green, linear leaves, applanate vernation, and a single apical mark on each inner perianth segment. In most cases, however, they are easily distinguished by their differences in leaf coloration and flowering time (see the discussion of *G. rizehensis*). The shape of the mark on each inner perianth segment can also be used as an aid to identification: *G. rizehensis* usually has a ⌒-shaped mark and *G. lagodechianus* a narrow ∧-shape (see FIGURE 8, T, U, and V). This character is not definitive, however, and often these marks are very similar. The leaves of *G. lagodechianus* are also usually longer and narrower than those of *G. rizehensis*, particularly in the variants collected from central Georgia.

The geographical distribution of *Galanthus lagodechianus* is much more extensive than *G. rizehensis*, and it is found throughout the Caucasus and into Armenia and Azerbaijan. It does not occur in the western Transcaucasus, however, within the range of *G. rizehensis*. Some distance separates *G. lagodechianus* from populations of *G. rizehensis*, which occurs around the eastern coast of the Black Sea. It is possible that an isolation event in the Caucasus separated a once more widely spread species, leading to the evolution of these two species from a common ancestor.

CULTIVATION. *Galanthus lagodechianus* is not well known in cultivation and is not very frequently reported in the horticultural literature; it was not included in Stern's *Snowdrops and Snowflakes*, for example, despite the fact that it had been described some 15 years earlier. The first truly accessible information on this species, at least for those outside Russian-speaking countries, was published by

Artjushenko (1967) in an article in the *Daffodil and Tulip Year Book*, based on an earlier paper in Russian (Artjushenko, 1965). Some time later the species was introduced into cultivation, probably via the botanic gardens at the Komarov Institute at St. Petersburg.

The garden variety known as *Galanthus lagodechianus* 'Anglesey Abbey', or just *G.* 'Anglesey Abbey', said to have originated from the gardens at Anglesey Abbey in Cambridge, does not belong to this species. Superficially, this clone looks very much like *G. lagodechianus*, but on closer inspection it is evident that it is a hybrid: probably the result of a cross between *G. nivalis* and one of the green-leafed species (perhaps *G. woronowii*). The leaf anatomy, and the markings on the outside and inside of the inner perianth segments suggests the influence of *G. nivalis*.

Galanthus lagodechianus requires no special treatment in cultivation, and once again, lightly shaded woodland conditions will probably suit it best. Because this species comes from high altitude locations in the Caucasus it should be very hardy and amenable to cultivation in the cooler parts of North America and the British Isles.

Galanthus lagodechianus is one of the last species of snowdrop to bloom, often flowering at the end of February or at the beginning of March in Britain.

Recently, new collections of this species have been introduced into cultivation from Azerbaijan and the northern Caucasus. These new introductions are robust and quick growing, and in time could provide us with some good garden plants.

Galanthus lagodechianus *Kem.-Nath.* in Makaschv. et al., Fl. Georgia 2: 526 (1941), *nom. nud.*; Kem.-Nath. in Zametki Sist. Geogr. Rast. 13: 6 (1947), *descr.*; Kem.-Nath. in Trudy Tbilissk Bot. Inst. ser. 2, 11: 180 (1947); Artjush. in Alp. Gard. Soc. Gr. Brit. 30(2): 121, 122 (1962); Artjush. in Bot. Zhurn. (Moscow & Leningrad) 50(10): 1445 (1965); Artjush. in Bot. Zhurn. (Moscow & Leningrad) 51 (10): 1450 (1966); Artjush. in Daffodil Tulip Year Book: 76, 81, (1967); Artjush. in Pl. Life 25(2–4): 151, (1969); Artjush., Amaryllidaceae SSSR: 82 (1970); C.D. Brickell in Walters et al. (eds.), Europ. Gard. Fl. 1: 318 (1986). Ind. loc.: Georgia orient. In silvis regionis inferioris. Prov. Tiflis. distr. Kachethi, circ. pag. Lagodechi, 10. II 1887. ex Herb. Medwedewi, 16. II. 1901. Mlokosievicz; 20. III. 1935. P. Zagareli; 10. IV. 1935. L. Kem.-Nath. et O. Kapeller. Type: (lectotype, designated here): Caucasus, Kachetia, prope Lago-

dechy, 16 ii 1901, *Mlokosievicz* 1 [annotated as 'paratype in shedae']
(lectotype TBI!, isolectotype LE!).

G. ketzkhovelii Kem.-Nath. in Trudy Tbilissk Bot. Inst. ser. 2, 11: 181
(1947). Ind. loc.: Caucasus Orientalis. Mons Khatschal-dag
5.IV.36 [?37], L. Kemularia-Nathadze! Ex Herbario vivo Instit.
Bot. Acad. Scien. G. SSR 5.IV.37. 10.III.47. L. Kemularia-Nathadze. Type: Georgia, Distr. Lagodechi, mons Khat-schal-dag,
reg. subalpina, 5 iv 1937, *Kemularia-Nathadze s.n.* (holotype TBI!).
Note: *G. lagodechianus* and *G. ketzkhovelli* were both published in
the same year, and by the same author, in two separate journals
from Tbilisi. *Galanthus lagodechianus* has a publication date
(9.6.1947), but *G. ketzkhovelli* does not, because the volumes of
Trudy Tbilissk Bot. Inst. were usually sent to print at the same
time at the end of the year. Until the date of publication for *G.
ketzkhovelli* is known *G. lagodechianus* has priority.

G. cabardensis Koss in Bot. Mater. Gerb. Inst. Kom. a Akad. Nauk
SSSR 14: 133, fig. 2 (1951); Galushko, Fl. N. Caucas. 1: 171
(1978) [as *G. carbardinicus* (*sic*)]. Ind. loc.: Caucasus septen-
trionalis, respublica Cabardensis, in districto Tschegemi, iii 1947,
G. Koss (Herb. Univ. Mosq.). Type: the region of Chegem and
Nalchick. In the mixed *Corylus* forest, east side of the hill at the al-
titude 900–1000 m, iii 1947, *Koss s.n.* (holotype *non vidi*; isotype
LE!).

G. kemulariae Kuth. in Zametki Sist. Geogr. Rast. 23: 128 (1963).
Ind. loc.: Georgia orientalis, pagum Saguramo in declivis septen-
trionalis prope monasterium Zedazeni, 1200 m.s.m., leg.
6.III.1962, A. Gagnidze, Sch. Kuthatheladze, I. Latscaschvili, E.
Mirenko, L. Chintibidze. (In herbario Instituti Botanici Ac. Sci-
ent. RSS Georgicae in Thbilissi conservatur). Type: Georgia,
Tbilisi, N slope of Zedazeni, 6 iii 1962, *Gagnidze, Kuthatheladze &
Latschaschvili s.n.* (holotype TBI!).

DESCRIPTION. *Bulb* ± spherical to ovoid, 1–2.5(–3) cm × 1.3–2.9
(–3) cm. *Sheath* 3–7 cm × 0.5–0.7 cm. *Leaves* applanate in vernation;
linear, at flowering 7.5–18 cm × 0.5–1(–1.2) cm, after flowering developing to 15–35(–45) cm × 0.6–1.1(1.5) cm, usually recurving or
nearly prostrate at maturity; adaxial surface bright to dark green,
glossy to matt, or infrequently becoming very slightly glaucescent,

178

abaxial surface bright, shiny green; surfaces smooth; midrib conspicuous; margins flat or slightly revolute; apex acute, flat. *Scape* 3.5–20(–30) cm long, green, with no clear disjunction in colour between scape and spathe-valves. *Pedicel* 1–3(–3.5) cm long. *Outer perianth segments* narrowly obovate, 1.5–2.7(–3) cm × 1–1.6 cm, slightly unguiculate. *Inner perianth segments* ± cuneate to ± obovate, 0.8–1(–1.2) cm × 0.3–0.6 cm, emarginate; each segment with a variable, ∧- to ∩-shaped mark on the adaxial surface above the apical notch; abaxial mark similar in shape and size to the adaxial mark, or larger and extending to almost half the length of the segment. *Anthers* tapering to an apiculum. *Capsule* almost spherical to ellipsoid, 1–1.5(–2) cm in diameter. *Seeds* brown, c. 0.5 cm long.

ILLUSTRATIONS. Koss in Bot. Mater. Gerb. Inst. Kom. a Akad. Nauk SSSR 14: 133, fig. 2 (1951); Artjush. in Alp. Gard. Soc. Gr. Brit. 30(2): 125 (1962). PLATES 17, 45, 46.

FLOWERING PERIOD. Spring (January–April).

HABITAT. Occurring in deciduous forest and mixed deciduous forest (*Carpinus* spp., *Fagus* spp., etc.), most commonly found at the subalpine to alpine zone, 800–2400 m.

DISTRIBUTION. Caucasus and Transcaucasus, in Armenia, Azerbaijan, Georgia, and southern Russia (only in the northern Caucasus: Karbardino-Balcaria and Severo-Ostenskaya). MAP 11.

16. GALANTHUS RIZEHENSIS

In 1934, G.P. Baker exhibited this species at the RHS shows under the name of *Galanthus latifolius* var. *rizehensis* (Anon., Proceedings-Scientific Committee. J. Roy. Hort. Soc. 59: cxvii, 1934). A year later it was shown again at the RHS show, but this time by Balfour-Gourlay as *G. latifolius rizaensis* [*sic*] (Anon., Proceedings-Floral Committee. J. Roy. Hort. Soc. 60: xxv, 1935). According to Stern and Gilmour (1946), these plants were introduced by E.K. Balls from a collection made at Soğuk Su near Trebizond (Trabzon) in 1934 (*Gourlay & Balls* B. 1600); and also from collections made by A. Baker near Rizeh, 80 km east of Trebizond [Trabzon].

Some years later, Stern (1956) described *Galanthus rizehensis* from plants that he cultivated at his garden at Highdown, Sussex, presumably from stock of the original collections made by Balfour-Gourlay and Balls, and Baker, although this is not indicated in his protologue. According to Stern, *G. rizehensis* is separated from other

179

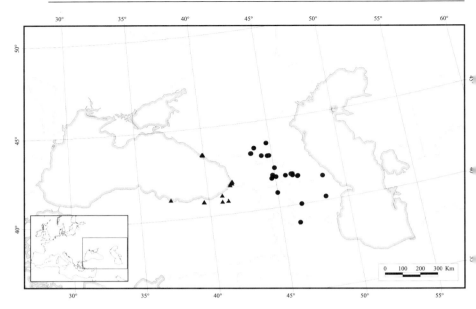

Map 11. Distribution of *Galanthus lagodechianus* [•] and *Galanthus rizehensis* [▲].

species in the following manner: '*Galanthus rizehensis* differs from *G. nivalis* by the dull green leaves which recurve during and after flowering and by the margin at the joint where the pedicel issues from the scape being altogether green; it differs from *G. ikariae* subsp. *latifolius* [*G. woronowii*] by the linear leaves and by the pedicel being longer than the spathe; it differs from all other known wild species of *Galanthus* by having a triploid form'; and, also according to Stern's description, this species has applanate vernation and a single apical mark on each inner perianth segment. *Galanthus rizehensis*, therefore, looks rather like a green-leafed variant of *G. nivalis*, making it a rather distinctive-looking species.

The marking on each inner perianth segment provides a further character for the identification of this species. The green mark on the inside of each inner perianth segment does not reach the base of the segment, as it does in *G. nivalis*; instead, it covers only about half the distance of the inner face; it is roughly the same size as the mark on the outside of the segment (see FIGURE 8, T).

Recurving of the leaves is a common feature of *Galanthus rizehensis*, but this is not exclusive to, or fixed within, this species. Similarly, the colour of the joint where the pedicel meets the spathe is

180

characteristic, but not a definitive taxonomic character. The relative length of the pedicel to the spathe is in my opinion a character of little or no taxonomic significance. Leaf colour is also variable, from dull green as described by Stern, to matt (a small amount of wax coating), or glossy, and the leaves of *G. rizehensis* often possess a faint median stripe.

The only species that one is likely to confuse with *Galanthus rizehensis* is the closely related *G. lagodechianus*. Indeed, these species are sometimes so similar that it is difficult to tell them apart. Originally, I considered that *G. rizehensis* should be a subspecies of *G. lagodechianus*, but I now think that the differences in leaf coloration, geographical distribution (see MAP 11, page 180, and distribution notes), chromosome number, and flowering time are enough to warrant their recognition at the level of species. *Galanthus lagodechianus* usually has leaves that are bright, shining green and only infrequently matt, whereas the leaves of *G. rizehensis* are usually matt with a faint median stripe. The chromosome number of *G. lagodechianus* is 2n = 72, and *G. rizehensis* is 2n = 24 or 36. It should also be noted that *Galanthus rizehensis* is predominately a species of lowland forest, occurring at comparatively low altitudes, from 25 m to 1100 m, whereas *G. lagodechianus* is found in the subalpine to alpine zone, between 800 m and 2400 m. In cultivation *G. rizehensis* usually finishes flowering two weeks or more before *G. lagodechianus* has started to produce its blooms.

When Stern described *Galanthus rizehensis* it was known only from the neighbourhood of Trebizond (Trabzon, northeastern Turkey), near the coast of the Black Sea. Since this time many more collections have been made, greatly extending the geographical distribution and the known morphological variability of this species. In 1966 Khokhrjakov described *G. glaucescens* as a new species from Adzhariya in Georgia, a taxon which has since been regarded as synonymous with *G. rizehensis* (Artjushenko, 1970). In 1982, collections were made in the Krasnodar region of southern Russia by A. Lebedeva (12 ii 1982, *Lebedeva s.n.*), further extending the distribution around the Black Sea coast area. And recently *G. rizehensis* was found on the south-facing side of the Pontus in northeastern Turkey.

In Georgia (Adzhariya) and Russia (Krasnodar) *Galanthus rizehensis* is very variable, and can often look quite different from the plants that occur in the Turkish Black Sea coast area (eastern Colchis), i.e., the plants that are presently known in cultivation. In these stations *G. rizehensis* is often larger than the variants known from Trabzon, particularly with regard to the size of the leaves. There is, however, considerable variation within the Georgian and Russian populations. During fieldwork in the Caucasian Biosphere Reserve near Sochi (Krasnodar), I observed individuals of the smaller type, as found in northeastern Turkey and populations nearby, near the village of Krasnaya Volyna (*Davis, Roskov, Tuniev, & Lebedeva* 466), and I located plants of larger dimensions similar to those described as *G. glaucescens*. Within larger populations, such as those near the village of Kashtanvka (*Davis, Roskov, Tuniev & Lebedeva* 471b.), a continuous range of variation was observed. On the south-facing side of the Pontus mountains similar variation is evident.

CULTIVATION. *Galanthus rizehensis* is long-lived in cultivation and not particularly fussy concerning location or soil requirements. It will grow in open positions, shade or half shade, and in most types of soil providing they are not too porous. In its native habitat it grows in a range of soil types, from rather heavy, calcareous soils to light, leafy, acidic ones. It is usually found in the shade of deciduous trees but also in more open places at the edge of woodlands.

Galanthus rizehensis usually sets seed freely in cultivation, producing large numbers of seedlings around the mother plants. If this happens the seedlings need to be removed and planted where they will get more space to grow and develop. Planting them slightly deeper than before helps to hasten their development to adult plants.

Most of the plants currently grown in cultivation probably originate from those grown at Highdown in Sussex, England, by Sir Frederick Stern, which in turn probably originated from the collections of Balfour-Gourlay and Balls, and Baker, from the Black Sea coast area of northeastern Turkey. These collections represent the smaller types of *G. rizehensis*, and include both the diploid and triploid forms that Stern (1956) describes in *Snowdrops and Snowflakes*. The larger forms of *G. rizehensis*, akin to the populations from further around the Black Sea in Georgia and Russia, are, to my knowledge at least, not yet in general cultivation. This is unfortunate as they have the potential to make fine garden plants, which could eclipse the clones already in cultivation.

Galanthus rizehensis *Stern*, in Snowdr. & Snowfl.: 37, fig. 8 (1956); Rix & R. Phillips, Bulb Book: 17, fig. c (p. 16) (1981); C.D. Brickell in P.H. Davis et al. (eds.), Fl. Turkey 8: 371, map 54 (1984); T. Baytop & B. Mathew, Bulb. Pl. Turkey: 23, fig. 2 (1984); C.D. Brickell in Walters et al. (eds.), Europ. Gard. Fl. 1: 318 (1986); N. Zeybek & E. Sauer, Türk. Kardelenleri 1: 49, fig. 10 (1995). Ind. loc.: Type in Herb. Mus. Brit., a F.C. Stern lectus i Feb. ex Hort. Highdown, Sussex. Type: garden of F.C. Stern, at Goring-by-Sea, Sussex, 1 ii 1946, Stern cult. (holotype BM!).

G. *latifolius* [var.] *rizaensis* [*sic*] Anon. in J. Roy. Hort. Soc. [Proc.] 60: xxv (1935), *nom. tant.*

G. *latifolius rizaensis* [*sic*] Anon. in J. Roy. Hort. Soc. [Proc.] 60: xxv (1935), *nom. tant.*

G. *latifolius* Rupr. var. *rizehensis* Stern & Gilmour in Bot. Mag. 164: t. 9669 (1946), *nom. tant.*

G. *glaucescens* A.P. Khokhr. in Byull. Glavn. Bot. Sada 62: 62 (1966). Ind. loc.: Adzharia, distr. Tschacva, pagus Chalo, in pratulis. 19 I 1966. A. Dimitrieva et A. Khokhrjakov legit. In herbario Horti botanici principalis conservatur. Type: not traced.

[G. *cilicicus auct. non* Baker: Artjush. in Bot. Zhurn. (Moscow & Leningrad) 51(10): 1449 (1966); Artjush. in Pl. Life 25(2–4): 151 (1969); Artjush., Amaryllidaceae SSSR: 82 (1970); Dimitr. in Opred. rast. Adzh. izd. 2(2): 152 (1990).]

DESCRIPTION. *Bulb* ± spherical to ovoid, 1.8–3 cm × 0.6–1.5 cm. *Sheath* 5–8.5 cm × 0.5–0.7 cm. *Leaves* applanate in vernation; ± linear, at flowering (4–)6.5–13(–16) cm × (0.3–)0.4–0.8(–1) cm, after flowering developing to 6.5–20(–33.5) cm × 0.4–1(1.4) cm, erect or recurving to ± prostrate at maturity; adaxial surface bright to dark green, shining to matt, or very slightly glaucous, often with a narrow, pale median stripe, abaxial surface bright shining green; surfaces smooth; midrib conspicuous; margins flat. *Scape* 8–12 cm long, green, with no clear disjunction in colour between scape and spathe-valves. *Pedicel* 1.5–3.5 cm long. *Outer perianth segments* narrowly obovate 1.5–2.2 cm × 0.6–1 cm, slightly unguiculate. *Inner perianth segments* ± obovate to cuneate, 0.8–1 cm × 0.4–0.6 cm, emarginate; each segment with a variable, ± ∧- to ∩-shaped mark on the adaxial surface above the apical notch; abaxial mark similar in

183

shape and size to the adaxial mark, or larger and extending to almost half the length of the segment. *Anthers* tapering to an apiculum. *Capsule* almost spherical, 1–1.5 cm in diameter. *Seeds* brown, c. 0.5 cm long.

ILLUSTRATIONS. Stern, Snowdr. & Snowfl.: 38, fig. 8 (1956); Rix & R. Phillips, Bulb Book: 16, fig. c (1981); T. Baytop & B. Mathew, Bulb. Pl. Turkey: 23, fig. 2 (1984); N. Zeybek & E. Sauer, Türk. Kardelenleri 1: 49, fig. 10 (1995). PLATES 16, 43, 44.

FLOWERING PERIOD. Spring (January–March, or infrequently April).

HABITAT. Occurring in deciduous and mixed deciduous forest (*Carpinus* spp., *Quercus* spp., *Fagus* spp., etc.), plantations (*Castanea* sp., etc.), and under small trees and shrubs (*Buxus colchica, Corylus* spp., *Aleurites* spp., *Paliurus spina-christi, Ruscus* spp., etc.). Found on slopes, stream banks, forest margins and clearings, cliff ledges, and small gulleys. Growing on calcareous and acidic soils, and on thin moss-covered soil on rocks. From 25–1200 m.

DISTRIBUTION. Western Transcaucasus, in Georgia (Adzhariya), Russia (Krasnodar region), and in the adjacent part of northeastern Turkey. Collectively, this distribution is within the ancient provinces of Colchis and Lazistan (the Euxine Province). MAP 11, page 180.

17. GALANTHUS KRASNOVII

Despite being described relatively recently (Khokhrjakov, 1963), the history of *Galanthus krasnovii* goes back to at least the beginning of this century. In 1913 Sakharov collected a *Galanthus* specimen (*Sakharov* 634) from Gagri in Abkhasia (Georgia), which he found growing on subalpine grassland at 1600 m. Twenty-five years later Panjutin determined this specimen as a new species, naming it *G. valentinae*. For some unknown reason this species was never published by Panjutin, although Grossheim took up this name (*G. valentinae* Panjutin ex Grossh.) for his account of *Galanthus* in *Flora Kavkaza* (1940). This species was not, however, validly published by Grossheim as his treatment did not include a Latin diagnosis, a practice contrary to the rules of the International Code of Botanical Nomenclature (ICBN). Some years later Khokhrjakov (1963) published *G. krasnovii* as a 'New Snowdrop from the Caucasus', which he described from material that he had collected in Adzhariya (Georgia). Artjushenko (1965) recognized that *G. krasnovii* was conspecific with *G. valentinae*, and accordingly placed the latter in synonymy. I have examined the herbarium specimen of *G. valentinae* (*Sakharov* 634) and type material of *G. krasnovii* (3 v 1959, *Khokhrjakov s.n.*) and concur with Artjushenko's decision.

Galanthus krasnovii is circumscribed mainly on the basis of floral features. Foremost, each of the inner perianth segments lacks the characteristic apical notch, which is present in the majority of the species. The outer perianth segments are spathulate in outline, due to the distictly unguiculate base; the inner perianth segments are more or less elliptic to oblanceolate.

In overall appearance, *Galanthus krasnovii* looks very different from other species. The leaves are broad (1.5–4 cm), and noticeably wider at the middle to upper part of the leaf. The vernation is conspicuously supervolute, and at maturity one leaf continues to clasp the other tightly at the base. The flowers are large and almost pear-shaped before they open fully.

Galanthus krasnovii is closely related to *G. platyphyllus*, these species sharing many common features: they have leaves of similar dimensions, shape, and colour, and they have flowers that lack the usual feature of a notch at the apex of each inner perianth segment. The shape of the inner perianth segments is, however, characteristic for each of these two species. In *G. krasnovii* the inner segments are more or less elliptic to oblanceolate, with a distinctly acute apex; in *G. platyphyllus* they are more or less obovate and the apex is obtuse to rounded (see FIGURE 8, x and y). It is also easy to separate these species by the shape of the anther apex which is pointed (apiculate) in *G. krasnovii* and blunt (obtuse) in *G. platyphyllus*.

Despite its unique appearance, *Galanthus krasnovii* has remained poorly known. It is rarely recorded in Floras, very few specimens of it are in any herbaria, and it is virtually unknown in cultivation, all this undoubtedly due to its rarity in nature. *Galanthus krasnovii* has a very restricted distribution and is known from only a few localities in the Black Sea coast region of Georgia (Abkhasia and Adzhariya), northeastern Turkey (Artvin Province), and at one locality in the southern Caucasus (Gagri, in Georgia).

In the *Flora of Turkey* Brickell (1984) noted that Khokhrjakov (1963) cited specimens of *Galanthus krasnovii* from Turkey (collected near Artvin, by Philippov) but, because no specimens were located, this species was given as 'a species doubtfully recorded'. However, study of material in the herbarium Tbilisi (TBI) shows that the specimens of Philippov (*Philippov* 1561 and 1562) are *G. krasnovii*, thus verifying the presence of this species in Turkey; recently, in 1987, *G. krasnovii* was rediscovered at Artvin, by Ole Sønderhousen (*Sønderhousen* 555).

CULTIVATION. Not much is known about the requirements for the successful cultivation of *Galanthus krasnovii*, as it has only rarely been grown in gardens. In its native habitat it experiences cold winters and high rainfall. According to Ole Sønderhousen's field notes it grows at the edge of deciduous woodlands in rich, moist soil. In 1995 John Drake and Liz Thompson located this species in northeastern Turkey, where it was growing in very wet conditions by the sides of streams and in wet flushes. In some places they found it growing in several centimetres of water. Based on these observations, it is likely that *G. krasnovii* will do well in similar conditions to those that suit *G. platyphyllus*. A site in the garden that has rich, deep soil and receives plenty of water during the growing season will probably suit it best. Plenty of air movement and sunlight are also important, and watering during periods of winter and spring drought could be advantageous. Another point to bear in mind is that *G. krasnovii* occurs on both calcareous and acidic soils.

Recently, some have succeeded with twin-scaling this species, and perhaps in a few years *Galanthus krasnovii* will be more widely available.

Galanthus krasnovii *A.P. Khokhr.* in Bjull. Moskovsk. Obsc. Isp. Prir. Otd. Biol. 68(4): 140, incl. photo (1963); Artjush. in Bot. Zhurn. (Moscow & Leningrad) 50(10): 1445 (1965); Artjush. in Bot. Zhurn. (Moscow & Leningrad) 51(10): 1449 (1966); Artjush. in Daffodil Tulip Year Book: 70 (1967); Artjush. in Pl. Life 25(2–4): 150, fig. 30 (1969); Artjush., Amaryllidaceae SSSR: 80, fig. 52 (map) and 54 (1970); C.D. Brickell in P.H. Davis et al. (eds.), Fl. Turkey 8: 372 (1984), *in adnot.*; Kolak., Fl. Abkhas. 4: 111 (1986); Dimitr. in Opred. rast Adzh. izd. 2, 2: 152 (1990). Ind. loc.: Adzharia, distr. Czakva. in angustis fluminis Czakvae inter Chalo et Czakvistavi, 3/V 1959. Ipse legi. In herbario Horti botanici principalis conservatur. Type: Adzhariya ASSR, between Chakhaty [Chakvistavi] and Khino [Khalo], in the river gorge of Kintrishi [Kintrish], beech-box wood, 3 v 1959, *Khokhrjakov s.n.* (holotype MHA!; isotype LE!, K! [label reads: Chakva district, gorge of river Chakvy between Khalo and Chakvistavi, 3 v 1959, *Khokhrjakov s.n.*]).

186

G. valentinae Panjut. [*in sched.* (1938), *leg.* 1913] ex Grossh., Fl. Caucas. edn. 2, 2: 194, map 212 (1940), *nom nud.*; Kem.-Nath. in Trudy Tbilissk Bot. Inst. ser. 2, 11: 179 (1947), *nom. nud.* Ind. loc.: Province of Colchis. Abkh. [Abkhasia] (Gagri mountain complex). In the lower alpine belt. In meadows. Specimen: Abkhasia, Gagri, *Abies* forest on the border with sub-alpine grassland, 1600 m, 12 iv 1913, *Sakharov* 634 (holotype LE!, isotype LE!).

G. krasnovii A.P. Khokhr. subsp. *maculatus* A.P. Khokhr. in Bjull. Glavn. Bot. Sada 62: 60 (1966). Ind. loc.: Abchasia angustia fluminis Pschirzcha. Legit Khokhrjakov, 5 iii 1961. Type: (holotype ?MHA, *non vidi*).

DESCRIPTION. *Bulb* ovoid to nearly obclavate, 1.7–3(–4) cm × 0.9–2.5 cm. *Sheath* (2–)4.5–8 cm × 0.5–0.8 cm. *Leaves* supervolute in vernation; lorate to oblanceolate, at flowering 7–19 cm × 1.5–3.5(–4) cm, after flowering developing to 10–24 cm × 2.2–4(–6) cm, erectopatent to recurving at maturity; bright green, shiny, surfaces concolorous; leaf blade smooth or with two to four fine, longitudinal furrows, often minutely puckered; midrib conspicuous to prominent; margins flat to slightly undulate; apex obtuse, frequently mucronate, ± flat. *Scape* 7–22(–27) cm long, green. *Pedicel* 1.5–2 cm long. *Outer perianth segments* narrowly obovate, 2.2–3.4 cm × 1–1.4 cm, unguiculate to distinctly unguiculate. *Inner perianth segments* ± elliptic to ± oblanceolate, 0.8–1 cm × 0.4–0.5 cm, apex acute, rounded at the very tip, slightly undulate, either marginate or with a very small apical notch; each segment with a variable, ± ∩-shaped mark, or often the mark is smaller and divided into two small cuneate marks, on the adaxial surface near the apex; abaxial surface with a similar mark to that on the adaxial face. *Anthers* tapering to an apiculum. *Capsule* almost spherical, 1–2 cm in diameter. *Seeds* mid- to dark brown, 0.55–0.65 cm long.

ILLUSTRATIONS. A.P. Khokhr. in Bjull. Moskovsk. Obsc. Isp. Prir. Otd. Biol. 68 (4): 141, inset photo (1963); Artjush. in Pl. Life 25(2–4): 150, fig. 30 (1969); Artjush., Amaryllidaceae SSSR: 80, fig. 54 (1970). PLATES 18, 52, 53, 54.

FLOWERING PERIOD. Spring to summer (March–May).

HABITAT. Occurring in low to medium altitude deciduous forest in clearings, in shrub understorey (*Buxus* spp.), in meadows, marshy places, and in river gorges. Often found at the edge of forest. In northeastern Turkey it gows in forest clearings through snow-flattened *Pteridium aquilinum*, and in light forest with *Crataegus* spp., *Rhododendron ponticum*, and *Cornus mas*. Occurring up to 1500 m; infrequently occurring near the subalpine zone at the edge of forest.

DISTRIBUTION. In close proximity to the eastern part of the Black Sea coast, in Georgia (Abkhazia and Adzhariya) and northeastern Turkey. Rare and only found in a few scattered locations. MAP 12.

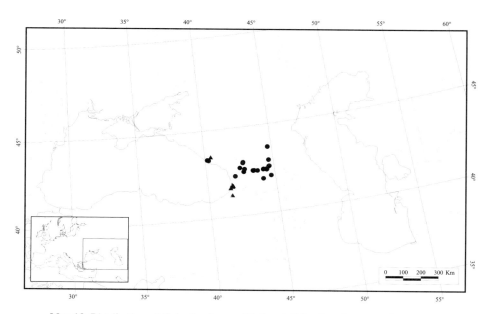

Map 12. Distribution of *Galanthus krasnovii* [●] and *Galanthus platyphyllus* [▲].

18. GALANTHUS PLATYPHYLLUS

Galanthus platyphyllus is probably the most distinctive of all *Galanthus* species due to the presence of a number of unique morphological features. Even from examination of herbarium specimens, three unique characters are clearly definable. Firstly, the apices of the anthers are blunt and not pointed as they are in all other *Galanthus* species; secondly, the bulb is large and rather elongated, more like the bulb of a *Narcissus* than a *Galanthus*; and thirdly, the apex of each inner perianth segment is obtuse and lacks the typical apical notch (FIGURE 8). The vernation of *G. platyphyllus* is distinctly super-

188

volute, and at maturity one leaf remains tightly clasped around the other. The leaves are bright to dark green, and usually shiny.

As the name implies, *Galanthus platyphyllus* has broad leaves. In fact, this species has the largest leaves of any *Galanthus*, up to 35 cm long and 4 cm wide. A plant once cultivated in Bakuriani Botanic Garden, and made into an herbarium specimen (*Artjushenko* 531), has leaves 6 cm wide—probably the largest *Galanthus* ever recorded!

Galanthus platyphyllus is, undoubtedly, closely related to *G. krasnovii*, and they look very similar in general appearance. The most distinctive feature linking *G. platyphyllus* with *G. krasnovii* is the lack of an apical notch on each inner perianth segment, a character which sets them apart from all the other species. The shape of the segment is, however, rather different for each of these two species: in *G. platyphyllus* the apex of the segment is obtuse, and in *G. krasnovii* it is acute (see FIGURE 8, X and Y). If in doubt as to the identity of these species, one should study the anthers, which are blunt at the apex of *G. platyphyllus* but pointed in *G. krasnovii*. A further useful distinguishing character for *G. platyphyllus*, but one that is usually only readily discernible on living material, is the presence of a light green patch at the base of each inner perianth segment. Occasionally this green patch can have a depth of colour that matches the apical mark (see FIGURE 8, X), or it can be faint and not very obvious and in some individuals absent.

For many years *Galanthus platyphyllus* was known under the more widely used name *G. latifolius*, a species described by Ruprecht (1868). After its description, however, it became evident that the epithet *latifolius* had been used in another context, in connection with *G. plicatus* M. Bieb. (noted by Beck, 1894; and Stern and Gilmour, 1946). The description of *G. latifolius* given by Salisbury (1866) represents *G. plicatus* and not species from the central high Caucasus with broad, green leaves. As Salisbury's article predates Ruprecht's, *G. latifolius* cannot be used in association with anything but *G. plicatus* (at this rank). This nomenclatural point was taken up by Traub and Moldenke (1948), who recognizing *G. latifolius* Rupr. as a later homonym, provided the new name of *G. platyphyllus*.

Despite its unique morphology *Galanthus platyphyllus* has often been treated as a synonym of other species, or it has been confused with other green-leafed snowdrops (Stern and Gilmour, 1946), particularly *G. woronowii* (as *G. ikariae* subsp. *latifolius*, Stern, 1956). The most likely reason for this mix-up is the fact that material of *G. platyphyllus*, especially living material, has not been readily accessible

189

during the greater part of this century. What most botanists and horticulturists cultivated under the name of *G. platyphyllus*, or *G. latifolius*, was actually *G. woronowii*. For Russian and Georgian botanists the availability of material was not a problem, however, and in nearly all of their treatments of *Galanthus* the name *G. platyphyllus* is recognized in the correct manner, in accordance with the original concept for this species.

In addition to its rather unique morphology, the ecology of *Galanthus platyphyllus* is unlike that of any other in the genus. *Galanthus platyphyllus* is most frequently recorded from high altitude localities, of approximately 2000 to 2700 m. It occurs in subalpine and alpine grassland, where abundant moisture is available from melting snow. It is often found growing amongst snow patches, and even in ephemeral water pools. The flowering time of this species is also very atypical for *Galanthus*, as this occurs from June onwards and up to the end of July, or later. In cultivation this characteristic is partially maintained, as *G. platyphyllus* often flowers up to a month later than the last of the late-flowering snowdrops.

CULTIVATION. When attempting to cultivate *Galanthus platyphyllus*, one should bear in mind the peculiar conditions in which this species grows in the wild. In the high Caucasus, it endures long, cold winters, and then in the growing season it receives an abundance of moisture and high light intensity. *Galanthus platyphyllus* is therefore probably more suited to cooler, and possibly wetter, garden climates. Dr Gwen Black, for example, grows this species admirably in her garden in northwest England (Carlisle), where it comes into flower in March. This is not to say that this species cannot be grown successfully further south. Colin Mason of Warwickshire, for example, has grown this species with little trouble for many years, and recently I have achieved encouraging results with plants grown in a dry, chalky garden in Kent.

Dr Gwen Black recommends watering *Galanthus platyphyllus* if the soil becomes dry during the growing period. In addition, she suggests a site in the coolest part of the garden, with the proviso that this location receives plenty of sunshine throughout flowering time.

Galanthus platyphyllus *Traub & Moldenke* in Herbertia 14: 110 (1948); Artjush. in Alp. Gard. Soc. Gr. Brit. 30(2): 127 (1962); Artjush. in Bot. Zhurn. (Moscow & Leningrad) 50(10): 1445 (1965); Artjush. in Bot. Zhurn. (Moscow & Leningrad) 51(10): 1448

(1966); Mordak in Spisok rast. Gerb. flory SSSR 16: 54 (1966); Art-jush. in Daffodil Tulip Year Book: 70 (1967); Artjush. in Pl. Life 25 (2–4): 150, fig. 27 (1969); Artjush., Amaryllidaceae SSSR: 80, fig. 53 (1970); Galushko, Fl. N. Caucas. 1: 171, fig. 39a (1978); Rix & R. Phillips, Bulb Book: 15, inset photo (1981); Kolak., Fl. Abkhas. 4: 112 (1986). Ind. loc.: [*ex descr. G. latifolius* Rupr.]: 'on the alpine meadows of Ossetien, or more exactly, on the Mount Gudgora, from the station of Godaur until the old wood to the Kreuzberg is met with, 1270–1200 m. or even lower; I received samples through Herr Bayern'. Type: [ex *G. latifolius* Rupr.] Gudgova, 8 v 1860, *Bayern s.n.* (holotype LE!, photo K(LE)!).

G. latifolius Rupr. in Gartenflora 17: 130, t. 578 (1868), *non G. latifolius* Salisb., Gen. Pl.: 95 (1866); Boiss., Fl. Orient. 5: 146 (1882); Baker, Handb. Amaryll.: 17, (1888); Burb. in J. Roy. Hort. Soc. 13: 204, fig. 30 (1891); Beck in Wiener Ill. Gart.-Zeitung 19: 49 (1894); C. Hansen in Gartenflora 48: 229, fig. 51 (1899); Sommier & Levier, Enum. Pl. Caucas.: 422 (1900); Gottl.-Tann. in Abh. K. K. Zool.-Bot. Ges. Wien 2(4): 41 (1904); J. Phillippow in Kuzn. et al., Fl. Caucas. Critic. 2.5: 7 (1916); Bowles in J. Roy. Hort. Soc. London 43: 34 (1918); Dykes in Gard. Chron. ser. 3, 65: 187 (1919); Grossh., Fl. Caucas. 1: 244 (1928); Losinsk. in Kom., Fl. SSSR 4: 477 (1935); Grossh., Fl. Caucas. edn. 2, 2: 193, tab. 24, fig. 7, map 226 (1940); Kem.-Nath. in Makaschv. et al., Fl. Georgia 2: 526 (1941); Kem.-Nath. in Trudy Tbilissk Bot. Inst. ser. 2, 11: 179 (1947). Type: as for *G. platyphyllus.*

G. latifolius Rupr. forma *typicus* Beck in Wiener Ill. Gart.-Zeitung 19: 49 (1894), *nom. invalid.*

G. latifolius Rupr. forma *typicus* Gottl.-Tann. in Abh. K. K. Zool.-Bot. Ges. Wien 2(4): 42 (1904), *nom. invalid.*

?*G. nivalis* L. var. *latifolius* (Rupr.) Harpur-Crewe in Gard. Chron. new ser., 11: (1879).

G. ikariae subsp. *latifolius* Stern, Snowdr. & Snowfl.: 50 (1956), *pro parte.*

DESCRIPTION. *Bulb* ovoid to obclavate, 3.5–5 cm × 1.7–2.5(–3) cm. *Sheath* 3–6.5 cm × 0.6–1 cm. *Leaves* supervolute in vernation; lorate to oblanceolate; at flowering 12.5–25(–32) cm × 1.7–3.4(–6) cm, after flowering developing to 14–28(–35) × 1.7–4(–6), ± erect to erecto-patent at maturity, or recurving; bright to dark green,

191

shiny, surfaces concolorous; adaxial surface smooth or two to four furrowed-lined; midrib rather inconspicuous; margins either flat or sometimes slightly undulate, apex obtuse, frequently mucronate, cucullate to flat. *Scape* 10–20 cm long, green. *Pedicel* 2–3.5 cm long. *Outer perianth segments* narrowly obovate, 2.2–3.4 cm × 1–1.4 cm, slightly unguiculate. *Inner perianth segments* obovate to broadly obovate, 0.8–1 cm × 0.4–0.5 cm, apex obtuse, marginate; each segment with a variable ± broad ∩-shaped mark, or the mark is smaller and divided into two small cuneate marks, mark located on the adaxial surface near the apex; at the base of each segment is a diffuse, light green mark; abaxial surface with a similar mark to that on the adaxial face. *Anthers* without a distinct apiculum, 0.5 cm × 0.12 cm. *Capsule* almost spherical, 1–1.5 cm in diameter. *Seeds* mid- to dark brown, 0.55–0.65 cm long.

ILLUSTRATIONS. Burb. in J. Roy. Hort. Soc. 13: 204, fig. 30 (1891); C. Hansen in Gartenflora 48: 229, fig. 51 (1899); Grossh., Fl. Caucas. edn. 2, 2: 193, tab. 24, fig. 7 (1940); Artjush. in Alp. Gard. Soc. Gr. Brit. 30(2): 125 (1962); Artjush. in Pl. Life 25(2–4): 150, fig. 27 (1969); Artjush., Amaryllidaceae SSSR: 80, fig. 53 (1970); Galushko, Fl. N. Caucas. 1: 171, fig. 39a (1978); Rix & R. Phillips, Bulb Book: 15, inset photo [habitat] (1981); Nutt, Garden (London) 107(2): front cover [habitat] (1982). PLATES 19, 55, 56.

FLOWERING PERIOD. Summer (April–July), except in cultivation when it usually flowers in spring (March–April).

HABITAT. A high altitude, alpine species, occurring at 2400–2600 m, sometimes at lower altitudes, between 1200 and 2000 m. Typically it grows on mountain pastures, amongst melting snow and where the ground is very wet, sometimes in close proximity to standing water; occasionally at the margins of forest and other woodlands.

DISTRIBUTION. Central Caucasus, in Georgia (incl. Abkhazia) and Russia (Severo-Ostenskaya). MAP 12, page 188.

192

Plate 36. Leaves of *Galanthus peshmenii*, growing in limestone rocks, eastern Mediterranean island of Kastellorhizo, Greece, 19 February 1992. Photo by A.P. Davis.

Plate 37. *Galanthus alpinus* var. *alpinus* in cultivation, from a collection made by W. McLewin in Borjomi, Georgia. Photo by J. Fielding.

Plate 38. *Galanthus alpinus* var. *bortkewitschianus*, growing in the University of Nalchik Botanic Gardens, Nalchik, Karbardino-Balcaria, southern Russia, 25 March 1992. Photo by A.P. Davis.

Plate 39. *Galanthus angustifolius*, growing in the University of Nalchik Botanic Gardens, Nalchik, Karbardino-Balcaria, southern Russia, 25 March 1992. Photo by A.P. Davis.

Plate 40. *Galanthus koenenianus*, close-up of leaf under-surface. Photo by M. Koenen.

Plate 41. *Galanthus koenenianus* in cultivation, February 1998. Photo by J. Fielding.

Plate 42. *Galanthus fosteri* growing in the shade of limestone rocks, Amasya, northern central Turkey. Photo by T. Baytop.

Plate 43. *Galanthus rizehensis* in the Krasnodar region of the western Transcaucasus, southern Russia, 1 April 1992. Photo by A.P. Davis.

Plate 44. *Galanthus rizehensis*, Maçka, near Trabzon in northeastern Turkey. Photo by T. Baytop.

Plate 45. *Galanthus lagodechianus* in cultivation at the Royal Botanic Gardens, Kew. Photo by B. Mathew.

Plate 46. *Galanthus lagodechianus* growing in the University of Nalchik Botanic Gardens, Nalchik, Karbardino-Balcaria, southern Russia, 25 March 1992. Photo by A.P. Davis

Plate 47. *Galanthus transcaucasicus*, Ramsar, northern Iran, 12 April 1976.

Plate 48. Collecting *Galanthus transcaucasicus* in the Talysh, northwest Iran. Photo by B. Mathew.

Plate 49. *Galanthus woronowii* in cultivation. Photo by B. Mathew.

Plate 50. *Galanthus ikariae* amongst ivy (*Hedera helix*) and Cyclamen (*Cyclamen hederifolium*), the central Aegean island of Ikaria, Greece, 1 March 1991. Photo by A.P. Davis.

Plate 51. *Galanthus ikariae* growing in the arboretum at the Royal Botanic Gardens, Kew, 26 February 1994. Photo by A.P. Davis.

Plate 52. *Galanthus krasnovii* near melting snow, northeast Turkey, 23 April 1997. Photo by A.P. Davis.

Plate 53. *Galanthus krasnovii*, northeast Turkey, 23 April 1997. Photo by A.P. Davis.

Plate 54. *Galanthus krasnovii*, close-up of flower. Photo by R. Hyam.

Plate 55. *Galanthus platyphyllus*, near the Krestovy Pass, Georgia, 25 June 1978. Photo by R.D. Nutt.

Plate 56. Habitat of *Galanthus platyphyllus*, near the Krestovy Pass, Georgia. Photo by E.M. Rix.

HYBRIDS

1. GALANTHUS × ALLENII

In 1891 Baker described *Galanthus allenii* as a species new to science, in honour of J. Allen who sent material to him at Kew. Baker considered *G. allenii* to be midway between *G. latifolius* Rupr. (now *G. platyphyllus* Traub & Moldenke) and *G. nivalis* subsp. *caucasicus* Baker (now known as *G. alpinus* Sosn.), having the short, broad leaves of the former species, but resembling the latter species by possessing slightly glaucous leaves (fully glaucous in *G. alpinus*). Baker also states that this plant sometimes has anthers with an apiculum (point) as in *G. nivalis* subsp. *caucasicus*, and sometimes without, as in *G. latifolius*. Although Baker did not explicitly state whether this species was a hybrid, Allen (1891) later wrote: 'Mr. Baker thinks it is probably a hybrid between *G. latifolius* and *G. caucasicus*, as it has some of the features of each species'.

Allen acquired material of *Galanthus allenii* by accident in 1883, when he ordered a consignment of *Galanthus latifolius* from the Austrian nurseryman Gusmus. Since this chance introduction no new collections have been made, and no record of the existence of *G. allenii* can be found in any herbaria or regional Floras of the Caucasus. Therefore, it seems likely that *G. allenii* is known only as a single collection—that sent to Allen by Gusmus, i.e., the type collection (26 ii 1889, Hort., *Allen s.n.*).

It is possible that *Galanthus allenii* could have arisen in cultivation as it is feasible that a cross occurred in either the nursery of Gusmus or the garden of Allen. It is likely that both growers had many other *Galanthus* in their collections, including species from the Caucasus, thus allowing any number of crosses to have occurred inadvertently. One must also remember that Allen did not send bulbs to Baker until five years after receiving them from Gusmus, which is enough time for a cross to occur and a seedling to grow to flowering size. Furthermore, it is not clear from Allen's communications to Baker (1891) whether he recognized this plant upon receiving his consignment of *G. latifolius* or some time after it had grown in his garden.

The origin of *Galanthus allenii* is ambiguous because although it is rumoured to have been collected in the Caucasus (see also Stern, 1956), nowhere in the literature is the place or time of collection stated with certainty. Baker states in his description that: 'he [Allen] received the bulb in 1883 amongst a stock of the Caucasian *G. latifolius*, from Gusmus'. No details of the origin for *G. allenii* were actually given; all that is implied is that *G. latifolius* is from the Caucasus. It is also possible that Gusmus collected his stocks some time before 1883. One further consideration to bear in mind is that *G. latifolius* is not the only species occurring in the Caucasus, as several other *Galanthus* species can also be found there.

On morphological evidence the theory of a hybrid origin for this species (Baker, 1891) can neither be proved or discounted, although *Galanthus allenii* does share characteristics of the species proposed as its parents (Baker, 1891): broad leaves (up to 2.5 cm), supervolute vernation as in *G. platyphyllus*, and semi-glaucous leaves which approach those of the glaucous-leafed *G. alpinus*.

In contrast to morphological studies, molecular data (Davis, 1994) provide a strong case for a hybrid origin. Analysis of chloroplast DNA (cpDNA) using RFLP (restriction fragment length polymorphisms) methodology shows that *Galanthus allenii* has a very similar chloroplast genome to *G. angustifolius*, *G. alpinus*, and *G. transcaucasicus*. A preliminary study of ribosomal DNA (rbDNA) indicates that *G. allenii* has the shared ribosomal genome of *G. alpinus* and *G. woronowii*. When two species hybridize the ribosomal genome of both parents is represented in the offspring. The chloroplast genome, however, is maternally inherited; therefore, a hybrid usually contains only one chloroplast genome, that of the female parent. Analysis of the ribosomal and chloroplast DNA of *G. platyphyllus* indicates that this species is not involved in the parentage of *G. allenii*.

To summarize, the molecular data show that *Galanthus allenii* is probably a hybrid, most likely between either *G. transcaucasicus*, *G. alpinus*, or *G. angustifolius* and *G. woronowii*. This probability is logically consistent with the other information we have about *G. allenii*, because we know that at least two of the possible parent species were in cultivation together at the end of the nineteenth century (i.e., *G. alpinus* and *G. woronowii*). That *G. platyphyllus* is one of the potential parents of *G. allenii* is less convincing because it has always been rare in cultivation; furthermore, it is far less likely that this species was collected frequently owing to its greater inaccessibility (the high Caucasus). Information on *G. platyphyllus* ties in well with the molecular evidence for *G. allenii*, which shows that there is very little similarity between the cpDNA and rbDNA of this species and the hybrid.

Based on the evidence presented above it seems reasonable to assume that *Galanthus allenii* is a hybrid. Accordingly, this hybrid should be written as *Galanthus × allenii*, using the × to indicate hybrid status. It seems unlikely that *G. × allenii* is a hybrid that was formed in nature, because, of the species indicated as its likely parents, none have been recorded as occurring in close proximity in the wild. A hybridization event between *G. platyphyllus* and *G. alpinus*, for example, is immediately excluded because these two species are separated by a considerable distance, and they occupy quite different ecological niches. It is more probable that *G. woronowii* and *G. alpinus* have hybridized, because their distributions overlap slightly. But even this scenario is not very realistic, as populations of these species have never been reported in the same area; it is more probable that these two species have hybridized in cultivation.

CULTIVATION. *Galanthus × allenii* is an attractive snowdrop and is coveted by many growers. It is available in commerce but never in large numbers, probably because it is relatively slow to bulk-up. It also has the habit of dying for no apparent reason, leaving the grower with the resolve never to try it again. I cannot offer any explanation for this phenomenon; in some gardens it does very well and looks splendid, but in others it never 'gets going'. Giving it optimal conditions will certainly help, and if one has several bulbs it is well worth placing them in separate parts of the garden to find a site that suits it. Personally, I find that *G. × allenii* does well on chalk and in locations that do not become too wet.

Galanthus × allenii *Baker* (?*G. alpinus* Sosn. × *G. woronowii* Losinsk.). *G. allenii* Baker in Gard. Chron. ser. 3, 9: 298 (1891), 'alleni'; J. Allen in J. Roy. Hort. Soc. 13: 177, 178, fig. 2 (1891); Ewbank in Garden (London) 39: 272 (1891); Bowles in J. Roy. Hort. Soc. 43: 34, fig 12 (1918); Traub & Moldenke in Herbertia 14: 110 (1948); Stern, Snowdr. & Snowfl.: 62, pl. 5 (1956); C.D. Brickell in Walters et al. (eds.), Europ. Gard. Fl. 1: 319 (1986). Ind. loc.: 'He [J. Allen] received the bulb in 1883 amongst a stock of the Caucasian *G. lati-folius,* from Austria, from Herr Gusmus . . . he [J. Allen] sent it to me [Baker] again in 1890'. Type: from Jas. Allen Esq., Shepton Mallet, 26 ii 1891 [Hort. Allen, Shepton Mallet 26 ii 1889]. (holotype K!).

G. latifolius Rupr. forma *allenii* (Baker) Beck in Wiener Ill. Gart.-Zeitung 19: 56, fig. 2,16 (1894).

G. nivalis L. subsp. *allenii* (Baker) Gottl.-Tann. in Abh. K. K. Zool.-Bot. Ges. Wien 2(4):37 (1904), *pro parte excl. G. ikariae* Baker.

G. perryi hort. Ware ex Baker in Gard. Chron. ser. 3, 13: 258 (1893); Traub & Moldenke in Herbertia 14: 109 (1948). Ind. loc.: 'My description is drawn from a plant kindly sent to me by Mr. Jas. Allen, with whom it flowered this year at Shepton Mallet, the second week in February'. Type: hort, Jas. Allen, 14 ii 1893, (holotype K!).

DESCRIPTION. *Bulb* ± ovoid, 1.5–3 cm × 1.3–3 cm. *Sheath* 4.5–7 cm × 0.5–0.7 cm. *Leaves* supervolute in vernation; lorate to narrowly oblanceolate, at flowering 8–15(–22) cm × 1–2 cm, after flowering developing to 10–18(–25) cm × 1–2.4 cm, erecto-patent to recurving at maturity; matt-green to glaucescent, often described as being like the colour of pewter, surfaces concolorous; surfaces smooth; midrib conspicuous; margins flat; apex obtuse to acute, flat. *Scape* 8–12 cm long, matt-green to glaucescent. *Pedicel* 2–3 cm long. *Outer perianth segments* narrowly obovate, 1.5–2.5(–3) cm × 0.7–1.1 cm, slightly unguiculate. *Inner perianth segments* ± cuneate to obovate, 0.7–1.2 cm × 0.4–0.6 cm, emarginate; each segment with a variable ± ∧-shaped mark on the adaxial surface above the apical notch; abaxial mark similar in size and shape to the adaxial marking, or extending to almost half the distance to the base of the segment. *Anthers* tapering to an apiculum. *Capsule* not known to develop.

ILLUSTRATIONS. J. Allen in J. Roy. Hort. Soc. 13: 177, 178, fig. 2 (1891); Bowles in J. Roy. Hort. Soc. 43: 34, fig. 12 (1918); Stern, Snowdr. & Snowfl.: 62, pl. 5 (1956).

FLOWERING PERIOD. Spring (February to March).

HABITAT. Not known.

DISTRIBUTION. Not known with certainty; said to have originated from the Caucasus but probably a garden hybrid.

2. GALANTHUS × GRANDIFLORUS

This hybrid was described by Baker (1893c) as *Galanthus maximus*, but he changed it to *G. grandiflorus* (Baker, 1893e) because Velenovsky (1891) had earlier used this name in connection with another plant (see account of *G. elwesii*). Baker (1893c) did not know if *G. maximus* was a new species or a hybrid, as he states: 'if not a true species, it is, no doubt, as Mrs R.O. Backhouse suggests, a hybrid between *G. plicatus* and one of the varieties of *nivalis*, such as Imperati, Melvilleior Redoutei'. Yeo (1963) investigated the origin of *G. grandiflorus* on the basis of morphology and came to the conclusion that it was a hybrid between *G. caucasicus* and *G. plicatus*. (Yeo was probably not using *G. caucasicus* in his experiments but the variant of *G. elwesii* with a single mark on each inner perianth segment). In spite of his investigation Yeo also states that *G. × grandiflorus* could be a hybrid between *G. nivalis* and *G. plicatus*, based on the fact that R.O. Backhouse had raised hybrids between these species.

After investigation of the type specimen of *Galanthus × grandiflorus* and with reference to the description given by Baker, I think it is impossible to determine the exact parentage of this hybrid. And as this plant is probably no longer in cultivation, a more detailed study cannot be made. It is quite obvious, however, that there is a strong influence of *G. plicatus*, due to the degree of folding in the leaves (i.e. nearly fully explicative, and thus approaching *G. plicatus*). The other parent of *G. × grandiflorus* could be *G. nivalis*, *G. elwesii*, or perhaps any of the large garden hybrids that were in cultivation in Backhouse's garden, such as those listed by Baker.

Galanthus × grandiflorus *Baker* in Gard. Chron. ser. 3, 13: 656 (1893). Ind. loc.: I have received a good supply of this living plant from R.O. Backhouse of Sutton Court, near Hereford. Type: J.E. Backhouse, Sutton Court, Hereford, 16 iii 1893 (K!).

G. × maximus Baker in Gard. Chron. ser. 3, 13: 354 (1893), *non* Velen.

?*G. × valentinei* Beck in Wiener Ill. Gart.-Zeitung 19: 57 (1894).

CULTIVARS

Despite the relatively small size and uniformity of the genus, well over 500 *Galanthus* cultivars have been named. To provide an exhaustive list of them is beyond the scope of this book, particularly as many have not been widely distributed, and information on the most recently introduced cultivars is scarce. What I have attempted to do here is provide an account of those cultivars that are either currently in cultivation and widely available, or recorded in the literature.

This list has been assembled from three main sources: published works (books and journals); sales catalogues; and miscellaneous notes, letters, and personal communication. Wherever I have used information from a published work I have cited the source, either directly in the text or under the subheading 'Literature'. The publications of Richard Nutt (mainly Nutt, 1993) and the sales catalogues of North Green Snowdrops (John Morley) were used extensively as a source of information for this checklist; the unpublished *A Gardener's Guide to Snowdrops* by Daphne Chappell and Phil Cornish was also very helpful.

Every effort has been made to follow the rules and guidelines of the *International Code of Nomenclature for Cultivated Plants* (ICNCP) to ensure the correct use and stability of names. I have made some nomenclatural changes, which are either explained in the text or under the subheading 'Note'. Where possible, I have identified the correct spelling for each epithet and placed spelling variants under the subheading 'Synonyms'.

After each cultivar name that does not have a species name preceding it is a number in parentheses. This number denotes either the most likely parentage of the hybrid or the species from which each cultivar has been modified; the main characters of species are fully described in the Taxonomy of *Galanthus*. An explanation of these codes is given below. The literature listed in this section has its own bibliography, located in Appendix 7.

In this section I have retained the use of ovary in place of receptacle. Ovary is not the correct botanical term for this structure, but as it is widely used in the horticultural literature I have kept it here to avoid confusion. Other descriptive terms are the same as those found in the Taxonomy of *Galanthus*.

I would like to acknowledge Ruby Baker, Matt Bishop, and Dr John Grimshaw for their help in correcting this annotated checklist.

Explanation of Codes Used in this Section

(1) A hybrid of unknown parentage, or a cultivar derived from a species that cannot be identified with certainty.

(2) A hybrid that has *Galanthus nivalis* as one of its parents, or a cultivar derived from *G. nivalis* that shows many of the main characteristics of *G. nivalis* but is not part of the natural variation of this species.

(3) A hybrid that has *Galanthus plicatus* as one of its parents, or a cultivar derived from *G. plicatus* that shows many of the main characteristics of *G. plicatus* but is not part of the natural variation of this species.

(4) A hybrid that has *Galanthus elwesii* as one of its parents, or a cultivar derived from *G. elwesii* that shows many of the main characteristics of *G. elwesii* but is not part of the natural variation of this species.

(5) A hybrid between *Galanthus nivalis* and *G. plicatus*, the gender and exact parentage of which are unknown, unless stated in the text.

(6) A hybrid between *Galanthus elwesii* and *G. plicatus*, the gender and exact parentage of which are unknown, unless stated in the text.

(*) Cultivar epithet previously used as a formal scientific name (e.g. as a species). See the Taxonomy of *Galanthus* and Appendix 5.

The awards listed in the following section are those given to *Galanthus* cultivars by The Royal Horticultural Society (RHS). The acronyms used in this chapter to denote those awards are: **AGM** (Award of Garden Merit), **FCC** (First Class Certificate), **AM** (Award of

199

Merit), and **PC** (Certificate of Preliminary Commendation). (See also the Glossary.)

ALPHABETICAL LIST OF CULTIVARS

G. elwesii **'Abington Green'** A selection made by Revd R.J. Blakeway-Phillips. Leaves supervolute in vernation, glaucous. Inner perianth segments with a large mark covering most of the segment except the base and margin.
Literature: Nutt (1993, p. 511).

G. 'Ace of Spades'—see *G. plicatus* 'Trym'

G. nivalis 'Albus'—see *G. nivalis* 'Poculiformis' (not an exclusive association)

G. **'Anglesey Abbey'** (2) Found in the garden at Anglesey Abbey, Cambridgeshire. This cultivar has often been associated with *G. lagodechianus*, because it has the same general features as this species: applanate vernation, green leaves, and a single mark at the apex of each inner perianth segment. Closer investigation, however, shows that this snowdrop is not *G. lagodechianus* but a hybrid. It is likely that *G. nivalis* is one of the parents. The inner perianth marks on the outer face of the segments are similar to *G. nivalis*; on the inner face of the inner segments the green lines run all the way to the base, another characteristic of *G. nivalis* but not of *G. lagodechianus* or most other green-leaved snowdrops.
Literature: Nutt (1993, p. 516, as a synonym of *G. lagodechianus*).

G. **'Anne of Geierstein'** (5) A seedling of *G. plicatus* raised by James Allen. Named by William Thomson after a character in Sir Walter Scott's novel *Anne of Geierstein*. A drawing of this snowdrop resides in the Lindley Library, marked by Bowles as: *G. plicatus* × *G. nivalis*, 'Anne of Geierstein', from Samuel Arnott, Dumfries, 29 February 1916. A tallish snowdrop with large, pure white flowers. The base of the outer perianth segments are unguiculate. Each inner perianth segment possesses a more or less ∧-shaped mark. Late flowering. A rare plant, said to require careful cultivation.
Literature: Arnott (1913, p. 154); Bowles (1956, p. 56); Stern (1956, p. 71); Nutt (1993, p. 511).

200

G. nivalis **'April Fool'** Found in the 1960s by Tony Venison of Hert-fordshire. Given this name because it is said to flower on 1 April, al-though it is very rarely this late. The inner perianth mark is typical of *G. nivalis* variants, i.e., more or less ∧-shaped with the ends of the ∧ thickened (see FIGURE 8, A and B).
Literature: Nutt (1993, p. 518).

G. **'Armine'** (3) A selected seedling from Hyde Lodge, Gloucester-shire, and named in the late 1950s after the daughter of Brigadier L.W.H. Mathias and Mrs W.V. Mathias (who at the time were the owners of Hyde Lodge, home of the Giant Snowdrop Company). A large, late-flowering *G. plicatus* hybrid. The inner perianth mark is very distinct and characteristic: at the apex of the segment is a pale, more or less ∧-shaped mark, and at the base are two elliptic marks resembling a pair of eyes.
Literature: Nutt (1993, p. 511).

G. 'Arnott's Seedling'—see *G.* 'S. Arnott'

G. **'Atkinsii'** * (2 or 5) According to Bowles (1914, pp. 48–49; 1956, p. 65), James Atkins of Painswick received this snowdrop from a friend in the late 1860s. Atkins passed it on to Canon Ellacombe, who in turn sent it to Bowles. In 1875 it was offered by Messrs. Barr under the name of *G. imperati*, who sent it out at 2s 6d per bulb. It was named *G. nivalis* 'Atkinsii' by James Allen (1891), but after this date it was often still associated with the epithet *imperati*, for exam-ple as *G. imperati* var. *atkinsii*. The exact parentage of *G.* 'Atkinsii' is not known, but is almost certainly involves *G. nivalis* and *G. plicatus*. One or both of the leaf margins may be slightly explicative, espe-cially near the base, indicating the influence of *G. plicatus* in the ge-netic make-up. Whatever its origin, this is undeniably an extremely good garden plant. *Galanthus* 'Atkinsii' is tall, well proportioned, handsome, and early flowering (January–February). The outer seg-ments are very long and rather narrow, which gives the flower a very characteristic shape, even when it is in bud. The inner perianth seg-ments bear a single, thick, ∧-shaped or inverted heart-shaped mark. Perhaps the most diagnostic feature of *G.* 'Atkinsii' is the presence of a misshapen outer perianth segment, although this is not a uni-versal feature, which brings us to a contentious issue regarding the identity of this snowdrop. Bowles (1918, p. 31) informs us that R.O. Backhouse distributed a variant similar to 'Atkinsii' that had the

201

tiresome habit of seldom producing a perfectly formed flower: 'Either they have an extra segment, or one of the inner ones is longer than the others, or again, a petaloid white bract may appear just below the ovary'. These are features that often appear in what we know today as *G.* 'Atkinsii'. A note in the proceedings of the Royal Horticultural Society of 1916 (Bowles, 1917b, p. xli) confirms that Bowles believed that this was not the form originally distributed by Atkins. Arnott (1917, pp. 100–101) referred to the form with an aberrant segment as "pseudo-Atkinsii". According to the early literature, it thus appears that the plant that we know today as *G.* 'Atkinsii' is not the original.

Literature: Allen (1891, p. 174); Burbidge (1891a, pp. 203, 204); Arnott (1899a, p. 130); Mallet (1905, p. 87); Arnott (1917, pp. 100–101); Bowles (1918, p. 31); Synge (1950, p. 64); Stern (1951, p. 75); Bowles (1956, p. 65); Stern (1956, p. 71); Wyatt (1956, p. 297); Mathias (1958, pp. 147, 149); Nutt (1974, p. 20); Trehane (1989, p. 201); Royal General Bulbgrowers' Association (1991, p. 239); Nutt (1993, p. 511).

Illustrations: Mathias (1958, b/w photo p. 149); Rix and Phillips (1981, p. 17, fig. g); Nutt (1974, fig. 10, b/w photo); Brown (1996, col. photo p. 56).

Awards: **AM** shown on 10 February 1920 by Revd W. Wilks, see J. Roy. Hort. Soc. 46 (1 and 2): lv (1920–21), as *G. nivalis*, Atkins' variety.

Synonyms: *G. imperati* var. *atkinsii*.

G. 'Atkinsii Moccas Form'—see *G.* 'Moccas'

G. 'Atkinsii Moccas Strain'—see *G.* 'Moccas'

G. 'Atkinsii' Moccas Strain—see *G.* 'Moccas'

G. plicatus **'Augustus'** A selection of *G. plicatus*, named after E.A. Bowles by Amy Doncaster. The leaves are broad (c. 2.5–3 cm), pale green to slightly yellowish, and lie flat to the ground. The flowers are large and rounded and have a large, thick, more or less X-shaped mark on the inner perianth segments. Often described as 'dumpy' or 'chubby'. An attractive and distinctive snowdrop which, despite its virused-looking leaves, is robust and quick to multiply.

Literature: Trehane (1989, p. 201); Nutt (1993, p. 511).

G. **'Backhouse No. 12'** (2 or 5) Originally produced by R.O. Backhouse and later distributed by Lady Beatrix Stanley, who probably obtained it from E.A. Bowles. Distributed by Oliver Wyatt during the 1950s and 1960s. Similar to *G.* 'Backhouse Spectacles' and other large *G. nivalis* hybrids. Not common and now probably confused with other snowdrops of the *G.* 'Atkinsii' ilk. Leaves glaucescent, one or both margins slightly explicative. Inner perianth segments with a *nivalis*-like, ∧-shaped mark. Ovary deep green, elongated.
Literature: Wyatt (1956, p. 297); Trehane (1989, p. 201); Royal General Bulbgrowers' Association (1991, p. 245); Nutt (1993, p. 517).
Synonyms: *G.* 'Mrs Backhouse', *G.* 'Mrs Backhouse No. 12'.

G. **'Backhouse Spectacles'** (2 or 5) According to Nutt (1993, p. 512), Lady Beatrix Stanley sent this snowdrop to Oliver Wyatt of Maidwell Hall, Northampton, and he distributed it in the 1950s and 1960s. Wyatt sent plants to R.D. Trotter, and according to him it was one of the hybrids raised by R.O. Backhouse of Sutton Court. (In the 1920s Backhouse experimented with crosses raised from *G. plicatus* and *G. nivalis* [note by E.A. Bowles in J. Roy. Hort. Soc. 46: xxxvi, 1920–21]). Two ideas explain the origin of the name *G.* 'Backhouse Spectacles'. Some say that it was so named because Mrs Backhouse left her spectacles by this snowdrop, and others say the name comes from the mark on each inner perianth segment that looks like a pair of spectacles. Similar to *G.* 'Atkinsii', although the outer segments are smaller and shorter and do not have misshapen segments.
Literature: Hellyer (1982, p. 475); Trehane (1989, p. 201); Royal General Bulbgrowers' Association (1991, p. 239); Nutt (1993, p. 512).
Synonyms: *G.* 'Mrs Backhouse's Spectacles'.

G. 'Barbara' and *G.* 'Barbara Double'—see *G. plicatus* 'Barbara's Double'

G. **'Barbara's Double'** Believed to have been collected by E.A. Bowles from Lady Beatrix Stanley's garden at Sibbertoft. Named after Lady Beatrix Stanley's daughter, Lady Barbara Buchanan. A double *G. plicatus* with a well proportioned habit and nicely rounded flowers. Outer perianth segments three, inner perianth segments c. 12–15, more or less uniform, forming a very neat, tight rosette. The outermost inner perianth segments have a single,

more or less ∧-shaped mark at the apex. The leaves are often rather short at flowering time.
Literature: Nutt (1981, p. 476); Nutt (1993, p. 512).
Synonyms: *G.* 'Barbara', *G.* 'Barbara Double'.

G. **'Benhall Beauty'** (1 or ?6) A snowdrop raised by John Gray, at his garden at Benhall, Suffolk, and named in 1961 by E.A. Bowles. A tall, upright snowdrop. Leaves applanate in vernation, linear, glaucous, and slightly explicative at the margins (suggesting the influence of *G. plicatus*). Inner perianth segments with two marks, apical and basal. The apical mark is ∩- to ∧-shaped with the tips of each mark enlarged and rounded. The basal mark is fainter than the apical mark and looks like a small pair of pincers, although sometimes it is divided into two smaller marks, and then it resembles a pair of single quotation marks. Ovary elongated. A charming snowdrop with a good scent.
Literature: Anderson (1973, p. 44); Trehane (1989, p. 201); Nutt (1993, p. 512).
Illustrations: Brown (1996, col. photo on p. 56).
Synonyms: *G.* 'Benthall Beauty'.

G. **'Benhall Seedling'** Another of the snowdrops raised by John Gray in his garden at Benhall, Suffolk, and named by E.A. Bowles. Rare and possibly no longer in cultivation.
Literature: Anderson (1973, p. 44).

G. 'Benthall Beauty'—see *G.* 'Benhall Beauty'

G. **'Bertram Anderson'** (?6) Selected and named by C.D. Brickell from seedlings found in the late E.B. Anderson's garden at Lower Slaughter, Gloucestershire. A large, chunky plant of great beauty. Leaves broad, glaucous, with explicative margins, indicating that *G. plicatus* is one of the parents of this hybrid. Flowers large, the outer perianth segments particularly well developed. Inner perianth segments with a single, large, broad, ∧-shaped mark. Sometimes confused with *G.* 'Mighty Atom' and *G.* 'Bill Bishop'. A first-class snowdrop.
Literature: Nutt (1993, p. 512); Bull. Alp. Gard. Soc. Gr. Brit. 64(4): 418 (1996).
Illustrations: Bull. Alp. Gard. Soc. Gr. Brit. 64(4): p. 414, b/w photo (1996).

204

Awards: **AM** shown at Vincent Square on 12 March 1996 by Dr R.M. Mackenzie, see Plant Awards 1995–96, Bull. Alp. Gard. Soc. Gr. Brit. 64(4): 418 (1996), author of article not given—includes history and description.

G. **'Bill Bishop'** (?6) Found in the garden of Bill Bishop. A large snowdrop similar to *G.* 'Bertram Anderson' and some of the plants known as *G.* 'Mighty Atom'. The flowers are very large and held on a long pedicel. The inner perianth segments have a single, bold, ∧-shaped mark at the apex. Not common but well worth growing.

G. **'Bitton'** (2) From Canon Ellacombe's garden at Bitton Rectory, Gloucestershire. A small but healthy-looking snowdrop, with an early-flowering habit. In overall dimensions this plant is like many of the other small to medium *G. nivalis* hybrids. The slightly folded leaf margins suggests the influence of *G. plicatus*. The inner perianth segments have a distinct, dark, more or less ∩-shaped mark. The ovary is pale green to yellowish, which is a consistent feature of this plant.
Literature: Trehane (1989, p. 200); Royal General Bulbgrowers' Association (1991, p. 245); Nutt (1993, p. 518).

G. **'Blewbury Tart'** (2) Found in the 1970s by Alan Street, in the churchyard of St. Michael's Church, Blewbury, Oxfordshire. A strange-looking, double snowdrop with upward-pointing flowers (i.e., held at an angle of c. 90°–140° to the scape). The leaves are like those of a medium-sized *G. nivalis*, with some folding at the margins. The rosette of inner perianth segments is uneven and strongly marked with green.

G. nivalis **'Boyd's Double'** Found by William Boyd in Miss Russell's garden at Ashiestiel (or sometimes spelt Ashiesteel) near Melrose, Berwickshire. A very curious and odd-looking double, with erect flowers. The outer and inner perianth segments do not fall into two easily defined whorls, as with most other snowdrops, although the outer ones are slightly larger. All the segments are very narrow, and can sometimes be partly fused together. The outer segments are streaked with green on their outer and inner faces. The inner perianth segments, which are also strongly marked with green, number c. 20, each with a more or less ∩-shaped mark at the apex. This is undoubtedly a very peculiar snowdrop, one that people seem to

205

either love or loathe. Not common in cultivation, because it is slow to increase. Hector Harrison has selected several similar snowdrops, including: *G. nivalis* 'Shuttlecock', *G. nivalis* 'Ermine Spikey', and *G. nivalis* 'Ermine Oddity'. Some of these are now making their way into wider cultivation.

Literature: Arnott (1907a, p. 264); Bowles (1914, pp. 55–56, without name); Wyatt (1966, p. 189); Nutt (1970a, p. 173); Royal General Bulbgrowers' Association (1991, p. 245); Nutt (1993, p. 518).

Synonyms: *G. nivalis* 'Boyd's Green', *G. nivalis* 'Boyd's Green Double', *G. nivalis* 'Double Green', *G. nivalis* 'Green Horror', *G. virescens* (double form), and *G. viridiflorus* flore pleno.

G. nivalis 'Boyd's Green'—see *G. nivalis* 'Boyd's Double'

G. nivalis 'Boyd's Green Double'—see *G. nivalis* 'Boyd's Double'

G. **'Brenda Troyle'** (5) This snowdrop most likely originated in Ireland, and it was probably named after one of the staff at Kilmacurragh Nurseries in Wexford (Nutt, 1974, p. 21). Another very good snowdrop of the *G.* 'S. Arnott' class. The leaves are narrower, and more heavily covered with a greyish bloom than many of the other *G. nivalis* hybrids; the leaf margins are slightly explicative. The flowers are nicely rounded and of good substance. The pedicel is longer than the spathe, unlike *G.* 'S. Arnott' where it is shorter. Each inner perianth segment is attractively marked with a deep green, broad, more or less inverted heart-shaped mark. The ovary is cone-shaped, tapering sharply towards the pedicel. The flowers are fragrant of honey. Another good snowdrop for those who like a refined, classical snowdrop.

Literature: Bowles (1956, p. 68); Stern (1956, p.71); J. Roy. Hort. Soc. 85(6): 276 (1960); Nutt (1974, p. 21); Nutt, in Lawrence (1986, p. 133); Trehane (1989, p. 201); Royal General Bulbgrowers' Association (1991, p. 240); Nutt (1993, p. 512).

Illustrations: (Nutt, 1974, fig. 16, b/w photo).

Awards: **AM** exhibited on 23 February 1960 by Sir Frederick Stern, see J. Roy. Hort. Soc. 85(6): 276 (1960)—includes description.

G. ikariae **'Butt's Form'** A selection of *G. ikariae* presumably made by the plantsman Walter Butt. This name dates back to around the mid-1960s and has occurred intermittently in specialist snowdrop catalogues. This is a neat, well-proportioned snowdrop, with good-sized flowers. The inner perianth segments are marked with a large, deep green blotch that extends over half the length of the outer face. Stronger growing and more robust than many other introductions of *G. ikariae*. This snowdrop does well when planted under deciduous trees.

G. reginae-olgae **'Cambridge'** A clone of *G. reginae-olgae* subsp. *reginae-olgae* from the Cambridge Botanic Garden, which was probably accessioned there in the 1960s. A large flowered variant of the species. The leaves are emergent at flowering time. The inner perianth mark is ∧-shaped, like the species, and bold. Sweetly scented. Awards: **AM** exhibited on 31 October 1989 by Mrs K.N. Dryden, see Proc. Roy. Hort. Soc. 115: 122 (1990); see also Plant Awards 1989–90, Bull. Alp. Gard. Soc. Gr. Brit. 58(4): 360 (1990), written by R.D. Nutt—includes short history and description.

G. 'Carpenter's Shop'—see *G.* 'Carpentry Shop'

G. **'Carpentry Shop'** (2) A seedling selected by Oliver Wyatt at Maidwell Hall, between 1950 and 1960. It was so named because it was found near the carpentry shop. It is similar to *G.* 'Atkinsii' but the outer perianth segments are said to be narrower. The inner perianth segments have a ∧-shaped mark. Not a very distinct selection.
Literature: Nutt (1993, p. 512).
Synonyms: *G.* 'Carpenter's Shop'.

G. elwesii **'Cassaba'** Introduced by Edward Whittall at the end of the eighteenth century from a collection made in Cassaba (now Turgutlu), near Izmir in southwest Turkey. This plant is very much like the many other variants of *G. elwesii* and does not differ from the species as represented in the wild. The following description is based on early articles covering this snowdrop. Bulbs very large, long. Leaves distinctly glaucous, very stout, long and erect, narrow at the base and broad towards the apex. Vernation supervolute. Flowers of good size, borne on tall stems, the inner perianth mark more or less X-shaped, i.e., apical and basal mark joined to form one large mark. Recent collections from near Izmir closely resemble *G.* 'Cassaba', although many of these plants have applanate instead of supervolute vernation. It is likely that the original clone, sent out by Whittall, is no longer in cultivation.
Literature: Arnott (1894, p. 179); Burbidge (1894, p. 127); Ewbank

(1894, p. 125); Arnott (1899a, p. 129); Burbidge (1899, p. 165); Arnott (1912, p. 10); Anon. (1920, p. 62); Stern (1956, p. 71); Trehane (1989, p. 200); Royal General Bulbgrowers' Association (1991, p. 240).

Illustrations: Burbidge (1899, fig. 57, line drawing); Anon. (1920, fig. 25, b/w photo, as *G. elwesii* var. Cassaba).

Synonyms: *G. elwesii* 'Cassalia'—a misspelling of *G. elwesii* 'Cassaba'.

G. elwesii 'Cassalia'—see *G. elwesii* 'Cassaba'

G. **'Celia Blakeway-Phillips'** (2) Another snowdrop produced by the Revd R.J. Blakeway-Phillips, this one selected from seedlings during the 1980s. The leaves are glaucescent with slightly explicative margins. The inner perianth segments have a more or less X-shaped mark, which is usually divided horizontally in the middle, leaving either two eye-like marks at the base or a weak, rounded ∧-shaped mark.

Literature: Nutt (1993, p. 513).

G. **'Clare Blakeway-Phillips'** (2) A selection made in the 1960s by Angela Marchant of Bishop's Stortford, Hertfordshire. The leaves are pale green to green-glaucescent, virused-looking, c. 1.5 cm wide, with explicative margins. If growing well this cultivar can have two scapes. The outer perianth segments are unguiculate at the base. The inner perianth marks are more or less X-shaped, sometimes becoming fainter and striped at the midpoint or base. The ovary is elongated and usually pale green. It is said to prefer a sunny situation, although John Grimshaw reports that it was superb in the woodland garden of the late Primrose Warburg.

Literature: Blakeway-Phillips (1980, p. 420); Trehane (1989, p. 201); Royal General Bulbgrowers' Association (1991, p. 240); Nutt (1993, p. 513).

Awards: **PC** shown on 28th January 1975 by Revd R.J. Blakeway-Phillips, see Proc. Roy. Hort. Soc. 100(2): 103; see also Plant Awards 1974–75, Bull. Alp. Gard. Soc. Gr. Brit. 43(4): 312 (1975). **AM** shown on 17th February 1976 by Revd R.J. Blakeway-Phillips, see Proc. Roy. Hort. Soc. 101(1): 36 (1976), written by R.D. Nutt—includes history and a description.

G. elwesii **'Clun Green'** A seedling selected by the Revd R.J. Blakeway-Phillips in the 1980s. Leaves glaucous, supervolute in verna-

tion, margins flat. Inner perianth segments with a large more or less X-shaped mark.
Literature: Nutt (1993, p. 513).

G. **'Colesborne'** (4) Found by Henry J. Elwes in grass at Colesborne, Gloucestershire. Shown to the Scientific Committee of the RHS on February 14th, 1911. Elwes sent this snowdrop to E.A. Bowles, and he thought it to be one of the 'most beautiful of all'; Bowles (1914) called it G. 'Colesborne Seedling'. During the early stages of flowering this plant is rather dwarf, and the flower buds are held close to the ground. As development continues the plant becomes much taller and the flowers are elevated above the ground several centimetres by the growing pedicel, like many other G. elwesii clones. When growing well, bulbs will produce a second flower scape. The most distinctive feature of this snowdrop, however, is the nearly all green inner perianth segments. The large, green mark extends from the apex to the base, with a slight narrowing in the middle, leaving only a thin edge of white segment. The flowers are large, and the ovary is long and narrow. Not an easy plant to keep, hence its scarcity.
Literature: Bowles (1914, p. 58, as 'Colesborne Seedling'); Bowles (1917b, p. xlii); Bowles (1918, p. 35), without direct reference to the name G. 'Colesborne'; J. Roy. Hort. Soc. 76: 332 and 421 (1951), erroneously as Galanthus 'Merlin' on p. 332; Bowles (1956, p. 68); Stern (1956, p. 72); Mathias (1958, p. 147); Nutt (1970a, p. 173); Nutt (1993, p. 513).
Illustrations: Nutt (1970a, fig. 10, b/w photo); Royal General Bulbgrowers' Association (1991, p. 241).
Awards: **AM** exhibited on 6th March 1951 by Mrs W.V. Mathias, see J. Roy. Hort. Soc. 76(9): 332(1951), as Galanthus 'Merlin' (see J. Roy. Hort. Soc. 76(11): 421, for correction).
Synonyms: G. 'Colesborne Seedling'.

G. **Colesborne Group** This group includes snowdrops with almost entirely green inner perianth segments. The majority of these clones are either G. elwesii or hybrids including this species, hence the leaves are usually supervolute in vernation and distinctly glaucous. The near total greening of the inner perianth segments occurs quite often in G. elwesii and naming new clones with this characteristic should be avoided.
Literature: Nutt (1993, p. 513).
Example: G. elwesii 'Washfield Colesborne'.

209

G. 'Colesborne Seedling'—see *G.* 'Colesborne'

G. elwesii **'Comet'** A selection made by John Morley at Stoven, Suffolk. A very substantial snowdrop, with a large and beautifully marked flower held on a long pedicel. The outer perianth segments are sometimes marked with about five short, green lines at the apex, but this feature is variable. The inner perianth segments have a deep green, more or less inverted heart-shaped mark. Pedicel longer than the spathe.
Literature: Trehane (1989, p. 200); Nutt (1993, p. 512).
Synonyms: *G. caucasicus* 'Comet'.

G 'Cool Ballin Taggart'—see *G.* 'Coolballintaggart'

G. **'Coolballintaggart'** (2) Raised by the O'Mahony (born Pierce Charles Mahony) of Kerry, Ireland. E.A. Bowles received *G.* 'Coolballintaggart' from Ireland, and distributed it to other growers. Very similar to *G.* 'Straffan', with which it might be synonymous.
Literature: Nutt (1970a, p. 166); Nelson (1992, p. 13); Nutt (1993, p. 513).
Synonyms: *G.* 'Cool Ballin Taggart', *G.* 'Cool Ballintaggert, *G.* 'The O'Mahony', *G.* 'The O'Mahoney'.

G. 'Cool Ballintaggert—see *G.* 'Coolballintaggart'

G. **'Cordelia'** (5) One of the Greatorex Doubles, raised and named by H.A. Greatorex, of Norwich, from stock of *G. plicatus.* The Greatorex Doubles are all quite similar and it takes a very practiced eye to identify one from the other. *Galanthus* 'Cordelia' has a relatively neat rosette of c. 20–22 inner perianth segments, and at the apex of each inner segment is a large green mark. Later flowering than most of the other Greatorex Doubles.
Literature: Bowles (1956, p. 70); Stern (1956, p. 72); Royal General Bulbgrowers' Association (1991, p. 241); Nutt (1993, p. 513).
Illustrations: Brown (1996, p. 59, col. photo).

G. nivalis **'Courteen Hall'** Selected by Oliver Wyatt in the late 1960s from amongst a large number of *G. nivalis* at Courteen Hall, near Northampton. The apex of each outer perianth segment is marked with faint green lines that touch at each apex. During flowering, the base of the outer segments elongate and become unguiculate.

The inner perianth segments possess a reasonably large, more or less, ∧-shaped mark. The flower is thus similar to *G. nivalis* 'Viridiapice'. Scarce in cultivation.
Literature: Nutt (1993, p. 518).

G. '**Cowhouse Green**' Found by Mark Brown, in a field in Buckinghamshire. Like *G. plicatus* subsp. *plicatus* except it has olive-green lines running down the outside of the outer perianth segments.
Literature: Baron (1995, p. 33); Brown (1996, p. 59).

G. '**Curly**' (?5) A seedling selected at Hyde Lodge, Chalford, Gloucestershire, during the early 1960s. So named because of the way the narrow, dark green leaves curl downwards at the tips. The flowers are rather long and narrow. The inner perianth mark is more or less X-shaped, the upper limbs of the mark gradually fading and not reaching to the base of the segment.
Literature: Nutt (1971, p. 208); Nutt (1993, p. 514).

G. '**Desdemona**' (5) A Greatorex Double, raised and named by H.A. Greatorex, of Norwich, from stock of *G. plicatus.* According to Greatorex, *G.* 'Desdemona' was one of his best doubles. The rosettes are a little more irregular than many of the other Greatorex Doubles, but the plants make up for it by increasing quickly and having large, bold flowers (larger than *G.* 'Ophelia').
Literature: Bowles (1956, p. 69); Stern (1956, p. 70); Trehane (1989, p. 201); Royal General Bulbgrowers' Association (1991, p. 241); Nutt (1993, p. 514).

G. 'Dionysius'—see *G.* 'Dionysus'

G. '**Dionysus**' (5) Another of the Greatorex Doubles, raised and named by H.A. Greatorex, of Norwich. The flowers are quite open and loose, due to the small number of inner perianth segments in the rosette (c. 10). Each segment of the outer whorl of inner perianth segments possesses an inverted heart-shaped mark; the inner whorl of inner perianth segments are usually misshapen and have no distinct mark. One of the earlier-flowering doubles.
Literature: Trehane (1989, p. 201); Royal General Bulbgrowers' Association (1991, p. 241); Nutt (1993, p. 514).
Synonyms: *G.* 'Dionysius'.

G. Dunrobin Seedling—see *G.* 'Melvillei'

G. caucasicus double—see *G.* 'Lady Beatrix Stanley'

G. nivalis 'Double Green'—see *G. nivalis* 'Boyd's Double'

G. elwesii **'Earliest of All'** According to Nutt (1993, p. 512) this snowdrop was found by E.B. Barnes, of Northampton, amongst a selection of bulbs obtained from Barrs in 1928. Later it was distributed by Oliver Wyatt. Similar to *G. elwesii* 'Hiemalis' but with longer, narrower outer perianth segments, and a thinner ∧-shaped inner perianth mark. The reports of flowering times seem to vary greatly, but it usually flowers at about the same time as *G. elwesii* 'Hiemalis'. In very warm gardens and in favourable sites this snowdrop can flower as early as November. Oliver Wyatt also distributed another early-flowering *G. elwesii* called 'Earliest', which is very similar to 'Earliest of All'.
Literature: Nutt (1993, p. 512).

G. 'Eleana Blakeway-Phillips'—see *G.* 'Eleanor Blakeway-Phillips'

G. **'Eleanor Blakeway-Phillips'** (6) Found in a churchyard near Little Abington, and named by Revd R.J. Blakeway-Phillips after his wife. A large snowdrop with pure white flowers and inner perianth segments heavily marked with green. Vernation supervolute; leaf margins slightly explicative.
Literature: Blakeway-Phillips (1980, p. 420); Trehane (1989, p. 201).
Awards: **PC** shown on 31st January 1989 by Revd R.J. Blakeway-Phillips, see Plant Awards 1988–89, Bull. Alp. Gard. Soc. Gr. Brit. 57(4): 335 (1989), written by Revd R.J. Blakeway-Phillips—includes history and description.
Synonyms: *G.* 'Eleana Blakeway-Phillips'.

G. nivalis 'Ermine Oddity'—see snowdrops listed under *G. nivalis* 'Boyd's Double'

G. nivalis 'Ermine Spikey'—see snowdrops listed under *G. nivalis* 'Boyd's Double'

G. **'Faringdon Double'** (4) Found in 1988 by Ruby Baker in a churchyard, in Faringdon, Oxfordshire. A large snowdrop with semi-double flowers. The vernation is supervolute, and the leaves

are glaucous. The inner perianth segments have a more or less X-shaped mark. Flowering in January.
Literature: Brown (1996, p. 59).

G. elwesii **'Fat Boy'** A seedling of *G. elwesii* found by E.A. Bowles at Myddelton House, Middlesex. Reginald Farrer suggested to Bowles that this snowdrop be called 'Fat Boy' on account of its 'solid obesity'. Very similar to some plants distributed at the present time as *G. elwesii* 'Cassaba', except the leaves are wider and less erect. Flowers large and globular, held near the ground at the start of flowering but lifted above the leaves by the time it is in full flower. Each inner perianth segment with a more or less X-shaped mark. It will produce two, or up to four, scapes when growing strongly. Scarce in cultivation.
Literature: Bowles (1914, p. 59); Nutt (1993, p. 514).

G. **'Fieldgate Superb'** (3) A *G. plicatus* hybrid raised and selected by Colin Mason in his garden at Fieldgate Lane, Kenilworth, Warwickshire. Leaves with a strong influence of *G. plicatus*. Flowers large, up to 4 cm long. Inner perianth segments with a more or less X-shaped mark, the upper limbs of the X shorter than those near the base. When growing well *G.* 'Fieldgate Superb' will produce two scapes. A fine snowdrop.

G. nivalis **'Flavescens'** * This snowdrop is usually placed into the synonymy of *G. nivalis* 'Sandersii', but there seems to be no good reason for doing so. *Galanthus nivalis* 'Flavescens' was discovered by W.B. Boyd of Faldonside, Melrose, in a cottage garden in Northumberland before 1890. We also know that *G.* 'Sandersii' was collected in Northumberland, but by a different person and in a different garden (see Allen, 1891, p. 181). According to Allen this snowdrop is: 'rather larger than *G. lutescens* (a synonym of *G.* 'Sandersii'), and all the yellow points are brighter in colour with the exception of the flower-stem, which in my two plants seem rather paler'. And he goes on to say that *G.* 'Flavescens': 'is a very beautiful variety, and will be a great favourite when it becomes known. It also has the recommendation of growing and increasing freely'. It is uncertain whether the original clone of *G.* 'Flavescens' is still with us, particularly as the yellow snowdrops are not very strong or long-lived.
Literature: Burbidge (1890, p. 268); Allen (1891, p. 181); Burbidge (1891a, p. 292); Ewbank (1891, p. 272); Arnott (1899a, p. 130); Ar-

nott (1900, p. 189); Bowles (1914, p. 53); Stern (1951, pp. 73–74); Royal General Bulbgrowers' Association (1991, p. 246).
Illustrations: Nutt (1970a, fig. 9, b/w photo).
Synonyms: *G. flavescens.*

G. flavescens—see *G. nivalis* 'Flavescens'

G. nivalis flavescens flore pleno—see *G. nivalis* 'Lady Elphinstone'

G. nivalis 'Flavescens flore pleno'—see *G. nivalis* 'Lady Elphinstone'

G. caucasicus flore pleno—see *G.* 'Lady Beatrix Stanley'

G. nivalis **'Flore Pleno'** This snowdrop has been in cultivation since at least the 1730s (Furber, 1733). Several clones no doubt exist under this name, most of which differ in their degree of doubling (which may also vary from year to year). There are usually three to five outer perianth segments, which may be either regular or misshapen. The rosette is made up of c. 7 to 15 inner perianth segments, which always contain a high proportion of aberrant segments. A common and well-known snowdrop, and very easy to grow. It is not, however, to everyones liking and many people consider this double a little on the ugly side. Flowering from February to March.
Literature: Herbert (1837, p. 330); Allen (1891, p. 174); Trehane (1989, p. 200); Royal General Bulbgrowers' Association (1991, p. 246).
Illustrations: Brown (1996, col. photo p. 53).
Synonyms: *G. nivalis* var. *hortensis* flore semipleno.

G. elwesii **'Fred's Giant'** Found growing at the base of an old hedge about 35 years ago by the then head gardener of the Cruickshank Botanic Garden, Mr Fred Sutherland. A large, and very vigorous form of *G. elwesii* with flowers up to 6 cm across. The leaves are distinctly glaucous and c. 3 cm wide. The inner perianth segment markings are variable, but usually the apex of each segment bears a single, straight-sided, inverted heart-shaped mark, and the base shows a pair of thick vertical dashes; sometimes the basal dashes fuse with the apical mark to form a more or less X-shaped mark.
Awards: **PC** shown on 22 February 1992 by the University of Aberdeen, Cruickshank Botanic Garden, see Plant Awards 1991–92, Bull. Alp. Gard. Soc. Gr. Brit. 60(4): 413 (1992), written by K.A.

Beckett—includes history and description. **AM** shown at Dunblane on 18 February 1995 by E. Hamilton, see Plant Awards 1994–95, Bull. Alp. Gard. Soc. Gr. Brit. 63(4): 371 (1971).

G. **'Galatea'** (2) A seedling raised by James Allen before 1890. A relatively tall snowdrop that often has two scapes per bulb. Leaves glaucescent, margins slightly explicative on one or both sides. The characteristic feature of this plant is the long pedicel that is crooked at an angle of c. 90°. The flowers are of a good size, just smaller than *G.* 'S. Arnott'. The inner perianth is of the typical *G. nivalis* type, that is, ∧-shaped and lobed at the ends. A charming snowdrop, but unfortunately it is often mixed up with other clones possessing an angled pedicel (e.g. *G.* 'Wisley Magnet').
Literature: Allen (1891, p. 174); Ewbank (1894, p. 125); Bowles (1914, p. 57); Bowles (1918, pp. 31, 32); Bowles (1956, p. 67); Stern (1956, p. 72); Trehane (1989, p. 201); Royal General Bulbgrowers' Association (1991, p. 242); Nutt (1993, p. 514).
Illustrations: Bowles (1918, fig. 8, painting by Bowles).

G. **'Ginns' Imperati'** (2) This plant was originally collected in the 1950s by R. Gathorne-Hardy, from a site north of Rome. It was grown for many years by R. Ginns of Desborough, Northamptonshire, and for this reason acquired the name *G.* 'Ginns' Imperati'. A large, strong-growing and attractive plant. The overall dimensions and leaf characteristics of this cultivar suggest that it has hybridized in cultivation. The leaves are like those of the large *G. nivalis* variants found in southern Europe: glaucescent, with a faint, glaucous median line running down the length of the upper leaf surface; the margins very slightly explicative on either side, especially near the base. The single mark at the apex of the inner perianth segment is typical of *G. nivalis* (see FIGURE 8, A and B).
Literature: Nutt (1993, p. 515).
Illustrations: Bull. Alp. Gard. Soc. Gr. Brit. 42(4): b/w photo on p. 334, (1974).
Synonyms: *G. imperati* 'Ginn's Form', *G.* 'Imperati Ginn's Form', *G. nivalis* subsp. *imperati* 'Ginn's Form'.

G. 'Grandiflorus'—see Appendix 6 and *G.* × *grandiflorus* in the Hybrids chapter

G. 'Grandis'—see *G.* 'Straffan'

G. caucasicus grandis—see *G.* 'Straffan'

G. nivalis grandis—see *G.* 'Straffan'

G. plicatus **'Greenfield'** Found sometime around the 1950s or 1960s by Leon Schofield in a neglected garden called Greenfield, in Ireland. Each inner perianth segment has a single, very broad, dark, ∩-shaped mark at the apex, which covers a large proportion of the segment with green. The ovary is pale green to yellowish and rather elongated.
Literature: Nutt (1993, p. 515).

G. nivalis 'Green Horror'—see *G. nivalis* 'Boyd's Double'

G. nivalis 'Green Tip'—see *G. nivalis* 'Pusey Green Tip'

G. nivalis 'Green Tip Double'—see *G. nivalis* 'Pusey Green Tip'

G. nivalis **'Hambutt's Orchard'** A double snowdrop found in the late 1960s by Brigadier L.W. Mathias in a garden called Hambutt's Orchard in Stroud, Gloucestershire. Similar to *G. nivalis* 'Pusey Green Tip' but slightly larger. Each outer perianth segment has a mark composed of two to three green lines near the apex.
Literature: Nutt (1993, p. 518).

G. **'Herbert Ransom'** (?5) Another of the snowdrops originating from Hyde Lodge, Stroud, Gloucestershire (The Giant Snowdrop Company). This one was formerly known as Seedling Hyde No. 2, and then later it was named after the gardener there. The leaves are quite broad, glaucescent, with the margins explicative at the very edge. The inner perianth bears a more or less X-shaped mark, which becomes fainter and does not extend to the base of the segment.
Literature: Nutt (1993, p. 515).
Synonyms: *G.* 'Herbert Ransome', *G.* 'Ransom'.

G. elwesii **'Hiemalis'** * This cultivar was originally listed by Stern (1956) in his *Snowdrops and Snowflakes* as *G. caucasicus* Early form, and then later described as *G. caucasicus* var. *hiemalis* (Stern, 1963, p. 137). It was selected from stock growing in Sir Frederick Stern's garden at Highdown, Goring, Sussex. The flowering time is variable depending on location and the weather conditions, but is usually from late November to late December, or sometimes during January. Typical of other early-flowering variants of *G. elwesii*, the leaves are not well developed during the first few days of flowering but expand and elongate very rapidly soon afterwards. The flowers are not very large, and have long, narrow outer perianth segments. Each inner perianth segment has a single ∧-shaped mark at the apex. Note: *Galanthus caucasicus* var. *hiemalis* (Stern, 1961, p. 324); Stern, 1963, p. 137) is not a valid name, as its publication does not conform with the rules of the ICBN. I have used the epithet *hiemalis* here to represent this garden plant.

Literature: Stern (1963, p. 137, as *G. caucasicus* var. *hiemalis*); Trehane (1989, p. 200)

Illustrations: Stern (1956, fig. 14, line drawing).

Awards: **AM** exhibited on 29th November 1960 at the RHS, Vincent Square, by Sir Frederick Stern, see Proc. J. Roy. Hort. Soc. 86: 15 (1961).

Synonyms: *G. caucasicus* Early form, *G. caucasicus* var. *hiemale*, *G. caucasicus* var. *hiemalis*.

G. gracilis **'Highdown'** This distinct little snowdrop was from Sir Frederick Stern's garden at Highdown, Sussex. The leaves are very narrow (c. 6 mm or less), almost grassy, grey-glaucous, and conspicuously twisted along their axes. The inner perianth marks are yellowish green, and may either consist of two separate marks, apical and basal, or one more or less X-shaped mark. The ovary is yellowish and elongated. Easily grown in a sunny spot and once settled will quickly produce a very pleasing, grass-like clump.

Literature: J. Roy. Hort. Soc. 86(4): 181 (1961); Royal General Bulbgrowers' Association (1991, p. 242).

G. plicatus **'Hill Poë'** Found about 85 years ago by James Hill Poë growing under a walnut tree near the dining room window at Riverston, Ireland. Blanche Poë looked after her father's find and propagated it. In the 1950s David Shackleton sent plants to The Giant Snowdrop Company, where it was propagated and then later distributed. A really good, neat, *G. plicatus* double. Outer perianth segments five, rarely less, and not misshapen. The inner rosette is very neat, made up of 18 to 24 inner perianth segments, which are roughly the same length and remarkably uniform in shape. Easy to grow and reasonably fast to increase.

Literature: Nutt (1970a, p. 170); Trehane (1989, p. 201); Royal

217

General Bulbgrowers' Association (1991, p. 242); Nelson (1992, p. 13); Nutt (1993, p. 515).
Illustrations: Bull. Alp. Gard. Soc. Gr. Brit. 42(4): b/w photo on p. 334, (1974).
Awards: **PC** shown on 19 February 1974 by Revd R.J. Blakeway-Phillips, see Proc. Roy. Hort. Soc. 100(1): 13 (1974); see also Plant Awards 1973–74, Bull. Alp. Gard. Soc. Gr. Brit. 42(4): 343, 334 (1974), written by R.D. Nutt—includes history and description. **AM** shown on 17 March 1979 by Revd R.J. Blakeway-Phillips, see Plant Awards 1978–79, Bull. Alp. Gard. Soc. Gr. Brit. 47(4): 347 (1979).

G. **'Hippolyta'** (3) A Greatorex Double, raised and selected by H.A. Greatorex in the 1940s.
Leaves glaucescent; margins explicative and slightly undulate. Flowers held away from the scapes on 3–4 cm pedicels. The outer perianth segments are sometimes green tipped. The inner perianth segments are arranged quite loosely, and have a broad horseshoe-shaped to inverted heart-shaped mark at the apex. The inner whorls of inner perianth segments are more heavily stained with green. Some anthers present. Ovary large, conical.
Literature: Nutt (1970b, p. 191); Nutt (1971, p. 207); Trehane (1989, p. 201); Royal General Bulbgrowers' Association (1991, p. 242); Nutt (1993, p. 515).
Illustrations: Nutt in J. Roy. Hort. Soc. 96(4): fig. 77, b/w photo (1970).
Awards: **AM** exhibited on 17 March 1970 by R.D. Nutt, see Proc. Roy. Hort. Soc. 95(2): 103 (1970); see also J. Roy. Hort. Soc. 96(4): 191 (1970)—includes description; see also Plant Awards 1969–70, Bull. Alp. Gard. Soc. Gr. Brit. 38(4): 398 (1970), written by D.E. Saunders and R. Gorer.

G. nivalis **'Hololeucus'** * A poculiform snowdrop, similar to *G. nivalis* 'Poculiformis' but with rounded flowers and neater perianth segments.
Literature: Čelakovsky (1891, p. 198); Beck (1894, p. 50); Stern (1956, p. 73).

G. nivalis var. *hortensis* flore semipleno—see *G. nivalis* 'Flore Pleno'

G. nivalis 'Horwick Yellow'—see *G. nivalis* 'Sandersii'

G. nivalis 'Howick Yellow'—see *G. nivalis* 'Sandersii'

G. nivalis 'Humberts Orchard'—see *G. nivalis* 'Hambutt's Orchard'

G. nivalis **'Imperati'** * Considered by some to be a separate species, or either a subspecies or variety of *G. nivalis*. It was originally collected from central and southern Italy (for more information see the Taxonomy of *Galanthus*). Owing to its large size and good performance in gardens, this snowdrop was quickly established in cultivation. Like a number of other snowdrops originally found in the wild and later brought into cultivation, this plant's species epithet has been adopted as the cultivar name. In essence this is a large variant of *G. nivalis*. It has tallish scapes, larger than average flowers and a good bold mark on each inner perianth segment. The leaf margins are often revolute (turned or rolled under), particularly at the base, but are not explicative (sharply folded under) like the hybrids between *G. nivalis* and *G. plicatus*. Clones with slightly, moderately (or distinctly) explicative leaf margins are not *G.* 'Imperati'.
Literature: Allen (1891, pp. 172, 173, 174); Burbidge (1891a, pp. 192, 195, 196, 200, 201, 203, 204, 207, 209); Arnott (1899a, p. 130); Bowles (1914, p. 48); Bowles (1918, pp. 31, 33, 34, 36); Bowles (1956, p. 73); Stern (1956, p. 73).
Illustrations: Bowles (1918, fig. 5, painting by Bowles).

G. imperati 'Ginn's Form'—see *G. nivalis* 'Ginn's Imperati'

G. 'Imperati Ginn's Form'—see *G. nivalis* 'Ginn's Imperati'

G. nivalis subsp. *imperati* 'Ginn's Form'—see *G. nivalis* 'Ginn's Imperati'

G. imperati var. *atkinsii*—see *G.* 'Atkinsii'

G. **'Jacquenetta'** (5) Raised and named by H.A. Greatorex, of Norwich, from stock of *G. plicatus*. A double with a rounded and compact inner rosette. The inner perianth segments number between 25 and 30, and possess a large, broad, more or less horseshoe-shaped mark at the apex of each segment. Bowles (1956) commented that the inner perianth markings turn to a delightful apricot colour, in some years. The outside face of the outer perianth segments sometimes has green tips. Anthers usually present.
Literature: Stern (1956, pp. 70, 73); Trehane (1989, p. 201); Royal General Bulbgrowers' Association (1991, p. 243); Nutt (1993, p. 515).
Synonyms: *G.* 'Jaquenetta'.

G. 'Janet'—see *G.* 'Jenny Wren'

G. 'Jaquenetta'—see *G.* 'Jacquenetta'

G. 'Jenny'—see *G.* 'Jenny Wren'

G. **'Jenny Wren'** (5) A pleasing double, said to be a cross between *G. nivalis* 'Flore Pleno' (male) and *G. plicatus* (female). It originated in H.A. Greatorex's garden in Norfolk and was distributed by Fred Buglass in the early 1970s. A relatively small flower but with a neat, open rosette consisting of c. 15 to 17 inner perianth segments. On each inner perianth segment is a thin, ∧-shaped mark, which may break down to form two separate marks, one on either side of the apical notch. Anthers present.
Literature: Stern (1956, p. 73); Nutt (1993, p. 515).
Synonyms: *G.* 'Janet', *G.* 'Jenny'.

G. **'John Gray'** (1, ?4) This snowdrop was found in the garden of the late John Gray of Benham, Suffolk. It was grown-on and later named by E.B. Anderson when he had his garden at Lower Slaughter, Gloucestershire. It was first shown as a cut flower at the RHS, Vincent Square, in January 1961. *Galanthus* 'John Gray' surely ranks amongst the best of snowdrop cultivars. It is bold, beautiful, and easy to grow. The leaves are applanate in vernation, linear, glaucous, with more or less flat margins. The flowers are of a robust constitution, large, and egg-shaped in outline. During the start of flowering the scape is held at approximately 45°, but as time goes on the scape gradually lowers towards the ground (probably due to the weight of the bloom) until the flowers are held close to the soil. Each inner perianth segment has a bold, more or less X-shaped mark, which is deep green at the apex, becoming lighter and fading towards the base. The pedicel is very long and gracefully curved. Two other attributes of this species are its early-flowering habit and its potential to produce two flowering scapes from each bulb. The one possible negative feature of *G.* 'John Gray' is that the flowers can be splashed with mud or soiled during heavy rains because they are held so close to the soil; a top-dressing of pea-gravel helps to keep the flowers clean.
Literature: Anderson (1973, pp. 44, 149); Trehane (1989, p. 201); Royal General Bulbgrowers' Association (1991, p. 243); Nutt (1993, p. 516); Bull. Alp. Gard. Soc. Gr. Brit. 64(4): 413 (1996).

Illustrations: Bull. Alp. Gard. Soc. Gr. Brit. 40(4): b/w photo on p. 317 (1972); Anderson (1973, fig. 51, b/w photo); Bull. Alp. Gard. Soc. Gr. Brit. 64(4): b/w photo on p. 414 (1996); Brown (1996, col. photo on p. 58).

Awards: **AM** exhibited on 1 February 1972 by E. Hodgkin, see Proc. Roy. Hort. Soc. 97(2): 107 (1972); see also Plant Awards 1971–72, Bull. Alp. Gard. Soc. Gr. Brit. 40(4): 320 (1972), written by R.D. Nutt—includes history and description. **FCC** shown at Vincent Square on 20 February 1996 by Monksilver Nursery, and Dr R. Mackenzie, see Plant Awards 1995–96, Bull. Alp. Gard. Soc. Gr. Brit. 64(4): 413 (1996)—includes history and description.

G. **'Ketton'** (2) Introduced by E.A. Bowles from the village of Old Ketton, near Peterborough, Leicestershire, in 1948. A tall, strong snowdrop with good-sized flowers. Leaves glaucescent. At the apex of each inner perianth segment is a thin mark, which is usually composed of two small triangles on either side of the apical sinus, that either just touch at the apex or are separate; sometimes the mark is more green, resembling a little stone bridge. The pedicel is usually shorter than the spathe. Ovary similar to *G.* 'Brenda Troyle'. One of the mid-season snowdrops. Note: Bowles had several clones from Ketton; therefore, some variation is likely in the characters of this cultivar.

Literature: Bowles (1956, p. 68); Stern (1956, p. 73); Mathias (1958, p. 152); Trehane (1989, p. 201); Royal General Bulbgrowers' Association (1991, p. 243); Nutt (1993, p. 516).

Illustrations: Mathias (1958, b/w photo p. 152, as *Galanthus* Ketton); Bull. Alp. Gard. Soc. Gr. Brit. 64(4): b/w photo on p. 414, 1996).

Awards: **AM** shown at Vincent Square on 12 March 1996 by Dr R.M. Mackenzie, see Plant Awards 1995–96, Bull. Alp. Gard. Soc. Gr. Brit. 64(4): 418 (1996), author of article not given—includes history and description.

G. elwesii **'Kingston Double'** Found by Elizabeth Parker-Jervis in the 1960s at Kingston House, Kingston Bagpuize, Oxon. A double *G. elwesii*. The outer perianth segments are faintly marked with green. The rosette is very loose, and made up of a small number of mis-shapen inner perianth segments.

Literature: Trehane (1989, p. 200).

Synonyms: *G. elwesii* 'Kingstone Double'.

G. elwesii 'Kingstone Double'—see *G.* 'Kingston Double'

G. **'Kite'** (4) An unusual snowdrop that usually has two flowers per scape. Selected by Oliver Wyatt from seedlings raised at Maidwell Hall. The leaves are supervolute in vernation, broad and distinctly glaucous. The manner in which the flowers are presented differs slightly from year to year, and is hardly ever constant. The scape usually bears two flowers on a single pedicel, but there can be two pedicels with a flower on each, or sometimes only a single flower per scape as in the majority of snowdrops. The ovaries of each flower are usually free but in some years they can be fused at the base. The outer perianth segments are of medium to large size. Each inner perianth segment bears a broad, more or less X-shaped mark.
Literature: Nutt (1971, p. 167); Royal General Bulbgrowers' Association (1991, p. 243); Nutt (1993, p. 516).
Illustrations: Nutt (1971, fig. 61, b/w photo).
Synonyms: *G.* 'Maidwell A'.

G. **'Lady Beatrix Stanley'** (4) According to Oliver Wyatt (see Nutt, 1981), this double came from Lady Buchanan, who probably brought it from Sibbertoft, Northamptonshire. Formerly known as *G. caucasicus* flore pleno or *G. caucasicus* double, it was given a cultivar name by Richard Nutt in 1981. The leaves are supervolute in vernation, erect, flat at the margins and pale glaucous. The outer perianth segments are narrow and develop an unguiculate base. The inner perianth segments number c. 15–18 and form a reasonably tidy rosette, although misshapen segments are usually present. Each inner segment has an ill-defined, more or less ∧-shaped mark. A very early-flowering plant, and usually the first of the doubles. A hybrid of unknown parentage, but almost certainly having a strong influence of *G. elwesii* (not *G. caucasicus*). A strong, attractive, easy to grow double, instantly recognizable from other doubles by its erect, glaucous leaves.
Literature: Nutt (1971, pp. 169–170); Nutt (1981, pp. 475–476); Trehane (1989, p. 201); Royal General Bulbgrowers' Association (1991, p. 243); Nutt (1993, p. 516).
Illustrations: Nutt (1974, fig. 11, b/w photo, as double *G. caucasicus*); Nutt (1981, col. photo on p. 476); Bull. Alp. Gard. Soc. Gr. Brit. 50(4): b/w photo on p. 284 (1982).
Awards: **AM** shown on 16 February 1982, by Revd R.J. Blakeway-

Phillips, see Plant Awards 1981–82, Bull. Alp. Gard. Soc. Gr. Brit. 50(4): 290, b/w photo on p. 284 (1982), written by B. Mathew—includes history and description.
Synonyms: *G. caucasicus* flore pleno, *G. caucasicus* double.

G. nivalis **'Lady Elphinstone'** Found by Sir Graham Elphinstone in 1890, in a garden at Heawood Hall, Cheshire. Named by Samuel Arnott. Very similar to *G. nivalis* 'Flore Pleno' but the inner perianth segments are marked with yellow instead of green. Unfortunately the yellow coloration is not stable, and can be influenced by environment and situation. In some years the yellow coloration is very weak and may revert to green. This is not a particularly easy plant to grow. Some say that it does better on a neutral to acid soil. Time and patience are rewarded, however, as this can be a very charming and unusual snowdrop. Note: Bowles exhibited a double yellow form of *G. nivalis* at the RHS on 19 March 1912, J. Roy. Hort. Soc. 28(3): xxxviii (1913), which was probably *G.* 'Lady Elphinstone'.
Literature: Arnott (1907b, p. 189, as *G. nivalis* flavescens fl. pl.); Stern (1956, p. 73); Nutt (1970a, p. 170); Trehane (1989, p. 200); Royal General Bulbgrowers' Association (1991, p. 246); Nutt (1993, p. 518).
Synonyms: *G. nivalis flavescens* flore pleno, *G. nivalis* 'Flavescens flore pleno'.

G. elwesii **'Latest of All'** Another of the large single-marked *G. elwesii* cultivars distributed by Oliver Wyatt. According to Nutt (1993), this one was sent to Bowles by Capt. Frank Sowles of Thetford, Norfolk. The outer perianth segments are long and on each inner perianth segment is a ∧-shaped mark. Usually flowering in March, but some report early April. More research is required as to whether this snowdrop is the same as that illustrated in *Snowdrops and Snowflakes* (Stern, p. 56, fig. 14), as *Galanthus caucasicus* Late form.
Literature: Nutt (1993, p. 513).

G. **'Lavinia'** (5) Raised and introduced by H.A. Greatorex. Leaves clearly showing the influence of *G. plicatus*. A double with an untidy, irregular rosette—not the best of Greatorex's doubles. The outer perianth segments are marked with green at the apex. The inner rosette is formed from a variable number of inner perianth segments, depending on how many and to what degree they are misshapen. The inner perianth mark is more or less horseshoe-shaped,

223

but can vary considerably depending on the shape of each segment.
Literature: Trehane (1989, p. 201); Royal General Bulbgrowers' Association (1991, p. 244); Nutt (1993, p. 517).

G. **'Lime Tree'** (2) A seedling found by Oliver Wyatt under a lime tree, at Maidwell Hall. Very similar to G. 'Atkinsii' but said to be earlier flowering. Several variants exist under this name but it would now be more or less impossible to say which is the correct one, particularly as it is not a very distinct cultivar.
Literature: Nutt (1993, p. 517).
Synonyms: G. 'Limetrees'.

G. 'Limetrees'—see G. 'Lime Tree'

G. **'Little Ben'** (4) Primrose Warburg grew this plant for many years as G. 'Mighty Atom', and according to her it came from John Gray's garden in Suffolk, via E.B. Anderson. The leaves are erect, grey-glaucous, more or less applanate in vernation; the margins are explicative. The flowers are large, particularly in relation to the overall dimensions of the plant, i.e., like G. 'Mighty Atom'.
Awards: **PC** shown at Vincent Square on 20th February 1996 by M.D. Myers, see Plant Awards 1995–96, Bull. Alp. Gard. Soc. Gr. Brit. 64(4): 434 (1996), written by M.D. Myers—includes history and a description by A. Leslie.

G. nivalis 'Lutescens'—see G. nivalis 'Sandersii'

G. nivalis 'Lutescens Flore Pleno'—see G. nivalis 'Lady Elphinstone'

G. nivalis var. lutescens—see G. nivalis 'Sandersii'

G. **'Magnet'** (2) Originally raised from seed of G. 'Melvillei' by James Allen, at Shepton Mallet, before 1894. The main feature is the long, slender, arching pedicel, which carries the flower well away from the spathe. The pedicel is so long and fine that the flowers swing to and fro in a slight breeze, which is very pleasing to the eye and makes this snowdrop easily recognized, even at some distance. Other bonuses are good-sized flowers and a robust constitution. Bowles (1956) considered this one of the best snowdrops, and there seems no reason to disagree with this point of view. The leaves show the basic characteristics of G. nivalis with slightly explicative margins, indicating the influence of G. plicatus in the genetic history.

224

The inner perianth segments have a thick ∧-shaped mark, similar to *G.* 'S. Arnott'. *Galanthus* 'Magnet' is sometimes muddled with *G.* 'Galatea', but the pedicel of the latter species is shorter and bent at an angle of c. 90°. Other snowdrops have very long pedicels: *G.* 'Benton Magnet', *G.* 'Wisley Magnet', and *G. elwesii* 'Sibbertoft Magnet'.

Literature: Ewbank (1894, p. 125); Arnott (1899a, p. 130); Bowles (1914, p. 57); Bowles (1918, pp. 30–32); Stern (1951, p. 76); Bowles (1956, p. 66); Stern (1956, p. 73); Mathias (1958, pp. 147, 150); Trehane (1989, p. 201); Royal General Bulbgrowers' Association (1991, p. 244); Nutt (1993, p. 517).

Illustrations: Bowles (1918, fig. 4, painting by Bowles, as *G. nivalis* Melvillei 'Magnet'); Stern (1951, fig. 46, b/w photo); Stern (1956, pl. 7 and 8, b/w photos.); Mathias (1958, b/w photo p. 150, as *Galanthus* Magnet); J. Roy. Hort. Soc. 92(4): fig. 83, b/w photo (1967); Brown (1996, col. photo p. 52).

Awards: **AM** exhibited on 7 February 1967 by Revd R.J. Blakeway-Phillips, see Proc. Roy. Hort. Soc. 92(1): 53 (1967); see also Plant Awards 1966–67, Bull. Alp. Gard. Soc. Gr. Brit. 35(4): 319 (1967), written by D.E. Saunders—includes description.

G. 'Maidwell A'—see *G.* 'Kite'

G. **'Maidwell C'** (3) A seedling selected by Oliver Wyatt, at Maidwell Hall. Leaves of medium width, glaucescent, margins explicative, showing the influence of *G. plicatus*. Flowers globose. Inner perianth segments with a ∧-shaped mark at the apex and two small, vertical marks near the base. Ovary rounded. The perianth markings and ovary are often quite pale.

Literature: Trehane (1989, p. 201); Royal General Bulbgrowers' Association (1991, p. 244); Nutt (1993, p. 517).

G. elwesii **'Maidwell L'** Raised by Oliver Wyatt, at Maidwell Hall. One of the snowdrops previously known as a cultivar of *G. caucasicus* (of gardens). The leaves are supervolute in vernation, broad, and glaucous. The flowers are large and very white. The inner perianth segments bear a large X-shaped mark. Most of the snowdrops formerly included under *G. caucasicus* (see page 120) make good garden plants and *G.* 'Maidwell L' is no exception.

Literature: Trehane (1989, p. 201); Royal General Bulbgrowers' Association (1991, p. 244); Nutt (1993, pp. 513, 517).

Synonyms: *G.* 'Oliver Wyatt', *G. caucasicus* 'Maidwell L'.

G. nivalis **'Margery Fish'** (or 1) Found at Margery Fish's garden at East Lambrook Manor, Somerset. This erect growing snowdrop has a greatly enlarged spathe-valve, like *G.* 'Modern Art', *G.* 'Viridiapicis' and *G.* 'Warei'. Indeed, it shares many other characteristics with these cultivars, particularly the last two. The pedicel is very long like *G.* 'Magnet'. The outer perianth segments are very narrow, and heavily marked with green at the apex; the inner perianth segments are covered with green for up to two-thirds of their length. Introduced in the late 1980s and rare in cultivation.

G. 'Maximus'—see *G.* × *grandiflorus* in the Hybrids chapter or *G. elwesii* var. *maximus* in the Taxonomy of *Galanthus*

G. **'Melvillei'** * (2) A seedling found and raised at Dunrobin Castle by Mr D. Melville. A *G. nivalis* hybrid, or perhaps a large form of this species, although considered to be rather dwarf by some specialists (Burbidge, 1891a; Bowles, 1914, 1918). The leaves are applanate in vernation, glaucescent, and 1.5–2 cm broad. Larger in all its parts than the normal garden form of *G. nivalis*. Flowers large, pure white, and globular. The inner-perianth-segment mark is typical of *G. nivalis*: more or less ∧-shaped with the ends expanded into the lobes of the segment to either side of the sinus. Rare in cultivation. Literature: Melville (1878, p. 308, as *G.* 'Dunrobin Seedling'); Harpur-Crewe (1879a, p. 237, as *G. nivalis* var. *Melvillei*); Correvon (1888, p. 140); D.K. (1888, p. 59); Allen (1891, p. 173, as *G. Melvillei major*); Baker (1891, p. 17, as var. *melvillei* hort.); Melville (1891, p. 189); Burbidge (1891a, p. 205); Allen (1899b, p. 173); Arnott (1911, p. 34, as *G. Melvillei major*); Bowles (1914, p. 58); Bowles (1917b, p. xli); Bowles (1918, p. 30); Stern (1956, p. 74, as Melvillei and Melvillei Major); Trehane (1989, p. 201); Royal General Bulb-growers' Association (1991, p. 244); Nutt (1993, p. 517).
Illustrations: Arnott (1911, fig. 19, b/w photo); Bowles (1918, fig. 2—'This drawing was made from specimens kindly sent me by Mr Melville in 1906, and it has never grown any taller'—as *G. nivalis* Melvillei).
Awards: **FCC** shown on 25 March 1879 by Mr D. Melville (gardener to the Duke of Sutherland), see J. Roy. Hort. Soc. 5: cxxix 1879, exhibited as *G. nivalis* var. *Melvillei*.
Synonyms: *G.* 'Dunrobin Seedling', *G.* Melvillei Major, *G. nivalis* var. *melvillei*

G. Melvillei Major—see *G.* 'Melvillei'

G. nivalis var. *melvillei*—see *G.* 'Melvillei'

G. **'Merlin'** (6) An old, well-established snowdrop raised by James Allen, probably from a chance cross between *G. plicatus* and *G. elwesii*. Noted for its nearly all-green inner perianth segments, although other cultivars have this feature. The leaves are broad, erect at flowering time, glaucous, and evenly coloured on the upper surface; one, or more often both, margins are explicative. The flowers are large and elongated. The green marks on the inner perianth segments usually cover almost the entire area of the segment, with just a thin border of white at the edges. Usually the mark has a very slight 'waist' in the apical third of the segment. Ovary rounded when first flowering, elongating afterwards. A distinctive and very beautiful snowdrop. The early literature reports that this is a robust, strong-growing plant, but some more recent publications, after the 1950s, conclude that this is not so.

Literature: Allen (1891, p. 185); Burbidge (1891a, p. 206); Ewbank (1894, p. 125); Stern (1951, pp. 74, 76); Nutt (1970a, p. 172); Rix and Phillips (1981, p. 13); Trehane (1989, p. 201); Royal General Bulbgrowers' Association (1991, p. 244); Nutt (1993, p. 517).

Illustrations: Stern (1956, pl. 10, b/w photo); Nutt (1970a, fig. 10, b/w photo); Brown (1996, col. photo p. 53).

Awards: **AM** exhibited on 2 February 1971 by Revd R.J. Blakeway-Phillips, see Proc. Roy. Hort. Soc. 96: 63 (1971); see also Plant Awards 1970–71, Bull. Alp. Gard. Soc. Gr. Brit. 39(4): 316 (1971), written by R. Gorer—includes history and description.

G. **'Mighty Atom'** (4) A snowdrop raised by John Gray and later grown and named by E.B. Anderson at Lower Slaughter, Gloucestershire. A very controversial snowdrop, because several quite different forms are going around under this name; each person who grows one of them claims to have the true *G.* 'Mighty Atom', a problem that is only to be resolved with more research. I offer a description of this cultivar. Leaves broad, more or less linear, and glaucous; margins slightly explicative. The flowers are large and globose, and during the first week or so of flowering they are held very close to the soil (c. 5 cm or less). The outer perianth segments are unguiculate at the base. The inner perianth segments have a single, large, more or less ∧-shaped mark at the base.

Literature: Anderson (1973, p. 149); Trehane (1989, p. 201); Royal General Bulbgrowers' Association (1991, p. 245); Nutt (1993, p. 517).

G. 'Mocca's'—see *G.* 'Moccas'

G. **'Moccas'** (2) Probably from the garden at Moccas Court, near Hereford. Very similar to and often associated with *G.* 'Atkinsii' (e.g. as *G.* 'Atkinsii' Moccas Strain), but it differs by its earlier-flowering habit and its perianth segments that are not misshapen.
Literature: Hellyer (1982, p. 475); Nutt (1993, p. 511); Brown (1996, p. 54).
Synonyms: *G.* 'Atkinsii Moccas Form', *G.* 'Atkinsii' Moccas Strain, *G.* 'Atkinsii Moccas Strain', *G.* 'Mocca's'.

G. **'Modern Art'** (3) A seedling selected by E.B. Anderson. Similar to *G. nivalis* 'Viridapicis' and *G. nivalis* 'Warei' but differing in several characters. The leaves are rather long and glaucous, and the margins are moderately explicative. The spathe is very large and divided at the apex but never to the base. The outer perianth segments are long and narrow, with a distinctly unguiculate base. At the base of each outer perianth segment is a faint green mark, and at the apex is a larger mark composed of four or five short, partially fused, green stripes. The inner perianth segments have a prominent ∩-shaped mark at the apex and two oval, eye-like marks near the base.
Literature: Nutt (1993, p. 517).

G. 'Mrs Backhouse No. 12'—see *G.* 'Backhouse No. 12'

G. 'Mrs Backhouse's Spectacles'—see *G.* 'Backhouse Spectacles'

G. **'Mrs Thompson'** (5) The origin of this unusual snowdrop is unclear, but it is said to have arisen during the 1940s or 1950s in connection with a Mrs Thompson of The Red House, Escrick, York. The leaves are glaucescent, with one or both margins explicative. In most years, two flower scapes are produced from each bulb; these may have either one or two pedicels, with a flower hanging from each. In some years, or depending on the growing conditions, only one scape and only one pedicel is produced. Probably the most characteristic feature of *G.* 'Mrs Thompson', however, is not the number of flowers but the number of perianth segments. It usually has five outer segments and four inner segments, but it can also have six and four, four and four, or four or three. The outer perianth segments are often misshapen, but never so much that they spoil the overall shape of the flowers. The markings on the inner perianth segments are slight and usually composed of two inward-pointing, narrow triangles, which a form a wide ∧-shaped mark. The ovary is either single or semi-double (two fused together). Literature: Proc. J. Roy. Hort. Soc. 75(12): lxi [7 March], lxx [4 April] (1950); Nutt (1971, p. 168); Nutt (1993, p. 517). Illustrations: Nutt (1971, fig. 9, b/w photo).

G. **'Neill Fraser'** (2) Selected and raised by Patrick Neill Fraser of Murrayfield, Edinburgh. Shortly before his death, Neill Fraser sent this snowdrop, then without a name, to Bowles. Bowles admired this snowdrop and grew it for many years at his garden at Myddelton House, as recorded in his book *My Garden in Spring*. Some years later he (Bowles, 1956) gave this snowdrop the name *G.* 'Neill Fraser'. According to Bowles (1914) it is similar to *G.* 'Straffan', but slightly smaller, and with more rounded flowers. The leaves are narrow, linear, glaucescent, and one or both of the margins is slightly explicative. The inner perianth segments have a broad, ∩-shaped mark at the apex, typical of *G. nivalis*. Also quite similar to *G.* 'Brenda Troyle', although the marks on the inner perianth segments are different.
Literature: Bowles (1914, pp. 50–51); Bowles (1917b, p. xli); Bowles (1956, p. 66); Stern (1956, p. 74); Royal General Bulbgrowers' Association (1991, p. 245); Nutt (1993, p. 518).

G. **'Nerissa'** (5) A double snowdrop raised from stock of *G. plicatus* and named by Mr H.A. Greatorex of Norwich. Very similar to other Greatorex Doubles, particularly *G.* 'Cordelia', but probably with smaller marks on the inner perianth segments.
Literature: Bowles (1956, p. 70); Stern (1956, p. 74); Royal General Bulbgrowers' Association (1991, p. 245).

G. nivalis **'Norfolk Small'** A small-flowered clone of *G. nivalis*, which as the name suggests, originated in Norfolk. Difficult to tell apart from other diminutive variants of *G. nivalis*. Probably no longer in cultivation.
Literature: Royal General Bulbgrowers' Association (1991, p. 246).

G. 'Oliver Wyatt'—see *G. elwesii* 'Maidwell L'

G. **'Ophelia'** (5) One of the better-known doubles raised and named by H.A. Greatorex of Norwich. Leaves green-glaucescent with a glaucescent median stripe, with one or both margins explicative. Flowers neat and compact. Outer perianth segments three, not aberrant, and large. The rosette is made of c. 15–20 inner perianth segments mostly not misshapen and in regular rows. The mark on the inner segments is bold and more or less ∩-shaped. The pedicel is longer than many other Greatorex Doubles (c. 3 cm), and it is probably the earliest to flower. Anthers present. One of Greatorex's earliest introductions, and according to him one of his best.

Literature: Bowles (1956, p. 69); Stern (1956, p. 70); Trehane (1989, p. 201); Royal General Bulbgrowers' Association (1991, p. 247); Nutt (1993, p. 519).

Illustrations: Brown (1996, col. photo p. 58).

G. nivalis **'Orwell Green Tip'** Found by the Revd R.J. Blakeway-Phillips at the vicarage at Orwell, Cambridgeshire. A variant of *G. nivalis* with green markings on the apex of each outer perianth segment. The inner perianth segments bear a typical *nivalis*-like mark.

Literature: Trehane (1989, p. 200); Nutt (1993, p. 518).

G. nivalis **'Pagoda'** Found in the garden of the Old Vicarage in the village of Wrockwardine, Shropshire. A small and very charming variant of *G. nivalis* with reflexed outer perianth segments. The leaves are short at flowering time (c. 5 cm) but develop during the flowering period to the more usual length for this species. Each outer perianth segment is sharply reflexed, fully exposing the inner perianth segments.

Awards: **PC** shown on 22 February 1994 by S.R.B. Savage, see Plant Awards 1993–94, Bull. Alp. Gard. Soc. Gr. Brit. 62(4): 445 (1994), written by S.R.B. Savage—includes history and description.

G. **'Peg Sharples'** (1) A seedling raised and selected in the 1960s by Peg Sharples, of Grange-over-Sands, Cumbria. The seed for this snowdrop was given to Peg Sharples by E.B. Anderson. Leaves applanate in vernation, broad, plane, and glaucous. The flowers are large, and bright white. The inner perianth segments bear an X-shaped green mark, which becomes lighter towards the base (similar to *G.* 'John Gray'). A robust, attractive, late-flowering snowdrop.

Literature: Trehane (1989, p. 201); Royal General Bulbgrowers' Association (1991, p. 247); Nutt (1993, p. 519).

230

G. nivalis **'Pewsey Green'** Originating from Pewsey, in the Vale of the White Horse, Wiltshire. A variant of *G. nivalis* 'Flore Pleno' with green marks at the apex of the outer perianth segments.
Literature: Nutt (1971, p. 205); Nutt (1993, p. 518).

G. nivalis **'Poculiformis'** * A snowdrop of multiple origins, which arises spontaneously from time to time, particularly amongst larger and older plantings of *G. nivalis*. Snowdrop literature dating from around 1900 reports several introductions. Allen (1891) tells us that it was first brought to his attention by D. Melville, who found it in the grounds at Dunrobin Castle. Then he remarks upon a collection from Penrhyn, Wales (see Webster, 1891, p. 233), and another from Ayr, in Scotland. It was probably first named by Harpur-Crewe, in 1880, from the Dunrobin stock. A very easy snowdrop to recognize, because the inner perianth segments are more or less the same size as the outer perianth segments, or nearly so, and because the inner ones lack the characteristic green markings of the snowdrop. Superficially the flowers resemble those of *Leucojum* (the snowflake), e.g. *L. autumnale*. Unfortunately this peculiar characteristic is accompanied by an unpleasant flaw: the inner perianth segments are often badly misshapen and malformed, partially reverting back to their normal size and shape. This aberration is not always present, however, and some clones are much neater than others (see *G. nivalis* 'Sandhill Gate'). At its best, this is a very beautiful snowdrop, one of purity and elegance. When the light is behind the flower the golden anthers appear to glow faintly inside the segments. Not one of the easiest snowdrops to grow, but do not treat it tenderly. Plant in light shade in a leafy, humus-rich soil.

From time to time poculiform specimens of *G. elwesii* have appeared, and Bowles tells us in his *My Garden in Spring* of one grown by Farrer (Bowles 1914, pp. 52–53). A good poculiform clone of *G. elwesii* arose in the 1970s and was named *G.* 'The Bride' by Phil Cornish.
Literature: Harpur-Crewe (1880, p. 249); Allen (1886, p. 75); Baker (1888, p. 17, as *G. nivalis* var. *poculiformis* hort.); Correvon (1888, p. 139); Allen (1891, p. 182); Burbidge (1891a, p. 207); Melville (1891, p. 189); Mallet (1905, p. 87); Bowles (1914, p. 51); Bowles (1918, p. 30); Mathias (1958, p. 156); Royal General Bulbgrowers' Association (1991, p. 246); Nutt (1993, p. 518).
Illustrations: Bowles (1918, fig. 3, painting by Bowles, as *G. nivalis*

231

poculiformis); Mathias (1958, b/w photo p. 156, as *G. nivalis* var. *poculiformis*).
Synonyms: *G. nivalis* 'Albus' (in part), *G. nivalis* var. *poculiformis*.

G. nivalis var. *poculiformis*—see *G. nivalis* 'Poculiformis'

G. **'Pride o' the Mill'** (1) A seedling selected and named by Daphne Chappell in her Mill House garden, Gloucestershire. The leaves are grey-glaucous, slightly explicative at the margins, becoming distinctly horizontal as they mature. The inner perianth segments are heavily covered with green due to the large, more or less X-shaped mark. Like many other snowdrops with a large X-shaped mark, the green is darkest nearer the apex and fades toward the base.
Literature: Chappell (1995, p. 24).

G. nivalis **'Pusey Green Tip'** Originating from the village of Pusey in Wiltshire. A variant of *G. nivalis* 'Flore Pleno' with a light green blotch on the apex of each outer perianth segment.
Literature: Nutt (1971, p. 169); Trehane (1989, p. 200); Nutt (1993, p. 518).
Illustrations: Nutt (1968, fig. 28, b/w photo); Nutt (1971, fig. 62, b/w photo).
Synonyms: *G. nivalis* 'Green Tip', *G. nivalis* 'Green Tip Double', *G. nivalis* 'Pusey Green Tips'.

G. nivalis 'Pusey Green Tips'—see *G. nivalis* 'Pusey Green Tip'

G. **'Richard Ayres'** (1) Discovered by Richard Nutt during a visit to Anglesey Abbey, Cambridge, in 1987. It was named by the National Trust (the present owners of Anglesey Abbey) after the head gardener, Richard Ayres. A tall, striking double snowdrop. Leaves weakly supervolute in vernation, rather narrow, glaucous. Outer perianth segments four, narrow. Inner perianth segments c. 20–25, forming a neat, splayed rosette. The markings on the inner perianth segments are variable but mostly based on an X-shape, although the X mark is often reduced in size to form two markings, apical and basal. The basal marks can be further reduced into two separate spots. Anthers present.
Literature: Nutt (1993, p. 519); Brown (1996, p. 59).

G. **'Robin Hood'** (6) An old, established snowdrop raised by James

232

Allen from a cross between *G. plicatus* and *G. elwesii*. Almost instantly recognized by its very erect habit, resembling a soldier standing to attention. Pedicel short, approximately half the length of the spathe, thus holding the flower close to the scape. Leaves more or less applanate in vernation, quite broad, glaucous, with explicative margins. Outer perianth segments narrow and long. Inner perianth segments with a large more or less X-shaped mark, which in outline looks rather like a spanner.

Literature: Allen (1891, p. 185); Arnott (1904, p. 166); Bowles (1914, p. 57); Bowles (1918, p. 35); Bowles (1956, p. 67); Stern (1956, p. 75); Nutt (1971, p. 209); Trehane (1989, p. 201); Royal General Bulbgrowers' Association (1991, p. 248); Nutt (1993, p. 520).

Illustrations: Brown (1996, col. photo opposite p. 54).

G. **'S. Arnott'** (2) Samuel Arnott, the provost of Dumfries, sent this snowdrop to Henry J. Elwes who grew it well at Colesborne and gave it to others as *G.* 'Arnott's seedling'. It was shown at the Royal Horticultural Society in 1951, when it received an Award of Merit (AM) under the more suitable name of *G.* 'S. Arnott'. Throughout the 1950s and 1960s it was widely distributed and has now become a firm favourite. In 1991 it received a First Class Certificate (FCC) from the RHS. Large drifts of *G.* 'S. Arnott' still grow at Colesborne. *Galanthus* 'S. Arnott' is a substantial snowdrop with clean, large, handsome flowers, borne on tall, robust scapes. Leaves glaucescent, erect at flowering time, narrowing towards the apices; margins slightly explicative along one or both margins. Outer perianth segments large but shorter and more concave than many other snowdrops, giving a rounded, more compact flower. The outer perianth segments have a tough constitution and are a good, bright white. Inner perianth segments with a single, thick, deep green, ∧-shaped mark at the apex. The ∧-shaped mark of this and other similar snowdrops is characteristic because the ends are enlarged, making the mark resemble two triangles that point inwards and touch at their tips. The pedicel is shorter than the spathe. The marking is broader than *G.* 'Ketton' but less heart-shaped (inverted) than *G.* 'Brenda Troyle'. Strongly scented. All in all a truly wonderful snowdrop, and excellent as a cut flower.

Literature: Bowles (1956, p. 68); Mathias (1958, pp. 147, 148); Trehane (1989, p. 201); Royal General Bulbgrowers' Association (1991, p. 248); Nutt (1993, p. 520).

Illustrations: Stern (1956, pl. 9, b/w photo); Mathias (1958, b/w photo p. 148, as *G. nivalis* 'S. Arnott'); Downard, in J. Roy. Hort. Soc. 85(12): fig. 158., b/w photo, as *G.* 'Samuel Arnott' (1960); Rix and Phillips (1981, p. 17, fig. j). Bull. Alp. Gard. Soc. Gr. Brit. 59(4): col. photo p. 369 (1991); Brown (1996, col. photo opposite p. 56). Awards: **AM** exhibited on 6 March 1951 by Mrs W.V. Mathias, see J. Roy. Hort. Soc. 76(9): 331(1951), as *G.* 'Arnott's Seedling'. **FCC** shown on 19 February 1991 by the Director, Royal Botanic Gardens, Kew, see Plant Awards 1990–91, Bull. Alp. Gard. Soc. Gr. Brit. 59(4): 368 (1991, col. photo p. 369), written by Tony Hall—includes history and description.
Synonyms: *G.* 'Arnott's Seedling', *G.* 'Sam Arnott', *G.* 'Samuel Arnott'.

G. **'Sally Ann'** (3) A seedling raised at Hyde Lodge, Stroud, Gloucestershire, and named after one of Herbert Ransom's daughters. Leaves glaucescent, margins moderately explicative, showing the influence of *G. plicatus*. At flowering time the leaves are held at c. 45°, but later they lie almost horizontally. The pedicel is longer than most cultivars. The flowers are globose, and the inner perianth segments have a bold X-shaped mark.
Literature: Nutt (1993, p. 520).

G. 'Sam Arnott'—see *G.* 'S. Arnott'

G. 'Samuel Arnott'—see *G.* 'S. Arnott'

G. nivalis **'Sandersii'** * This snowdrop was found in about 1876 by a Mr Sanders of Newham, near Cambridge, in an old farmhouse garden in a remote part of Northumberland. It was sent to Harpur-Crewe (1879b) for identification and he called it *G. nivalis* var. *sandersii*, in honour of its discoverer. It was also sent to James Allen (see Burbidge 1891a), who decided to call it *G. lutescens*, a name that does not have priority and is therefore a synonym of *G.* 'Sandersii'. A variant of a medium- to small-sized *G. nivalis*, having a yellow ovary and yellow markings on the inner perianth segments. This is a very delicate snowdrop and is not easy to grow. However, perseverance will be rewarded, as it can be a charming little plant. Bowles remarked that this yellow-flowered snowdrop comes well and true from seed (see J. Roy. Hort. Soc. 47(2 and 3): xxvii (1922) [Scientific Committee, January 25, 1921]).

Literature: Harpur-Crewe (1879b, p. 342); Stern (1956, p. 75); Nutt (1970a, p. 171); Nutt (1993, p. 518); Baker (1997, pp. 9–10). In the following references as *lutescens* or 'Lutescens': Harpur-Crewe (1880, p. 249); Allen (1886, p. 75); Baker (1888, p. 17, as *G. nivalis* var. *lutescens* hort.); Correvon (1888, p. 139); Burbidge (1890, p. 268); Burbidge (1891a, p. 205); Allen (1891b, p. 181); Ewbank (1891, p. 272); Arnott (1899a, p. 130); Arnott (1900, p. 189); Mallet (1905, p. 87); Arnott (1912, p. 10); Bowles (1914, p. 53); Bowles (1918, p. 33); Stern (1951, p. 74); Stern (1956, p. 73); Mathias (1958, p. 154); Trehane (1989, p. 200, as *G. nivalis* var. *lutescens*); Royal General Bulbgrowers' Association (1991, p. 246).
Illustrations: Mathias (1958, b/w photo p. 154); Rix and Phillips (1981, p. 17, fig. h, as *G.* 'Lutescens'); Baker (1997, col. photo p. 10).
Synonyms: *G. nivalis* 'Howick Yellow', *G. nivalis* 'Horwick Yellow' (misspelling), *G. nivalis* 'Lutescens', *G. nivalis* var. *lutescens*.

G. nivalis **'Sandhill Gate'** Found by the Revd R.J. Blakeway-Phillips during the 1960s in the garden of a cottage called Sandhill Gate, at Crawley Down, Sussex. It is a variant of *G. nivalis* 'Poculiformis' and very similar to it except that the segments of *G. nivalis* 'Sandhill Gate' are much more uniform and less inclined to be misshapen. It is sometimes said that the anthers can be seen more easily through the translucent segments of this version of *G.* 'Poculiformis'. These characters are an improvement on other poculiform *G. nivalis*, and 'Sandhill Gate' is thus well worth growing.
Literature: Blakeway-Phillips (1980, p. 420); Trehane (1989, p. 200); Nutt (1993, p. 519).
Illustrations: Brown (1996, col. photo p. 59).

G. nivalis **'Scharlockii'** * First named in 1868 by Professor Caspary as *G. nivalis* var. *scharlockii* in honour of its discoverer, Herr Julius Scharlock. Scharlock found this snowdrop in 1818 in the valley of the Nahe, a tributary of the Rhine. A very distinct and well-known snowdrop. The main diagnostic feature is the enlarged, leaf-like spathe valve. Unlike the normal green-sided, membranous-bodied spathe of most snowdrops, this spathe is all green, opaque, and divided into two leaf-like structures. The enlarged spathe is also about twice the size of those in other snowdrops, and when divided, each half is slightly curved downwards. When mature the spathe resembles a pair of miniature, elongated donkey's ears. In addition to this peculiar feature, the outer perianth segments are marked at their tips with a large spot of green (composed of three to five fused green lines). Each inner perianth segment has a broad, ∧-shaped mark. Usually very easy to grow although some gardeners report otherwise (see Blakeway-Phillips, 1980, p. 420). Note: (1) The spelling of *G.* 'Scharlockii' has encountered a considerable amount of inconsistency. I have followed the spelling used by Caspary when he described *G. nivalis* var. *scharlockii*. (2) Several variants of *G. nivalis* 'Scharlockii' exhibit differences in size and in the shape and extent of the green coloration on the perianth segments. All of the variants have the enlarged, leaf-like spathe valve characteristic of this cultivar, however, and I see no merit in either recognizing them as a cultivar group or selecting individual clones as separate cultivars.

Literature: Harpur-Crewe (1879a, p. 237); Harpur-Crewe (1879b, p. 342); Allen (1886, p. 75); Correvon (1888, p. 140); Allen (1891, p. 182); Baker (1891, p. 17); Burbidge (1891a, pp. 208, 209); Ewbank (1891, p. 272); Arnott (1899a, p. 130); Mallet (1905, p. 87); Bowles (1914, p. 54); Bowles (1918, pp. 32, 33); Stern (1951, p. 73); Stern (1956, p. 27); Bowles (1956, p. 75); Mathias (1958, pp. 147, 153); Nutt (1971, p. 166); Trehane (1989, p. 200); Nutt (1993, p. 519).

Illustrations: Harpur-Crewe (1879b, p. 342, fig. 48, line drawing); Burbidge (1891a, p. 208, fig. 32, line drawing); Bowles (1918, fig. 9, painting by Bowles, as *G. nivalis* Scharlockii); Stern (1951, fig. 44, b/w photo); Stern (1956, fig. 4, as *G. nivalis* 'Scharlokii' [*sic*], line drawing; plate 6, as *G. nivalis* 'Scharlockii', b/w photo); Mathias (1958, b/w photo p. 153, as *G. nivalis* forma *scharlocki*); Nutt (1968, fig. 30, b/w photo); Blakeway-Phillips (1980, p. 420); Rix and Phillips (1981, p. 14, fig. a).

Synonyms: *G. nivalis* 'Scharlokii', *G. nivalis* forma *scharlockii*, *G. nivalis* var. *scharlockii*, *G. nivalis* var. *shaylockii*.

G. nivalis 'Scharlokii' and other spelling variants—see *G. nivalis* 'Scharlockii'

G. nivalis forma *scharlocki*—see *G. nivalis* 'Scharlockii'

G. nivalis var. *scharlockii*—see *G. nivalis* 'Scharlockii'

G. nivalis var. *shaylockii*—see *G. nivalis* 'Scharlockii'

G. **'Sir Herbert Maxwell'** (2) Found by Sir Herbert Maxwell of Monreith, Galloway, and later sent to E.A. Bowles, who named it. An early-flowering *G. nivalis* hybrid. The leaves are glaucescent and very slightly explicative along one or both margins. Inner perianth segments with a splayed, ∧-shaped mark. Uncommon.
Literature: Nutt (1993, p. 519).

G. **'St Anne's'** (5) Originally found in a wood in north Norfolk and later grown on at St Anne's Manor, Sutton Bonington, Nottingham. Leaves glaucescent; leaf margins slightly explicative, particularly at the base. The inner perianth segments possess a single, small, ∧-shaped mark at the apex.
Literature: Trehane (1989, p. 200); Nutt (1993, p. 519).

G. **'Straffan'** (2) Bowles (1918) tells us that this snowdrop appeared spontaneously in Lord Clarina's garden at Straffan, County Kildare, Ireland. Frederick Bedford, the head gardener, was the first to notice it in 1858, when a plant with two flowers, superior to its neighbours, caught his eye. Its ancestors are said to be *G. plicatus*, brought back from the valley of Tchernaya in the Crimea by Lord Clarina (according to Nelson [1992, p. 13] it was Major Massey). It is recorded that some 4000 plants were eventually raised at Straffan. The characteristic feature of this snowdrop is the regularity with which it produces two scapes per bulb. The leaves are glaucescent, flat at the margins or very slightly explicative. In most years two scapes are produced from each bulb, the first scape always taller than the second, and the flower larger. The presence of two flowering scapes means that this cultivar always provides a rich mass of flowers. The outer perianth segments are bright white, large, and slightly elongated. The inner perianth segments bear a thick, open ∩- to ∧-shaped mark at the apex. The flowering season is very late, which combined with the potential for plentiful flowers means that this snowdrop is a real show when many others are past their best.
Literature: Burbidge (1891a, pp. 196, 199, 203); Burbidge (1894, p. 127); Arnott (1912, p. 10); Bowles (1914, p. 49)—as 'the Straffan Snowdrop' and *G. caucasicus grandis*: Bowles (1918, p. 31, called *G. caucasicus grandis*, in parentheses); Synge (1950, p. 64); Bowles (1956, p. 66); Stern (1956, p. 75); Mathias (1958, p. 151); Nutt (1970a, p. 165); Blakeway-Phillips (1980, p. 420); Trehane (1989, p. 201); Royal General Bulbgrowers' Association (1991, p. 249); Nutt (1993, p. 520); Brown (1996, p. 53).

Illustrations: Bowles (1918, fig. 6, painting by Bowles, as *Galanthus* 'Straffan' Seedling); Synge (1950, fig. 19, opposite p. 66, b/w photo); Mathias (1958, b/w photo p. 151, as *Galanthus* Straffan); J. Roy. Hort. Soc. 94(5): fig. 98, b/w photo (1969); Blakeway-Phillips (1980, b/w photo p. 419).

Awards: **AM** exhibited on 19 March 1968 by R.D. Nutt, see Proc. Roy. Hort. Soc. 93(1): 48 (1968); see also Plant Awards 1967–68, Bull. Alp. Gard. Soc. Gr. Brit. 36(4): 358 (1968), written by D.E. Saunders—includes description.

Synonyms: *G. caucasicus grandis, G. nivalis grandis.*

G. 'The O'Mahoney'—see *G.* 'Coolballintaggart'

G. 'The O'Mahony'—see *G.* 'Coolballintaggart'

G. elwesii **'Three Leaves'** A large handsome snowdrop, which has three leaves instead of the usual two. The leaves are erect, broad, and bluish glaucous. Each inner perianth segment has a single ∧-shaped mark at the apex. A robust and interesting snowdrop, but presently uncommon in cultivation. A similar multi-leafed snowdrop is *G.* 'Six Leaves', which originated in Lady Barbara Buchanan's garden at Sibbertoft, Northamptonshire. It seems, however, that this snowdrop rarely has more than four leaves.
Literature: Nutt (1993, p. 513).

G. plicatus **'Three Ships'** Found in the former garden of Henham Hall, Suffolk, growing under an old cork oak, later propagated and distributed by John Morley. Named after the Christmas carol: 'I saw three ships come sailing in . . .'. An early-flowering variant of *G. plicatus* subsp. *plicatus*, which often flowers around Christmas time. The leaves are deep green, with a broad, glaucescent median stripe. The main leaf characters are the same as the species. The flower is held on a long pedicel, similar to but shorter than *G.* 'Magnet'. The inner perianth segments have a bold, more or less X-shaped or Y-shaped mark, which fades out near the base.
Literature: Nutt (1993, p. 512).

G. nivalis **'Tiny'** Another dwarf variant of *G. nivalis*, very similar to *G. nivalis* 'Tiny Tim'. A number of clones seem to exist under this name.
Literature: Trehane (1989, p. 200); Nutt (1993, p. 518).

238

G. nivalis **'Tiny Tim'** A diminutive clone of *G. nivalis*. Smaller in all parts than the average *G. nivalis*, particularly in the leaves, which can be less than 5 mm wide. Delightful, but often not producing many flowers.
Literature: Blakeway-Phillips (1980, p. 420); Royal General Bulbgrowers' Association (1991, p. 246).

G. **'Titania'** (5) A double, raised and introduced by H.A. Greatorex; probably the result of a cross between *G. plicatus* and *G. nivalis*. The leaves are glaucescent, characteristically semi-erect, and not fully developed at flowering time; the margins are slightly explicative. Flowers globular and held on a tall, upright scape. Inner perianth segments c. 10–15, forming a reasonably tidy rosette. At the apex of each inner perianth segment is a single, more or less ∩-shaped mark. Anthers conspicuous. Note: Allen (1891, p. 185; and Appendix 6) named a single-flowered *G.* 'Titania' before the double-flowered *G.* 'Titania' of Greatorex. However, it seems likely that Allen's 'Titania' is no longer in cultivation, in which case the modern and more widely used concept of the double 'Titania' could be upheld. The ICNCP states that a name cannot be reused unless sanctioned by the International Registration Authority (Articles 26.1, 26.2). I have pre-empted this decision here, by retaining the popular and widespread use of this cultivar name for use in this checklist of cultivars.
Literature: Trehane (1989, p. 201); Nutt (1993, p. 520).

G. **'Trotter's Merlin'** (?3) Introduced by Elizabeth Parker-Jervis in the 1960s; the original plants came from her father, R.D. Trotter. Similar to *G.* 'Merlin' but with less green on the inner perianth segments. Leaves glaucescent, more or less linear. Outer perianth segments elongated, elliptic in outline. Inner perianth segments with a large, broad, X-shaped mark that covers a good deal of the surface area of each segment, although small white areas appear at the place where the X crosses, and at the base, and around the edges. The inner segments are rather fleshy and are turned sharply upwards at the apex. Ovary large and angular, pale green.
Literature: Royal General Bulbgrowers' Association (1991, p. 247, as *G.* 'Trotter Merlin'); Nutt (1993, p. 517).

G. plicatus **'Trym'** A bizarre snowdrop which arose by chance in Mrs Gibb's garden at Westbury-on-Trym, Bristol, during the 1970s. Leaves matt green, with a broad, glaucous central stripe. Very odd

239

because the outer perianth segments have been replaced with what appears to be enlarged inner perianth segments. Thus, the flower is composed of two whorls of inner perianth segments. All the segments flare outwards, especially at the apex, the outer ones more so. Each segment bears a single, more or less inverted heart-shaped mark at the apex, and an apical notch.

Literature: Nutt (1993, p. 520).

Synonyms: *G.* 'Ace of Spades'.

G. **'Tubby Merlin'** (1 or ?6) A neat, compact variant from the *Galanthus* Merlin Group. It was Raised by E.B. Anderson in the early 1960s when he was at Lower Slaughter. Leaves glaucescent, margins either slightly explicative or flat. Outer perianth segments nearly circular in outline, giving the flower a good, rounded shape. Inner perianth segments almost entirely covered by the green mark, except for a white band around the margin. Ovary distinctly rounded, pale yellow. Early flowering and nicely scented.

Literature: Nutt (1970a, pp. 172–173); Nutt (1993, p. 520).

Illustrations: Nutt (1970a, fig. 10, b/w photo).

G. nivalis **'Virescens'** * According to Burbidge (1819, p. 209), Professor Fenzl, the director of the Vienna Botanical Garden, originally grew this greenish flowered variant of *G. nivalis*. Max Leichtlin obtained two bulbs from Professor Fenzl, and thereafter sent a bulb to Revd Harpur-Crewe, and another to James Allen. From these few bulbs it was distributed to other English gardens. The outer perianth segments are heavily marked with light green, and the inner perianth segments are almost entirely covered with dark green, except for the margins. Very late flowering; usually the last of the *G. nivalis* cultivars to flower. A very interesting plant but often quite difficult to grow and slow to increase, hence its rarity.

Literature: Leichtlin (1879, p. 342); Harpur-Crewe (1880, p. 249); Allen (1886, p. 75); Baker (1891, p. 17, as *G. caucasicus* var. *virescens* hort.); Correvon (1888, p. 140); Allen (1891, p. 182); Burbidge (1891a, p. 209); Ewbank (1891, p. 272); Bowles (1819, p. 33, as *G. caucasicus virescens*); Anon. (1907, p. 264); Bowles (1914, p. 54); Stern (1956, p. 75); Trehane (1989, p. 200); Royal General Bulbgrowers' Association (1991, p. 247); Nutt (1993, p. 519).

Illustrations: Burbidge (1891a, fig. 33, line drawing); Ewbank (1891, fig. p. 276, line drawing); Nutt (1970a, fig. 10, b/w photo); Nutt (1971, fig. 63, b/w photo).

240

Awards: **PC** shown on 10 March 1990 by A.M. Edwards, see Plant Awards 1989–90, Bull. Alp. Gard. Soc. Gr. Brit. 58(4): 360 (1990), written by A.M. Edwards—includes short history and a description.
Synonyms: *G. caucasicus* var. *virescens*, *G. caucasicus virescens* [*sic*]

G. caucasicus var. *virescens*—see *G. nivalis* 'Virescens'

G. caucasicus virescens—see *G. nivalis* 'Virescens'

G. virescens (double form)—see *G. nivalis* 'Boyd's Double'

G. nivalis **'Virgin'** Raised from seed of *G. nivalis* 'Poculiformis' by James Allen. The inner perianth segments are about two-thirds the length of the outer ones, and the margins are conspicuously rolled inwards. Each inner perianth segment has two small green marks at the apex. Scarce in cultivation.
Literature: Arnott (1904, p. 166); Bowles (1914, p. 52); Stern (1956, p. 75).

G. nivalis **'Viridapice'** Selected in the nurseries of Van Tubergen, in the Netherlands. In 1922 Messrs Barr showed it to the RHS Scientific Committee as the 'Green tipped Snowdrop'. A large variant of *G. nivalis* with an enlarged spathe-valve and green spots on the outer perianth segments. Leaves glaucescent, usually erect or semi-erect at flowering time. The outer perianth segments are large and elongated. At the apex of each outer perianth segment is a single green mark, either made of several vertical lines or evenly stained with green to form a blotch. Each inner perianth segment has a single apical mark, which is either inverted heart-shaped or shaped like a thick moustache with turned-up ends. The spathe-valve is greatly enlarged and either not divided or slightly divided into two at the apex. The spathe normally forms a hood-like structure above the flower. A vigorous snowdrop that grows strongly and multiplies quickly. Not the most elegant snowdrop but still a very good garden plant. Note: This cultivar has at least seven different spellings. The use of the epithet 'Viridapice' has been adopted here since it is the original spelling (as given by Arnott). In common with all the other spelling variants of this cultivar, this is not the preferred Latin spelling, but I have maintained the original name rather than introduce another spelling.
Literature: J. Roy Hort. Soc. 48(2 and 3): xxxi (1923—Scientific

Committee, 14 February, 1922); Arnott (1929, p. 297); Stern (1956, p. 76); Mathias (1958, pp. 147, 155); Nutt (1968, p. 84); (Nutt, 1974, p. 21); Trehane (1989, p. 200); Royal General Bulbgrowers' Association (1991, p. 247).

Illustrations: Mathias (1958, fig. p. 155, as *G. nivalis* var. *viridapicis*); Nutt (1968, fig. 27); Nutt (1974, fig. 20, b/w photo).

Synonyms: *G. nivalis* var. *viridapicis*; *G. nivalis* 'Viridi-apice', *G. nivalis* 'Virdiapicis' and other spelling variants.

G. nivalis var. *viridapicis*—see *G. nivalis* 'Viridapice'

G. nivalis 'Viridi-apice'—see *G. nivalis* 'Viridapice'

G. nivalis 'Viridiapicis'—see *G. nivalis* 'Viridapice'

G. viridiflorus flore pleno—see *G. nivalis* 'Boyd's Double'

G. 'W. Thompson'—see *G.* 'William Thomson'

G. nivalis **'Walrus'** A curious double snowdrop selected by Oliver Wyatt at Maidwell Hall, Northamptonshire, during the 1960s. The three outer perianth segments are very long and thin, like the tusks of a walrus. The apex of each inner perianth segment is heavily stained with green. Inner perianth segments longer and thinner than the species, c. 7–12, forming a loose rosette. At the apex of each inner perianth segment is a single, more or less ∧-shaped mark.

Literature: Trehane (1989, p. 200); Royal General Bulbgrowers' Association (1991, p. 249); Nutt (1993, p. 519).

G. nivalis **'Warei'** Named by James Allen (1891, p. 183). Allen received this snowdrop from W. Boyd, who had in turn obtained it from a Mr Ware under the name of *G. scharlockii*. Very similar to *G. nivalis* 'Viridapice' but differs due to the spathe being undivided or only partially so. Also perhaps a little larger than *G. nivalis* 'Viridapice'.

Literature: Allen (1891, p. 183); Burbidge (1891a, p. 210); Bowles (1914, p. 55); Stern (1956, p. 76); Nutt (1993, p. 519).

G. plicatus **'Warham'** Found in a garden at Warham, Norfolk, by the Revd C. Digby. According to Lady Beatrix Stanley (1939, p. 226) it was originally introduced from the Crimea during the Crimean War, in about 1855. A snowdrop that continues to cause debate amongst galanthophiles because of the lack of agreement on its essential diagnostic features. The shape of the markings on the inner perianth segments is the most contentious point of discussion. Personally, I feel that *G. plicatus* is so variable that the matter is mostly academic. Furthermore, it is likely that the original clone of *G. plicatus* 'Warham' has been replaced a number of times by seedling progeny. Despite the disagreements, *G. plicatus* 'Warham' is nearly always represented by a large, bold snowdrop. The leaves are very broad, light to dull green, with a broad, glaucous stripe running along the middle of the upper surface. The flowers are very large and elliptic in outline. The inner perianth segments either have a single, chunky, ∩-shaped mark at the apex, or an X-shaped mark with short upper limbs (see FIGURE 8, E).

Literature: Beatrix Stanley (1939, p. 226); Synge (1950, p. 64); Stern (1951, p. 74); Stern (1956, p. 76); Wyatt (1956, p. 297); Trehane (1989, p. 200); Nutt (1993, p. 519).

Illustrations: Stern (1951, fig. 47, b/w photo).

Awards: **AM** shown on 22 February 1927 by Lady Beatrix Stanley, see J. Roy. Hort. Soc. 53(2): xlv (1928). **FCC** shown on 9 February 1937 by Lady Beatrix Stanley, see J. Roy. Hort. Soc. 62(4): 174 (1937).

Synonyms: *G. plicatus* 'Warham Variety'.

G. plicatus 'Warham Variety'—see *G. plicatus* 'Warham'

G. elwesii **'Washfield Colesborne'** One of the *Galanthus* Colesborne Group, which has been sold for some time by Washfield Nursery, Hawkhurst, Kent. Similar to *G.* 'Colesborne' but without the narrow ovary. Leaves grey-glaucous. Easier in cultivation than its namesake and probably more garden worthy.

Literature: Nutt (1993, p. 513).

G. plicatus **'Wendy's Gold'** Found in 1985 by Mrs Sharman at Wandlebury Ring, Cambridgeshire. A fine clone of *G. plicatus* subsp. *plicatus*, with yellow perianth markings and yellowish ovary. Outer perianth segments short and wide, giving a rounded flower. The inner perianth segments bear a large, yellow mark, which covers almost the entire outside surface of each segment; the yellow fades to white near the ovary and a narrow white margin surrounds each

243

segment. Ovary and pedicel yellow. A snowdrop of great beauty and quick to multiply. The yellow perianth markings and the sometimes pale green leaves are said by some to be the result of virus, but this is a vigorous snowdrop that shows no other indications of ill health.
Literature: Nutt, in Lawrence (1986, p. 133); Royal General Bulb-growers' Association (1991, p. 249); Nutt (1993, p. 519).
Illustrations: Brown (1996, front cover of journal, col. photo).
Awards: **PC** 1992, but not written up for Bull. Alp. Gard. Soc. Gr. Brit. **AM** shown at Vincent Square on 20 February 1996 by Monksilver Nursery, see Plant Awards 1995–96, 64(4): 417 (1996), by R. Rolfe—includes history and description.

G. **'White Swan'** (5) A lesser-known Greatorex Double, raised by H.A. Greatorex from a cross between *G. nivalis* 'Flore Pleno' (male) and *G. plicatus* (female).
Literature: Bowles (1956, p. 70); Stern (1956, p. 76); Brown (1996, p. 58).

G. **'William Thomson'** (5) Raised by William Thomson at his garden in High Blantyre, Lanarkshire. William Thomson sent bulbs to Samuel Arnott, who named it in honour of its discoverer. According to Arnott (1911, p. 34) this is a hybrid between *G. nivalis* and *G. plicatus*. Very close to *G.* 'S. Arnott' and other similar hybrids such as *G.* 'Brenda Troyle'. Each inner perianth segment has a large, deep green, more or less ∩-shaped mark at the apex, or sometimes this mark is reduced to two inward-pointing, eye-shaped marks (see Arnott, 1911, fig. 20). Pedicel distinctly shorter than the spathe, not longer as stated by Bowles (1917a, p. 4).
Literature: Arnott (1911, p. 34, as *G.* 'William Thomson'); Bowles (1917a, p. 4); Bowles (1956, p. 69); Stern (1956, p. 76); Nutt (1971, p. 165); Royal General Bulbgrowers' Association (1991, p. 249); Nutt (1993, p. 520).
Illustrations: Arnott (1911, fig. 20, b/w photo).
Synonyms: *G.* 'W. Thompson', *G.* 'William Thompson'.

G. 'William Thompson'—see *G.* 'William Thomson'

G. **'Winifrede Mathias'** (2). A seedling raised at Hyde Lodge and named after Mrs Mathias, who with her husband Brigadier Mathias ran the Giant Snowdrop Company at the same address. Shown at the RHS on 19 February 1974 by R.D. Nutt. (see Proc. Roy. Hort.

Soc. 100(1): 13 (1975)). Leaves narrow, glaucescent, one or both margins slightly explicative. Flowers small. Inner perianth segments bear a single, inverted heart-shaped or broad ∩-shaped mark at the apex.

Literature: Trehane (1989, p. 201); Nutt (1993, p. 520).

Synonyms: *G.* 'Winifred Matthias'.

G. 'Winifred Matthias'—see *G.* 'Winifrede Mathias'

G. **'Wisley Magnet'** (5) Found by C.D. Brickell at the RHS Gardens at Wisley, Surrey, in the early 1960s. Very similar to *G.* 'Magnet' because it possesses a very long pedicel. Leaves glaucescent, margins slightly explicative. Inner perianth segments with a single, *nivalis*-like, ∧-shaped mark at the apex. The pedicel is bent sharply downwards at a point just over half of its length, a character it shares with *G.* 'Galatea'. *Galanthus* 'Magnet' has no bend in the pedicel. *Galanthus* 'Wisley Magnet' is often confused with *G.* 'Galatea' and at Wisley both snowdrops seem to coexist in one large drift.

Literature: Nutt (1993, p. 520).

G. elwesii **'Zwanenburg'** Probably named after the nursery of the same name in The Netherlands. A rather ordinary clone of *G. elwesii*.

GLOSSARY, ABBREVIATIONS, AND TERMS

A List of Acronyms, Abbreviations, Latin, and Technical or Special Terms and Words

Terms in italics are Latin. Terms followed by a full stop are abbreviations. Terms consisting of capital letters only are acronyms.

abaxial the side or face positioned away from the axis; dorsal or lower surface

acapitate non capitate; without a head

acidic soil with a pH of less than 7

acuminate having a gradually diminishing point

acute sharp, ending in a point; sharply pointed but not drawn out

adaxial the side or face next to the axis; ventral or upper surface

AGM Award of Garden Merit: an award given to plants by The Royal Horticultural Society (not at shows) based on a plant's appearance and performance in the garden

allopatric species distributions that neither overlap nor touch; distributions that are geographically separate

AM Award of Merit: an award given to plants at Royal Horticultural Society shows, primarily based on the appearance of a plant at a show

anatomy the study of the internal structures of an organism

androecium the 'male' parts of the flower, including the anther sacs, filaments, and pollen

anon. anonymous; without author or author unknown

anthesis the stage of flowering at which the anthers dehisce, or split open, and release their pollen

apex the tip or end of a plant structure, such as a leaf, perianth segment, or anther

apiculate furnished with an apiculum

apiculum a sharp and short but not rigid point

applanate (vernation) with both leaves flat together in bud; the adaxial, or upper, surfaces facing each other in bud

246

auct. auctorum: of authors

autopolyploid a form of polyploidy resulting from the multiplication of chromosome sets in a cell within a single species, not as the result of hybridization

axile placentation (ovary) ovules positioned in the centre of the ovary, against the axis

basifixed (anthers) anthers attached by their base, or end, to the filaments

binomial a two-part name used in the Linnaean classification system: the first denotes the genus, the second the species

BCE before the common era (often BC, "before Christ")

bulblet small bulb produced from the parent bulb; often called an 'offset'

bulliform cells enlarged cells of the epidermis or upper mesophyll (e.g. of the leaf)

calcareous soils soils occurring over calcareous substrates, such as limestone and chalk; the pH is usually greater than 7

campanulate bell-shaped

capitate headed; having a head-like structure

capsule a dry or semi-succulent seed pod which splits (lengthways in *Galanthus*) to expose the seeds

carinate keeled; having a projecting, central, longitudinal line or ridge on the abaxial surface

chasmophyte a plant growing on rocks, in rock crevices, or in fissures, rooted in small soil pockets or in detritus and debris

chloroplast a green organelle, or specialized cellular part, found in the cells of green plants that plays an essential role in photosynthesis

chromosome number the number of chromosomes within one cell of a living organism; the number is usually given as either the haploid number (n) or diploid number (2n)

chromosomes threadlike structures within the cells of all living organisms that carry the genetic information of an organism

clinal see cline

cline a gradual change in a character, or suite of characters, that occurs over the range of a species

cochleariform concave like a spoon

coexist to occur in the same area or habitat as one or more other species

comb. illegit. combinatio illegitima: an illegitimate combination; a combination that meets the requirements for a valid combination according to the ICBN but which must be rejected because of the rules of priority

comb. nov. *combinatio nova*: new combination; indicates a new name resulting from a change in the position but not rank of an epithet, such as the transference of a species name from one genus to another

combination the name of a taxon below the rank of genus (e.g. species, subspecies), consisting of the name of the genus followed by the one or more epithets peculiar to the taxon (e.g. *Galanthus* series *Latifolii; Galanthus nivalis, Galanthus plicatus* subsp. *byzantinus*)

concolorous of the same colour, uniform in colour

conspecific two or more species considered to represent a single species; belonging to the same species

cpDNA chloroplast DNA

cross to hybridize; the transfer of pollen from the anthers of one flower to the stigma of another flower in order to affect hybridization between different species, cultivars, etc.

cryptic species two or more species which look very similar (appearing morphologically indistinguishable) but which are in fact separate; closer inspection shows the existence of characters that can be used to circumscribe these species, such as molecular data, anatomy, and reproductive isolation

cucullate having the shape of a hood, particularly in the tip of a leaf or spathe

cultivar a plant variant produced and normally maintained by cultivation

cultivation the raising of plants by horticulture or gardening; not taken immediately from the wild

cuneate wedge-shaped; triangular

cytology the study of cell biology, such as the study of chromosomes

dehiscence the natural rupture or opening of a biological structure, such as the splitting of a seed capsule

descr. *descriptio*: the description of a species or other taxonomic unit

diam. diameter

dicotyledon (often shortened to dicot) a flowering plant having embryos with two cotyledons (seed leaves); general features usually include having broad leaves with branching veins and flower parts in fours and fives (cf. monocotyledon)

diffluent flowing in different directions

diploid having a double set of homologous chromosomes in each cell, the typical state of most organisms; usually written as 2n

discolorous of another colour; not uniform in colour

distribution geographical location in which plants are found growing in the wild

DNA Deoxyribonucleic acid; the primary genetic material of the cell

ed. editor

edn. edition of a book or journal

eds. editors

elaiosome a swollen seed appendage containing substances that are nutritious to insects and other invertebrates (e.g. ants)

electrophoresis a technique for separating mixtures of organic molecules (e.g. DNA) on the basis of their different rates of travel in an electric field

electrophoretic gel a block of semi-solid gel used in electrophoresis

ellipsoid a plane or solid in the shape of an ellipse: oblong with regularly rounded ends

elliptic having the shape of an ellipse, oval in outline: narrowed to rounded ends and widest at or about the middle

emarginate having a notched margin, or border; margin not entire

emend. *emendatus*: emended

entire having a continuous margin, or border; not indented or toothed, whole

epidermal cells the uppermost, or outermost, layer of cells of a biological structure

epiphyte a plant growing on another plant for support and anchorage but not for a direct supply of water or nutrients, such as an orchid growing on a tree branch

epithet the ultimate word of a species or infraspecific name

erecto-patent semi-erect; held at an angle of c. 45°

escape a plant which has left the boundaries of cultivation (e.g. a garden) and is found occurring in natural vegetation

et and

ex after; may be used between the names of two authors, the second of whom validly published the name indicated or suggested by the first author

excl. exclusus: excluded

exine the outer part of the wall of a pollen grain

explicative (vernation) the leaf margins folded sharply under in bud, so that they almost touch the abaxial surface of the same leaf

exserted protruding, exposed; said of stamens or style that are longer than the inner perianth segments

FCC First Class Certificate: an award given to plants at Royal Horticultural Society shows, primarily based on the appearance of a plant at a show

filiform very slender, thread-like

fl. flower

fl. pl. *flore pleno*: having a double flower

forma in the hierarchy of classification, a unit arranged below the rank of variety

fr. fruit

galanthophile a person with a love of snowdrops

garrigue low-growing vegetation consisting of short scrub, spiny plants, and aromatics, typical of the Mediterranean and usually found on thin, poor soils overlying calcareous substrates

gene the basic unit of inheritance, consisting of a specific sequence of DNA subunits (nucleotides) on a DNA chain; the gene usually has a specific function and occupies a particular location on a chromosome

geneaology a list of ancestors of common descent

gene exchange (or gene flow) the exchange of genetic factors (e.g. genes) within and between populations and individuals by interbreeding or migration; the genetic factors are carried in the pollen, seed, or the whole plant, etc.

genome the complete, basic set of chromosomes for a particular organism

genus the category in the nomenclatural hierarchy into which species are placed; species may be grouped into subgenera or sections within the genus

geophyte a plant that exists completely underground for a significant part of its life cycle

glaucescent becoming glaucous; green-grey

glaucous covered with a bluish grey, silvery, or greyish bloom

globose nearly spherical

globular ball-like, globose

gynoecium the 'female' parts of the flower, including the ovary, ovules, style, and stigma

habit the external appearance or form of an organism

habitat the area and conditions in which an organism lives; including such factors as soil, geology, altitude, aspect, and surrounding vegetation or type of plant community in which an organism lives

heteropolar having unequally sized or shaped poles; said of pollen grains

hippocrepiform horseshoe-shaped

holotype a single specimen or illustration used or designated by the author of a name as the nomenclatural type of a particular species, subspecies, etc.

hort. *hortorum*: of gardens; horticulture

hybrid an individual produced from a cross between two different species

ICBN *International Code of Botanical Nomenclature*: a publication outlining the procedures, rules, and recommendations for the naming of plants (Greuter et al., 1994)

ICNCP *International Code of Nomenclature for Cultivated Plants*: a publication outlining the procedures, rules, and recommendations for the naming of cultivated plants (Trehane et al., 1995)

in adnot. *in adnotatione*: in annotation; in a note

in prep. in preparation

in sched. *in scheda*: on a herbarium specimen or label

in syn. *in synonymia*: in synonymy

ined. *ineditus*: unpublished

inferior (ovary) an ovary that is positioned below or encased within the tissue of the receptacle

inflorescence the flowering part of the plant; in *Galanthus* this includes the scape, spathe-valves, pedicel, and flower

infrageneric pertaining to any taxon below the rank of genus, such as subgenus, section, or species.

infraspecific pertaining to any taxon below the rank of species, such as subspecies, variety, or form

introduction a plant that does not naturally occur in a particular country or region, but which occurs in the wild due to human influence (through purpose or chance)

introrse (anthers) anthers that point inwards and usually dehisce towards the centre of the flower

isotype a duplicate specimen of the holotype

karyotype a photographic or diagrammatic representation of the chromosomes from a single cell, showing their size, shape, and number.

lectotype a specimen or illustration selected as the nomenclatural type when no holotype, or single specimen, was indicated in the first publication of a new name

leg. *legit*: he gathered; used to indicate the collector

251

lineage a line of common descent

linear long and narrow, with parallel sides or nearly so

Linnaean of Linnaeus; for example, Linnaean classification

Linnaean classification the system of hierarchical classification of the plant world and binomial nomenclature established by Linnaeus and still in use today

Linnaeus (Carl, 1707–1778) Swedish botanist, physician, and zoologist who devised the binomial system of classification

locule the chamber of the ovary

locus classicus the place from which the type specimen, or nomenclatural type, was collected

longitudinal lengthways; running along the length

lorate strap-shaped

maquis stunted woodland or scrub woodland found in semi-arid regions, such as the Mediterranean, that have been deforested, burned, or otherwise affected by agriculture; the thin, poor soil often associated with this habitat supports shrubs and dwarf trees up to about 3 m in height

marginate with a complete margin, or border; without notches or indentations

matt lacking lustre, dull

median pertaining to the middle; the longitudinal axis

membranous membrane-like, papery, dry but flexible, often translucent

meristem the growing point of plant structures from which new cells originate, develop, and expand

mesophyll the unspecialized cells that make up the bulk of leaf tissue

microclimate the climate in the immediate surroundings or local environment of an organism; differs from the larger regional climate, or macroclimate; many local factors may govern the microclimate, including natural and manufactured features

monocotyledon (often shortened to monocot) a flowering plant having embryos with one cotyledon (seed leaf); general features usually include having narrow leaves with parallel veins, and having flower parts in threes or multiples of three (cf. dicotyledon)

monograph a definitive written account of a group of related organisms

monosulcate having one groove or furrow

morphology the external features and characteristics of an organism; the study of these

morphometrics the quantitative study of the shape and form of biological structures

mucronate possessing a short and straight point

native an organism that occurs naturally in a country, region, etc.

naturalized describes an alien or introduced species that has become successfully established and which reproduces itself in its new environment

nectary a nectar-secreting gland

neotype a specimen or illustration selected to serve as the nomenclatural type when all the original material on which a name was based is missing or assumed to be destroyed

nom. *nomen*: name

nom. ambig. *nomen ambiguum*: ambiguous name

nom. cons. prop. *nomen conservandum propositum*: a name formally proposed for conservation according to the rules of the ICBN

nom. illeg. *nomen illegitimum*: an illegitimate name; a name which meets the requirements for valid publication according to the ICBN but which must be rejected because of the rules of priority

nom. invalid. *nomen invalidum*: invalid name; names which are not validly published according to the rules of the ICBN

nom. rej. prop. *nomen rejiciendum propositum*: a name formally proposed for rejection according to the rules of the ICBN

nom. superfl. *nomen superfluum*; name superfluous when published

nom. tant. *nomen tantum*: name only; indicates the author had no desire to publish the name in question

nomenclature branch of science concerned with the naming of organisms

non not

non vidi not seen; usually pertaining to specimens and particularly used by authors to state that they have not seen the type(s)

obclavate club-shaped, with the thickest end downward

oblanceolate a shape, especially of a leaf, that is lance-like, broader in the terminal upper third than in the middle, tapering towards the base; the reverse of lanceolate

obovate a shape, especially of a leaf, that is egg-like, broader in the terminal upper third than in the middle, tapering towards the base; the reverse of ovate

obovoid a structure that is obovate in outline

obtuse blunt, rounded; said of the apex

organism any living thing, such as a plant, animal, fungus or bacteria

orthographical variant an alternative spelling for the same name

ovary the 'female' part of the flower containing the ovules, which after fertilization become the seeds

ovoid a structure that is oval in outline

PC Certificate of Preliminary Commendation: an award given to plants at Royal Horticultural Society shows, primarily based on the appearance of a plant at a show

pedicel the stalk of a single flower

perforate having many holes

perianth the showy parts of the flower: the petals, or corolla, the calyx, or both together; *Galanthus* (and many other monocotyledons) have no calyx, and the flowers are referred to in terms of perianth segments instead of petals

perianth segment one part of the perianth; *Galanthus* have six segments to each perianth

pers. comm. personal communication, such as through conversation or written correspondence

petaloid petal-like

petaloid monocotyledons the group of monocots that have showy flower parts, or 'petals', i.e., excluding grasses and sedges

petiole a leaf stalk

pl. plate; and illustration, painting, or photograph

plantsman one who has a large and/or specialist knowledge of plants, and grows them

poculiform cup-shaped; for *Galanthus*, results when the two whorls of perianth segments have approximately the same dimensions

pollen grains borne by the anthers, containing the 'male' element of the plant

pollination the process by which pollen is transferred from anther to stigma

polyploid having more than two sets of chromosomes in the same cell; the typical condition is diploid, having two sets of chromosomes per cell

porandrous (anthers) anthers that shed pollen through a pore

pre-Linnaean pertaining to works published before 1 January 1753 (the publication date of Linnaeus' *Species Plantarum*)

priority the principal of nomenclature (after the ICBN) whereby the first published name takes precedence over later names for the same taxon at the same rank

pro min. part. pro minore parte: for the smaller part

pro parte pro parte: partly, in part

progenitor ancestor

propagule the product of sexual or non-sexual reproduction and propagation

prostrate lying flat (e.g. leaves lying flat on the ground)

protologue all the information, including text and illustration(s), associated with a name at its place of first valid publication

rank any category in the hierarchy of nomenclatural classification

rbDNA ribosomal DNA

receptacle the enlarged end of a flower stem, or pedicel, on which some or all of the flower parts are borne; in a flower with a inferior ovary (such as *Galanthus*) the receptacle encloses the ovary and becomes the external wall of the fruit

recurving bent or curved downwards

reflexed abruptly bent downwards or backwards

revolute rolled back from the margin or apex

RFLP restriction fragment length polymorphisms, a method of DNA analysis that may be used for systematic purposes

RHS Royal Horticultural Society

ribosome an inclusion within the cells of living organisms that plays an essential role in the production of proteins

s.n. *sine numero*: without a number; used mainly for indicating that a herbarium specimen does not have a number associated with the collector

scape a leafless stalk arising from the ground, bearing one or many flowers

scapose bearing flowers or inflorescence on a scape

selection in the case of horticulture, a process by which plants are chosen for their attributes and potential to make good garden subjects

semi-cryptic species a species that is almost a cryptic species

sensu in the sense of; the manner in which an author interpreted or used a name

sens. lat. *sensu lato*: in the broad sense; a taxon, usually a species, including all its variants and subordinate taxa and/or other taxa which are sometimes considered as distinct entities

ser. series; pertaining to series in a journal or book

sic used after a word that looks wrong or absurd, to show that it has been quoted correctly

sp. species (singular); also *sp.* for *species*

sp. nov. *species nova*: a new species

spathe a modified leaf or leaves forming a structure that encloses the bud of the inflorescence or flower

spathulate more or less spoon-shaped; a shape, often of a leaf, that is distinctly broader in the upper, terminal third, narrowing quickly at about the middle, and then tapering to the base

species the basic unit of classification; the lowest principal taxonomic rank

spp. species (plural); also *spp.* for *species*

stat. status: rank

stigma the tip of the style; the area of the style that receives the pollen

style the stalk connecting the stigma and the ovary; the pollen travels through this structure

subgeneric pertaining to any taxon below the rank of genus: subgenus, section, subsection, species, etc.

subsp. subspecies; also *subsp.* for *subspecies*

subspecies the rank in the nomenclatural hierarchy immediately below the level of species

sulcate grooved or furrowed lengthways

supervolute (vernation) having one leaf fully or partially enveloping the other; leaves rolled towards the adaxial surface (in *Galanthus*)

sympatric when two species, populations, or other taxa occur in the same geographical area, overlap, or are contiguous

sympodial (inflorescence) an inflorescence with a determinate growing point, with any further growth of the inflorescence occurring below it

synonym a name that is applied to a taxon but that cannot be used because it is not the accepted name; the synonym or synonyms form the synonymy

systematics the study of the relationships between groups of organisms (e.g. plant species); systematic studies are usually undertaken within a genealogical framework

tab. tabula: plate (a full page illustration)

taxa plural of taxon

taxon a taxonomic entity or group of any rank; a taxon must include all its subordinate taxa (e.g. *Galanthus nivalis*, *Galanthus alpinus* var. *bortkewitschianus*)

taxonomy the science, study, or act of classifying organisms (e.g. plants)

tectum the outermost wall of the pollen grain wall (exine), on which the sculpturing is usually found

terricolous living on or in the soil

trilocular (ovary) an ovary with three locules

triloculate having three locules

triploid a polyploid having three sets of chromosomes; written as 3n

type (specimen) a herbarium specimen or illustration which fixes the application of a name; the type is used as the definitive reference for the name it represents

type locality the location in which the type specimen (e.g. holotype) was collected

typification the process by which types are designated

unguiculate narrowed into a petiole-like base; clawed

var. variety; also *var.* for *varietas*

variant any organism or group of organisms (e.g. a plant) that is different from the type species or normal range of variation but to which no taxonomic rank is given; a term used to indicate an individual with atypical or unusual characteristics but one which does not warrant recognition within a taxonomic framework

variety a unit of classification arranged in the hierarchy of classification below the rank of subspecies

vernation the order of unfolding of leaf buds; the arrangement of leaves in bud; in *Galanthus* it is usually possible to ascertain the type of vernation after the bud stage and during maturity by looking at how the leaves are folded at the base of the plant

APPENDIX 1

An outline of Stern's classification, based on his Key to the Series of *Galanthus* (1956)

A. Flowers appearing before the leaves in autumn, or more usually, appearing with the leaves; leaves narrow (usually less than 1cm wide), of almost equal width throughout; leaves pressed flat against each other in vernation.

Series 1 *NIVALES* Beck
  1. *G. nivalis* subsp. *nivalis* L.
    G. nivalis subsp. *cilicius* (Baker) Gottl.-Tann.
    G. nivalis subsp. *reginae-olgae* (Orph.) Gottl.-Tann.
  2. *G. corcyrensis* (Beck) Stern
  3. *G. rizehensis* Stern
  4. *G. graecus* Orph. ex Boiss.

AA. Flowers always appearing with the leaves; leaves broad (usually more than 1cm wide) with margins rolled or folded in vernation.

B. Leaves plicate in vernation with margins folded outwards.

Series 2 *PLICATI* Beck
  5. *G. plicatus* M. Bieb.
  6. *G. woronowii* Losinsk.
  7. *G. byzantinus* Baker

BB. Leaves convolute in vernation, the outer leaf rolled around the inner which has margins folded inwards on non-flowering bulbs.

Series 3 *LATIFOLII* Stern
  8. *G. ikariae* subsp. *ikariae* Baker
    G. ikariae subsp. *latifolius* Stern

9. *G. fosteri* Baker
10. *G. caucasicus* (Baker) Grossh.
11. *G. elwesii* var. *elwesii* Hook. f.
    G. elwesii var. *maximus* (Velen.) Beck
12. *G. allenii* Baker

APPENDIX 2

Classification of *Galanthus* into groups of no taxonomic rank, after Artjushenko (1965)

Anatomical Group I—Rectangular Epidermal Cells—The Caucasus

Group 1. Caucasus and Aegean Island of Ikaria
[Right-angled epidermal cells, leaves without hollows, vernation convolute]
    G. ikariae Baker (incl. *G. woronowii* Losinsk., *in syn.*)
    G. krasnovii A.P. Khokhr.
    G. platyphyllus Traub & Moldenke
Group 2. Caucasus
[Right-angled epidermal cells, leaves with hollows, vernation convolute]
    G. alpinus Sosn.
    G. bortkewitschianus Koss
    G. caucasicus (Baker) Grossh.
Group 3. Caucasus and Asia Minor
[Right-angled epidermal cells, leaves with big hollows, vernation applanate]
    G. lagodechianus Kem.-Nath.
    G. transcaucasicus Fomin (incl. *G. rizehensis* Stern, *in syn.*)

Anatomical Group II—Tapering Epidermal Cells—Europe

Group 4. Europe and Asia Minor
[Epidermal cells tapering to the ends, leaves with big hollows, vernation applanate]
    G. corcyrensis (Beck) Stern
    G. nivalis L.
    G. reginae-olgae Orph.

Group 5. Europe and Asia Minor
[Epidermal cells severely constricted towards the ends, leaves with big hollows, vernation plicate]
G. *plicatus* M. Bieb.
G. *byzantinus* Baker

APPENDIX 3

An outline of the classification of *Galanthus*, after Artjushenko (1966 and 1970)†

Section 1 *GALANTHUS* L.
Leaves glaucous, epidermal cells tapering to the ends. Species growing in central southern Europe and in northwest Asia Minor.
[*Foliorum epiderma e cellulis elongatis plerumque subrhombeis (non rectangularibus) constans. Species Europae mediae et australis ac paris boreali-occidentlasi Asiae Minoris.*]

1a. *G. nivalis* L. subsp. *nivalis*
1b. *G. nivalis* L. subsp. *angustifolius* (Koss) Artjush.
2. *G. reginae-olgae* Orph.
3. *G. corcyrensis* (Beck) Stern
4. *G. graceus* Orph. ex Boiss.*
5. *G. elwesii* Hook. f.*
6. *G. plicatus* M. Bieb.
7. *G. byzantinus* Baker

Section 2 *VIRIDIFOLII* Kem.-Nath.
Leaves glaucous, shiny or matt-surfaced, with rectangular epidermal cells. Species growing in the Caucasus and Asia Minor, including only the northeastern part of the latter (*G. ikariae* is the only exception).
[*Foliorum epiderma e cellulis rectangularibus constans. Species Caucasi et Asiae Minoris (parte eius boreali-occidentali exclusua).*]

8. *G. caucasicus* (Baker) Grossh.
9. *G. alpinus* Sosn.
10. *G. bortkewitschianus* Koss
11. *G. ikariae* Baker (incl. *G. woronowii* Losinsk., *in syn.*)
12. *G. platyphyllus* Traub & Moldenke
13. *G. krasnovii* A.P. Khokhr.
14. *G. fosteri* Baker*

15. *G. transcaucasicus* Fomin (incl. *G. rizehensis* Stern, *in syn.*)
16. *G. cilicicus* Baker**
17. *G. lagodechianus* Kem.-Nath.

†The Latin descriptions of Section 1 and Section 2, included in brackets, are taken from Artjushenko (1966).

*Species marked with one asterisk were not included in previous classification (Artjushenko, 1965). *Galanthus cilicicus* Baker, marked with two asterisks (**), was included in the text of the 1965 publication but not in the classification.

APPENDIX 4

A guide to pre-Linnaean literature

This list is intended as a guide for those interested in the early literature on *Galanthus*. It is not an exhaustive survey of pre-Linnaean works. Further editions and reprints of these titles have not been included here, except in a few instances.

With Illustrations

1554 Mattioli, P.A. *Medici Senensis commentarii, in sex libros Pedacii Dioscoridis,* book 3, cap. 160, p. 537. Venice.

As **Narcissus** (An illustration of a *Galanthus* with many leaves, therefore probably combining the morphology of *Galanthus* and *Leucojum*).

1568 Dodoens, R. *Florum et coronarium odorataumque nonnullarum herbarum historia,* p. 192. Antverpiae: ex Christophori Plantini.

As **Leucoium bulb. triphyllon** [*sic*] (= *Galanthus nivalis*).

1576 Lobel, M. de. *Plantarum seu stirpium historia,* p. 64 [plate in lower left-hand corner]. Antverpiae: ex officina Christophori Plantini Architypographi Regii.

As **Leuconarcissolirion minum** (= *Galanthus nivalis*).

1581 Lobel, M. de. *Plantarum seu stirpium [icones],* p. 123. Antwerp: Christopher Plantin.

As **Leuconarcisso-lirion minum** (= *Galanthus nivalis*).

1581 Lobel, M. de. *Kruydtboeck* oft beschrijvinghe van allerleye ghewassen, p. 160 [left-hand plate]. t'Antwerpen: by Christoffer Plantyn.

As **Leuconarcisso-lirion minimum (Leucoium bulbosum triphyllum)** (= *Galanthus nivalis*).

264

1583 Clusius, C. *Rariorum aliquot stirpium, per Pannonian, Austriam & vicinas . . . historia,* pp. 181, 183. Antwerpen: ex officina Christophori Plantini.

As **Leucoium bulbosum praecox minus** (= *Galanthus nivalis*) [fig. p. 182], and **Leucoium bulbos. praecox byzantinum*** (= *Galanthus plicatus*) [fig. not included].

1583 Dodoens, R. *Stirpium historiae pemptades sex,* p. 230. Antverpiae: ex officina Christophori Plantini Architypographi Regii.

As **Leucoion bulbosum triphyllon** (= *Galanthus nivalis*).

1586 Daléchamps, J. *Historiae generalis plantarum* in libros XVIII, vol. 2, lib 15, p. 1527. Lyon: apud Gulielmum Rouillium.

As **Viola alba bulbosa (Leucoion bulbosa)** (mixed plate of *Galanthus* and *Leucojum*).

1590 Tabernmontanus, J.T. *Eicones plantarum,* p. 614. Frankfurt: Nicolao Bassaeo.

As **Leucoium bulbosum II** (= *Galanthus* sp.).

1591 Tabernmontanus, J.T. *Neuw Kreuterbuch,* p. 308. Frankfurt: Nicolao Bassaeo.

As **Leucoium bulbosum II** (= *Galanthus* sp.).

1596 Mattioli, P.A. *Kreutterbuch,* p. 456 [plate D. opposite p. 456]. Florent.

As **Narcissus VII, Leucoion Theophrasti Triphyllon** (= *Galanthus nivalis*).

1597 Gerard, J. *Herball,* p. 120. London: John Norton.

As **Leucoium bulbosum preacox. Timely flowring** [*sic*] **Bulbus violet** (= *Galanthus nivalis*) [illustration the same as Tabernmontanus, 1590].

1601 Clusius, C. *Rariorum plantarum historia,* p. 169. Antverpiae: ex officina Plantiniana apub Ioannem Moretum.

As **Leucoium bulbosum praecox minus** (= *Galanthus nivalis*), and **Leucoium bulbosum praecox Byzantinus** (= *Galanthus* sp.).

1611 De Bry, J.T. *Florilegium novum* [no page or plate numbers].

As **Leucoium bulbos. praecox minus** [*sic*] (= *Galanthus nivalis*) and **Leucoium bul. praecox Byzant.** [*sic*] (= *Galanthus plicatus*).

1612 Sweert, E. *Florilegium,* pl. 20, no 3. Frankfurt: ad Moenum Apud Anthoricum Kempner Sumptibus Autoris.

As **Narcisolyrion maius praecox album** (= *Galanthus* sp.) In this plate the outer and inner whorl of segments are the same size. The same plate is shown in Rabel, 1621, with the error corrected.

1613 Besler, B. *Hortus eystettensis,* vol. 2, primo ordo, icones plantarum autmnalium, collectarum plantarum Hyemalium, nos. II and III [no page numbers]. Nürenburg.

As **Leucoium bulbosum triphyl. Maius Byzantinum*** [*sic*] (= *Galanthus* sp.) and **Leucoium bulbosum triphyl. Minus** [*sic*] (= *Galanthus nivalis*).

1614 Pas, C. *Hortus floridus,* pl. 4. (of Hyemalis). Arahemy apud Ioannem Iansonium Bibliopalem ibid.

As **Leucoium bulb.** [*sic*] **Triphyllon** (= *Galanthus nivalis*) and **Leucoium Triph.** [*sic*] **Byzant.** (= *Galanthus plicatus*).

1621 Rabel, D. [based on Sweerts, 1612]. *Theatrum florae,* pl. 20, no 3.

As **Narcisolyrion maius praecox album** (= *Galanthus* sp.). The plate in this work is based on that found in Sweerts, 1612; the plate is coloured. A new edition of this work was published in 1633.

1626 Bry, J.T. *Anthologia magna, sive florilegium novum . . .,* pl. 6. Frankfurt.

As **Leucoium bulbos. praecox minus** [*sic*] (= *Galanthus nivalis*) and **Leucoium bul. praecox Byzant.** [*sic*] (= *Galanthus plicatus*).

1629 Parkinson, J. *Paradisi in sole paradisus terrestris,* p. 109, pl. 9 [ii] p. 107. London.

As **Leucoium bulbosum praecox minus—The lesser early bulbous violet** (= *Galanthus nivalis*).

1636 Gerard, J. *Herball,* Lib. 1, p. 147, pl. 1, 2. London: Adam Norton.

As **Leucoium bulbosum minus. Timely flowring** [*sic*] **Bulbous violet** (= *Galanthus nivalis*) and **Leucoium bulbosum preacox Byzantinum.*** **The Byzantine early bulbous violet** (= *Galanthus plicatus*).

1641 De Bry, J.T. *Florilegium renovatum et auctum,* pl. 20. Oppenheim: J.T. de Bry.

266

As **Leucoium bulbos. praecox minus** [*sic*] (= *Galanthus nivalis*) and **Leucoium bul. praecox Byzant.** [*sic*] (= *Galanthus plicatus*).

1642 Mattioli, P.A. *Les Commentaris*, p. 45.
As **Narcisse VI** (= *Galanthus* sp.). Many other editions and reprints of this work were published from the mid-sixteenth to the late seventeenth centuries.

1664 Tabernmontanus, J.T. *New vollkommenlich Kräuter Buch*, p. 1005. Basel.
As **Leucojum bulbosum secundum** (= *Galanthus* sp.).

1666 Chabrey, D. *Stirpium icones et sciagraphia*, p. 211, [2 plates]. Geneve: Phil. Gamoneti & alc de la Piere.
As **Leucoium bulbosum minus triphyllum** (= *Galanthus nivalis*) and **Leucoium bulbosum praecox Byzantinum*** (= *Galanthus plicatus*).

1676 Cause, D.H. *De koninglycke Hovenier* 2nd pl. [after p. 72]. Amsterdam: Marcus Doornick.
As **Leucojon triphyllon** (= *Galanthus nivalis*).

1694 Tournefort, J.P. de. *Élemens de botanique*, vol. 1, p. 306; vol. 2, pl. 208. Paris: de L'Imprimerie Royale.
As **Narcissoleucoium trifolium minus—Le Percenége** (= *Galanthus nivalis*).

1700 Tournefort, J.P. de. *Institutiones rei herbariae*, vol. 2, tab. 208. Paris: Joanne Anisson.
As **Narcissoleucoium—Le Percenege** (= *Galanthus nivalis*).

1713 Besler, B. *Hortus eystettensis*: vol. 1, pl. 1, nos. 2 and 3. Ioannis Antonii I.
As **Leucoium bulbosum triphyllon Majus Byzantinum*** (= *Galanthus plicatus*) and **Leucoium bulbosum triphyllon Minus** (= *Galanthus* ? *nivalis*).

1715 Morison, R. *Plantarum historiae universalis oxoniensis*, sect. 4, p. 364 tab. 9, fig. 23 [after page 450]. Oxonii: E Theatro Sheldoniano et Prostant Londini Apud Paulum & Isaacum Vaillart.
As **Leocoion bulbosum praecox minus** (= *Galanthus nivalis*) and

267

Leucoium bulbosum triphyllon majus praecox Bizantinum* [*sic*]
(= *Galanthus* ?*plicatus*).

1732 Furber, R. *The Flower-Garden Displayed*, p. 2 (January), nos. 3
and 4 [figs. in a mixed bouquet of flowers. London: printed for J.
Hazard et al.

As **Greater early Snowdrop** (= *Galanthus* sp.) and **Single Snowdrop** (= *Galanthus nivalis*).

1737 Lonicer, A. *Krauter-Buch*, p. 422, cap. 253. Bohn: Daniel Bar-
tholomai.

As **Leucoion Theophrasti** (= *Galanthus* sp.).

[**1747** Anon., *Compleat florist*, pl. 57. London: J. Duke.

As **Greater early snowdrop** (= *Leucojum vernum*—not *Galanthus*).]

Without Illustrations

1611 Reneaulme, P. *Specimen historiae plantarum*, p. 97. Paris: apud
Hadrianum Beys.

As **Erangelia** (= *Galanthus*).

1623 Bauhin, C. *Pinax theatri botanici*, p. 56. Baisileae Helvet. Sumptibus & typis Ludovici Regis.

As **Leucoium bulbosum trifolium minus** (= *Galanthus nivalis*) and
Leucoium bulbosum trifolium majus (= *Galanthus* sp.—Leucoium
bulbosum Byzant. [Clusius] and Leucoium bulbosum triphyllum
majus Byzantinum* [Besler] in synonymy = *Galanthus plicatus*).

1651 Bauhin, J. *Historia plantarum universalis*, vol. 2, pp. 591–592.
Ebroduni [= Yverdon].

As **Leucoium bulbosum minus Triphyllum** (= *Galanthus nivalis*)
and **Leocoion bulbosum praecox Byzantinum*** (= *Galanthus plicatus*).

1688 Ray, J. *Historia plantarum*, vol. 2, pp. 1144–1145. Londini: Typis
Mariae Clark: prostant apud Henricum Faithorne.

As **Leucoium bulbosum minus triphyllon**—The lesser early bulbous Violet, or Snow-drops [*sic*] (= *Galanthus nivalis*) and **Leucoium
bulbosum praecox byzantinum*** (= *Galanthus nivalis*—'Neapoli
etiam á Fer. Imperato, è monte Virgino erutus').

1700 Rudbeck, O.J. *Campus Elysius* 2: p. 96. Uppsala.
As **Leucoium bulbosum triphyllum minus**.

1700 Tournefort, J.P. *Institutiones rei herbariae*, vol. 1, p. 387. Etypographia Regia.
As **Narcisso-Leucojum trifolium minus** (= *Galanthus nivalis*).

1733 Furber, R. *A Short Introduction to Gardening or a Guide to Gentlemen and Ladies in Furnishing their Gardens*, p. 38, no. 4; p. 39, nos. 19 and 21. London: H. Woodfall.
As **Single Snow-Drop** (= *Galanthus nivalis*), **The greater Snow-Drop** (= *Galanthus* or *Leucojum*) and **Double Snow-Drop** (= *Galanthus nivalis* 'Flore Pleno').

1736 Siegesbeck, J.G. *Primitae florae petropolitanae*, p. 3. Rigae: Charactere Samuel Laur. Frölich.
As **Chianthemum** (= *Galanthus* and *Leucojum*).

1737 Clifford, G. *Hortus Cliffortianus*. Amsteleadami, p. 134.
As **Galanthus** [after Linnaeus, *Genera Plantarum*, p. 288 (1735)].

1748 Heister, L. *Systema plantarum generale*, p. 19. Helmstadii: apud Christian Frederic Weygand.
As **Nivaria** (= *Galanthus*).

*In most cases the epithet *byzantinum* refers to *Galanthus plicatus*, but it may also refer to the larger variants of *G. nivalis* from central and southern Italy. See the discussion of *G. plicatus* in the Taxonomy of *Galanthus*.

APPENDIX 5

Synonyms for *Galanthus nivalis*

During the late nineteenth and early twentieth centuries, the use of standard conventions and guidelines for the naming of plants was neither so widely nor so strictly in force as it is today, particularly for names used in the horticultural literature. In many publications of that era no clear distinction is made between botanical units of classification (e.g. species, subspecies and varieties) and cultivar names for plants of garden and horticultural origin (e.g. those resulting from hybridization or selection by man). In some publications it is unclear whether the author of the article was referring to a botanical unit of classification or a cultivar. This problem is compounded because these names often do comply with the conditions for effective publication outlined in the ICBN (*International Code of Botanical Nomenclature*), which is retrospectively less rigorous when applied to earlier publications. In most circumstances it is possible to deduce that the author was using a name without any desire to name a new species, variety, etc., but many works did describe new taxa in the horticultural literature, such as *The Garden* and *The Gardeners Chronicle*, and therefore these publications need to be checked carefully. Indeed, there are many examples of explicitly and legitimately published taxa, such as those in which the author described and discussed a plant of wild provenance, listed the characters that distinguish one taxa from another, or provided a Latin description. Other names are ambiguous, however, and it is often difficult or impossible to be clear as to the author's intentions. For the purposes of this work I have removed most of the equivocal names from the main body of the monograph. Those names that I think might be of garden origin have been listed here. All these names represent synonyms of *G. nivalis*, and many of them have been reclassified as cultivars (see the Cultivars chapter and Appendix 6).

Names are arranged alphabetically. The symbol † denotes invalid names or those not validly published.

Galanthus nivalis *L.*

G. aestivalis Burb. in J. Roy. Hort. Soc. 13(2): 200 (1891).†

G. boydii Burb. in J. Roy. Hort. Soc. 13(2): 200 (1891).†

G. cathcartiae (hort. J. Allen) Burb. in J. Roy. Hort. Soc. 13(2): 200 (1891).

G. flavescens Boyd ex Ewbank in Garden (London) 39: 272 (1891).†

G. flavescens Burb. in Gard. Chron. ser. 3, 7: 268 (1890).†

G. flavescens Burb. in J. Roy. Hort. Soc. 13(2): 202 (1891).†

G. flavescens J. Allen in Garden (London) 40: 272 (1891).†

G. flavescens J. Allen in J. Roy. Hort. Soc. 13(2): 181 (1891).

G. lutescens hort. ex Correvon in Le Jardin 32: 139 (1888).†

G. lutescens J. Allen in Garden (London) 29: 75 (1886).

G. melvillei hort. ex Burb. in J. Roy. Hort. Soc. 13(2): 205, fig. 31 (1891).†

G. melvillei hort. ex Correvon in Le Jardin 32: 139 (1888).†

G. melvillei hort. ex Siebert & Voss in Vilm. Blumengärt. edn. 3, 1: 1006 (1895).†

G. melvillei [var.] *major* J. Allen in J. Roy. Hort. Soc. 13(2): 173 (1891).†

G. nivalis L. forma *virescens* Leichtlin in Gard. Chron. new ser., 11: 342 (1879).

G. nivalis L. [var.] *albus* J. Allen in J. Roy. Hort. Soc. 13(2): 182 (1891).

G. nivalis L. [var.] *cathcartiae* J. Allen in J. Roy. Hort. Soc. 13(2): 184 (1891).

G. nivalis L. var. *europaeus* Beck in Wiener Ill. Gart.-Zeitung 19: 50 (1894).

G. nivalis L. var. *europaeus* Beck forma *aestivalis* (Burb.) Beck in Wiener Ill. Gart.-Zeitung 19: 51 (1894).

G. nivalis L. var. *europaeus* Beck forma *albus* (J. Allen) Beck in Wiener Ill. Gart.-Zeitung 19: 50 (1894).

G. nivalis L. var. *europaeus* Beck forma *biflorus* Beck in Wiener Ill. Gart.-Zeitung 19: 52 (1894).

G. nivalis L. var. *europaeus* Beck forma *biscapus* Beck in Wiener Ill. Gart.-Zeitung 19: 52 (1894).

G. nivalis L. var. *europaeus* Beck forma *candidus* Beck in Wiener Ill. Gart.-Zeitung 19: 52 (1894).

G. nivalis L. var. *europaeus* Beck forma *cathcartiae* (J. Allen) Beck in Wiener Ill. Gart.-Zeitung 19: 52 (1894).

G. nivalis L. var. *europaeus* Beck forma *pallidus* (Smith) Beck in Wiener Ill. Gart.-Zeitung 19: 51 (1894).

G. nivalis L. var. *europaeus* Beck forma *platytepalus* Beck in Wiener Ill. Gart.-Zeitung 19: 50, fig. 1,2 (1894).

G. nivalis L. var. *europaeus* Beck forma *plenissimus* Beck in Wiener Ill. Gart.-Zeitung 19: 50 (1894).

G. nivalis L. var. *europaeus* Beck forma *poculiformis* (hort.) Beck in Wiener Ill. Gart.-Zeitung 19: 50 (1894).†

G. nivalis L. var. *europaeus* Beck forma *sandersii* (Harpur-Crewe) Beck in Wiener Ill. Gart.-Zeitung 19: 50 (1894).

G. nivalis L. var. *europaeus* Beck forma *stenotepalus* Beck in Wiener Ill. Gart.-Zeitung 19: 50, fig. 1,1 (1894).

G. nivalis L. var. *europaeus* Beck forma *trifolius* Beck in Wiener Ill. Gart.-Zeitung 19: 52 (1894).

G. nivalis L. var. *europaeus* Beck forma *virescens* (Leichtlin) Beck in Wiener Ill. Gart.-Zeitung 19: 51, fig. 1,4 (1894).

G. nivalis L. var. *europaeus* Beck forma *viridans* Beck in Wiener Ill. Gart.-Zeitung 19: 51, fig. 1,3 (1894).

G. nivalis L. var. *lutescens* hort. ex Baker, Handb. Amaryll.: 17 (1888).†

G. nivalis L. var. *lutescens* Mallett in Garden (London) 67: 87 (1905).†

G. nivalis L. [var.] *melvillei* Bowles in J. Roy. Hort. Soc. 43: 30, fig. 2 (1918).†

G. nivalis L. var. *melvillei* Harpur-Crewe in Gard. Chron. new ser., 11: 237 (1879).

G. nivalis L. var. *poculiformis* (Beck) Bowles in J. Roy. Hort. Soc. 43: 30 (1918).†

G. nivalis L. var. *poculiformis* hort. ex Baker, Handb. Amaryll.: 17 (1888).†

G. nivalis L. var. *poculiformis* Mallett in Garden (London) 67: 87 (1905).†

G. nivalis L. var. *sandersii* Harpur-Crewe in Gard. Chron. new ser., 11: 342 (1879).

G. nivalis L. [var.] *serotinus* hort. ex Correvon in Le Jardin 32: 140 (1888).

G. pallidus Smith ex Burb. in J. Roy. Hort. Soc. 13(2): 206 (1891).†

G. poculiformis hort. ex Burb. in J. Roy. Hort. Soc. 13(2): 207 (1891).†

G. poculiformis hort. ex Correvon in Le Jardin 32: 139 (1888).†

G. poculiformis J. Allen in Garden (London) 29: 75 (1886).†

G. serotinus D. Melville in Gard. Chron. new ser., 15: 181 (1881).†

G. serotinus hort. [Dunrobin] ex. Burb. in J. Roy. Hort. Soc. 13(2): 209 (1891).†

G. umbrensis [*sic*] hort. [Dammann] ex Burb. in J. Roy. Hort.Soc. 13(2): 209 (1891).†

G. umbricus Dewar in Gard. Chron. ser. 3, 7: 107 (1890).†

G. umbricus J. Allen in J. Roy. Hort. Soc. 13(2): 184 (1891).†

G. umbricus Wolley Dod in Gard. Chron. ser. 3, 7: 207 (1890).†

G. virescens Anon. in Garden (London) 25: 371 (1884).

G. virescens Burb. in J. Roy. Hort.Soc. 13(2): 209, fig 33. (1891).†

G. virescens Ewbank in Garden (London) 39: 273, fig. p. 276 (1891).†

G. virescens J. Allen in Garden (London) 29: 75 (1886).†

G. virescens J. Allen in Garden (London) 40: 272 (1891).†

G. virescens (Leichtlin) Correvon in Le Jardin 2: 140 (1888).

G. warei Burb. in J. Roy. Hort. Soc. 13(2): 210 (1891).†

G. warei J. Allen in J. Roy. Hort. Soc. 13(2): 183 (1891 [10 March]); J. Allen in Garden (London) 40: 273 (1891 [19 September]).

APPENDIX 6

Galanthus cultivars no longer in cultivation

The following list includes all the cultivars thought to be no longer in cultivation. The use of this list is twofold: firstly it can be used to check if a newly proposed name has been used before, and secondly it provides a ready means of accessing the available data, should any of these cultivars be rediscovered. Many cultivar names listed here have been used as epithets for species, subspecies, and varieties. In order to cross reference these names an asterisk (*) or a double asterisk (**) has been used to indicate that a name has been included in the taxonomic parts of this work: at a single asterisk (*), see the Taxonomy of *Galanthus*; at a double asterisk (**), see Appendix 5. The references in this section are included in Appendix 7, the bibliography for *Galanthus* cultivars.

G. nivalis **'Acme'** Arnott (1904, p. 166); Stern (1956, p. 71).

G. nivalis **'Aestivalis'** Burbidge (1891a, p. 200); Stern (1956, p. 71).**

G. nivalis **'Aestivum'** Melville (1891, p. 190); Stern (1956, p. 71).

G. **'Afterglow'** Allen (1891, p. 174); Ewbank (1894, p. 125); Stern (1956, p. 71).

G. elwesii **'Aidin'** Arnott (1894, p. 179); Burbidge (1894, p. 127); Ewbank (1894, p. 125); Stern (1956, p. 71).

G. nivalis **'Albus'** (Allen 1891, p. 182); Robinson (1893, p. 429); Arnott (1913, p. 154); Stern (1956, p. 71).

G. **'Allen's Perfection'** Exhibited by R.D. Nutt, see Proc. J. Roy. Hort. Soc., 95(2): 103 (1970a); Nutt (1971, p. 208).

G. **'Allen's Seedling'** Bowles (1918, pp. 31, 32).

G. **'Anacreon'** Ewbank (1894, p. 125); Stern (1956, p. 71).

G. **'Anamus'** Arnott (1894, p. 180). Probably a provisional name used to indicate a locality.

G. nivalis **'Angustifolius'** D.K. (1888, p. 59); Stern (1956, p. 71).

G. **'Aurora'** Ewbank (1894, p. 125); Arnott (1899a, p. 130); Stern (1956, p. 71).

G. elwesii **'Balloon'** Allen (1891, p. 176); Stern (1956, p. 71).

G. plicatus **'Belated'** Bowles (1914, p. 60); Stern (1956, p. 71).

G. nivalis **'Biflorus'** Beck (1894, p. 52); Stern (1956, p. 71).**

G. nivalis **'Biscapus'** Beck (1894, p. 52).**

G. nivalis **'Boydii'** Burbidge (1891a, p. 200); Stern (1956, p. 71).**

G. plicatus **'Breviflos'** Stern (1956, p. 71).

G. nivalis **'Candidus'** Beck (1894, p. 52); Stern (1956, p. 71).**

G. elwesii **'Cassaba Boydii'** Arnott (1905a, p. 173).

G. nivalis **'Cathcarti'** Ewbank (1894, p. 125); Stern (1956, p. 71). Possibly an alternative spelling for *G. nivalis* 'Cathcartiae'.

G. nivalis **'Cathcartiae'** Allen (1891, p. 184); Burbidge (1891a, pp. 195, 200); Beck (1894, p. 52); Stern (1956, p. 71).**

G. plicatus **'Chapeli'** Allen (1891, p. 175); Robinson (1893, p. 427, as *plicatus* 'Chapel var.'); Burbidge (1891a, p. 207); Beck (1894, p. 57); Stern (1956, p. 71); as *G. plicatus chapelensis*: Burbidge (1894, p. 127); Bowles (1917b, p. xlii).

G. nivalis **'Charmer'** Allen (1891, p. 174); Burbidge (1891a, p. 206); Ewbank (1894, p. 125); Burbidge (1894, p. 128); Arnott (1899a, p.130); Bowles (1914, p. 57); Stern (1956, pp. 66, 72); Royal General Bulbgrowers' Association (1991, p. 240).

G. nivalis **'Charmer Flore Pleno'** Ewbank (1894, p. 125); Bowles (1918, pp. 32, 33); Stern (1956, p. 72).

G. **'Claudia'** Ewbank (1894, p. 125); Stern (1956, p. 72).

G. **'Clown'** Ewbank (1894, p. 125); Stern (1956, p. 72).

G. **'Creole'** Allen (1891, p. 185); Stern (1956, p. 72).

G. **'Cupid'** Allen (1891, p. 185); Ewbank (1894, p. 125); Stern (1956, p. 72).

G. nivalis **'Demo'** Arnott (1894, p. 180); Stern (1956, p. 72).

G. elwesii **'Distinction'** Burbidge (1891a, p. 201); Stern (1956, p. 72).

G. **'Dora Parker'** Nutt (1974, p. 21, fig. 18).

G. plicatus **'Dragoon'** Bowles (1917b, p. xlii); Stern (1956, p. 72).

G. **'Early Bird'** Palmer (1967, p. 10).

G. plicatus **'Elegans'** Allen (1891, p. 175); Burbidge (1890, p. 268); Burbidge (1891a, p. 207); Stern (1956, p. 72).

G. **'Elise Scharlok'** Stern (1956, p. 72).

G. **'Elsae'** Allen (1891, p. 181); Burbidge (1891a, p. 201); Bowles (1918, p. 32); Stern (1956, p. 72); Nelson (1992, p. 13).*

G. plicatus **'Emerald'** Burbidge (1891a, pp. 195, 198, 207); Burbidge (1894, p. 128); Stern (1956, p. 72).

G. elwesii **'Erythrae'** (Roozen); Stern (1956, p. 72); 'Erithrae' in J. Roy. Hort. Soc. 26: xxxi (1901–1902).

G. plicatus **'Esmeralda'** Ledger (no reference); Stern (1956, p. 72).

G. **'Fascination'** Ewbank (1894, p. 125); Stern (1956, p. 72).

G. plicatus **'Fenella'** Thompson (without reference); Stern (1956, p. 72).

G. **'Flavus'** in J. Roy. Hort. Soc. 26: 961 (1901–1902).

G. plicatus **'Frazeri'** Arnott (1899a, p. 129); Arnott (1912, p. 10); Arnott (1905b, p. 173); Arnott (1923, p. 103); Stern (1956, p. 72).

G. elwesii **'Gem'** Burbidge (1891a, pp. 201, 202).

G. elwesii **'Globosus'** Burbidge (1891a, pp. 202, 203); Wilks (1887, p. 393); Baker (1888, p. 17); Stern (1956, p. 72).*

G. elwesii **'Globosus'** hort. Correvon (1888, p. 140).*

G. plicatus **'Gottwaldi'** Irving (1906a, p. 105); Stern (1956, p. 72).

G. **'Grandiflorus'** Baker (1893a, p. 656); Bowles (1918, p. 36); Stern (1956, p. 72). See the Hybrids chapter; this clone is probably no longer in cultivation.

G. nivalis **'Grandior'** Schult. & Schult. f. (1830, p. 781, as *G. nivalis* var. *grandior*); Beck (1894, p. 53); Stern (1956, p. 72).*

G. **'Gusmusi'** Allen (1886, p. 74); Allen (1891, p. 174); Stern (1956, p. 73).

G. nivalis **'Hololeucus'** Čelakovsky (1891, p. 198); Beck (1894, p. 50); Stern (1956, p. 73).*

G. **'Hortensis'** Herbert (1837, p. 330); Beck (1894, p. 50); Stern (1956, p. 73).

G. **'Hybridus'** Beck (1894, p. 57).

G. **'Jason Scharlock'** Stern (1956, p. 73).

G. **'Kew'** Nutt (1971, p. 208).

G. **'Lanarth'** Exhibited by Mrs. G. Anley, see Proc. Roy. Hort. Soc. 90(1): 20 (1965).

G. **'Lazybones'** Allen (1891, p. 174); Ewbank (1894, p. 125); Stern (1956, p. 73).

G. fosteri **'Leopard'** Allen (1891, p. 183); Stern (1956, p. 73).

G. nivalis **'Longiflorus'** Harpur-Crewe (1879a, p. 342); Stern (1956, p. 73).

G. **'Lop Ears'** Palmer (1967, p. 10).

G. **'Macedonicus'** Stern (1956, p. 73).

G. nivalis **'Maculatus'** Kew Hand-list of Herbaceous Plants (1895); Stern (1956, p. 73).

G. **'Majestic'** Allen (1891, p. 185); Ewbank (1894, p. 125); Stern (1956, p. 73).

G. elwesii **'Major'** Burbidge (1894, p. 127); Correvon (1888, p. 140); Burbidge (1891a, pp. 201, 202).

G. plicatus '**Majus**' Burbidge (1891a, p. 207).

G. '**Maximus**' Baker (1893b, p. 354); Stern (1956, p. 73). See *G.* × *grandiflorus* in the Hybrids chapter.

G. nivalis '**Maximus**' Bowles (1918, p. 30).

G. plicatus '**Maximus**' Burbidge (1894, p. 127); Allen (1891, p. 175).

G. elwesii '**Minnie Warren**' Stern (1956, p. 74).

G. '**Miss Hassell's**' (Fish, 1965, p. 26).

G. '**Newry Giant**' (Nelson, 1992, p. 13).

G. ikariae '**Nicana**' Wood (1897, p. 283); Anon. (1898, p. 46); Stern (1956, p. 74).

G. elwesii '**Novelty**' Burbidge (1891a, p. 201); Stern (1956, p. 74).

G. plicatus (subsp. *byzantinus*) '**November**' Receiving an RHS **AM**, see J. Roy. Hort. Soc. 51(2): cxxvi (1926); Arnott (1925, p. 480).

G. '**Octobrensis**' Allen (1891, pp. 179, 180); Burbidge (1891a, p. 206).*

G. plicatus '**Omega**' Allen (1891, p. 175); Stern (1956, p. 74).

G. nivalis '**Pallidus**' (Smith) Burbidge (1891a, p. 206); Stern (1956, p. 74).

G. '**Paris**' Ewbank (1894, p. 125); Stern (1956, p. 74).

G. '**Pearl**' Exhibited by Sir Frederick Stern, see Proc. Roy. Hort. Soc. 92(1): 53 (1967). and J. Roy. Hort. Soc. 92(5): 195 (1967).

G. nivalis '**Pendulus**' Kew Hand-list of Herbaceous Plants (1895); Stern (1956, p. 74).

G. '**Perfection**' Arnott (1904, p. 166); Arnott (1911, p. 42); Arnott (1920, p. 203); Stern (1956, p. 74).

G. '**Pictus**' Maly (1904, p. 302, as *G. nivalis* L. forma *pictus* Maly); Stern (1956, p. 74).*

G. '**Phaenika Samos**' Arnott (1894, p. 180). Possibly only a provisional name used to indicate a locality.

G. nivalis '**Platytepalus**' Beck (1894, p. 50).**

G. nivalis '**Plenissimus**' Allen (1891, p. 174).**

G. elwesii '**Poculiformis**' Bowles (1912, p. 144); Farrer in Gard. Chron. ser. 3, 51: 33 (1912).

G. nivalis '**Praecox**' Harpur-Crewe (1880, p. 249); Baker (1883, p. 54); Stern (1956, p. 74).

G. '**Praecox**' Allen (1891, p. 180); Burbidge (1891a, pp. 201, 207); Stern (1956, p. 74).

G. plicatus '**Praecox**' Allen (1891, p. 175); Stern (1956, p. 74).

G. '**Pumilis**' Kew Hand-list of Herbaceous Plants (1895); Stern (1956, p. 74).

G. **'Punctatus'** Beck (1894, p. 56); Stern (1956, p. 74).

G. **'Quadripetala'** D.K. (1888, p. 59); Stern (1956, p. 74).

G. **'Rachelae'** Allen (1891, pp. 179, 180); Burbidge (1891a, p. 207); Bowles (1918, p. 32); Nelson (1992, p. 13).*

G. **'Raphael'** Allen (1891, p. 185); Stern (1956, p. 74).

G. **'Rebecca'** Bowles (1956, p. 67); Stern (1956, p. 74).

G. **'Redoutei'** Burbidge (1891a, p. 207); Stern (1956, p. 74).*

G. **'Reflexus'** Lindley (1845, p. 35, as *G. reflexus*); Baker (1888, p. 17); Allen (1891, pp. 181, 185); Burbidge (1891a, p. 208); Stern (1956, p. 75).*

G. plicatus **'Reflexus'** Allen (1886, p. 74, as *G. plicatus reflexus*).

G. **'Robin'** Ewbank (1894, p. 125); Stern (1956, p. 75).

G. elwesii **'Robustus'** Baker (1893a, p. 226); Arnott (1894, p. 180); Allen (1894, p. 385); Stern (1956, p. 75).*

G. **'Romeo'** Burbidge (1891a, p. 207); Stern (1956, p. 75).

G. **'Saundersi'** D.K. (1888, p. 59); Stern (1956, p. 75). Probably a misspelling of 'Sandersii'.

G. nivalis **'Serotinus'** Melville (1881, p. 189); Correvon (1888, p. 140); Burbidge (1891a, p. 209, as *G.* 'Serotinus' hort. Dunrobin); Stern (1956, p. 75).

G. fosteri **'Spot'** Allen (1891, p. 183); Stern (1956, p. 75).

G. nivalis **'Stenopetalus'** Beck (1894, p. 50); Stern (1956, p. 75).**

G. plicatus **'Steveni'** Beck (1894, p. 57); Stern (1956, p. 75).

G. elwesii **'Tauricus'** Burbidge (1894, p. 127); Stern (1956, p. 75).

G. **'Taurus'** [*sic*] Arnott (1894, p. 180); Burbidge (1894, p. 127).

G. **'Titania'** Allen (1891, p. 185); Ewbank (1894, p. 125); Stern (1956, p. 75); Royal General Bulbgrowers' Association (1991, p. 248). Not the double-flowered *G.* 'Titania'.

G. **'Tomtit'** Allen (1891, p. 174); Stern (1956, p. 75).

G. **'Trifolius'** Beck (1894, p. 52); Stern (1956, p. 75).**

G. **'Umbrensis'** Burbidge (1891a, p. 209, as *G.* 'Umbrensis' hort. Dammann).

G. nivalis **'Umbricus'** Dewar (1890, p. 107, as *Galanthus umbricus*]); Allen (1891, p. 184); Beck (1894, p. 53); Stern (1956, p. 75).**

G. **'Unguiculatus'** Arnott (1891, p. 206); Anon. (1895, p. 361); Arnott (1899a, p. 129); Arnott (1912, p. 10); Stern (1956, p. 75).

G. **'Valentinae'** Burbidge (1891a, p. 206, as *nivalo-plicatus* 'Valentinae').

G. **'Valentine'** Allen (1891, p. 174); Burbidge (1891a, pp. 195, 206); Arnott (1899a, p. 130); Stern (1956, p. 75); Nutt, in Lawrence (1986, p. 132).

G. **'Valentinei'** Beck (1894, p. 57); Stern (1956, p. 75). (See the Hybrids chapter).

G. **'Van Houttei'** Burbidge (1891a, p. 209); Ewbank (1894, p. 125); Stern (1956, p. 75).

G. **'Victor'** Arnott (1894, p. 180); Stern (1956, p. 75).

G. **'Victoria Gibbs'** Blakeway-Phillips (1980, p. 420).

G. **'Viridans'** Beck (1894, p. 51); Stern (1956, p. 76); Nutt (1970a, p. 172).**

G. elwesii **'Whittallii'** Arnott (1898, p. 466); Arnott (1912, p. 10); Stern (1956, p. 76); Stern (1960, p. 20).*

G. elwesii **'Winner'** Burbidge (1891a, p. 201); Stern (1956, p. 76).

G. **'Wraysbury'** Exhibited at the RHS by J.R. Williams Esq., see Proc. Roy. Hort. Soc. 88(3): 20 (1963).

APPENDIX 7

Bibliography for *Galanthus* cultivars

Allen, J. (1886). The snowdrops. *Garden (London)* 29: 74–75.

Allen, J. (1891). Snowdrops. *J. Roy. Hort. Soc.* 13(2): 172–188. Also published in *Garden (London)* 40: 272–275 (1891).

Allen, J. (1894). The new snowdrops. *Garden (London)* 45: 385.

Anderson, E.B. (1973). *Seven Gardens or Sixty Years of Gardening.* London: Michael Joseph Ltd.

Anon. (1895). *Galanthus elwesii* var. *unguiculatus. Gard. Chron.* ser. 3, 17: 361.

Anon. (1898). New garden plants of the year 1897. *Bull. Misc. Inform.*, appendix 2: 46.

Anon. (1920). *Galanthus Elwesii* var. *Cassaba. Gard. Chron.* ser 3, 67: 62.

Arnott, S. (1894). [no article title] *J. Hort. Cottage/ Prac. Gard*, ser. 3, 28: 179–180.

Arnott, S. (1899a). Snowdrops. *Gard. Chron.* ser. 3, 25: 129–130.

Arnott, S. (1899b). *Galanthus melvillei. Gard. Chron.* ser. 3, 25: 173.

Arnott, S. (1900). The 'yellow' snowdrops. *Gard. Chron.* ser. 3, 27: 189.

Arnott, S. (1904). Bulb garden. Four new snowdrops. *Gard. Chron.* ser. 3, 35: 166.

Arnott, S. (1905a). *Galanthus Cassaba Boydii. Garden (London)* 67: 173.

Arnott, S. (1905b). A fine variety of snowdrop (*Galanthus plicatus Fraseri*). *Garden (London)* 67: 173.

Arnott, S. (1907a). The alpine garden: *Galanthus nivalis* var. *virescens. Galanthus virescens* (double-flowered form). *Gard. Chron.* ser. 3, 41: 264.

Arnott, S. (1907b). The alpine garden: *Galanthus nivalis flavescens* fl. pl. *Gard. Chron.* ser. 3, 41: 198.

Arnott, S. (1911). Two garden-raised snowdops. *Gard. Chron.* ser. 3, 49: 34.

Arnott, S. (1912). The value of snowdrops in early spring. *Garden*

(London) 76: 9–10. Abstracted by H. R. Darlington in *J. Roy. Hort. Soc.* 39(1): 305–306 (1913).

Arnott, S. (1913). Snowdrops in the grey moraine. *Garden (London)* 77: 154.

Arnott, S. (1917). *Galanthus Imperatii Atkinsii. Gard. Chron.* ser. 3, 61: 100–101.

Arnott, S. (1920). The alpine garden: *Galanthus nivalis* Perfection. *Gard. Chron.* ser. 3, 67: 203.

Arnott, S. (1923). The bulb garden: *Galanthus plicatus* Fraseri. *Gard. Chron.* ser 3, 73: 103.

Arnott, S. (1925). Bulb garden: *Galanthus byzantinus* var. November. *Gard. Chron.* ser 3, 78: 480.

Arnott, S. (1929). Bulb garden: *Galanthus nivalis* var. *viridapice. Gard. Chron.* ser 3, 85: 297.

Baker, J.G. (1888). *Handbook of the Amaryllideae.* London: George Bell & Sons.

Baker, J.G. (1893a). New or noteworthy plants: *Galanthus elwesii* var. *robustus. Gard. Chron.* ser. 3, 13: 226.

Baker, J.G. (1893b). *Galanthus maximus,* Baker, n. sp., or hybrid? *Gard. Chron.* ser. 3, 13: 354.

Baker, J.G. (1893c). New or noteworthy plants. *Gard. Chron.* ser. 3, 13: 656.

Baker, R. (1997). *Galanthus lutescens/ flavescens. Bull. Alp. Gard. Soc. Gr. Brit.* 65(1): 9–10.

Baron, M. (1995). Treasures of spring. *Garden (London)* 120(1): 30–35.

Beck, G. von M. (1894). Die Schneeglocken, Eine monographische Skizze der Gattung *Galanthus. Wiener Ill. Gart.-Zeitung* 19: 45–58.

Blakeway-Phillips, R. (1980). Snowdrops. *Garden (London)* 105(10): 419–421.

Bowles, E.A. (1912). *Galanthus Elwesii poculiformis.* A new variety. *J. Roy. Hort. Soc.* 38(1): 144.

Bowles, E.A. (1914). *My Garden in Spring.* London: T.C. & E.C. Jack.

Bowles, E.A. (1917a). Autumn-flowering snowdrops. *Garden (London)* 81: 4. Abstracted by H.R. Darlington in *J. Roy. Hort. Soc.* 43(2 and 3): 574 (1919).

Bowles, E.A. (1917b). [no article title] *J. Roy. Hort. Soc.* 42(2 and 3): li–lii.

Bowles, E.A. (1918). Snowdrops. *J. Roy. Hort. Soc.* 43: 28–36.

Bowles, E.A. (1956). In *Snowdrops and Snowflakes* by F.C. Stern. London: The Royal Horticultural Society, Vincent Square.

Brown, M. (1996). Cold comfort charm. *Gardens Ilustrated* 23: 52–59.

Burbidge, F.W. (1890). The giant snowdrops. *Gard. Chron.* ser. 3, 7: 268–269, 271.

Burbidge, F.W. (1891a). Snowdrops. *J. Roy. Hort. Soc.* 13(2): 191–209.

Burbidge, F.W. (1891b). Autumn-blooming snowdrops. *Garden (London)* 39: 243.

Burbidge, F.W. (1894). The time of snowdrops. *Garden (London)* 45: 127–128.

Čelakovsky, L. (1891). Popis noveho druhu 'snezenky' *Galanthus gracilis* n. sp. *Sitzungsber. Königl. Böhm. Ges. Wiss. Prag. Math.-Naturwiss. Cl.* 1891: 198.

Chappell, D. (1995). Snowdrop enthusiasts in for a treat with *Galanthus* 'Pride o' the Mill' from Gloucestershire. *New, Rare and Elusive Plants* 2: 24.

Correvon, H. (1888). Les perce-neiges. *Le Jardin* 32: 139–140.

D.K. (1888). Snowdrops and winter aconites. *Garden (London)* 34: 58–59.

Ewbank, H. (1891). Snowdrops. *Garden (London)* 39: 272–273.

Ewbank, H. (1894). Snowdrops. *Garden (London)* 45: 125–126.

Farrer, R. (1912). *Galanthus elwesii poculiformis. Gard. Chron.* ser. 3, 51: 33–34.

Fish, M. (1965). *A Flower for Every Day.* London: Studio Vista Limited.

Furber, R. (1732). *The Flower-Garden Displayed*: 2. London: printed for J. Hazard et al.

Harpur-Crewe, H. (1879a). Snowdrops. *Gard. Chron.* new ser., 11: 236–237

Harpur-Crewe, H. (1879b). Snowdrops. *Gard. Chron.* new ser., 11: 342.

Harpur-Crewe, H. (1880). *Garden (London)* 17: 249.

Herbert, W. (1837). *Amaryllidaceae*: 330. London: James Ridgeway and Sons.

Irving, W. (1906a). The Alpine garden. '*Galanthus* Gottwaldi'. *Gard. Chron.* ser. 3, 39: 105.

Irving, W. (1906b). The alpine garden: *Galanthus nivalis flavescens. Gard. Chron.* ser. 3, 29: 165.

Lawrence, W. (1986). Bulbs in the alpine garden. *Bull. Alp. Gard. Soc. Gr. Brit.* 54(2): 130–146, with notes on *Galanthus* by R. Nutt [First printed in *Bull. Alp. Gard. Soc. Gr. Brit.* 1: (1933)].

Leichtlin, M. (1879). Snowdrops. *Gard. Chron.* new ser., 11: 342.

Lindley, J. (1845). *G. reflexus. Edward's Bot. Reg.* 31: misc. 44, p. 35.

Malay, K. (1904). Beiträge zur Kenntnis der Flora Bosniens und der Herzegowina. *Verh. Zool.-Bot. Ges. Wien* 54: 302.

Mallet, G.B. (1905). The snowdrops. *Garden (London)* 67: 53–54, 70, 87.

Mathias, L.W.H. (1958). A portfolio of snowdrop portraits. *Natl. Hort. Mag.* 37(3): 147–164.

Melville, D. (1878). Snowdrops. *Gard. Chron.* new ser., 9: 308.

Melville, D. (1891). Snowdrops. *J. Roy. Hort. Soc.* 13(2): 188–191.

Myers, M.D. (1996). *Galanthus* 'Little Ben' PC. *Bull. Alp. Gard. Soc. Gr. Brit.* 64(4): 434.

Nelson, E.C. (1992). Fair maids of February. *Irish Garden* 1(1): 12–13.

Nutt, R. (1968). Some thoughts on growing snowdrops. *Daffodil Tulip Year Book* 34: 80–83.

Nutt, R. (1970a). Snowdrop freaks or natural variations. *Daffodil Tulip Year Book* 36: 165–174.

Nutt, R. (1970b). Plants to which awards were made in 1970. *J. Roy. Hort. Soc.* 96(4): 191.

Nutt, R. (1971). Snowdrop cultivars and colchicum in cultivation. *J. Scott. Rock Gard. Club* No. 48, 12(3): 190–209.

Nutt, R. (1974). White flowers in winter. *J. Roy. Hort. Soc.* 99(1): 19–22.

Nutt, R. (1981). *Galanthus caucasicus* 'Double'. *J. Roy. Hort. Soc.* 106 (11): 475–476.

Nutt, R. (1993). *Galanthus.* In K. Beckett [ed.], *Encyclopedia of Alpines* 1: 510–520. Pershore: AGS Publications Ltd.

Palmer, L. (1967). A cold chalk garden throughout the year. *J. Roy. Hort. Soc.* 92(1): 8–17.

Rix, M. and R. Phillips. (1981). *The Bulb Book.* London: Book Club Associates.

Royal General Bulbgrowers' Association/ Koninklijke Algemeene Vereeniging voor Bloembollencultuur (1991). *International Checklist for Hyacinths and Miscellaneous Bulbs.* Alblasserdam: Offsetdrukkerij Kanters B.V.

Schultes, J.A., and J.H. Schultes. (1830). *Systema Vegetabilium* 7(2): 781. Stuttgardtiae: sumtibus J.G. Cottae.

Stanley, Lady Beatrix (1939). New or interesting plants—two snowdrops. *New Fl. and Silva* 11(3): 226.

Stern, F.C. (1951). Snowdrops and snowflakes. *J. Roy. Hort. Soc.* 76 (3): 73–77.

Stern, F.C. (1956). *Snowdrops and Snowflakes*. London: The Royal Horticultural Society, Vincent Square.

Stern, F.C. (1960). *A Chalk Garden*. Edinburgh: Thomas Nelson and Sons Ltd.

Stern, F.C. (1961). Plants to which awards have been made in 1960–61. *Galanthus caucasicus* var. *hiemalis. J. Roy. Hort. Soc.* 86(7): 324.

Stern, F.C. (1963). Comments on the notes of Dr Schwarz. *Bull. Alp. Gard. Soc. Gr. Brit.* 31(2): 136–138.

Trehane, P. (1989). *Index Hortensis, Volume 1: Perennials.* Wimborne: Quarterjack Publishing.

Synge, P.M. (1950). The garden in winter. *J. Roy. Hort. Soc.* 75(2): 57–68.

Webster, A.D. (1891). *Galanthus nivalis poculifomis. Garden (London)* 39: 233.

Wilks, W. (1887). *Galanthus globosus. Garden (London)* 31: 393.

Wood, J. (1897). *Galanthus nicana. Garden (London)* 51: 283.

Wyatt, O.E.P. (1956). The Gardens at Maidwell Hall. *J. Roy. Hort. Soc.* 81(7): 294–302.

Wyatt, O.E.P. (1966). 'Double Green' Snowdrop. *Daffodil Tulip Year Book* 326: 189.

BIBLIOGRAPHY

Agapova, N.D. (ed.), K.B. Arkharova, L.I. Vakhtina, E.A. Zemskova, and L.V. Tarvis. (1990). *Numeri Chromsomatum Magnoliophytorum Florae URSS (Aceraceae—Menyanthaceae)*. Leninopoli—Nauka—Sectio Leninopolitana.

Allen, J. (1891). Snowdrops. *J. Roy. Hort. Soc.* 13(1): 172–188.

Anderson, E.B. (1973). *Seven Gardens or Sixty Years of Gardening*. London: Michael Joseph Ltd.

Andriyenko, T.L., V.I. Melnik, and L.A. Yakushina. (1992). Distribution and structure of *Galanthus nivalis* (Amaryllidaceae) coenopulations in Ukraine. *Bot. Zhurn. (Moscow & Leningrad)* 77(3): 101–107.

Anon. (1934). [RHS] Proceedings—Scientific Committee. *J. Roy. Hort. Soc.* 59: cxvii.

Anon. (1935). [RHS] Proceedings—Floral Committee. *J. Roy. Hort. Soc.* 60: xxv.

Artjushenko, Z.T. (1962). Early spring in the Caucasus. *Alp. Gard. Soc. Gr. Brit.* 30(2): 106–129.

Artjushenko, Z.T. (1965). A contribution to the taxonomy of the genus *Galanthus* L. *Bot. Zhurn. (Moscow & Leningrad)* 50(10): 1430–1447.

Artjushenko, Z.T. (1966). A critical review of the genus *Galanthus* L. *Bot. Zhurn.(Moscow & Leningrad)* 51(10): 1437–1451.

Artjushenko, Z.T. (1967). Taxonomy of the genus *Galanthus* L. *Daffodil Tulip Year Book* 32: 62–82, 87.

Artjushenko, Z.T. (1969). A critical review of the genus *Galanthus* L. *Plant Life* 25(2–4): 137–152.

Artjushenko, Z.T. (1970). *Amaryllidaceae J. St. Hil. SSSR. Morphology, Systematics and Uses*: 41–83. Leningrad: Akademii Nauk SSSR. Botanicheskii Institut V.L. Komarova.

Artjushenko, Z.T. (1974). *Galanthus* L. (Amaryllidaceae) in Greece. *Ann. Mus. Goulandris* 2: 9–21.

Baker, J.G. (1887). New or noteworthy plants, *Galanthus nivalis* L. subsp. *caucasicus*. *Gard. Chron.* ser. 3, 1: 313.

Baker, J.G. (1888). *Handbook of the Amaryllideae.* London: George Bell & Sons.

Baker, J.G. (1889). New or noteworthy plants, *Galanthus fosteri* Baker n. sp. *Gard. Chron.* ser. 3, 5: 458.

Baker, J.G. (1891). New or noteworthy plants, *Galanthus alleni* Baker n. sp. *Gard Chron.* ser. 3, 9: 298.

Baker, J.G. (1893a). New or noteworthy plants, *Galanthus ikariae* Baker n. sp. *Gard. Chron.* ser. 3, 13: 226.

Baker, J.G. (1893b). *Galanthus perryi* Hort. Ware. ex Baker. *Gard. Chron.* ser. 3, 13: 258.

Baker, J.G. (1893c). New or noteworthy plants, *Galanthus maximus* Baker n. sp. or hybrid. *Gard. Chron.* ser. 3, 13: 354.

Baker, J.G. (1893d). New or noteworthy plants, *Galanthus byzantinus* Baker n. sp. *Gard. Chron.* ser. 3, 13: 506.

Baker, J.G. (1893e). New or noteworthy plants [*Galanthus grandiflorus*]. *Gard. Chron.* ser. 3, 13: 656.

Baker, J.G. (1897). New or noteworthy plants, *Galanthus cilicicus* Baker n. sp. *Gard. Chron.* ser. 3, 21: 214.

Beck, G. von M. (1894). Die Schneeglocken, Eine monographische Skizze der Gattung *Galanthus. Wiener Ill. Gart.-Zeitung* 19: 45–58.

Bertoloni, A. (1839). *Flora italica* 4: 3–5. Bologna: Richardii Masii.

Boissier, E. (1882). *Flora orientalis* 5: 144–146. Basel, Geneve: H. Georg.

Bowles, E.A. (1918). Snowdrops. *J. Roy. Hort. Soc.* 43: 28–36.

Brickell, C.D. (1984). *Galanthus.* In P.H. Davis et al. (eds.), *Flora of Turkey and the East Aegean Islands* 8: 365–372. Edinburgh: University Press.

Brickell, C.D. (1986). *Galanthus* L. In S.M. Walters et al. (eds.), *European Garden Flora* 1: 317–319. Cambridge: Cambridge University Press.

Bridson, G.D.R., and E.R. Smith. (1991). *B-P-H/ S (Botanico-Periodicum- Huntianum/ Supplementum).* Pittsburgh: Hunt Institute for Botanical Documentation.

Brummitt, R.K., and C.E. Powell. (1992). *Authors of Plant Names.* Royal Botanic Gardens, Kew.

Budnikov, G., and V. Kricsfalusy. (1994). Bioecological study of *Galanthus nivalis* L. in the East Carpathians. *Thaiszia—J. Bot., Kosice* 4: 49–75.

Burbidge, F.W. (1891). Snowdrops. *J. Roy. Hort. Soc.* 13(1): 191–209.

Burbidge, F.W. (1896). Snowdrops. *Garden (London)* 49: 330 (1896).

Čelakovsky, L. (1891). Popis noveho druhu "snezenky" *Galanthus gracilis* n. sp. *Sitzungsber. Königl. Böhm. Ges. Wiss. Prag. Math.-Naturwiss.* Cl. 1891: 195.

Chabrey, D. (1566). *Stirpium icones et sciagraphia*: 211.Geneve: Phil. Gamoneti & alc de la Piere.

Church, A.H. (1908). *Types of Floral Mechanism: A Selection of Diagrams and Descriptions of Common Flowers*, part 1, types I–XII. Oxford: Clarendon Press.

Clusius, C. (1583). *Rariorum aliquot stirpium, per Pannonian, Austriam & vicinas . . . historia*: 183. Antwerpen: ex officina Christophori Plantini.

Cullen, J. (1978). A preliminary survey of ptyxis (vernation) in the Angiosperms. *Notes Roy. Bot. Gard. Edinb.* 37: 161–214.

Davis, A.P., and C.D. Brickell. (1993). *Galanthus peshmenii*: a new snowdrop from the eastern Aegean. *New Plantsman* 1(1): 14.

Davis, A.P. (1994). *A systematic study of the genus* Galanthus *L. (Amaryllidaceae J. St. Hil.)*. PhD thesis. University of Reading.

Davis, A.P., H. Mordak, and S.L. Jury. (1996). Taxonomic status of three Caucasian snowdrops: *Galanthus alpinus* Sosn., *G. bortkewitschianus* Koss and *G. caucasicus* (Baker) Grossh. *Kew Bull.* 51 (4): 741–752.

Davis, A.P. (1997). Proposal to conserve the name *Galanthus elwesii* (Amaryllidaceae) with a conserved type (1307). *Taxon* 46: 553–554.

Davis, A.P., and J.R. Barnett. (1997). The leaf anatomy of the genus *Galanthus* L. (Amaryllidaceae J. St. Hil.). *Bot. J. Linn. Soc.* 123: 333–352.

Davis, P.H., and F.C. Stern. (1949). On the flora of the near east: 23. Miscellaneous new species and records. *Kew Bull.* 1: 112–113.

Davis, P.H., R.R. Mill, and K. Tan (eds.). (1988). *Flora of Turkey and the East Aegean Islands* 10: 226–227. Edinburgh: University Press.

Delipavlov, D. (1971). The genus *Galanthus* L. (snowdrop) in Bulgaria. *Izv. Bot. Inst.* 21: 161–168.

Dykes, W.R. (1919). Snowdrops. *Gard. Chron.* ser. 3, 65: 188.

Endlicher, S.L. (1836). Tribe *Narcisseae. Genera Plantarum*: 178. Wien: Fr. Beck.

Erik, S., and N. Demirkus. (1986). Contributions to the flora of Turkey. *Doga Turk. J. Biol.* 10(1): 100–105.

Evelyn, J. (1664). *Kalendarium hortense: or the Gard'ner's Almanac, &c.* London.

Fomin, A.V., and G.J.N. Woronow. (1909). *Identification Key to the Plants of the Caucasus and Crimea* 1: 280–281. Tiflis.

Furber, R. (1732). *The Flower-Garden Displayed*: 2. London: printed for J. Hazard et al.

Gabrieljan, E.T. (1988). *Galanthus alpinus* Sosn. In V. Kazarien, *Red Data Book of Armenia*: 49–50. Yerevan: Ajestan Press.

Gabrieljan, E.T., and K.G. Tamanian. (1982). The genus *Galanthus* in Armenia. *Biol. Zhurn. Armenii* 35(5): 410–412.

Gottlieb-Tannenhain, P. von. (1904). Studien uber die Formen der Gattung *Galanthus*. *Abh. K. K. Zool.-Bot. Ges. Wien* 2(4): 1–93.

Greuter, W., F. Barrie, H.M. Burdet, W.G. Chaloner, V. Demoulin, D.L. Hawksworth, P.M. Jørgensen, D.H. Nicolson, P.C. Silva, P. Trehane, and J. McNeill. (1994). *International Code of Botanical Nomenclature (Tokyo Code)*. [Regnum Vegetabile No. 131]. Königstein: Koeltz Scientific Books.

Grossheim, A.A., and B.K. Schischkin. (1924). *Schedae ad herbarium "Plantae orientalis, exsiccatae"* fasc. 1: 4, 1(6). Tiflis.

Grossheim, A.A. (1928). *Flora Kavkaza* [Flora Caucasus] 1: 288. Tiflis. Narodyni Komissariat Zemledeliya SSR Armenii Baku.

Grossheim, A.A. (1940). *Flora Kavkaza* [Flora Caucasus] edn. 2, 2: 193. Tiflis. Narodyni Komissariat Zemledeliya SSR Armenii Baku.

Halácsy, E. de. (1904). *Conspectus florae graecea* 3: 206. Leipzig: Sumptibus Guilelmi Engelmann.

Holmgren, P.K., N.H. Holmgren, and L.C. Barnett (eds.). (1990). *Index Herbariorum. Part 1: The Herbaria of the World. Eighth Edition.* New York Botanic Garden: International Association for Plant Taxonomy.

Hooker, J.D. (1875). *Galanthus elwesii. Bot. Mag.* tab. 6166.

Jarvis, C.E., F.R. Barrie, D.M. Allen, and J.L. Reveal. (1993). *A list of Linnaean Generic Names and Their Types.* Konigstein, Germany: The International Association for Plant Taxonomy.

Kamari, G. (1981). A biosystematic study of the genus *Galanthus* L. in Greece, part II (Cytology). *Bot. Chron.* 1(2): 60–98.

Kamari, G. (1982). A biosystematic study of the genus *Galanthus* L. in Greece, part I. *Bot. Jahrb. Syst.* 103(1): 107–135.

Kemularia-Nathadze, L.M. (1941). In A.K. Makaschvili, D.I. Sosnowsky, and A.L. Kharadze (eds.), *Flora Gruzii* [Flora Georgia] 2: 526. Tbilisi: AN Gruzinskoj SSR Press.

Kemularia-Nathadze, L.M. (1947a). Galanthi generis species novae in 'Flora Georgica' descriptae. *Zametki Sist. Geogr. Rast.* 13: 6.

288

Kemularia-Nathadze, L.M. (1947b). A study of the Caucasian representatives of the genus *Galanthus* L. *Trudy Tbilissk. Bot. Inst.* ser. 2, 11: 165–190.

Kemularia-Nathadze, L.M. (1977). Ad cognitionem duram speciens *Galanthus* L. Esc talysh descriptae. *Zametki Sist. Geogr. Rast.* 34: 34–37.

Khokhrjakov, A.P. (1963). A new snowdrop from the Caucasus. *Bjull. Moskovsk. Obsc. Isp. Prir. Otd. Biol.* 68(4): 140–141.

Koss, G.I. (1951). Species Caucasicae novae generis *Galanthus* L. *Bot. Mater. Gerb. Inst. Kom. a. Akad. Nauk. SSSR* 14: 130–138.

Kuthathaladze, S.I. (1963). Generis *Galanthus* species nova ex Iberia Orientalis. *Zametki Sist. Geogr. Rast.* 23: 128–129.

Lawrence, G.H.M., A.F. Günther Buchheim, G.S. Daniels, and H. Dolezal. (1968). *B-P-H (Botanico-Periodicum-Huntianum)*. Pittsburgh: Hunt Botanical Library.

Linnaeus, C. (1735). *Systema naturae*, edn. 1. Leiden: apud Theodorum Haak; ex typographia Joannis Wilhelmi de Groot.

Linnaeus, C. (1753). *Species plantarum*, edn. 1: 288. Stockholm: Impensis Laurentii Salvii.

Lobin, W., C.D. Brickell, and A.P. Davis. (1994). *Galanthus koenenianus* (Amaryllidaceae), a remarkable new species of snowdrop from northeast Turkey. *Kew Bull.* 48(1): 161–163.

Loudon, J.W. (1841). *Ladies' Flower Garden—Of Ornamental Bulbous Plants*: 180. London: William Smith.

Lozina-Lozinskaya, A.S. (1935). *Galanthus*. In V.L. Komarov (ed.), *Flora SSSR* 4: 476–480. Leningrad: Editio Academiae Scientarum URSS.

Marschall von Bieberstein, F.A.F. (1819). *Flora Taurico-Caucasica* 3: 255. Charkov: Typis academicus.

Marshall, N.T. (1993). *The Gardener's Guide to Plant Conservation*. Washington, D.C.: World Wildlife Fund.

Mattioli, P.A. (1554). *Medici senensis commentari, in sex libros Pedacii Dioscoridis*. Venice.

Melnik, V.I. (1994). *Galanthus elwesii* Hook. f. (Amaryllidaceae) in the Ukraine. *Ukrajins'k. Bot. Zhurn.* 51(1): 29–33.

Melville, D. (1891). Snowdrops. *J. Roy. Hort. Soc.* 13(1): 188–191.

Müller-Doblies, D. (1971). *Galanthus* ist doch sympodial gebaut! *Ber. Dtsch. Bot. Ges.* 84(11): 665–682.

Müller-Doblies, D., and U. Müller-Doblies. (1978). Studies on tribal systematics of *Amaryllidoideae* I. The systematic position of *Lapiedra* Lag. *Lagascalia* 8(1): 13–23.

Nutt, R.D. (1974). White flowers in winter. *J. Roy. Hort. Soc.* 99(1): 19–22.

Orphanides, T.G. (1876). *Atti Congresco Internazionale Botanico*: 214. Firenze.

Papanicolaou, K., and E. Zacharof. (1983). Cytological notes and taxonomic comments on four *Galanthus* L. taxa from Greece. *Israel J. Bot.* 32: 23–32.

Parker, G. (1963). Tentative key to the wild species of *Galanthus* L.—Comments on Schwarz and Stern. *Bull. Alp. Gard. Soc. Gr. Brit.* 31: 138–141.

Pax, F.A. (1887). Subtribe *Galanthinae.* In H.G.A. Engler and K.A.E. Prantl, *Die Natürlichen Pflanzenfamilien* div. 2, 5: 105. Leipzig: Wilhelm Engelmann.

Pax, F.A., and K. Hoffman. (1930). Subtribe *Galanthinae.* In H.G.A. Engler, *Die Natürlichen Pflanzenfamilien* edn. 2, 15a: 403. Leipzig: Wilhelm Engelmann.

Ray, J. (1688). *Historia plantarum* 2: 1144–1145. Londini: Typis Mariae Clark: prostant apud Henricum Faithorne.

Rix, M., and R. Phillips. (1981). *The Bulb Book.* London: Book Club Associates.

Ruprecht, F. (1868). Originalabhandlungen, b) *Galanthus latifolius. Gartenflora* 17: 130.

Salisbury, R.A. (1866). *The Genera of Plants*: 95. London: John van Voorst.

Schwarz, O. (1963). Tentative key to the wild species of *Galanthus* L. *Bull. Alp. Gard. Soc. Gr. Brit.* 31: 131–136.

Sell, P.D. (1996). *Galanthus.* In P.D. Sell and G. Murrell, *Flora of Great Britain and Ireland* 5: 283–285, 363. Cambridge: Cambridge University Press.

Somerus, J.D. (1820). *Galanthus plicatus.* Clusius's snowdrop. *Bot. Mag.* tab. 2162.

Sosnowsky, D. (1911). The flora of the Caucasus. *Galanthus alpinus* n. sp. *Vestn. Tiflissk. Bot. Tiflissk. Sada* 19: 26.

Stafleu, F.A., and R.S. Cowan. (1976–1988). *Taxonomic Literature,* edn. 2, vol. 1–7. Bohn, Scheltema, and Holkema: Utrecht/Antwerpen; dr. W. Junk b.v. Publishers: The Hague/ Boston.

Stanley, Lady B. (1939). New or interesting plants—two snowdrops. *New Fl. & Silva* 11(3): 226.

Stern, F.C., and J.S.L. Gilmour. (1946). *Galanthus latifolius. Bot. Mag.* tab. 9669.

Stern, F.C. (1956). *Snowdrops and Snowflakes.* London: The Royal Horticultural Society, Vincent Square.

Stern, F.C. (1963). Tentative key to the wild species of *Galanthus* L.—Comments on the notes of Dr. Schwarz. *Bull. Alp. Gard. Soc. Gr. Brit.* 31: 136–138.

Steudel, E.G. (1840). *Nomenclator botanicus*, edn. 2, 1: 653. Stuttgardiae et Tubingae: typis et sumptibus J.G. Cottae.

Sveshnikova, L.I. (1965). Chromosome numbers of species of the genus *Galanthus* L. (Amaryllidaceae). *Bot. Zhurn. (Moscow & Leningrad).* 50(5): 689–692.

Sveshnikova, L.I. (1967). Chromosome numbers of some species of *Galanthus* from south Europe and Asia Minor. *Bot. Zhurn. (Moscow & Leningrad)* 52(3): 359–362.

Sveshnikova, L.I. (1971a). A comparative karyological investigation of *Galanthus* L.: I. Section *Galanthus. Bot. Zhurn. (Moscow & Leningrad)* 56(1): 118–126.

Sveshnikova, L.I. (1971b). A comparative karyological investigation of the *Galanthus* L.: II. Section *Viridifolii. Bot. Zhurn. (Moscow & Leningrad)* 56(2): 282–293.

Sveshnikova, L.I. (1975). On the origin of karyotype of the genus *Galanthus* L. *Bot. Zhurn. (Moscow & Leningrad)* 60: 12. 1760–1768.

Sveshnikova, L.I., and S.S. Fodor. (1983). Intraspecies caryotypical polymorphism in *Galanthus nivalis* L. *Ukrajins'k. Bot. Zhurn.* 40 (5): 32–35.

Traub, H.P., and H.N. Moldenke. (1948). The tribe *Galantheae. Herbertia* 14: 85–116.

Trehane, P., C.D. Brickell, B.R. Baum, W.L.A. Hetterscheid, A.C. Leslie, J. McNeill, S.A. Spongberg, and F. Vrugtman. (1995). *International Code of Nomenclature for Cultivated Plants—1995.* Wimborne: Quarterjack Publishing.

Turril, W.B. (1937). *Galanthus ikariae. Bot. Mag.* tab. 9474.

Velenovsky, J. (1891). *Flora bulgarica*: 540. Pragae.

Webb, D.A. (1978). The European species of *Galanthus* L. *Bot. J. Linn. Soc.* 76(4): 307–313.

Webb, D.A. (1980). *Galanthus.* In T.G. Tutin et al. (eds.), *Flora Europaea* 5: 77–78. Cambridge: Cambridge University Press.

Wendelbo, P. (1970). Amaryllidaceae—*Galanthus.* In K.L. Rechinger (ed.), *Flora Iranica* 67: 6–7. Graz-Austria: Akademische Druck-u. Verlagsanstalt.

Wendelbo, P. (1977). *Tulips and Irises of Iran and their Relatives.* Tehran: Botanical Institute of Iran, Ariamehr Botanical Garden.

Wyatt, O.E.P. (1967). Two snowdrop problems, *Galanthus cilicicus* and *Galanthus caucasicus. Daffodil Tulip Year Book* 32: 83–87.

Yeo, P.F. (1963). The identity of *Galanthus grandiflorus* Baker. *Baileya* 11: 59–61.

Zeybek, N. (1988). Taxonomic investigations on Turkish snowdrops. *Tu. J. Botany* 12(1): 89–102.

Zeybek, N., and E. Sauer. (1995). *Türkiye Kardelenleri (Galanthus L.) I./ Beitrag Zur Türkischen Schneeglöckhen (Galanthus L.) I.* VSB Altinova-Karamürsel.

INDEX OF
SCIENTIFIC NAMES

Accepted names are given in **bold** type; synonyms are in *italic* type.